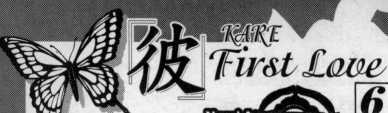

KARE First Love

6

Karin chose an all-girls' school because she was never really comfortable around boys. It might not have been bliss, but she managed.

Everything changed when she met Kiriya on the morning bus. Her classmate, Yuka, tried to sabotage them, but with Nanri's support, Karin and Kiriya started going out.

For their first summer vacation together, the two went to Okinawa with their friends. They stayed on the beach near the spot where Kiriya's older brother died a few years before. It was an emotional trip, but it brought Karin and Kiriya closer. They spent the night together, but Karin was so nervous that she drank too much ... and the vacation ended with Karin's virginity intact.

Karin's father became convinced that Kiriya was a bad influence, and he forbade the two to see each other. But on Christmas Eve, Kiriya called on Karin in secret. When her family accidentally bumped into Kiriya on New Year's Day, Karin's father softened and allowed them to continue their relationship with a few conditions. Then one weekend, while visiting a video shoot they got caught in a rainstorm...

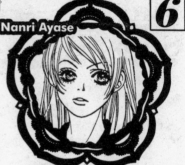

Nanri Ayase

Karin's classmate. She recently broke up with her married boyfriend.

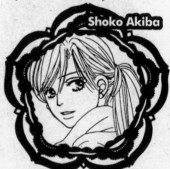

Shoko Akiba

The widow of Kiriya's older brother, the famous photographer Yuji.

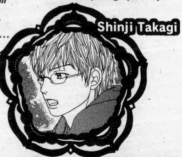

Shinji Takagi

A professional photographer who works in many genres. He was Yuji's colleague.

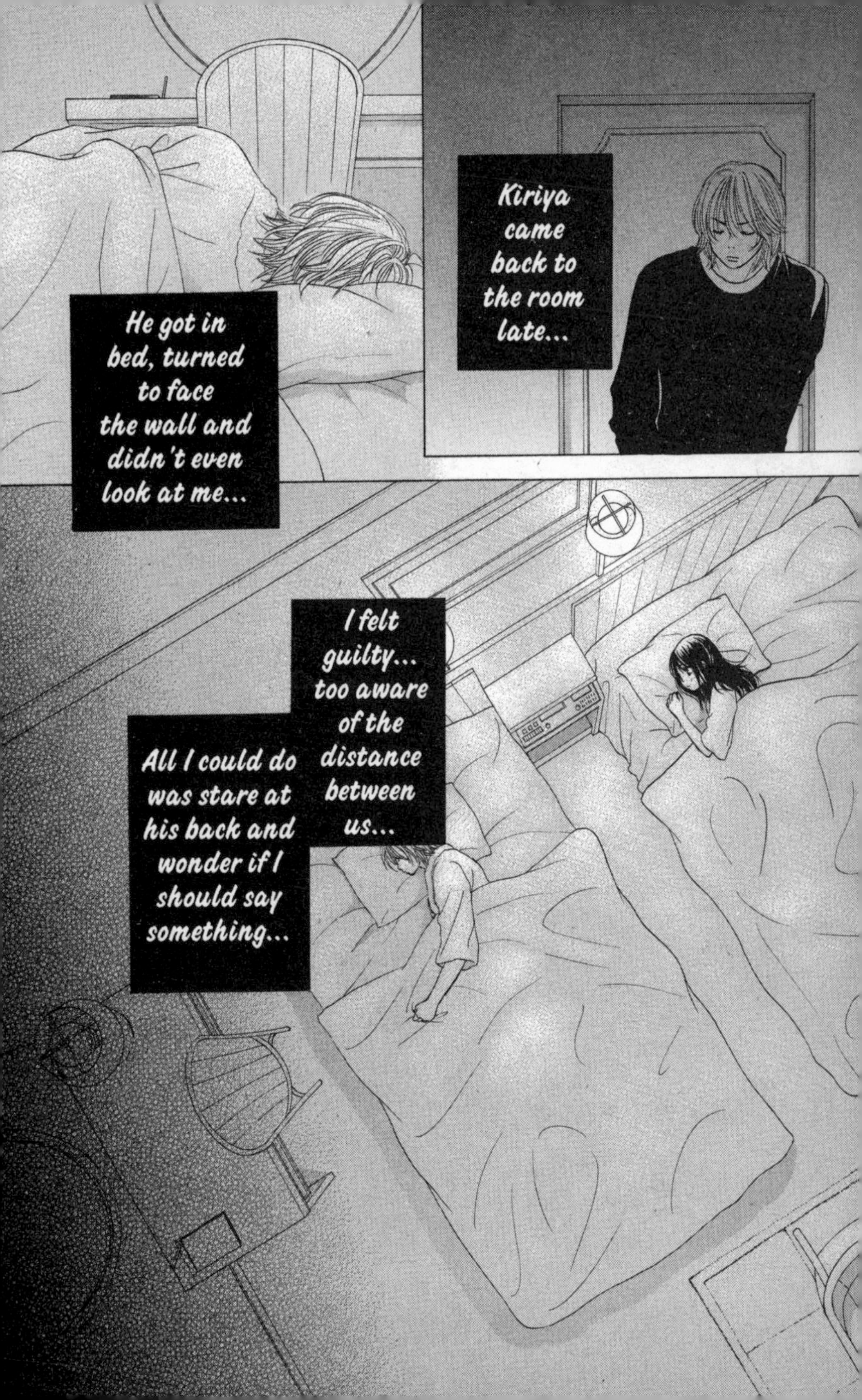
Kiriya came back to the room late...
He got in bed, turned to face the wall and didn't even look at me...
I felt guilty... too aware of the distance between us...
All I could do was stare at his back and wonder if I should say something...

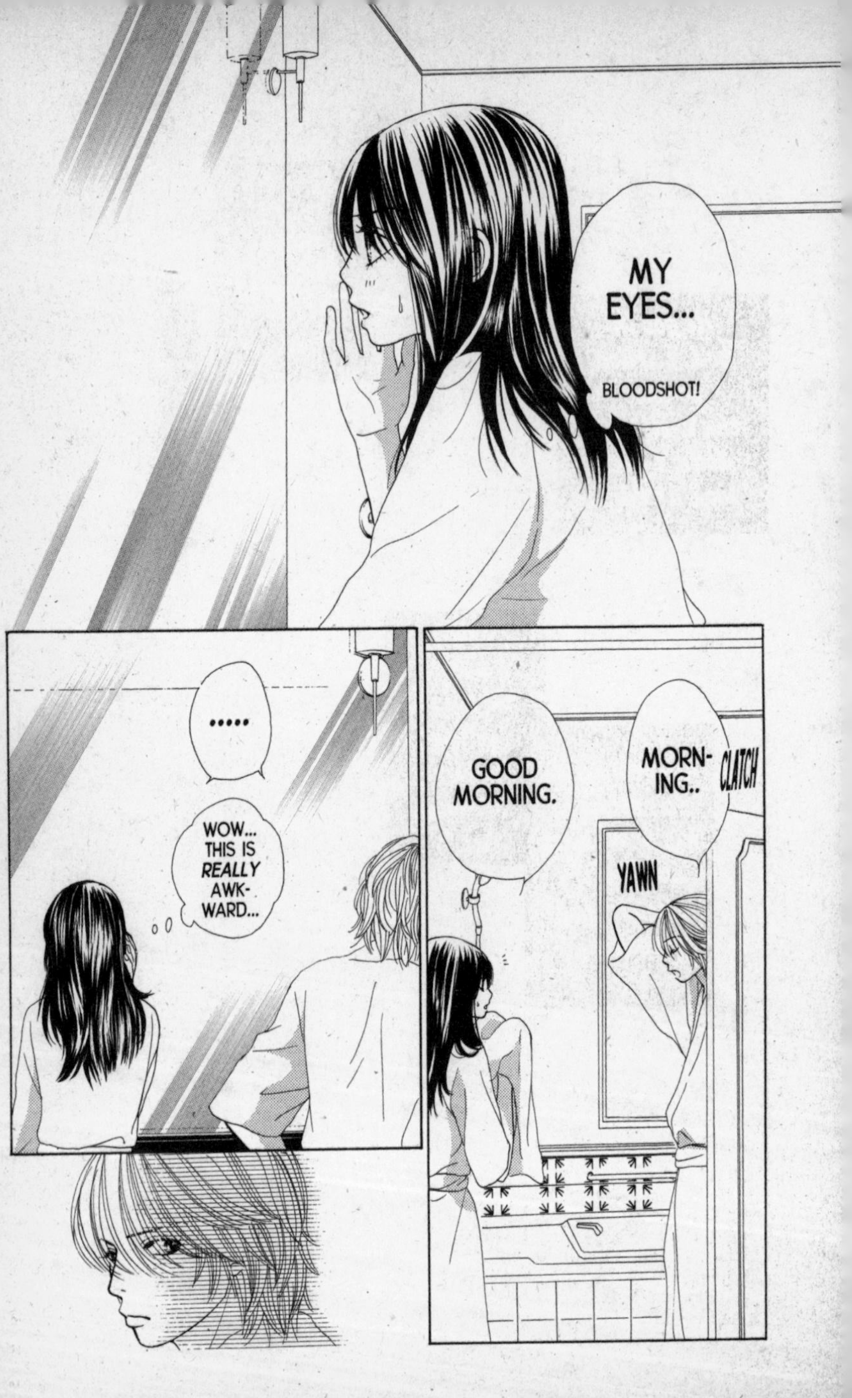
MY EYES...
BLOODSHOT!
CLATCH
MORN-ING..
GOOD MORNING.
YAWN
......
WOW... THIS IS *REALLY* AWK-WARD...

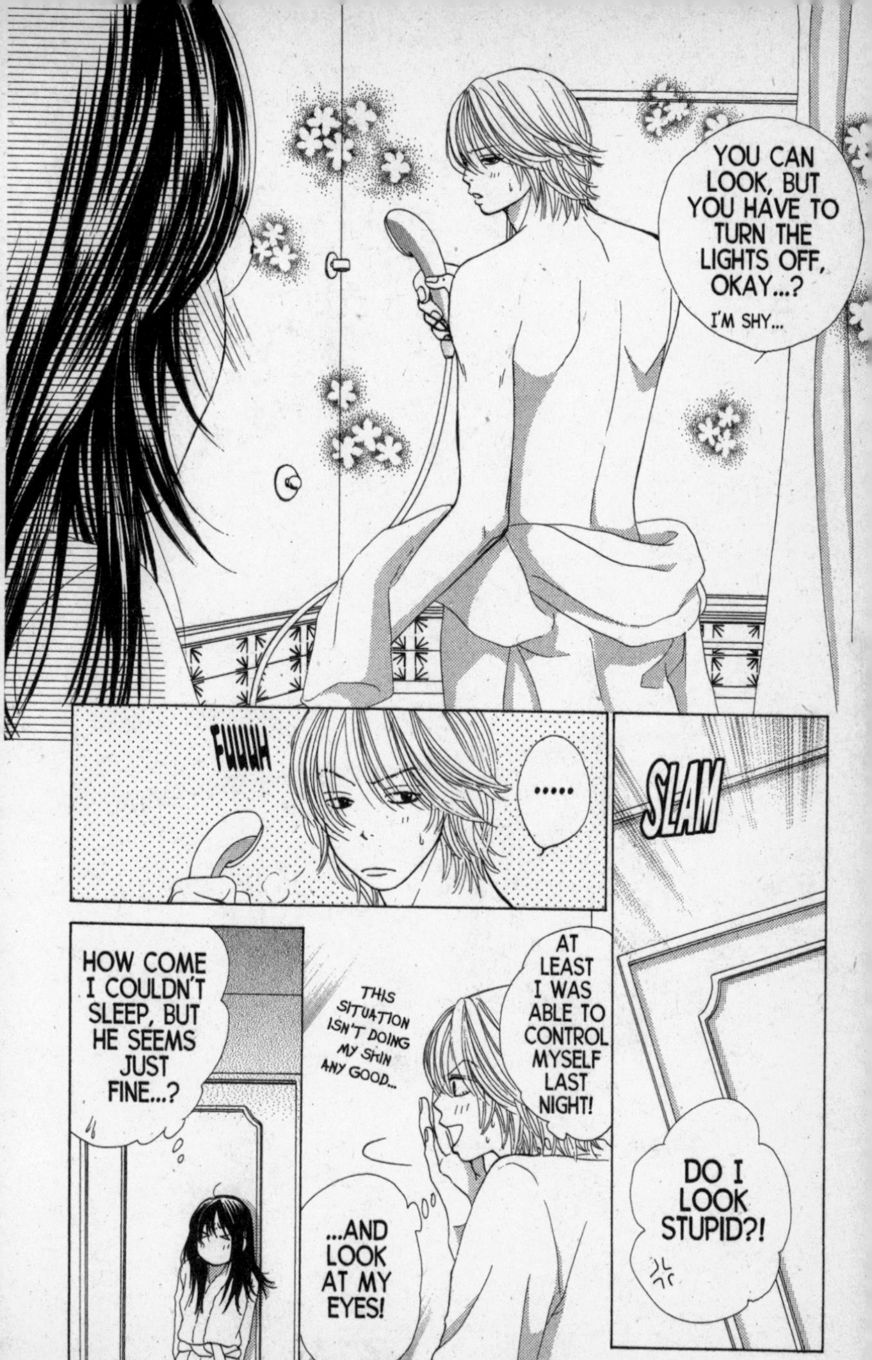
YOU CAN LOOK, BUT YOU HAVE TO TURN THE LIGHTS OFF, OKAY...?
I'M SHY...
SLAM
DO I LOOK STUPID?!
FUUUH
.....
AT LEAST I WAS ABLE TO CONTROL MYSELF LAST NIGHT!
THIS SITUATION ISN'T DOING MY SKIN ANY GOOD...
...AND LOOK AT MY EYES!
HOW COME I COULDN'T SLEEP, BUT HE SEEMS JUST FINE...?

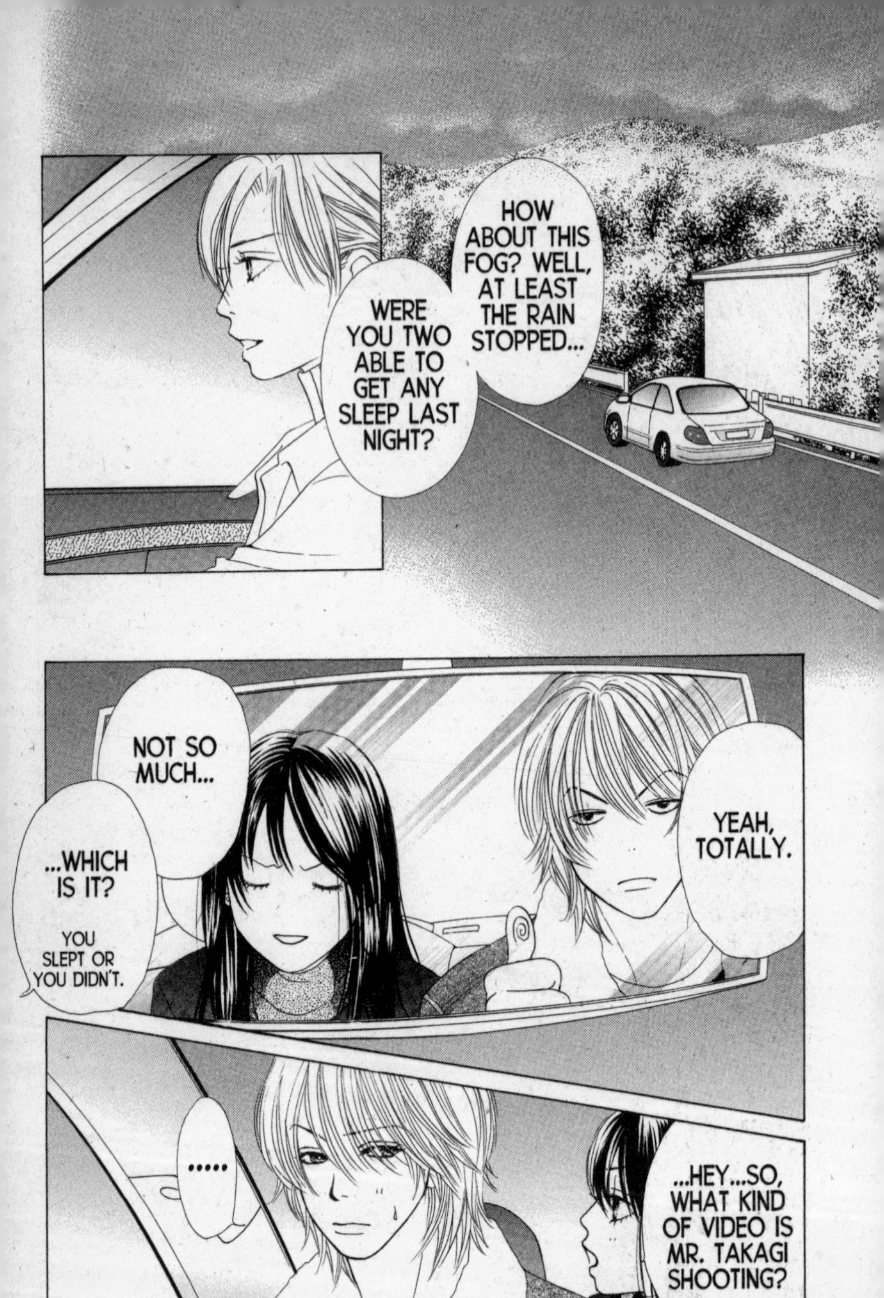
HOW ABOUT THIS FOG? WELL, AT LEAST THE RAIN STOPPED...
WERE YOU TWO ABLE TO GET ANY SLEEP LAST NIGHT?
YEAH, TOTALLY.
NOT SO MUCH...
...WHICH IS IT?
YOU SLEPT OR YOU DIDN'T.
...HEY...SO, WHAT KIND OF VIDEO IS MR. TAKAGI SHOOTING?
......

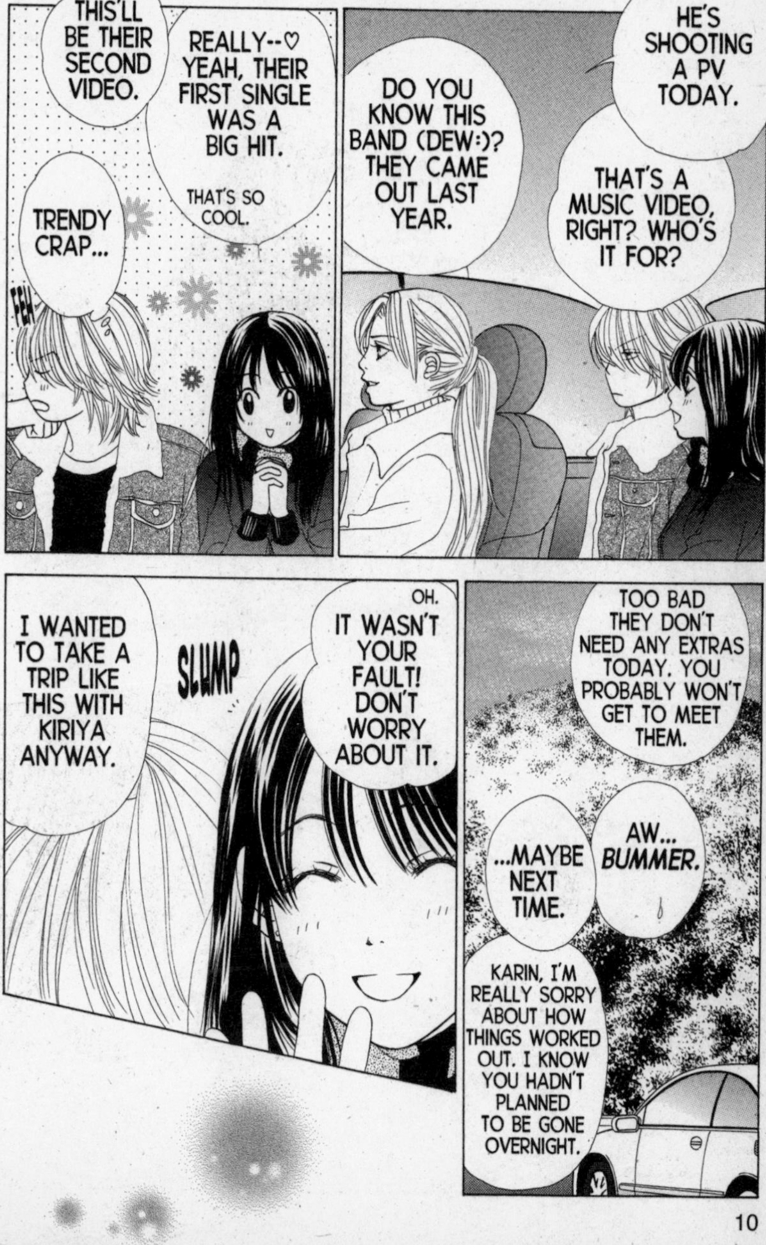
HE'S SHOOTING A PV TODAY.
THAT'S A MUSIC VIDEO, RIGHT? WHO'S IT FOR?
DO YOU KNOW THIS BAND (DEW:)? THEY CAME OUT LAST YEAR.
REALLY--♡ YEAH, THEIR FIRST SINGLE WAS A BIG HIT.
THAT'S SO COOL.
THIS'LL BE THEIR SECOND VIDEO.
TRENDY CRAP...
FEH
TOO BAD THEY DON'T NEED ANY EXTRAS TODAY. YOU PROBABLY WON'T GET TO MEET THEM.
AW... *BUMMER.*
...MAYBE NEXT TIME.
KARIN, I'M REALLY SORRY ABOUT HOW THINGS WORKED OUT. I KNOW YOU HADN'T PLANNED TO BE GONE OVERNIGHT.
OH.
IT WASN'T YOUR FAULT! DON'T WORRY ABOUT IT.
SLUMP
I WANTED TO TAKE A TRIP LIKE THIS WITH KIRIYA ANYWAY.

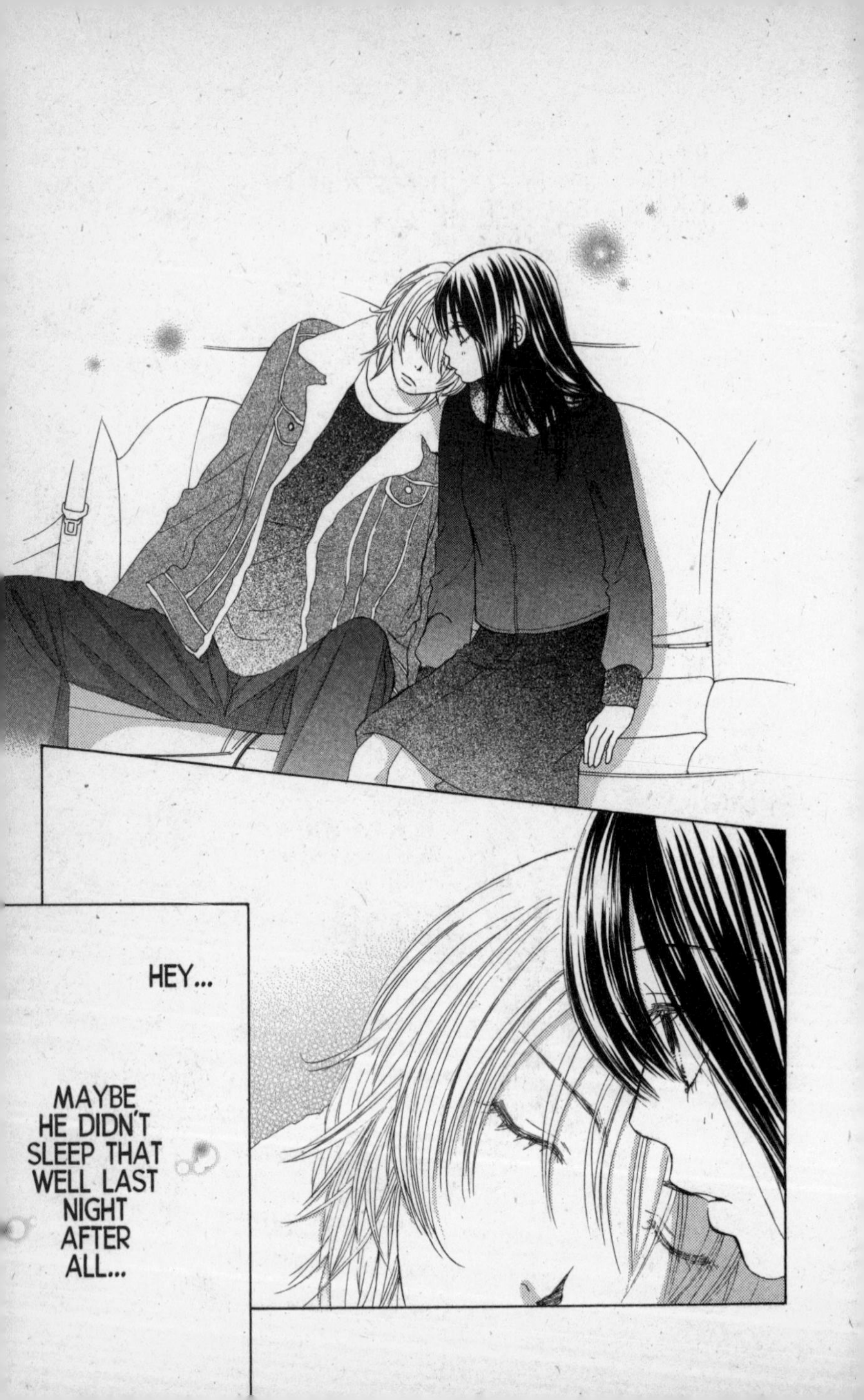
HEY...
MAYBE HE DIDN'T SLEEP THAT WELL LAST NIGHT AFTER ALL...

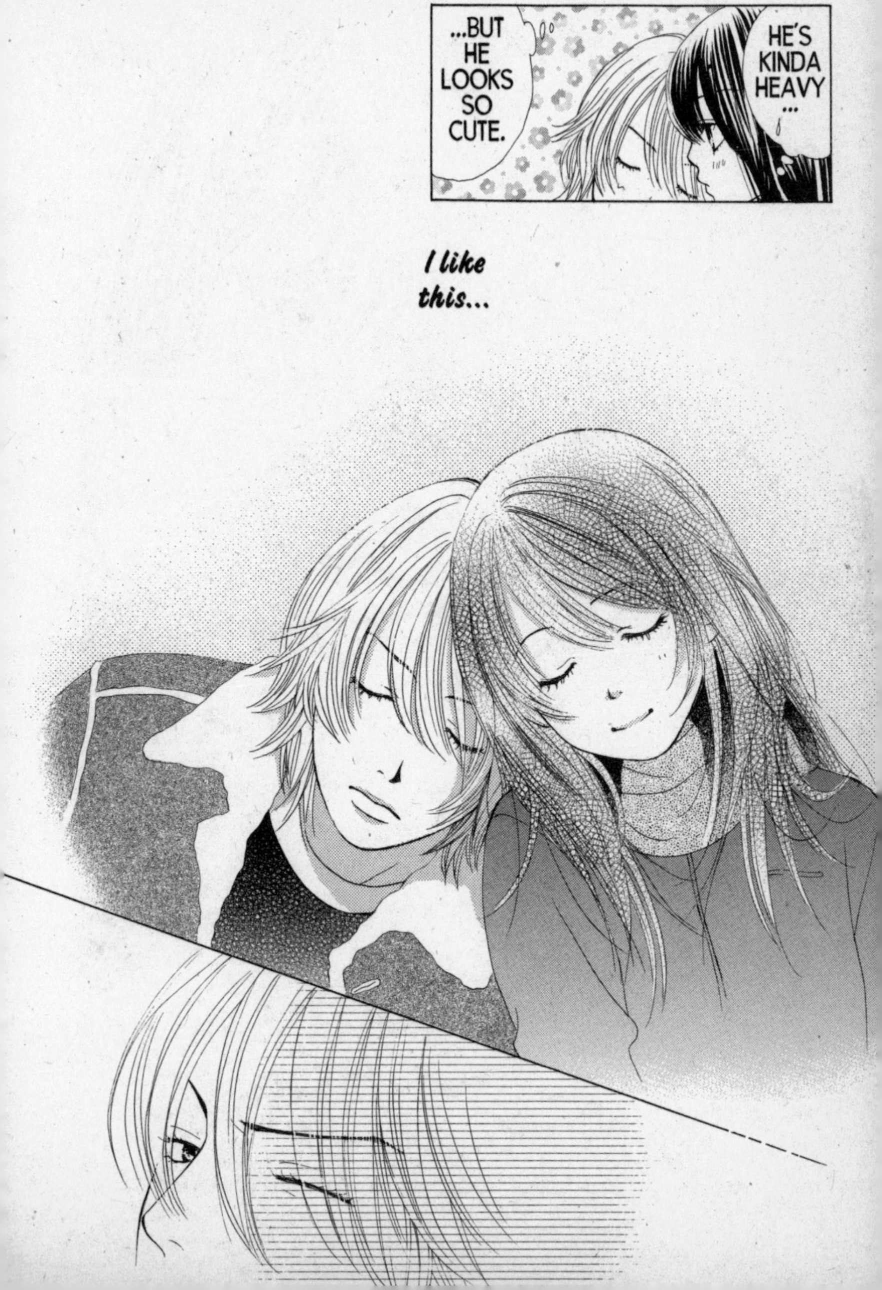
HE'S KINDA HEAVY ...
...BUT HE LOOKS SO CUTE.
I like this...

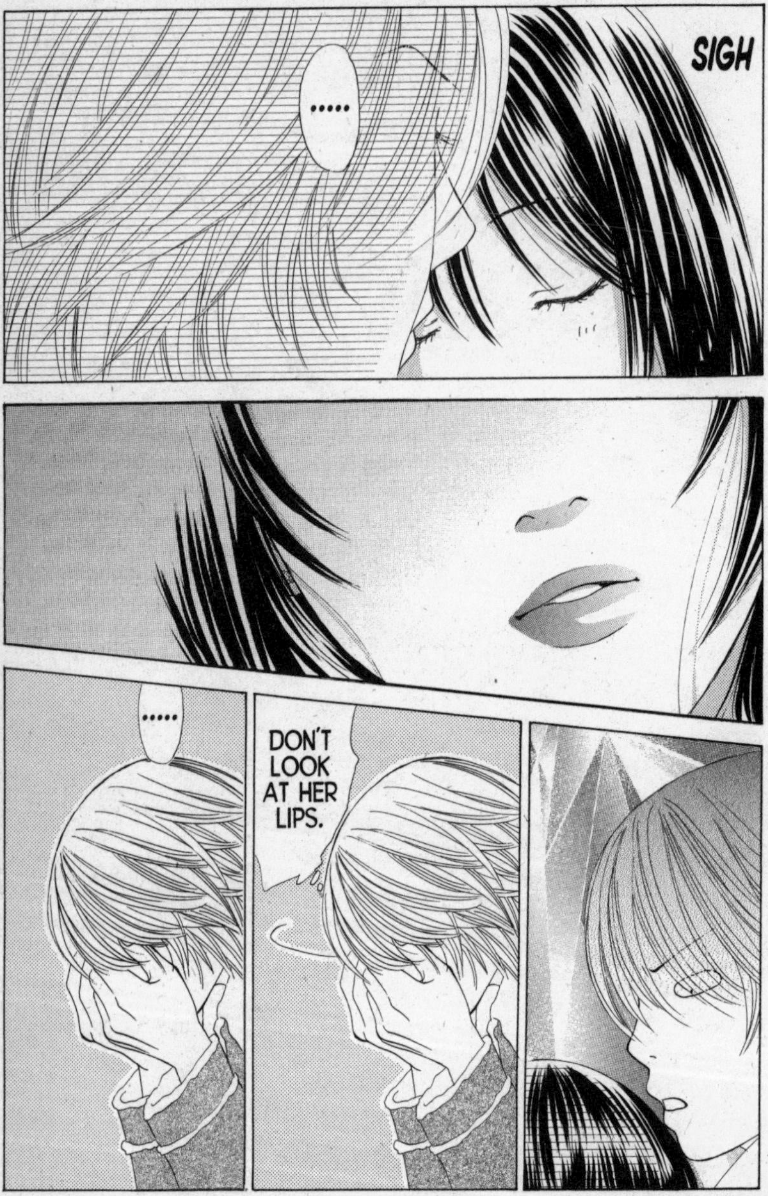
SIGH
......
DON'T LOOK AT HER LIPS.
......

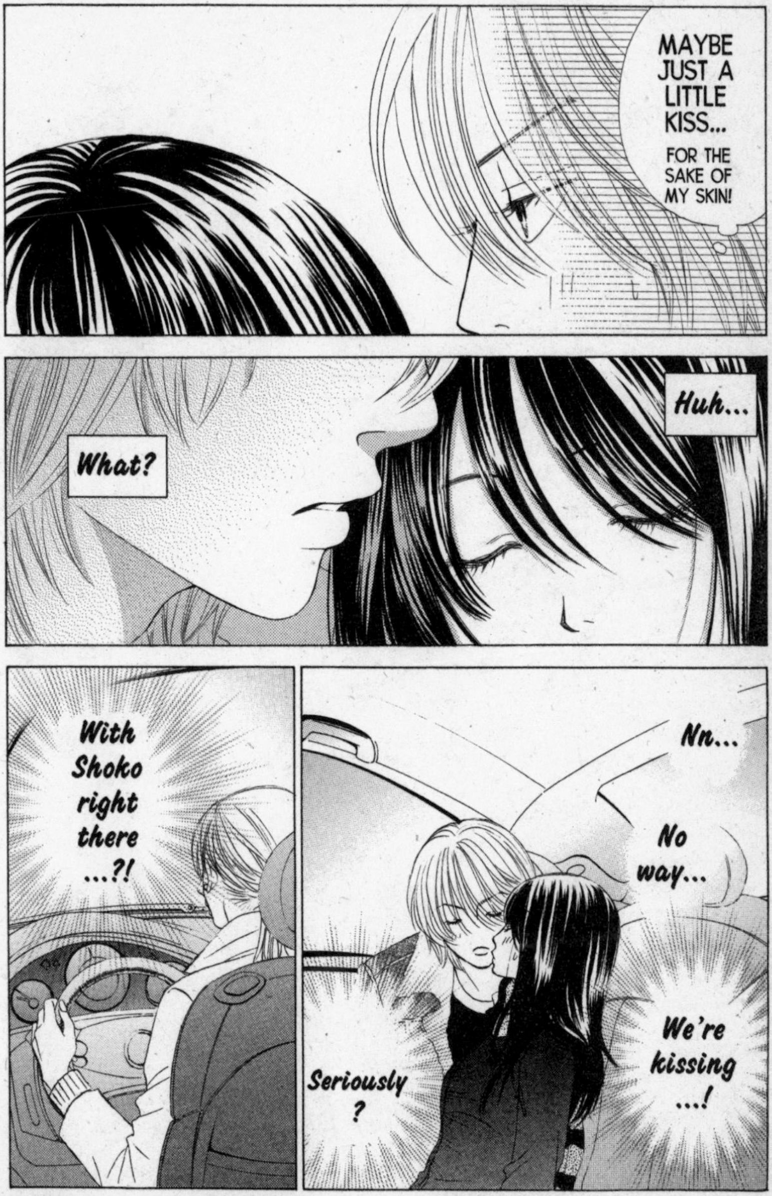
MAYBE JUST A LITTLE KISS...
FOR THE SAKE OF MY SKIN!
Huh...
What?
Nn...
No way...
We're kissing ...!
Seriously ?
With Shoko right there ...?!

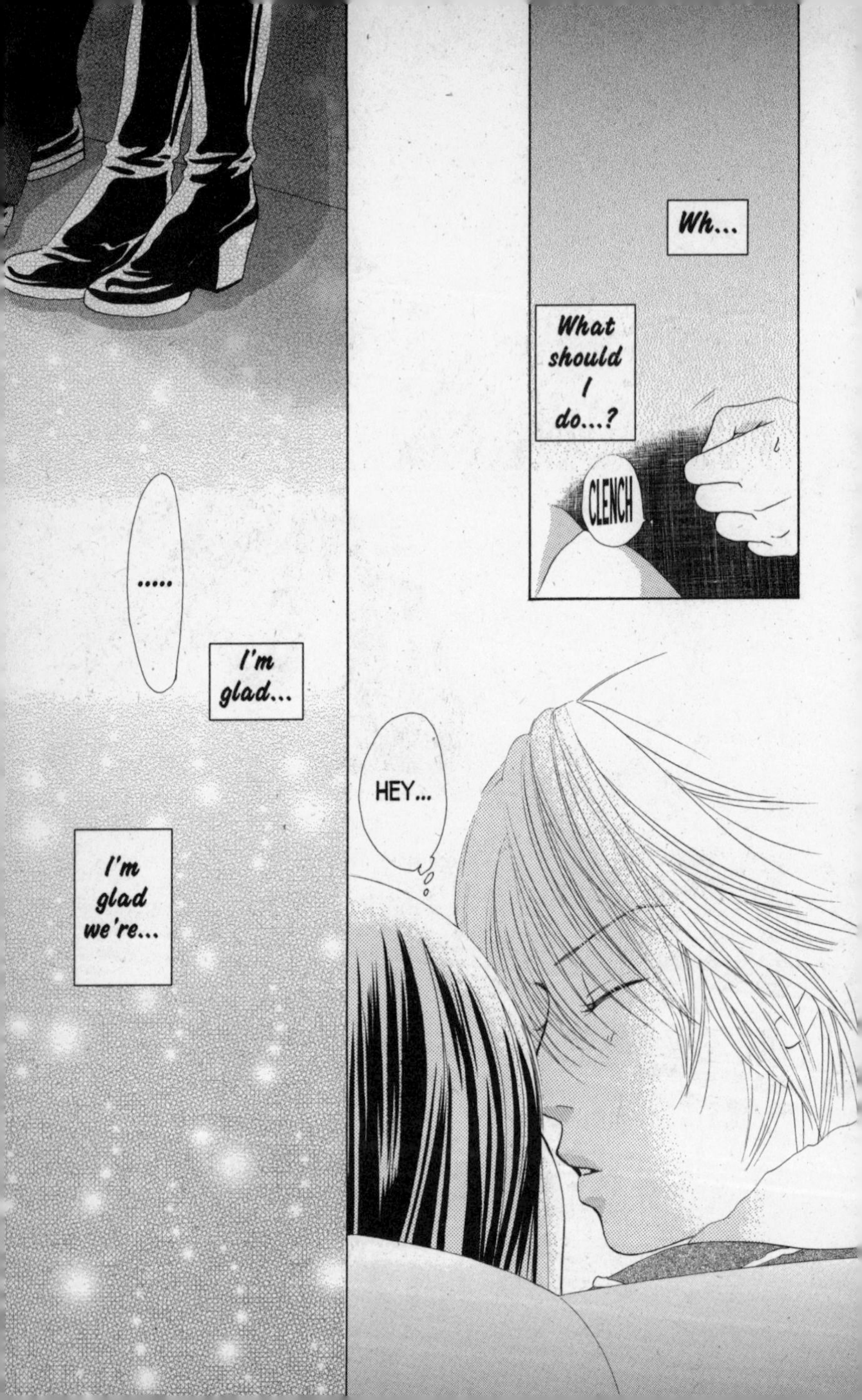
Wh...
What should I do...?
CLENCH
HEY...
......
I'm glad...
I'm glad we're...

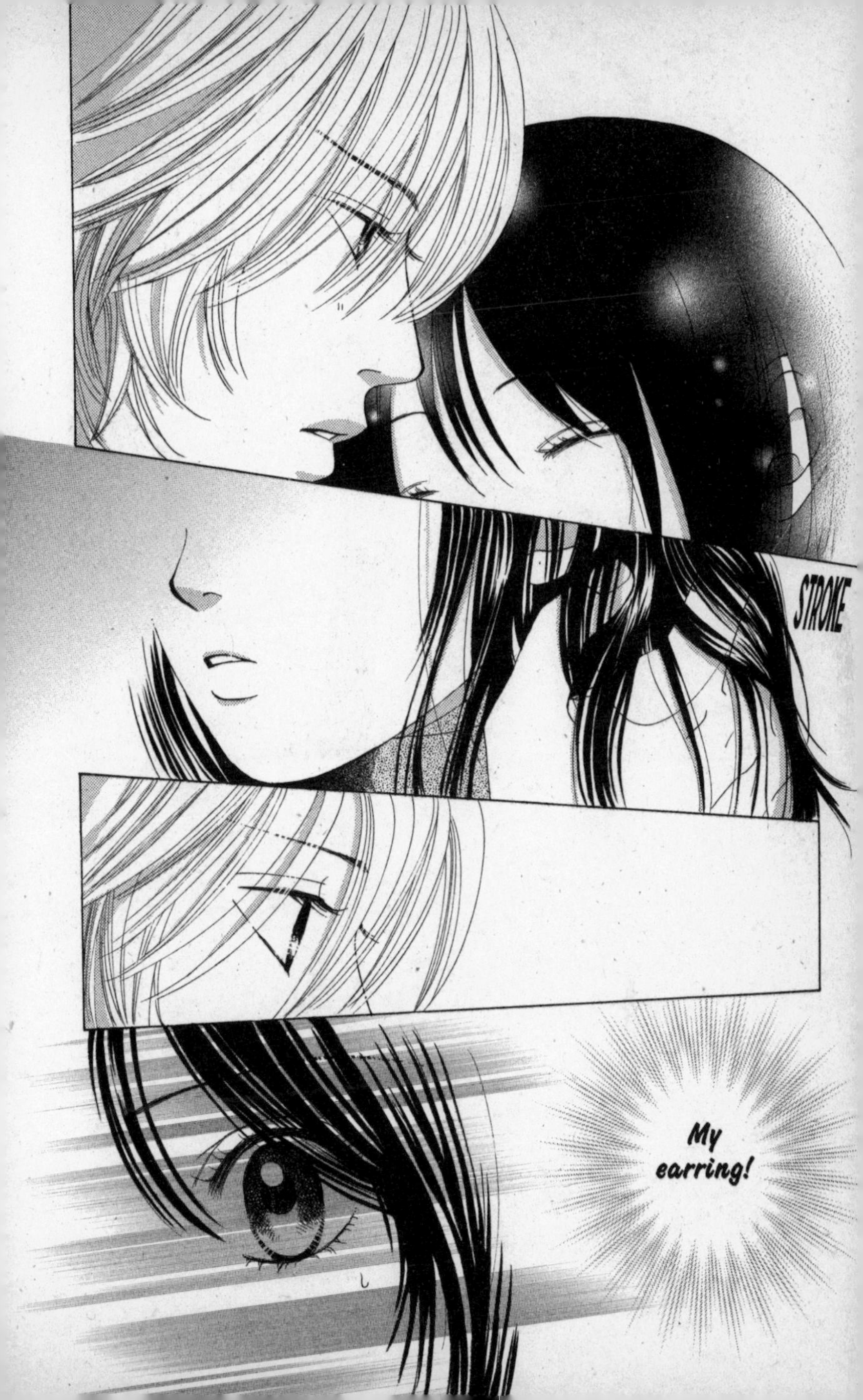
STROKE
My earring!

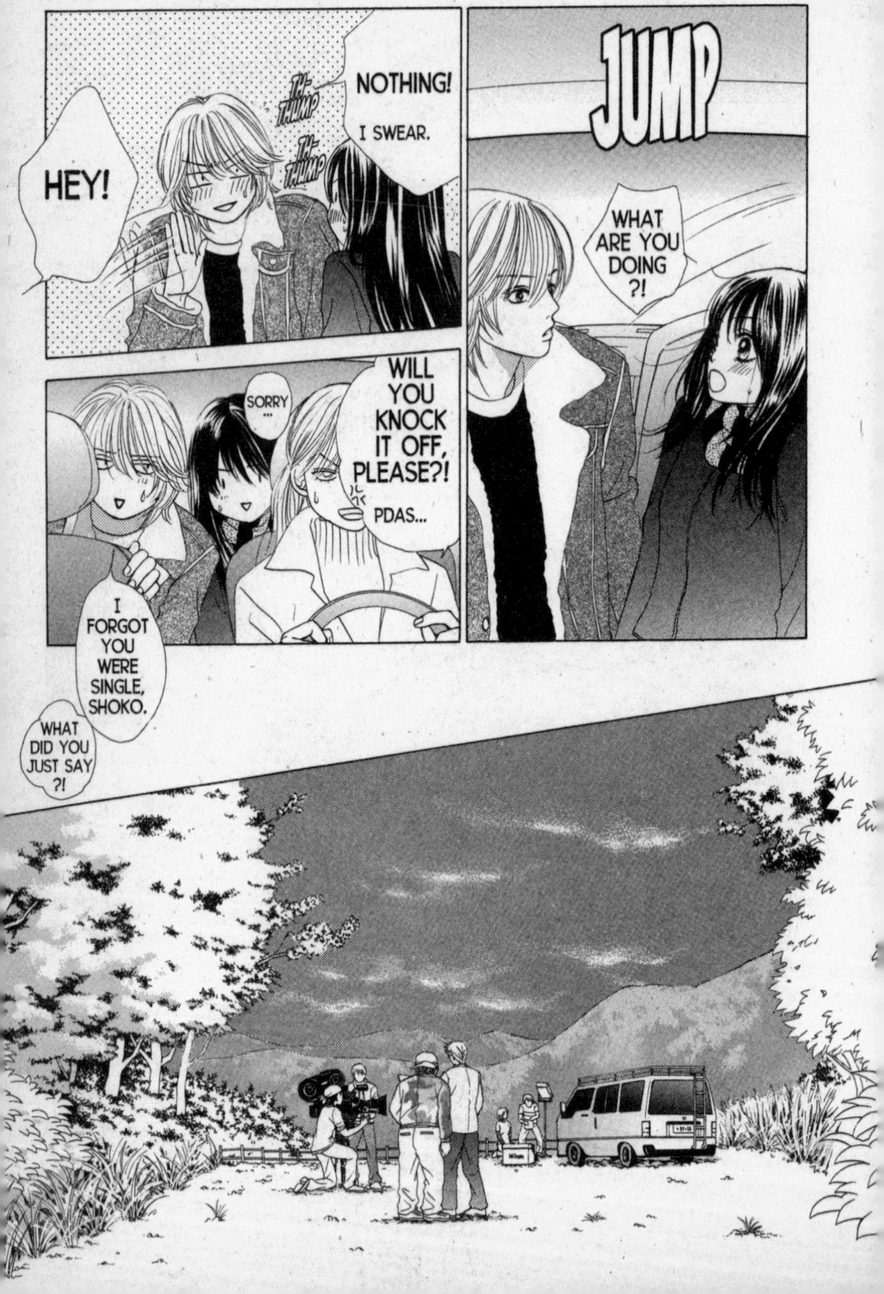
JUMP
WHAT ARE YOU DOING ?!
NOTHING!
I SWEAR.
TH-THUMP
TH-THUMP
HEY!
WILL YOU KNOCK IT OFF, PLEASE?!
PDAS...
SORRY ...
I FORGOT YOU WERE SINGLE, SHOKO.
WHAT DID YOU JUST SAY ?!

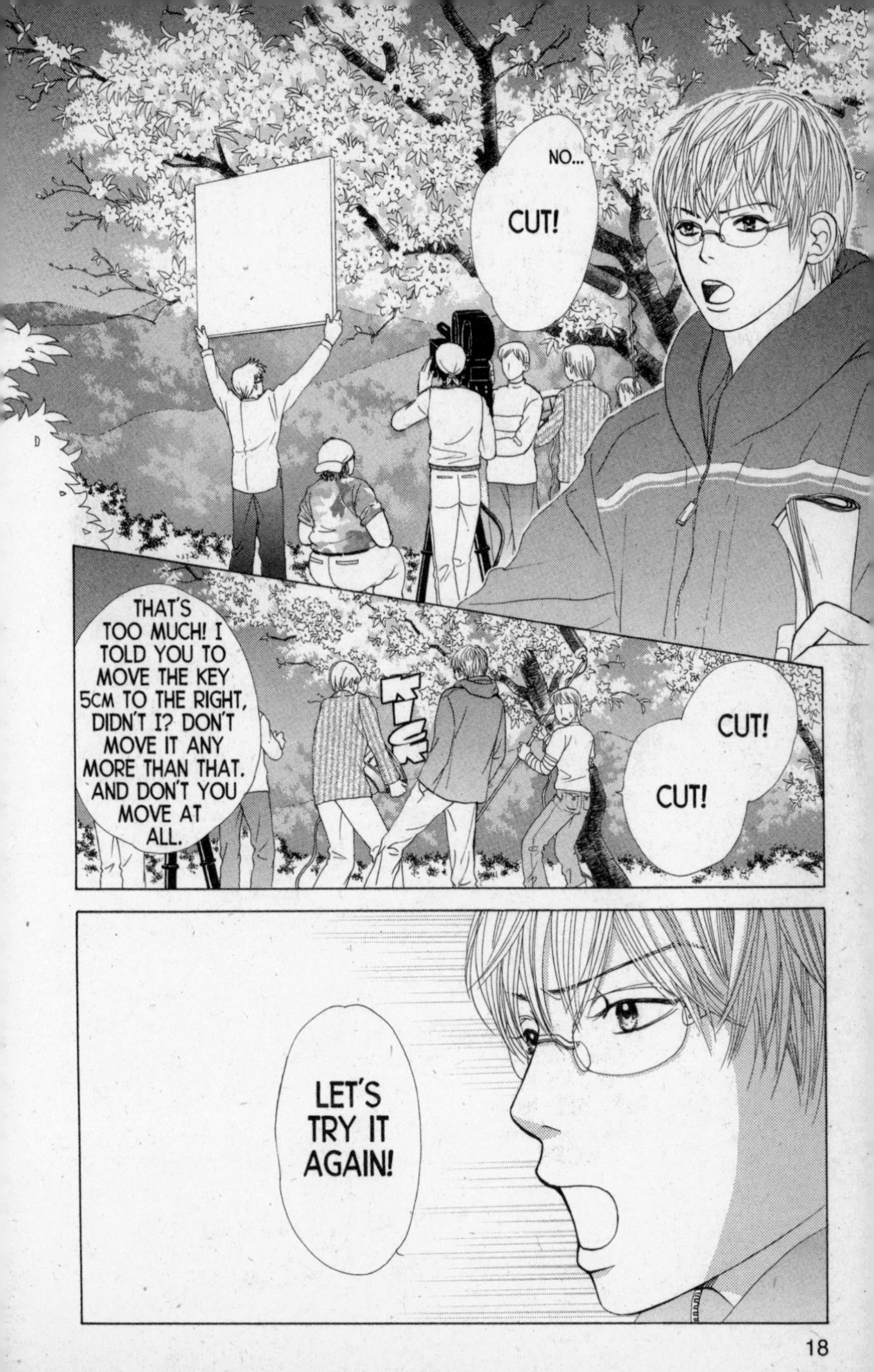
NO...
CUT!
CUT!
CUT!
KICK
THAT'S TOO MUCH! I TOLD YOU TO MOVE THE KEY 5CM TO THE RIGHT, DIDN'T I? DON'T MOVE IT ANY MORE THAN THAT. AND DON'T YOU MOVE AT ALL.
LET'S TRY IT AGAIN!

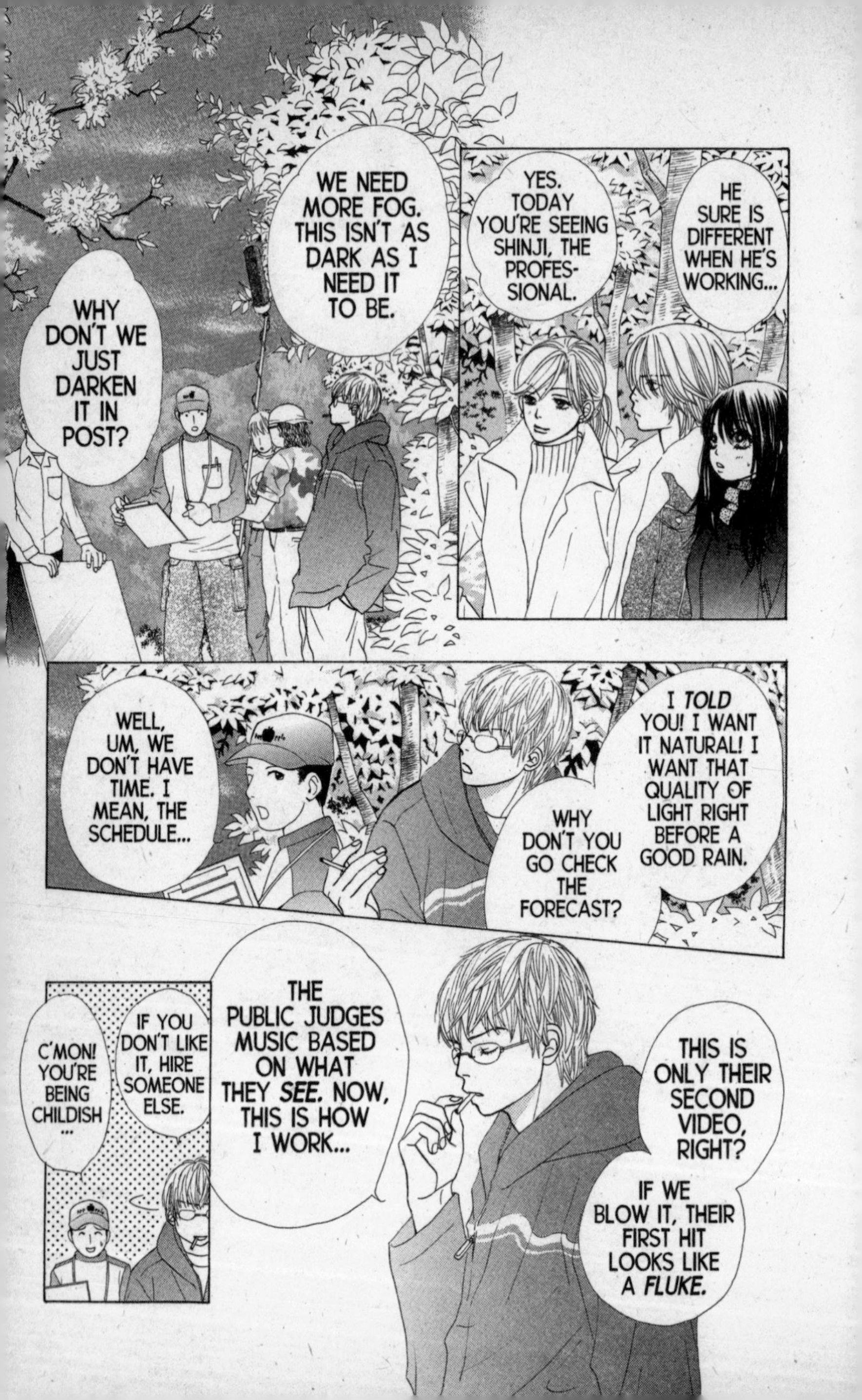
WE NEED MORE FOG. THIS ISN'T AS DARK AS I NEED IT TO BE.
WHY DON'T WE JUST DARKEN IT IN POST?
HE SURE IS DIFFERENT WHEN HE'S WORKING...
YES. TODAY YOU'RE SEEING SHINJI, THE PROFES-SIONAL.
I *TOLD* YOU! I WANT IT NATURAL! I WANT THAT QUALITY OF LIGHT RIGHT BEFORE A GOOD RAIN.
WHY DON'T YOU GO CHECK THE FORECAST?
WELL, UM, WE DON'T HAVE TIME. I MEAN, THE SCHEDULE...
THIS IS ONLY THEIR SECOND VIDEO, RIGHT?
IF WE BLOW IT, THEIR FIRST HIT LOOKS LIKE A ***FLUKE.***
THE PUBLIC JUDGES MUSIC BASED ON WHAT THEY *SEE.* NOW, THIS IS HOW I WORK...
IF YOU DON'T LIKE IT, HIRE SOMEONE ELSE.
C'MON! YOU'RE BEING CHILDISH...

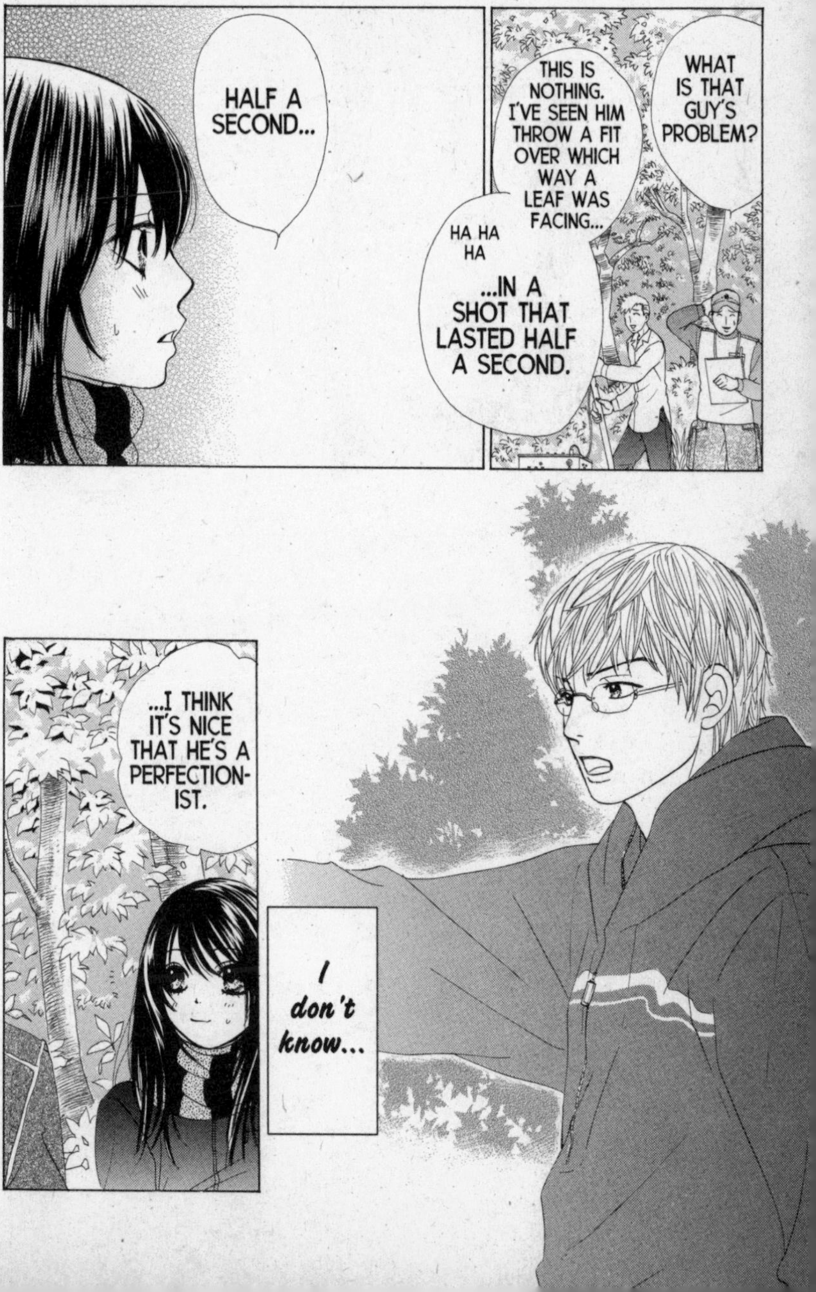
WHAT IS THAT GUY'S PROBLEM?
THIS IS NOTHING. I'VE SEEN HIM THROW A FIT OVER WHICH WAY A LEAF WAS FACING...
HA HA HA
...IN A SHOT THAT LASTED HALF A SECOND.
HALF A SECOND...
I don't know...
...I THINK IT'S NICE THAT HE'S A PERFECTION-IST.

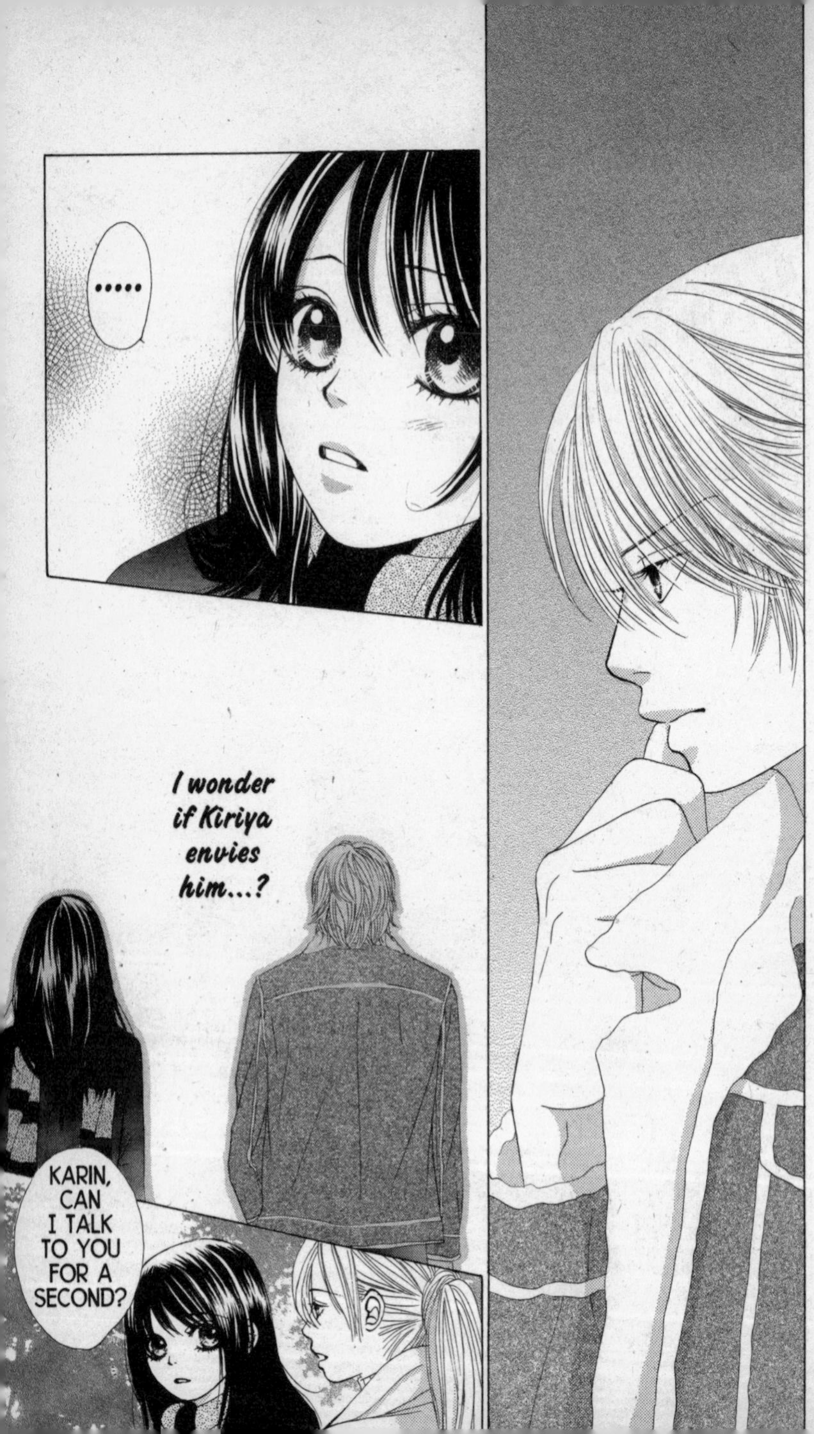
.....
I wonder if Kiriya envies him...?
KARIN, CAN I TALK TO YOU FOR A SECOND?

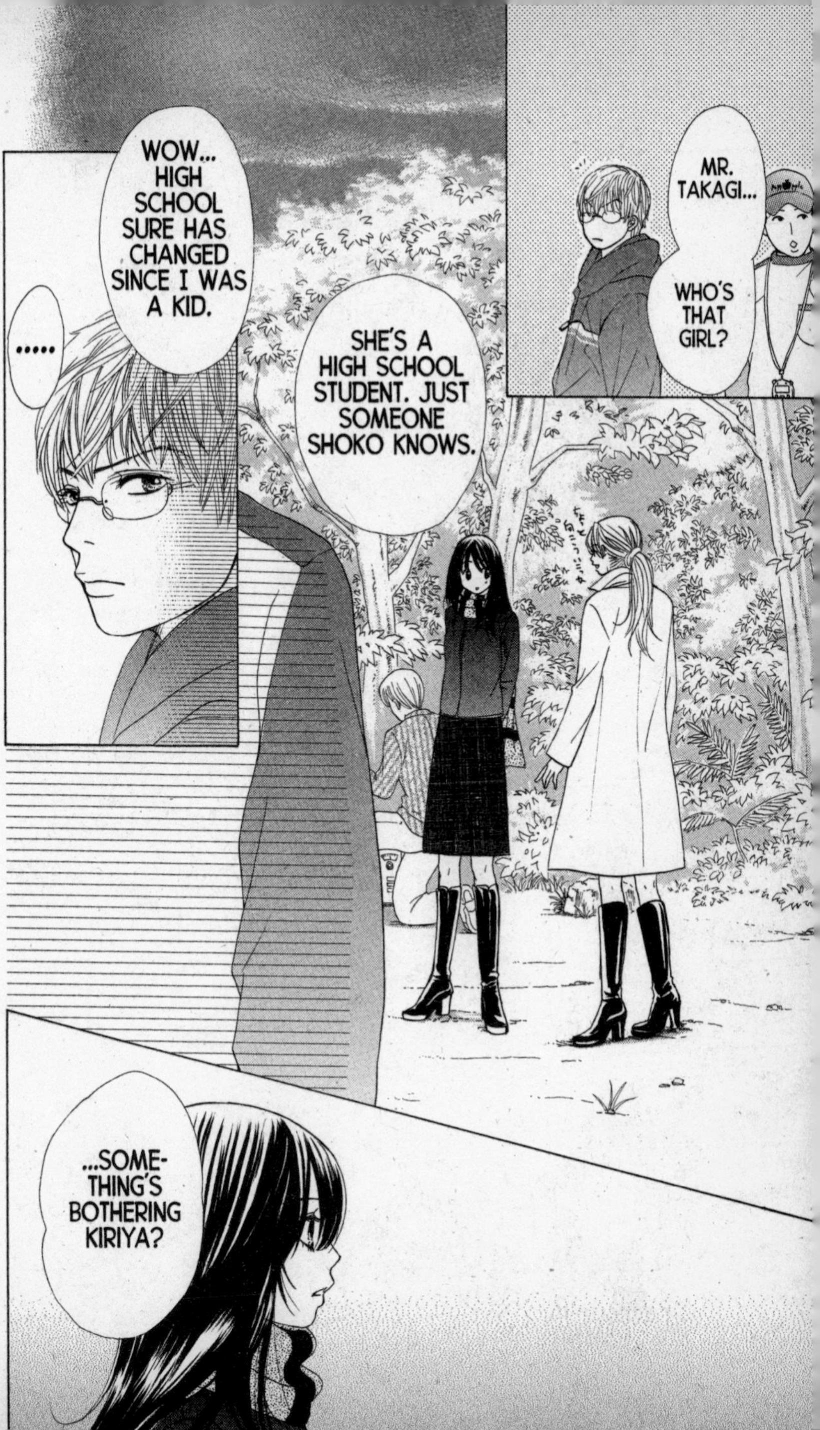
MR. TAKAGI...
WHO'S THAT GIRL?
SHE'S A HIGH SCHOOL STUDENT. JUST SOMEONE SHOKO KNOWS.
WOW... HIGH SCHOOL SURE HAS CHANGED SINCE I WAS A KID.
......
...SOME-THING'S BOTHERING KIRIYA?

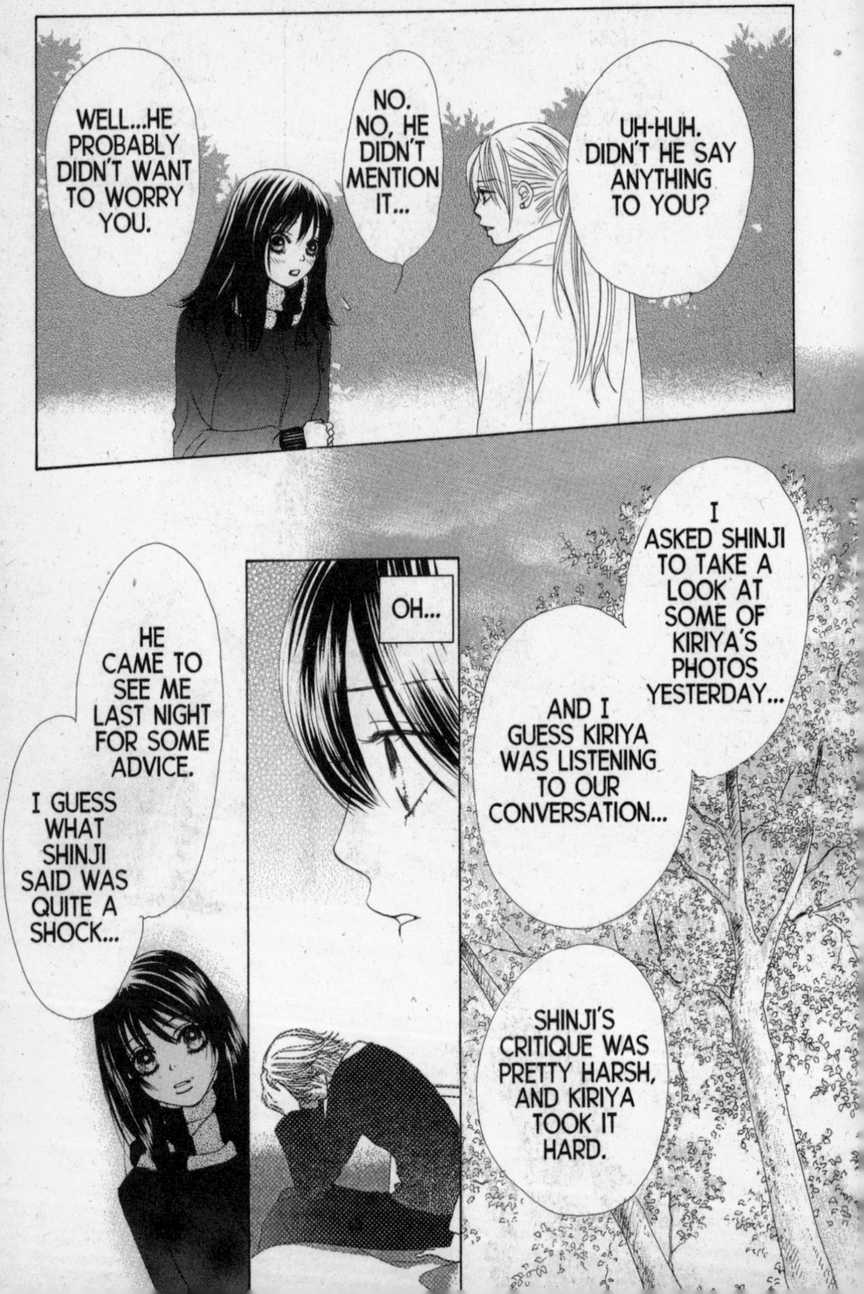
UH-HUH. DIDN'T HE SAY ANYTHING TO YOU?
NO. NO, HE DIDN'T MENTION IT...
WELL...HE PROBABLY DIDN'T WANT TO WORRY YOU.
I ASKED SHINJI TO TAKE A LOOK AT SOME OF KIRIYA'S PHOTOS YESTERDAY...
AND I GUESS KIRIYA WAS LISTENING TO OUR CONVERSATION...
SHINJI'S CRITIQUE WAS PRETTY HARSH, AND KIRIYA TOOK IT HARD.
OH...
HE CAME TO SEE ME LAST NIGHT FOR SOME ADVICE.
I GUESS WHAT SHINJI SAID WAS QUITE A SHOCK...

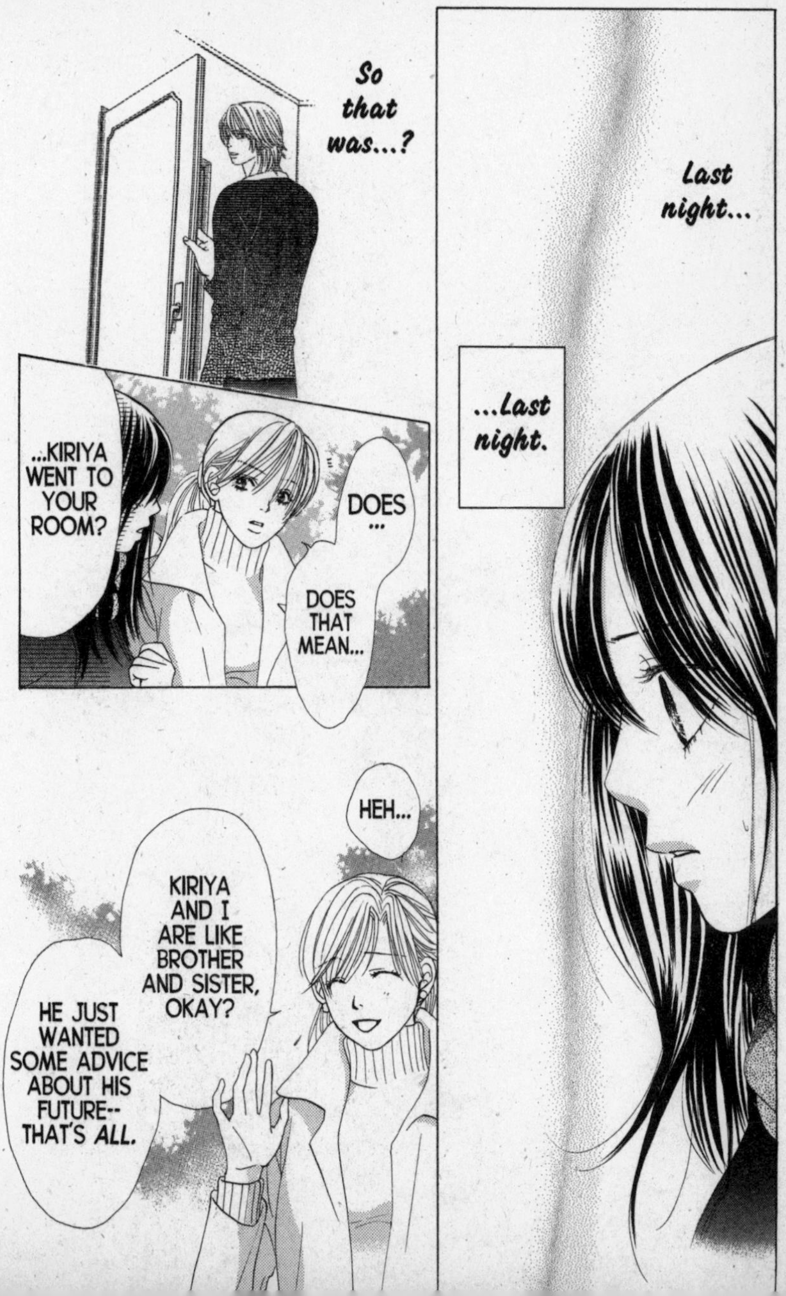
Last night...
...Last night.
So that was...?
DOES...
DOES THAT MEAN...
...KIRIYA WENT TO YOUR ROOM?
HEH...
KIRIYA AND I ARE LIKE BROTHER AND SISTER, OKAY?
HE JUST WANTED SOME ADVICE ABOUT HIS FUTURE-- THAT'S *ALL*.

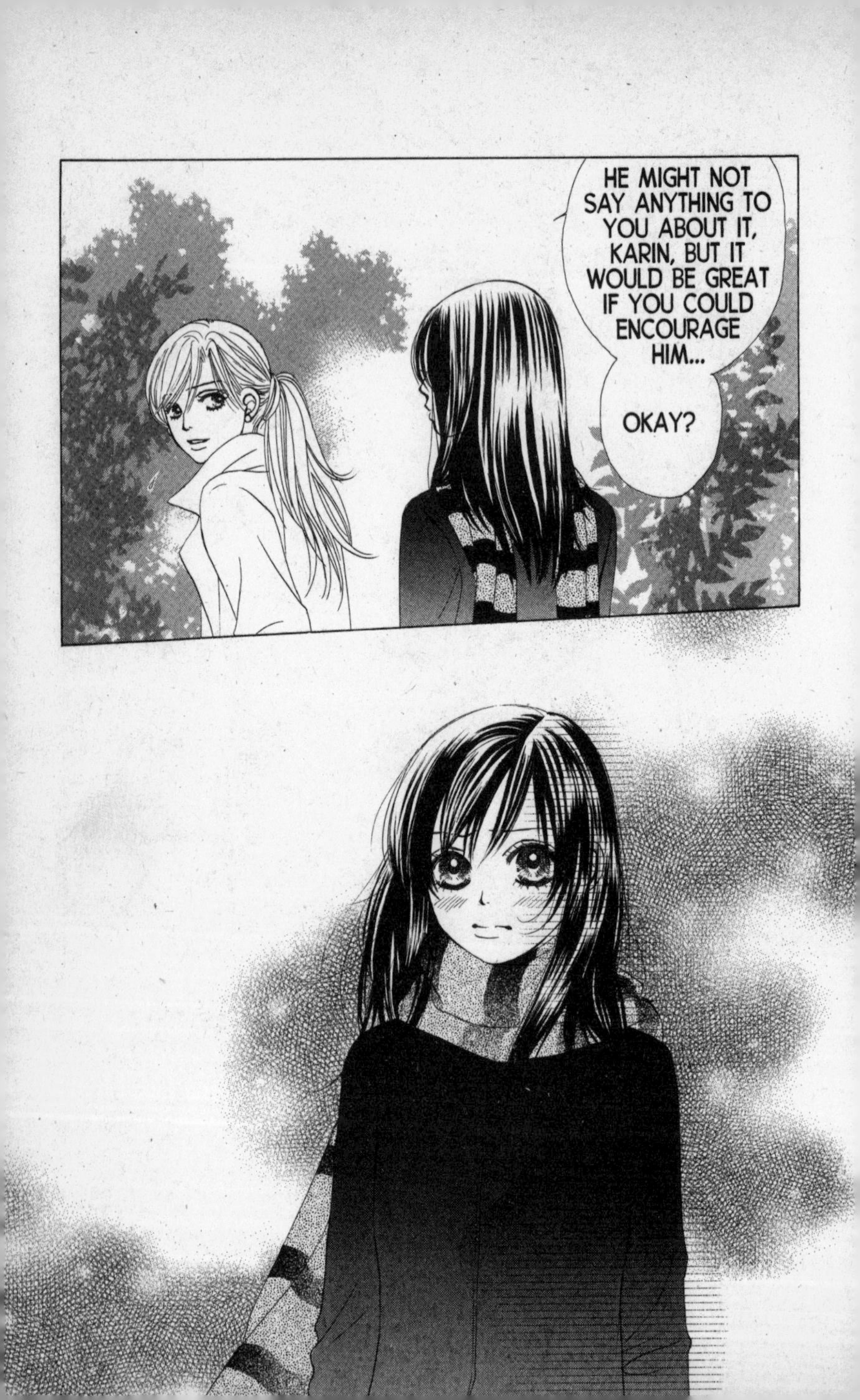
HE MIGHT NOT SAY ANYTHING TO YOU ABOUT IT, KARIN, BUT IT WOULD BE GREAT IF YOU COULD ENCOURAGE HIM...
OKAY?

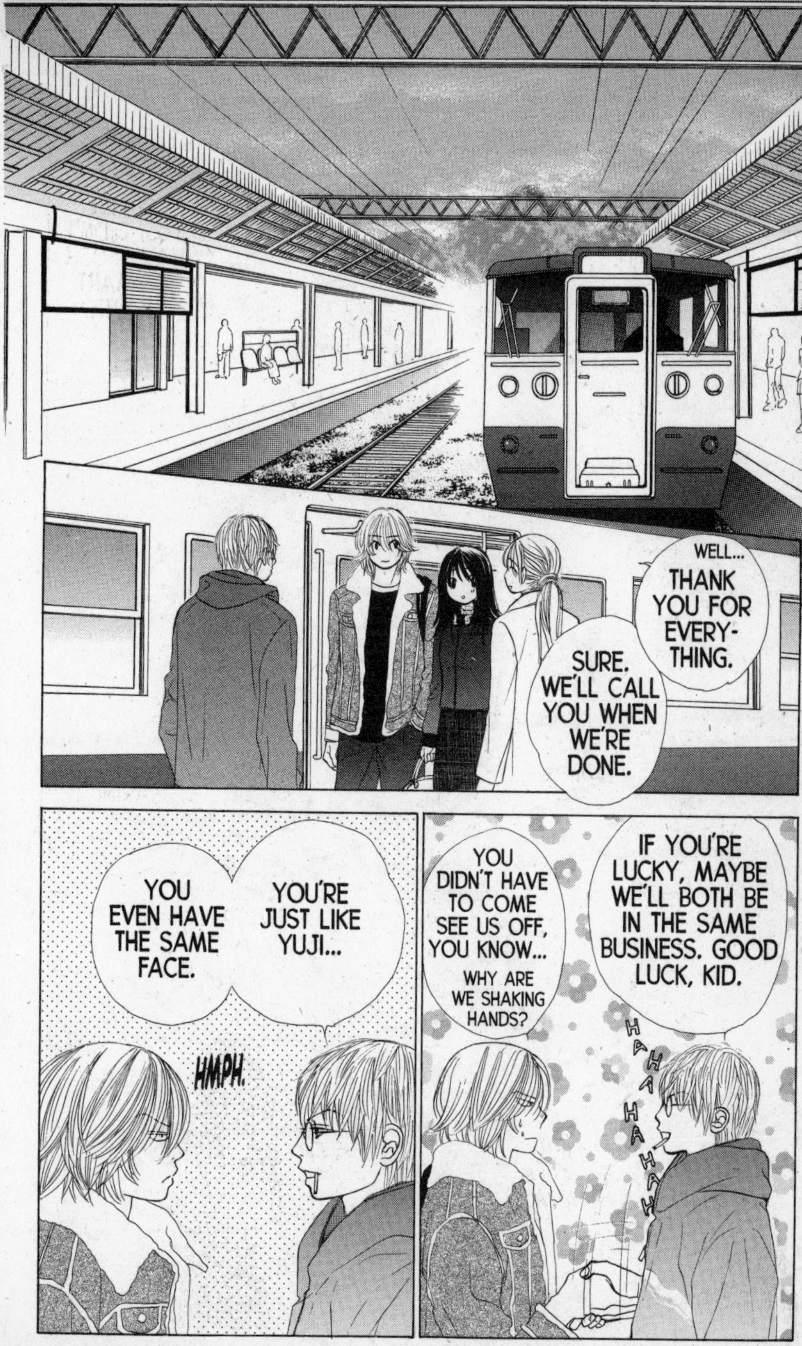
WELL... THANK YOU FOR EVERY-THING.
SURE. WE'LL CALL YOU WHEN WE'RE DONE.
IF YOU'RE LUCKY, MAYBE WE'LL BOTH BE IN THE SAME BUSINESS. GOOD LUCK, KID.
HAHAHAHA
YOU DIDN'T HAVE TO COME SEE US OFF, YOU KNOW...
WHY ARE WE SHAKING HANDS?
YOU'RE JUST LIKE YUJI...
YOU EVEN HAVE THE SAME FACE.
HMPH.

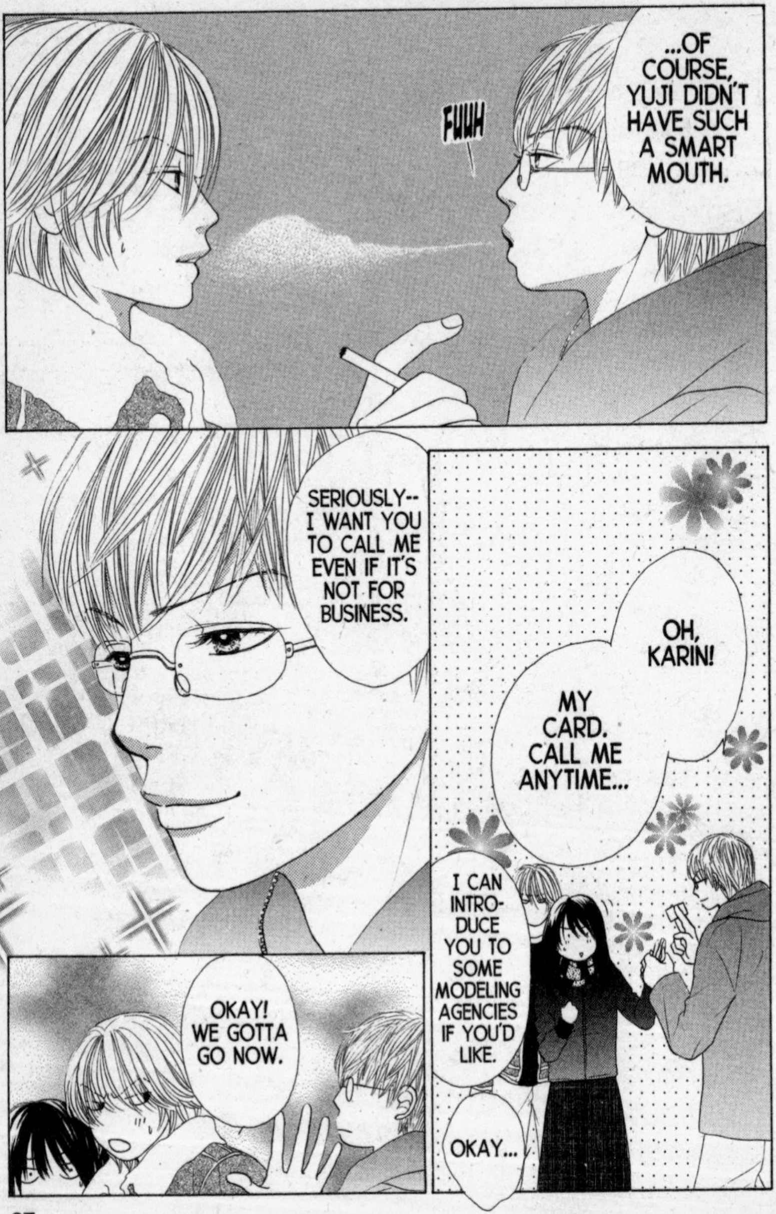
...OF COURSE, YUJI DIDN'T HAVE SUCH A SMART MOUTH.
FUUH
OH, KARIN!
MY CARD. CALL ME ANYTIME...
I CAN INTRO-DUCE YOU TO SOME MODELING AGENCIES IF YOU'D LIKE.
OKAY...
SERIOUSLY-- I WANT YOU TO CALL ME EVEN IF IT'S NOT FOR BUSINESS.
OKAY! WE GOTTA GO NOW.

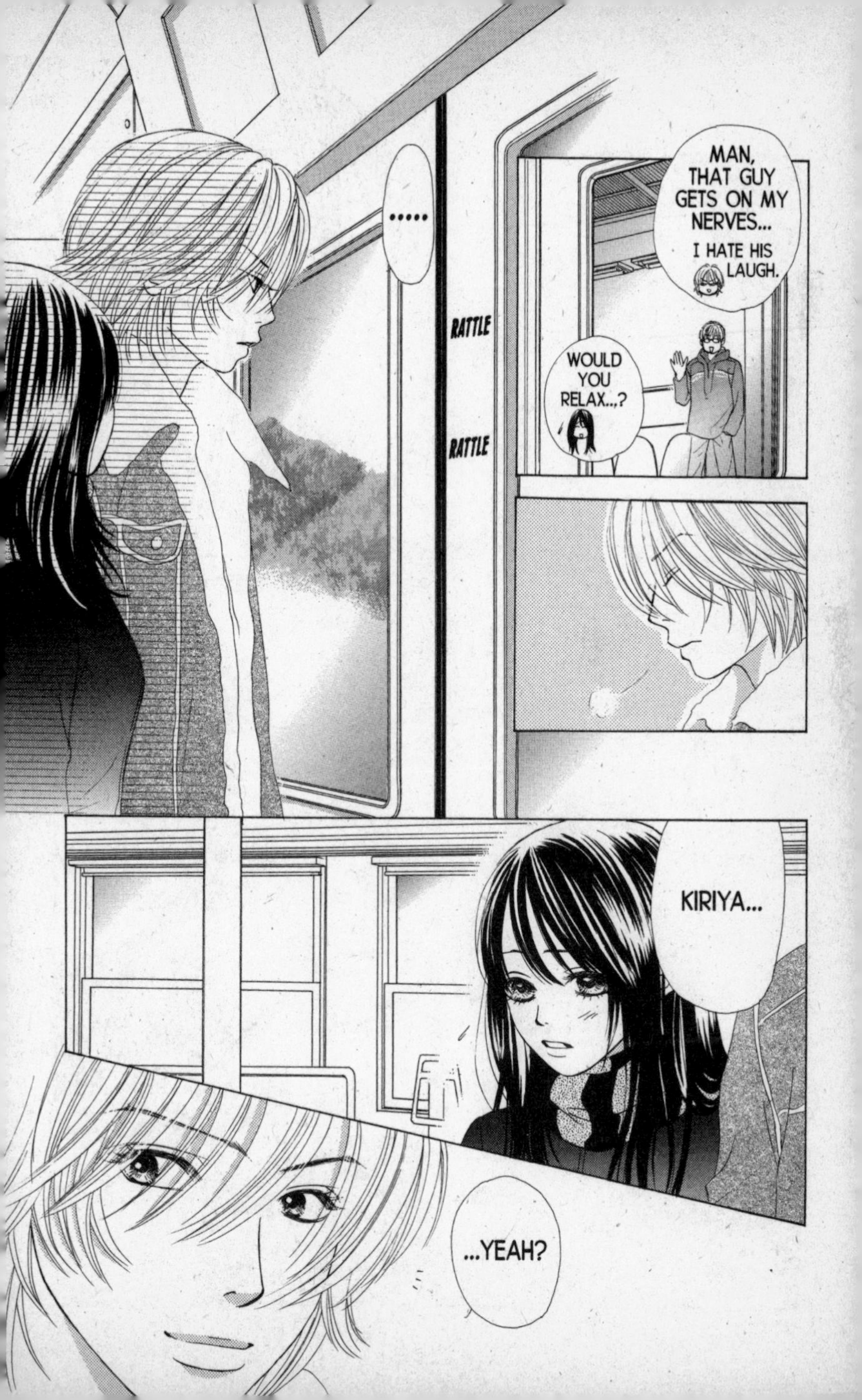
MAN, THAT GUY GETS ON MY NERVES...
I HATE HIS LAUGH.
WOULD YOU RELAX...?
.....
RATTLE
RATTLE
KIRIYA...
...YEAH?

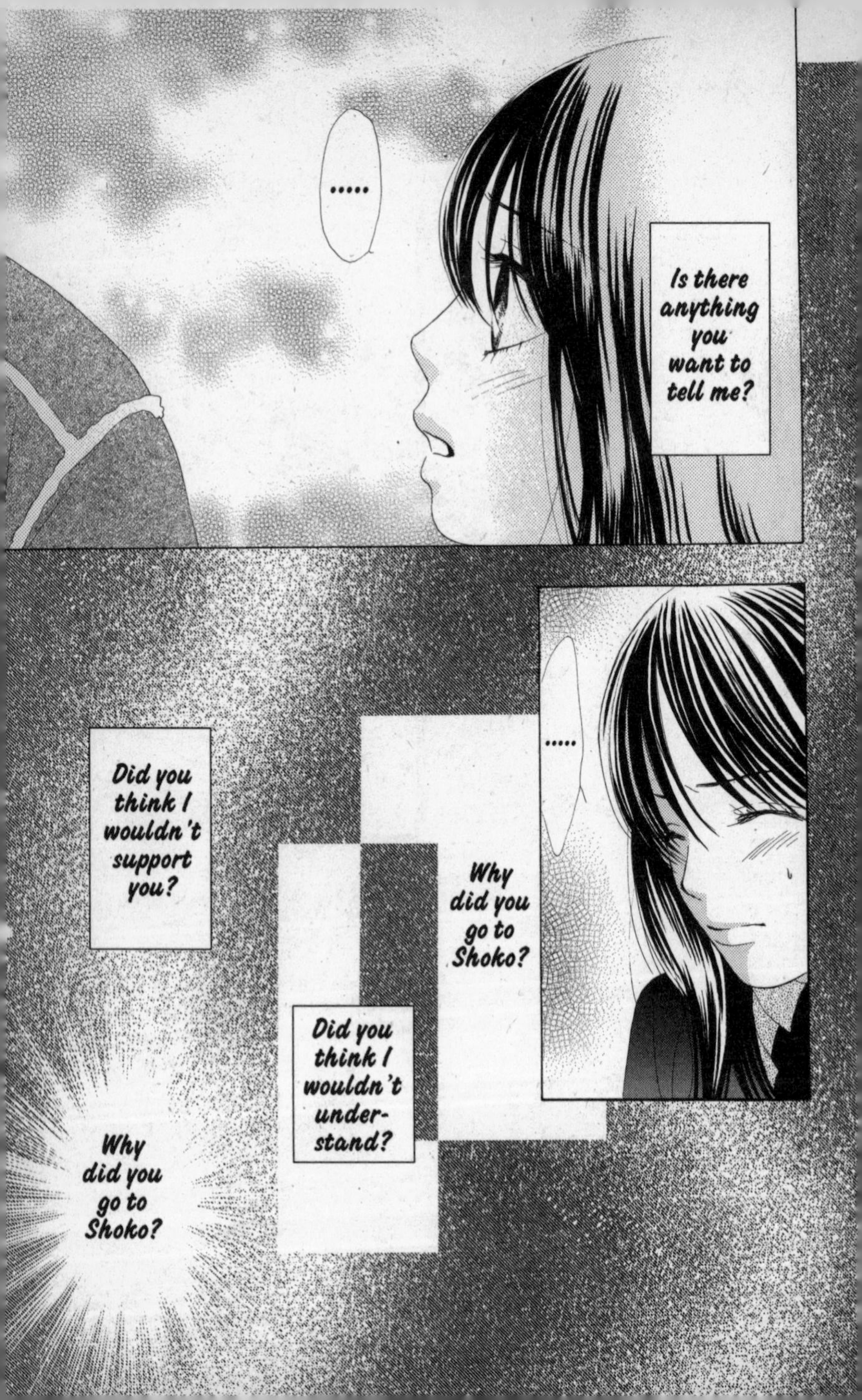
Is there anything you want to tell me?
.....
.....
Why did you go to Shoko?
Did you think I wouldn't understand?
Did you think I wouldn't support you?
Why did you go to Shoko?

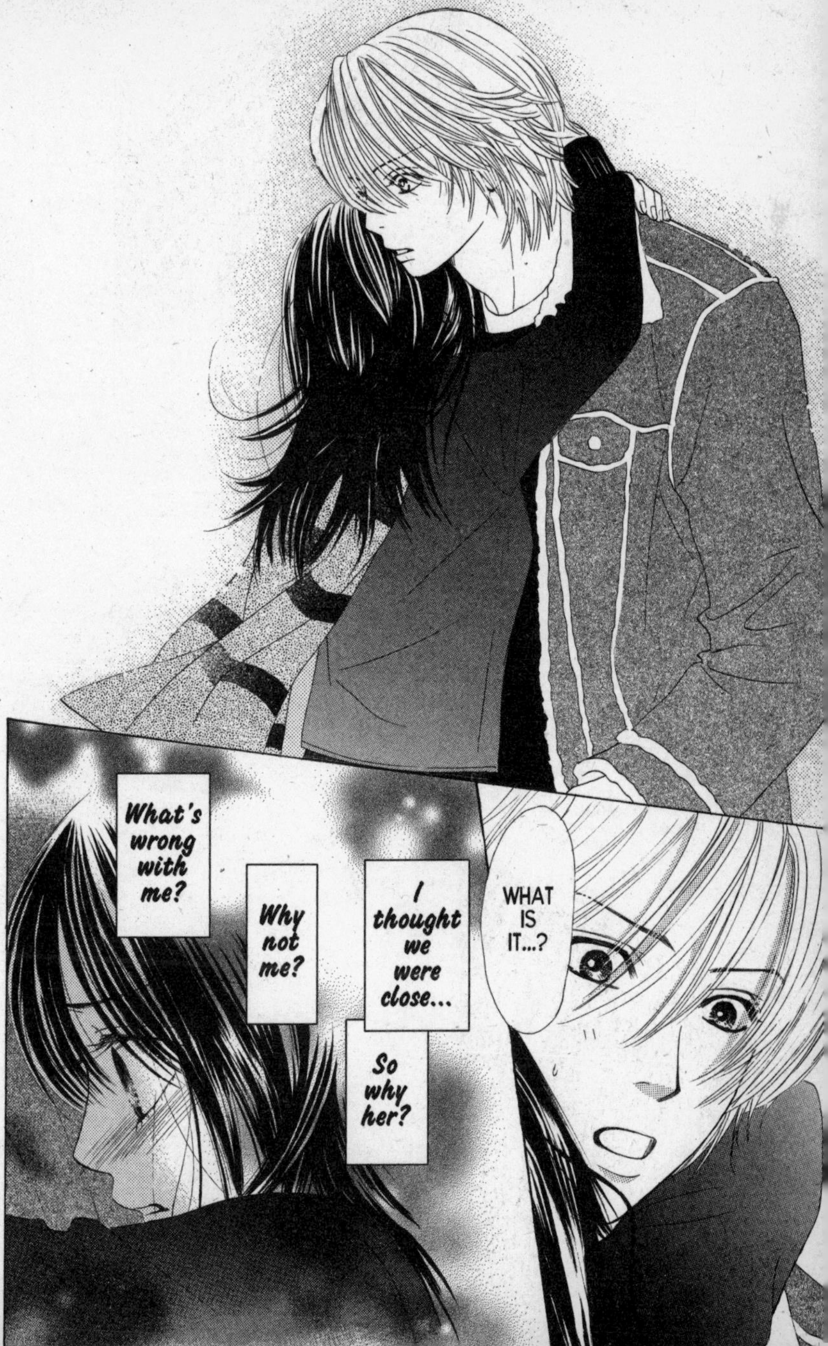
WHAT IS IT...?
I thought we were close...
So why her?
Why not me?
What's wrong with me?

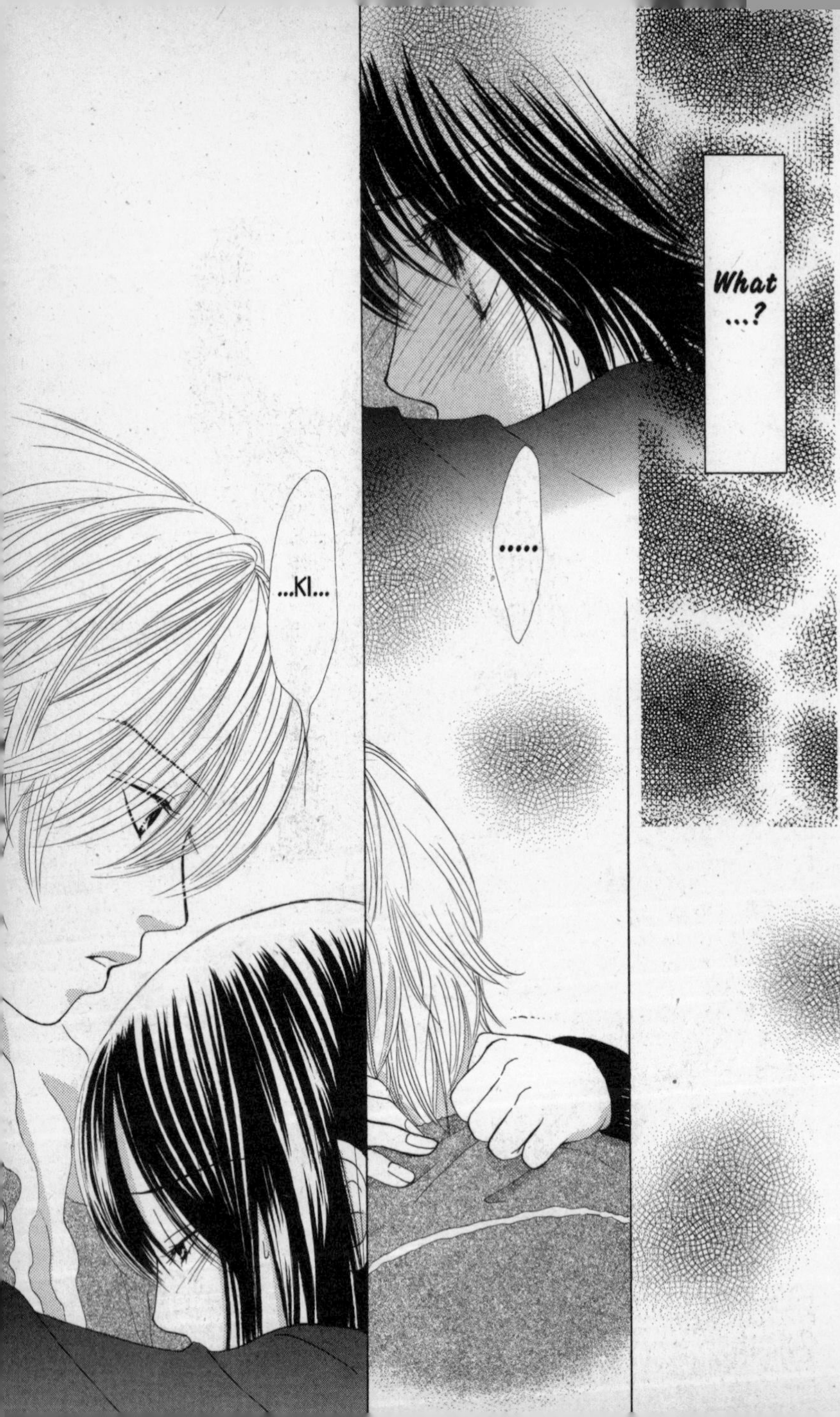
What ...?
......
...KI...

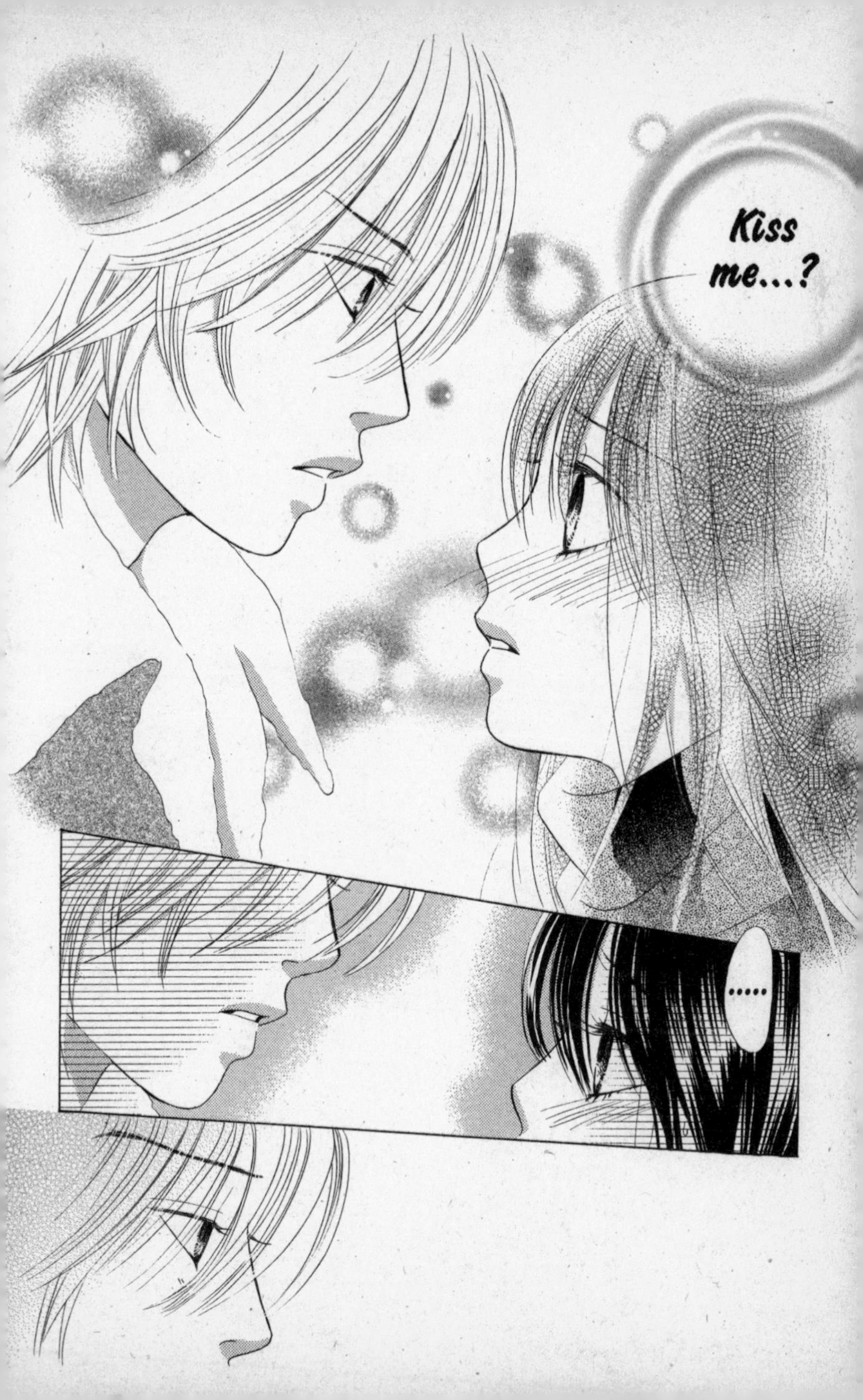
Kiss me...?
......

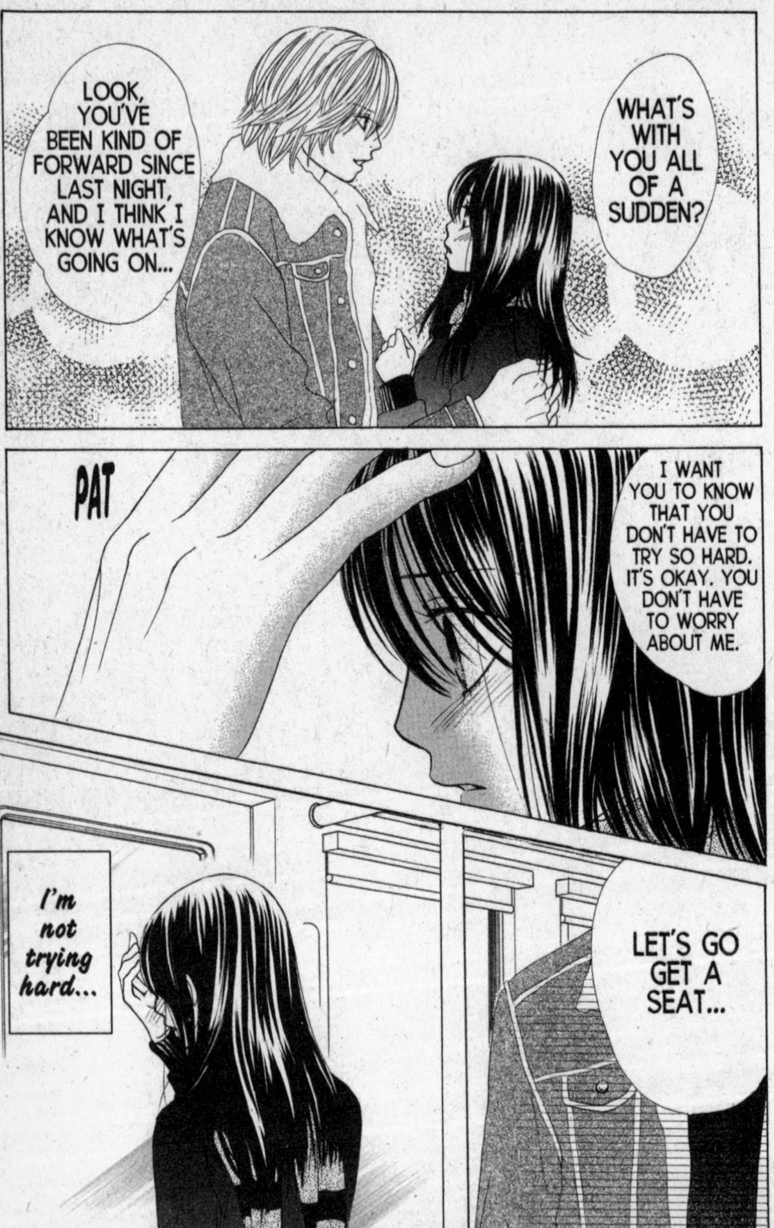
WHAT'S WITH YOU ALL OF A SUDDEN?
LOOK, YOU'VE BEEN KIND OF FORWARD SINCE LAST NIGHT, AND I THINK I KNOW WHAT'S GOING ON...
I WANT YOU TO KNOW THAT YOU DON'T HAVE TO TRY SO HARD. IT'S OKAY. YOU DON'T HAVE TO WORRY ABOUT ME.
PAT
LET'S GO GET A SEAT...
I'm not trying hard...

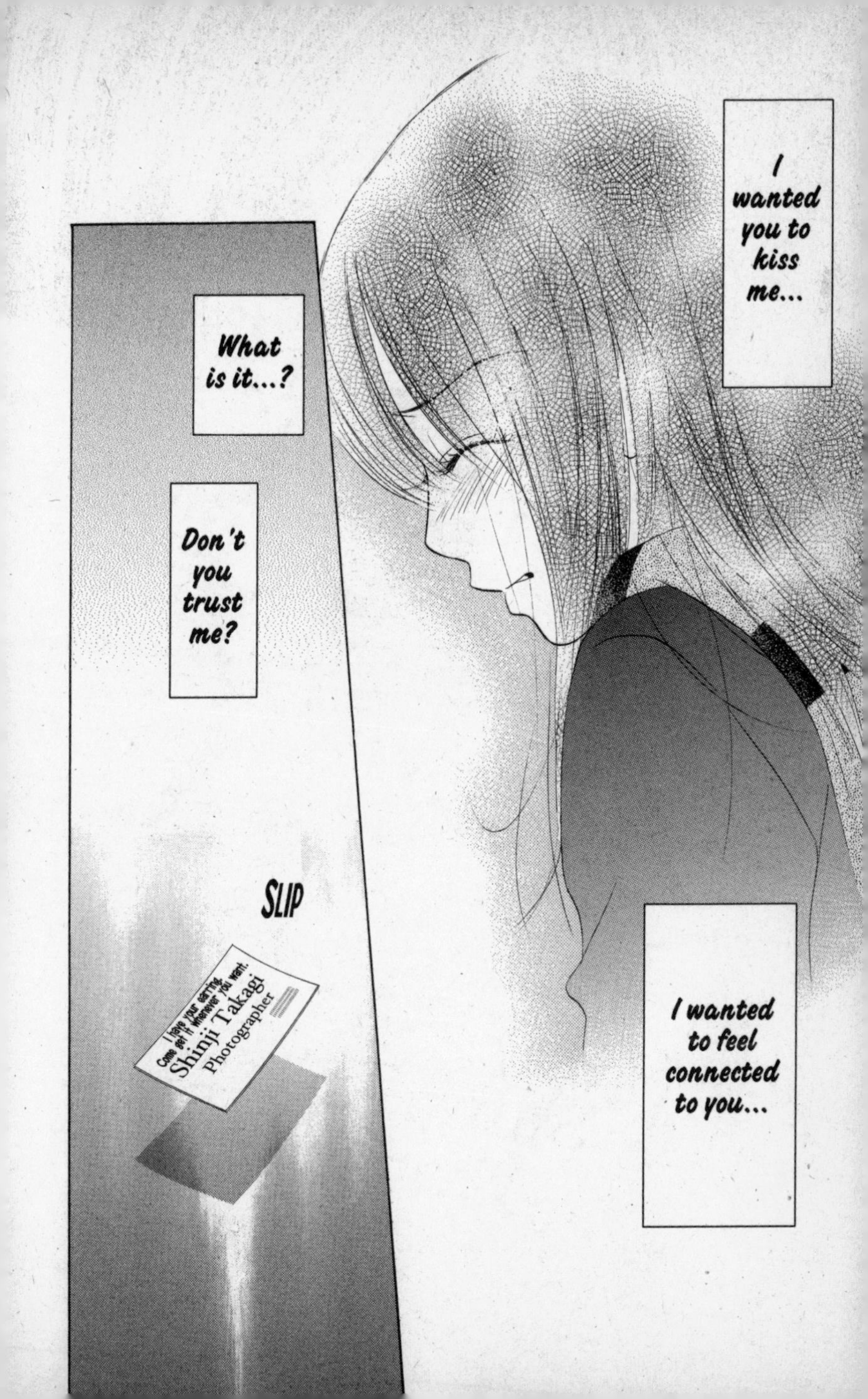
I wanted you to kiss me...
I wanted to feel connected to you...
What is it...?
Don't you trust me?
SLIP
I have your earring.
Come get it whenever you want.
Shinji Takagi
Photographer

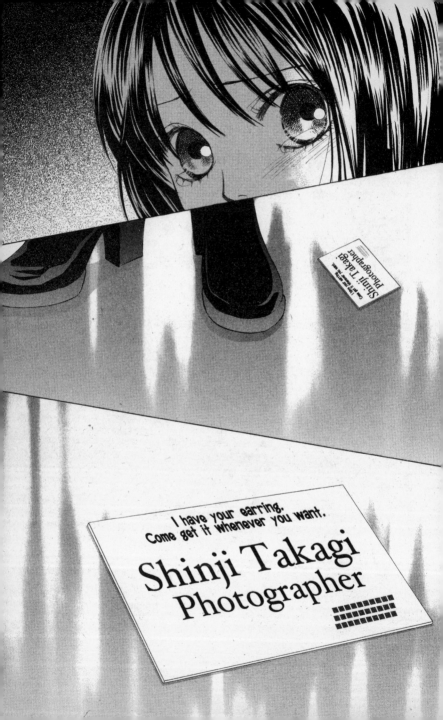

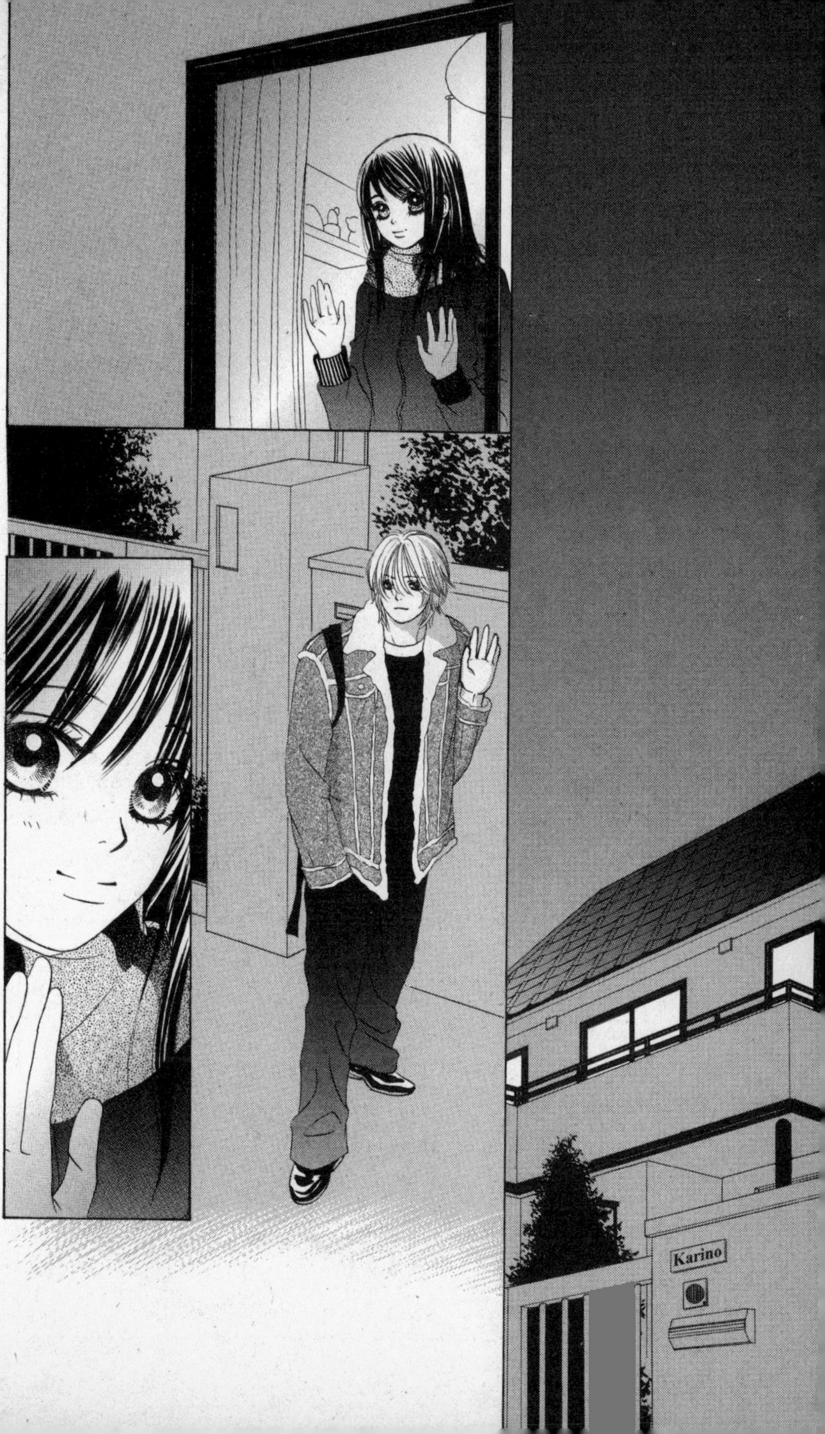
Karino

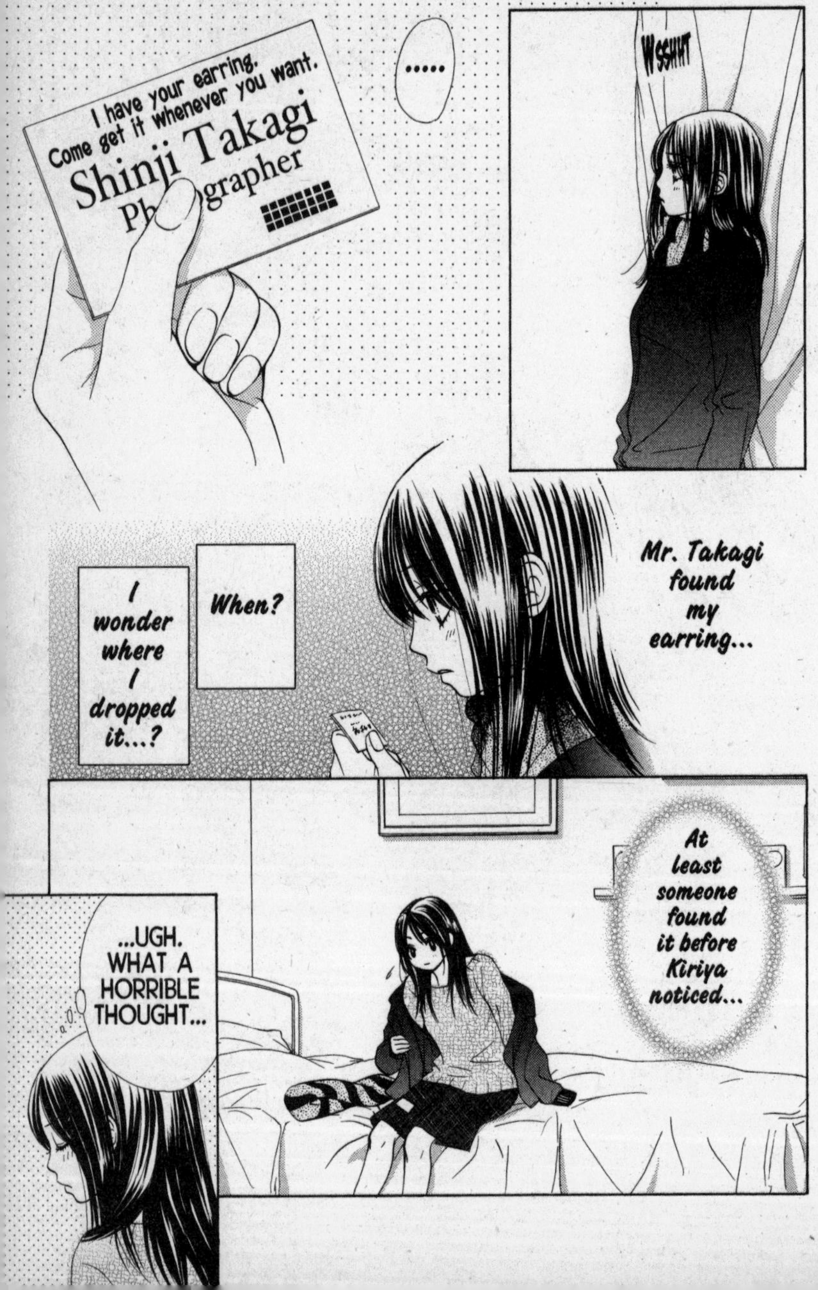
WSSHUT
.....
I have your earring.
Come get it whenever you want.
Shinji Takagi
Photographer
Mr. Takagi found my earring...
When?
I wonder where I dropped it...?
At least someone found it before Kiriya noticed...
...UGH. WHAT A HORRIBLE THOUGHT...

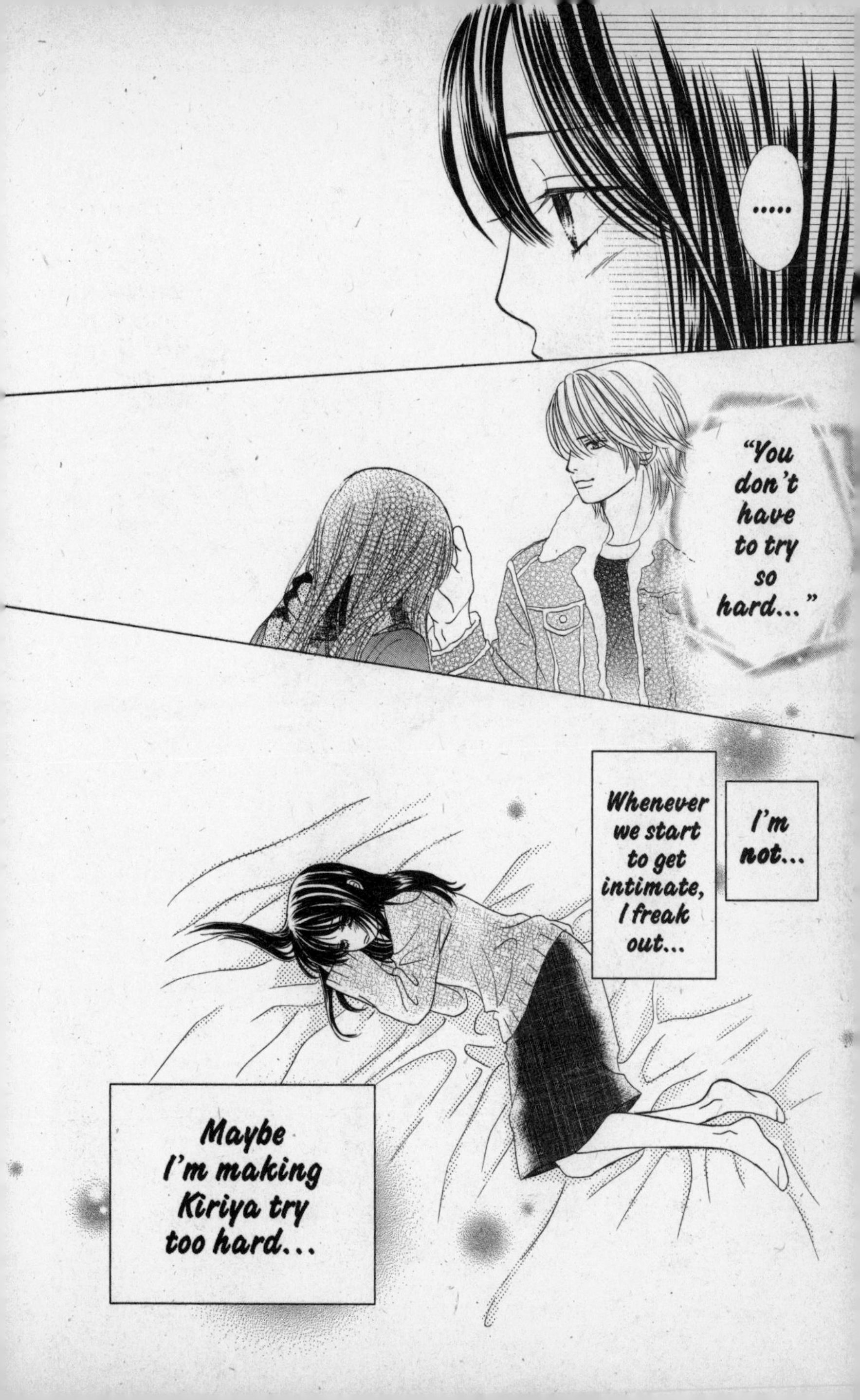
.....
"You don't have to try so hard..."
I'm not...
Whenever we start to get intimate, I freak out...
Maybe I'm making Kiriya try too hard...

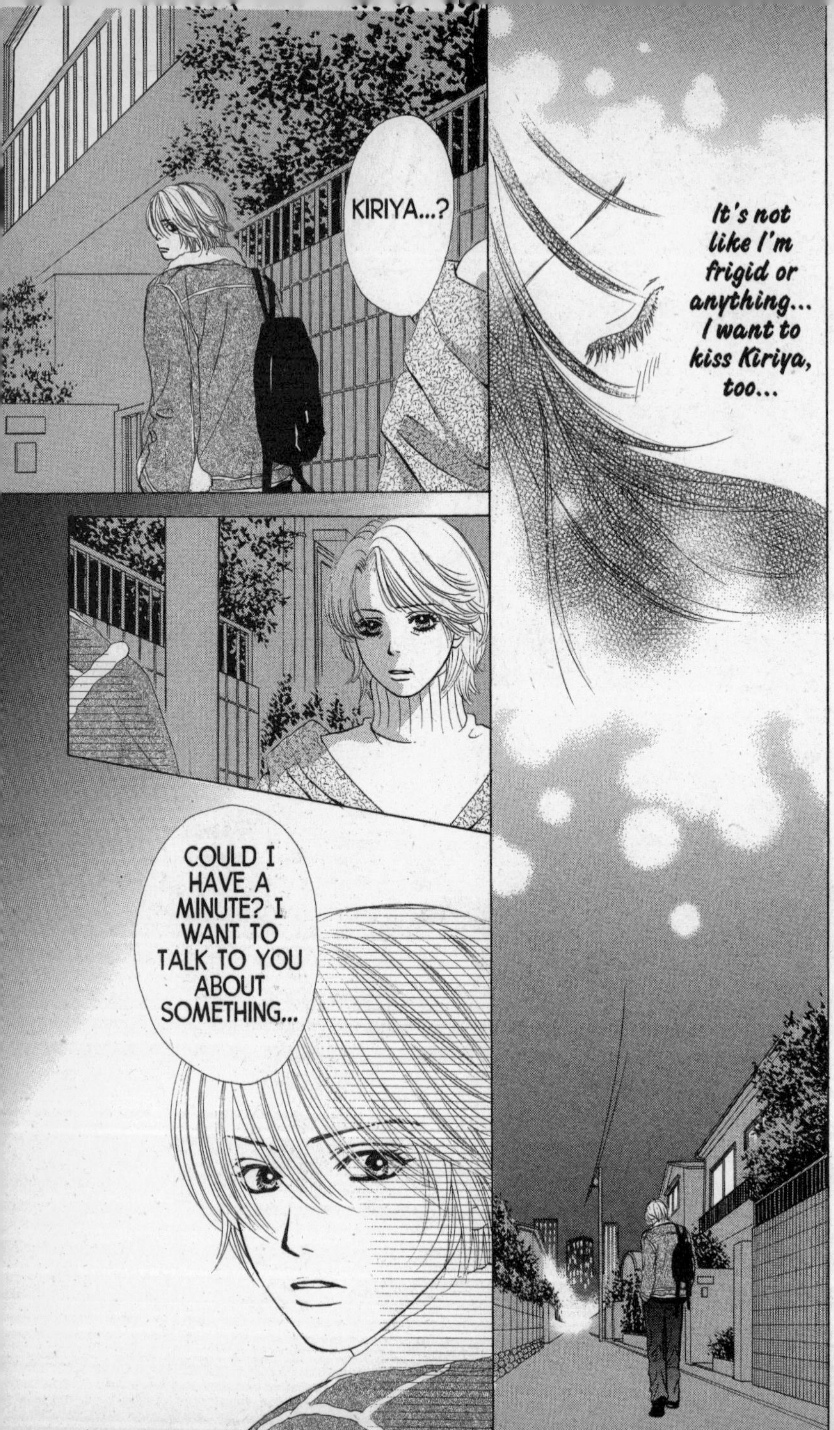
It's not like I'm frigid or anything... I want to kiss Kiriya, too...
KIRIYA...?
COULD I HAVE A MINUTE? I WANT TO TALK TO YOU ABOUT SOMETHING...

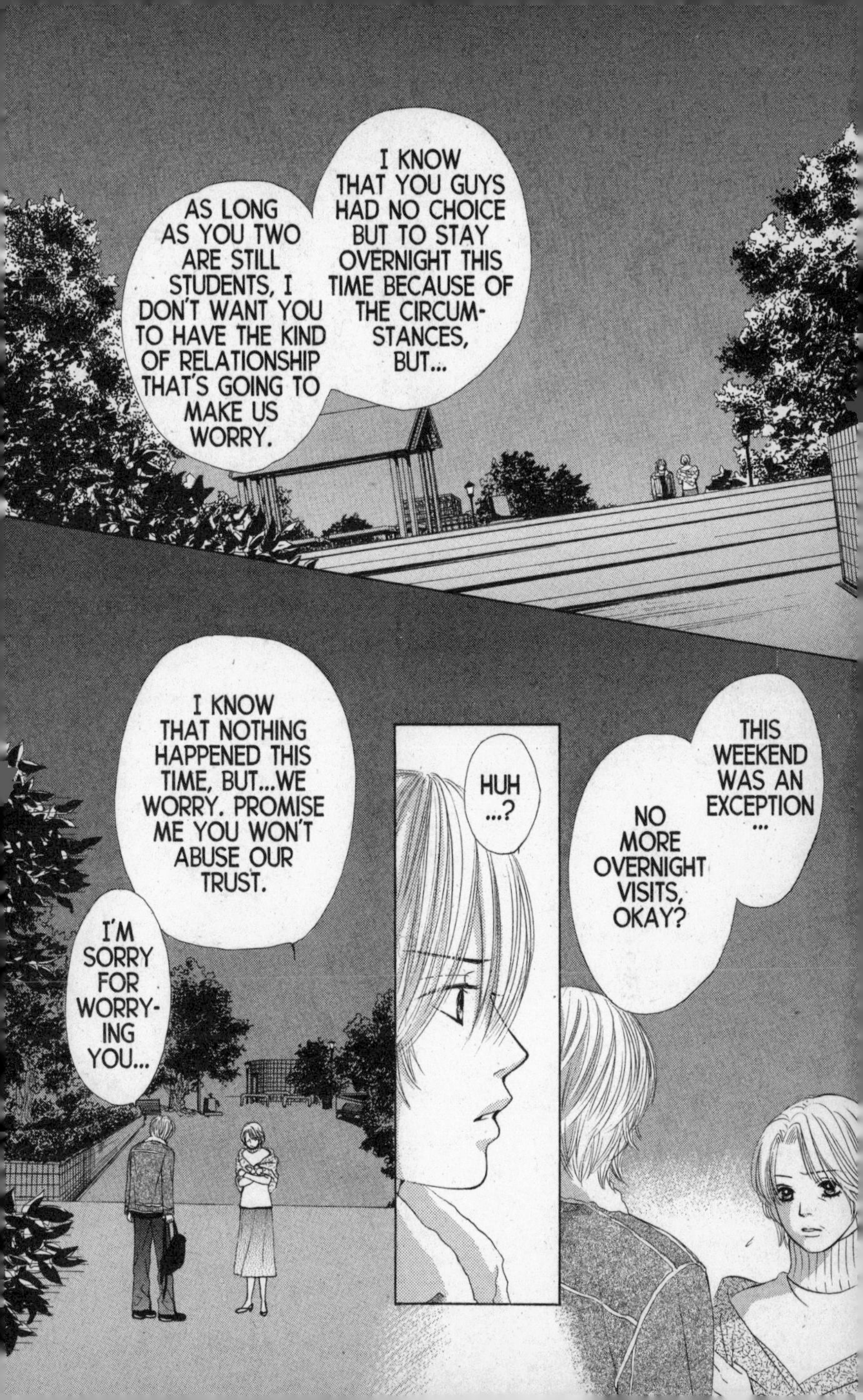
I KNOW THAT YOU GUYS HAD NO CHOICE BUT TO STAY OVERNIGHT THIS TIME BECAUSE OF THE CIRCUM-STANCES, BUT...
AS LONG AS YOU TWO ARE STILL STUDENTS, I DON'T WANT YOU TO HAVE THE KIND OF RELATIONSHIP THAT'S GOING TO MAKE US WORRY.
THIS WEEKEND WAS AN EXCEPTION...
NO MORE OVERNIGHT VISITS, OKAY?
HUH...?
I KNOW THAT NOTHING HAPPENED THIS TIME, BUT...WE WORRY. PROMISE ME YOU WON'T ABUSE OUR TRUST.
I'M SORRY FOR WORRY-ING YOU...

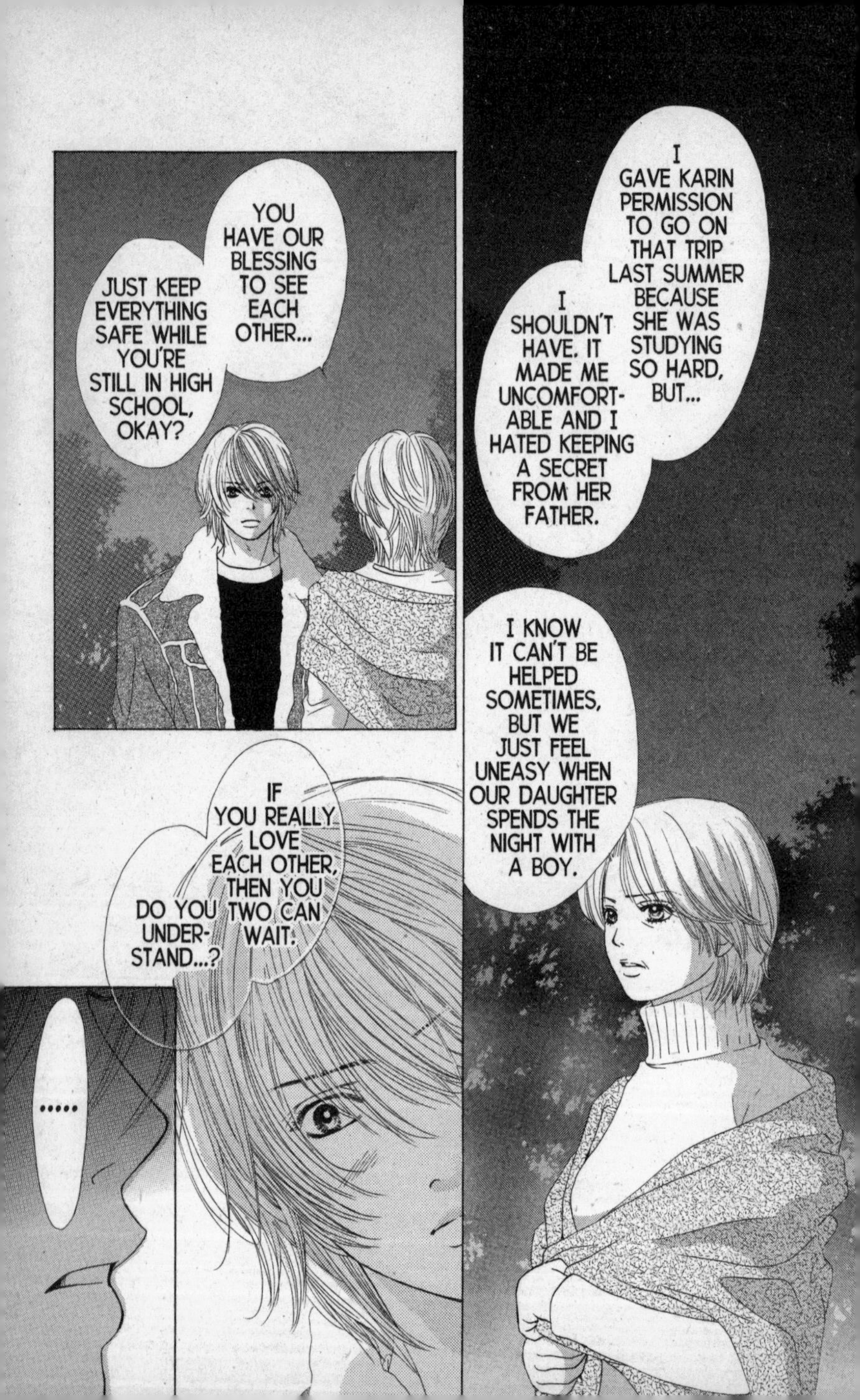
I GAVE KARIN PERMISSION TO GO ON THAT TRIP LAST SUMMER BECAUSE SHE WAS STUDYING SO HARD, BUT...
I SHOULDN'T HAVE. IT MADE ME UNCOMFORT-ABLE AND I HATED KEEPING A SECRET FROM HER FATHER.
I KNOW IT CAN'T BE HELPED SOMETIMES, BUT WE JUST FEEL UNEASY WHEN OUR DAUGHTER SPENDS THE NIGHT WITH A BOY.
YOU HAVE OUR BLESSING TO SEE EACH OTHER...
JUST KEEP EVERYTHING SAFE WHILE YOU'RE STILL IN HIGH SCHOOL, OKAY?
IF YOU REALLY LOVE EACH OTHER, THEN YOU TWO CAN WAIT.
DO YOU UNDER-STAND...?
......

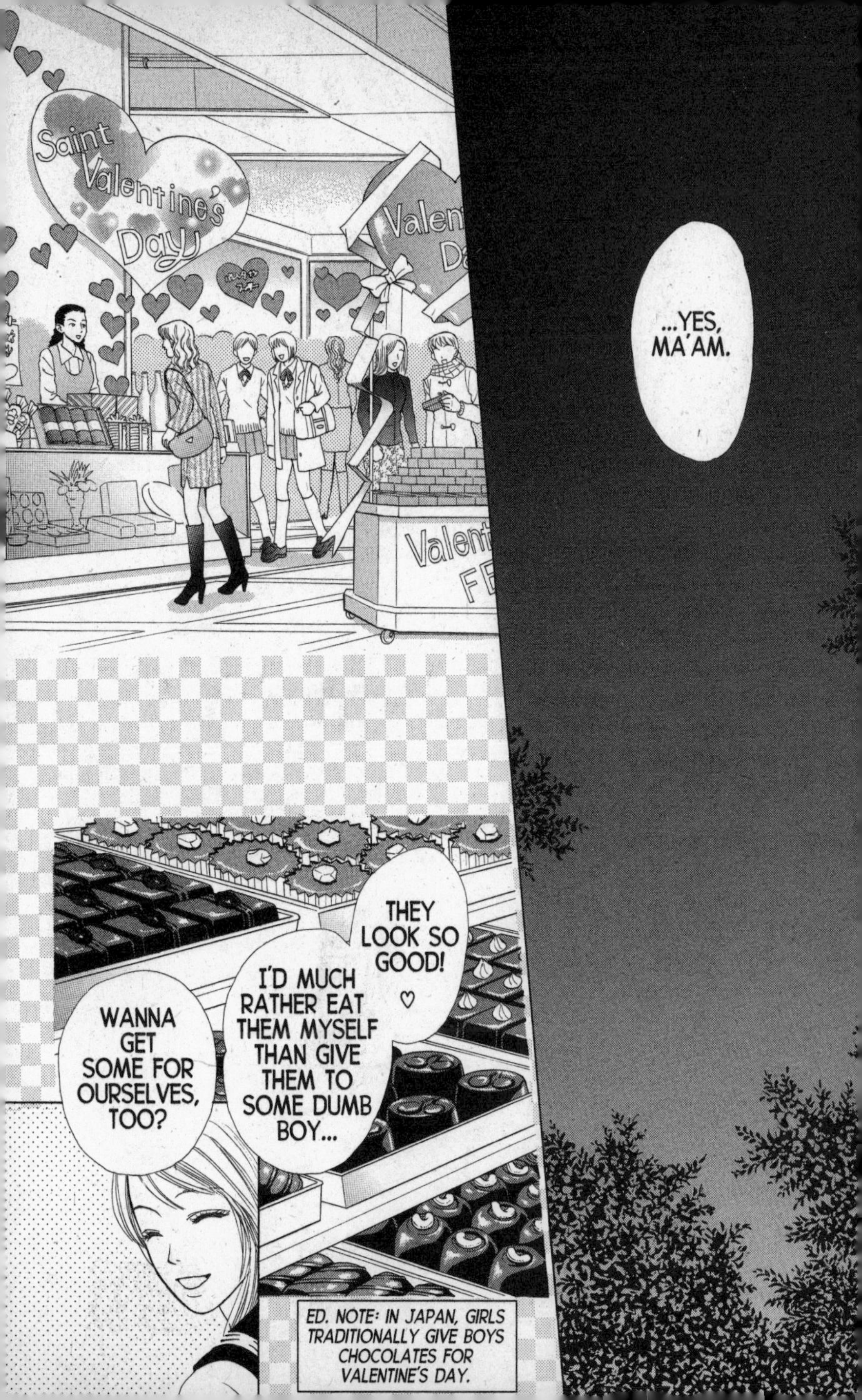
...YES, MA'AM.
Saint Valentine's Day
THEY LOOK SO GOOD! ♡
I'D MUCH RATHER EAT THEM MYSELF THAN GIVE THEM TO SOME DUMB BOY...
WANNA GET SOME FOR OURSELVES, TOO?
ED. NOTE: IN JAPAN, GIRLS TRADITIONALLY GIVE BOYS CHOCOLATES FOR VALENTINE'S DAY.

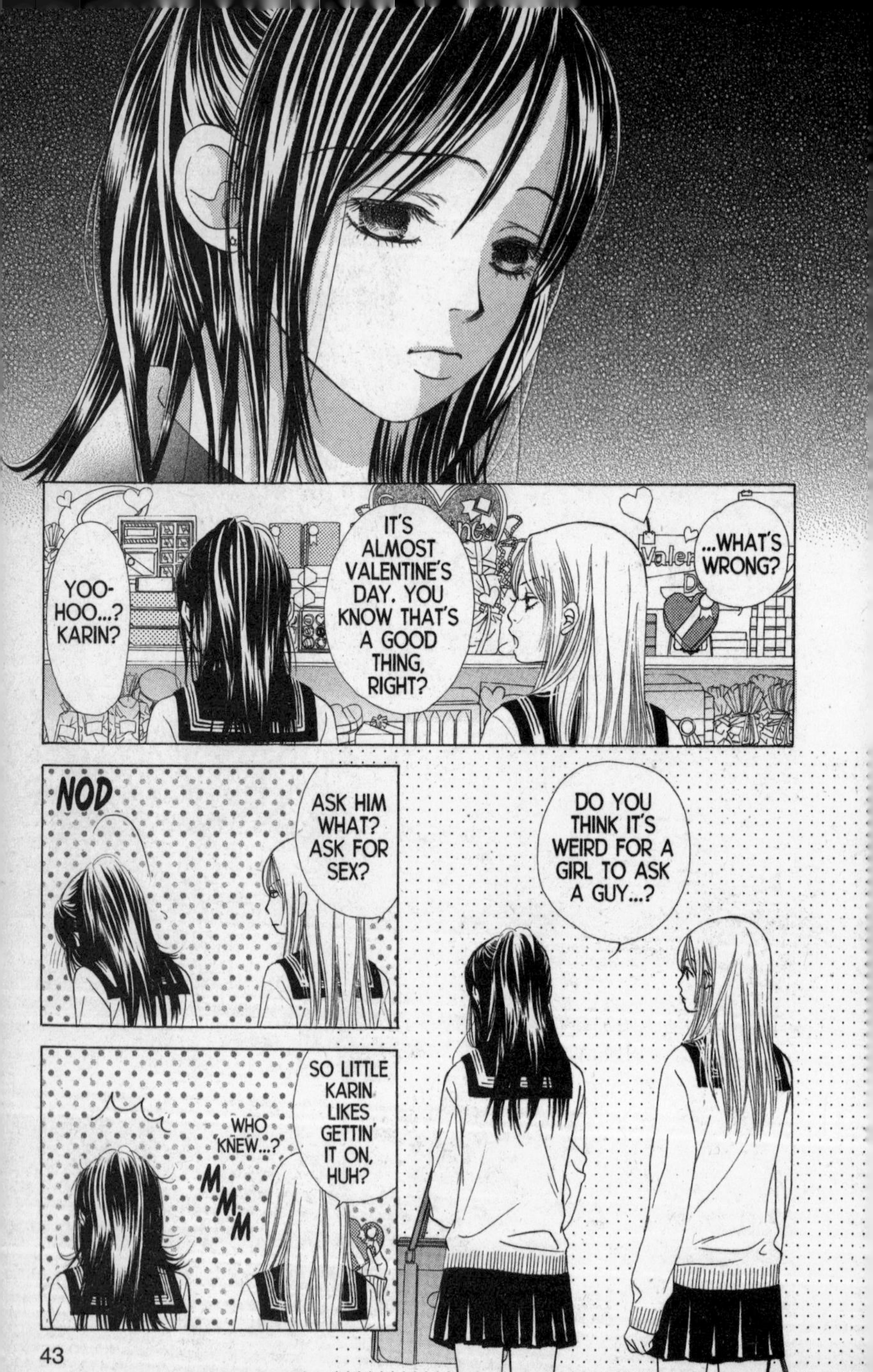
...WHAT'S WRONG?
IT'S ALMOST VALENTINE'S DAY. YOU KNOW THAT'S A GOOD THING, RIGHT?
YOO-HOO...? KARIN?
DO YOU THINK IT'S WEIRD FOR A GIRL TO ASK A GUY...?
ASK HIM WHAT? ASK FOR SEX?
NOD
SO LITTLE KARIN LIKES GETTIN' IT ON, HUH?
WHO KNEW...?
MMM

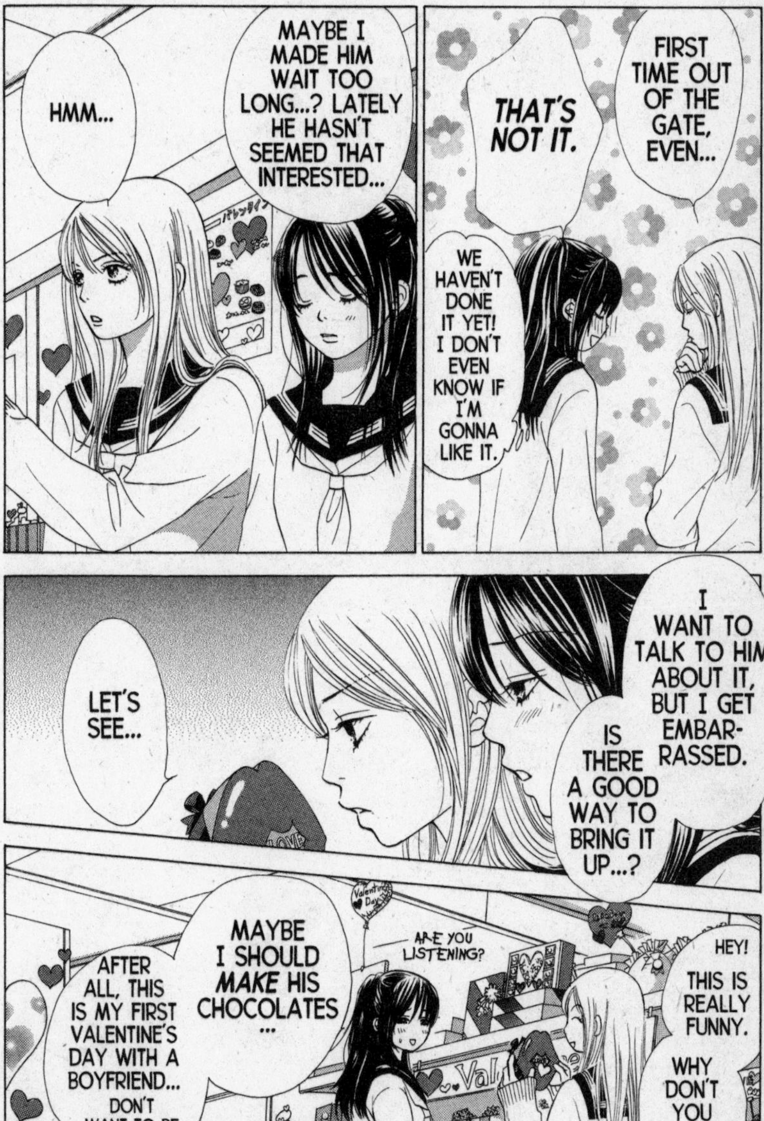
FIRST TIME OUT OF THE GATE, EVEN...
THAT'S NOT IT.
WE HAVEN'T DONE IT YET! I DON'T EVEN KNOW IF I'M GONNA LIKE IT.
MAYBE I MADE HIM WAIT TOO LONG...? LATELY HE HASN'T SEEMED THAT INTERESTED...
HMM...
I WANT TO TALK TO HIM ABOUT IT, BUT I GET EMBARRASSED.
IS THERE A GOOD WAY TO BRING IT UP...?
LET'S SEE...
HEY!
THIS IS REALLY FUNNY.
WHY DON'T YOU GET HIM THIS?
ARE YOU LISTENING?
MAYBE I SHOULD *MAKE* HIS CHOCOLATES...
AFTER ALL, THIS IS MY FIRST VALENTINE'S DAY WITH A BOYFRIEND...
DON'T WANT TO BE TACKY...

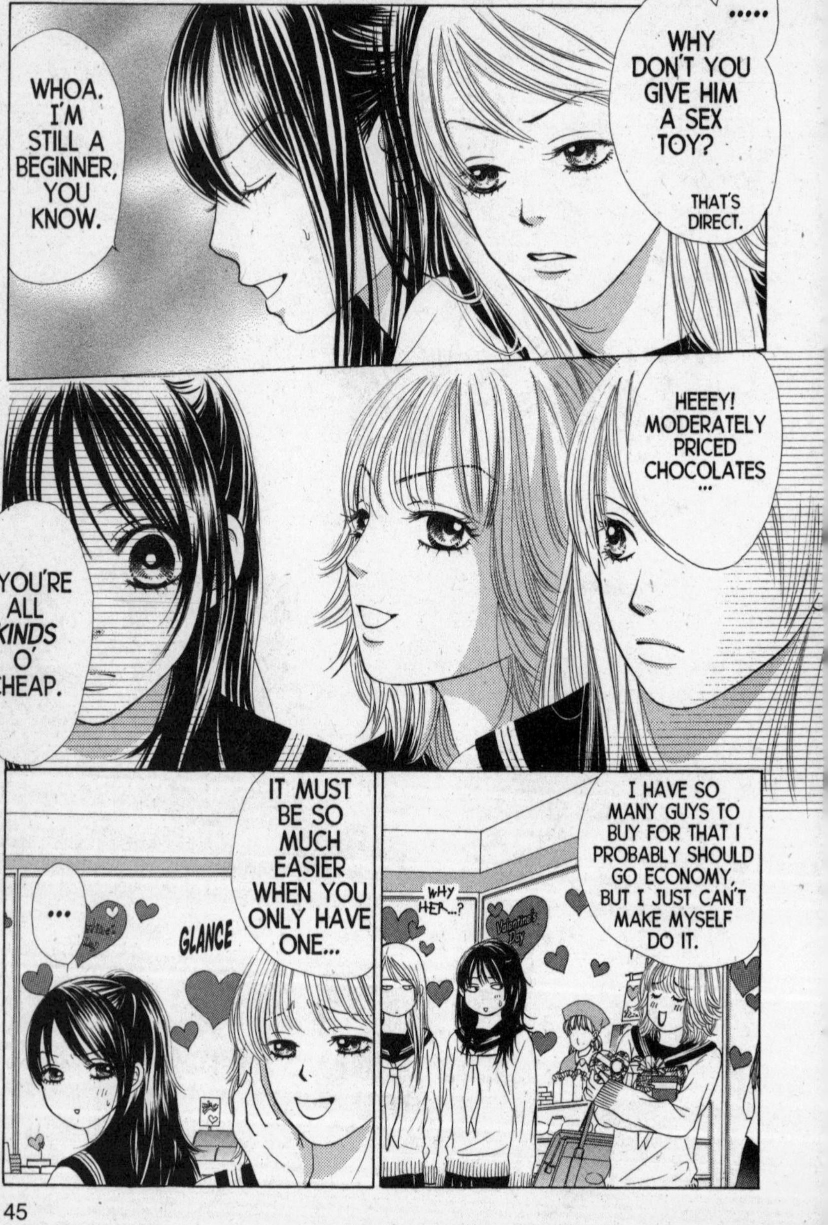
......
WHY DON'T YOU GIVE HIM A SEX TOY?
THAT'S DIRECT.
WHOA. I'M STILL A BEGINNER, YOU KNOW.
HEEEY! MODERATELY PRICED CHOCOLATES ...
...YOU'RE ALL *KINDS* O' CHEAP.
I HAVE SO MANY GUYS TO BUY FOR THAT I PROBABLY SHOULD GO ECONOMY, BUT I JUST CAN'T MAKE MYSELF DO IT.
WHY HER...?
IT MUST BE SO MUCH EASIER WHEN YOU ONLY HAVE ONE...
GLANCE
...

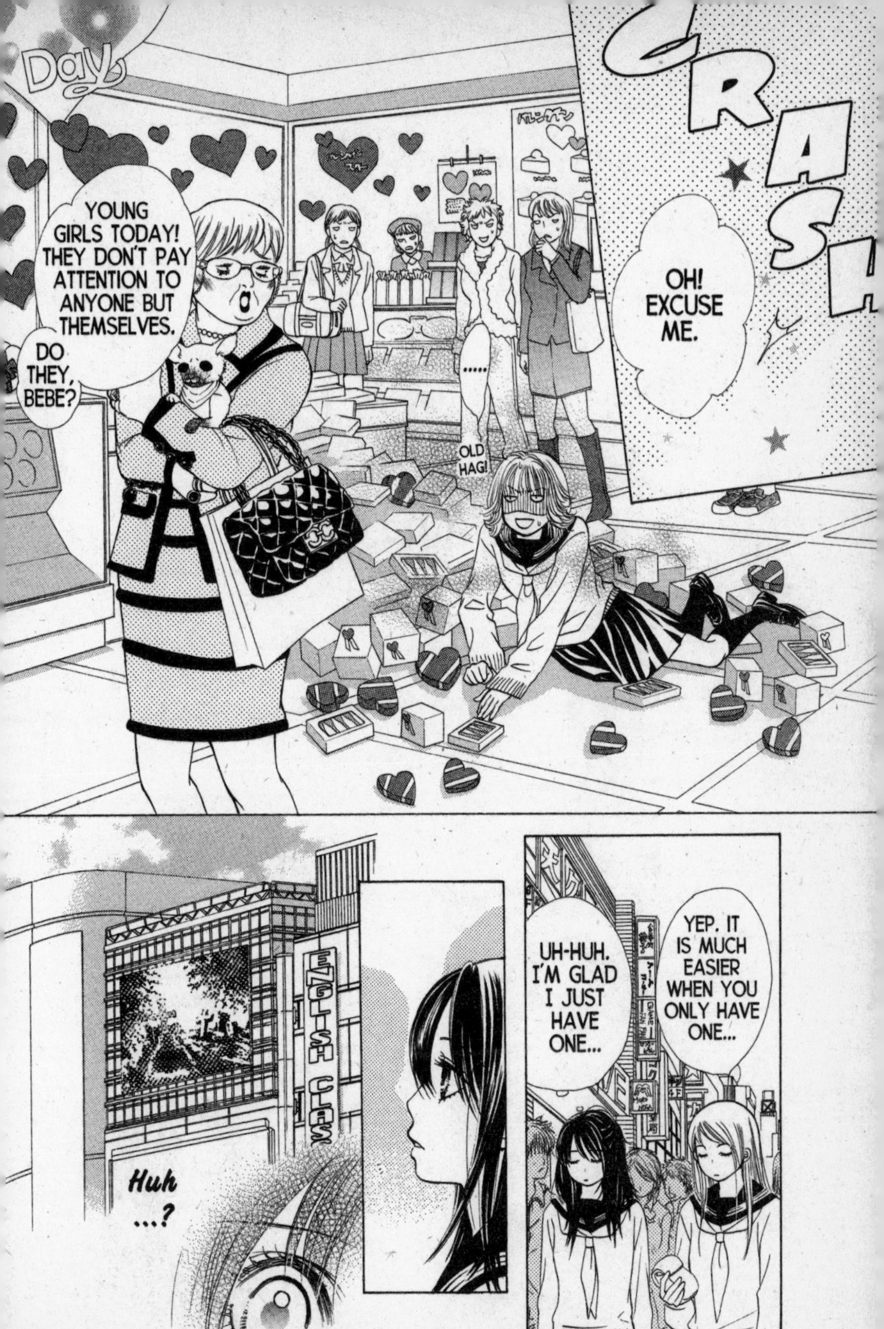
CRASH
Day
OH! EXCUSE ME.
......
OLD HAG!
YOUNG GIRLS TODAY! THEY DON'T PAY ATTENTION TO ANYONE BUT THEMSELVES.
DO THEY, BEBE?
YEP. IT IS MUCH EASIER WHEN YOU ONLY HAVE ONE...
UH-HUH. I'M GLAD I JUST HAVE ONE...
ENGLISH CLAS
Huh ...?

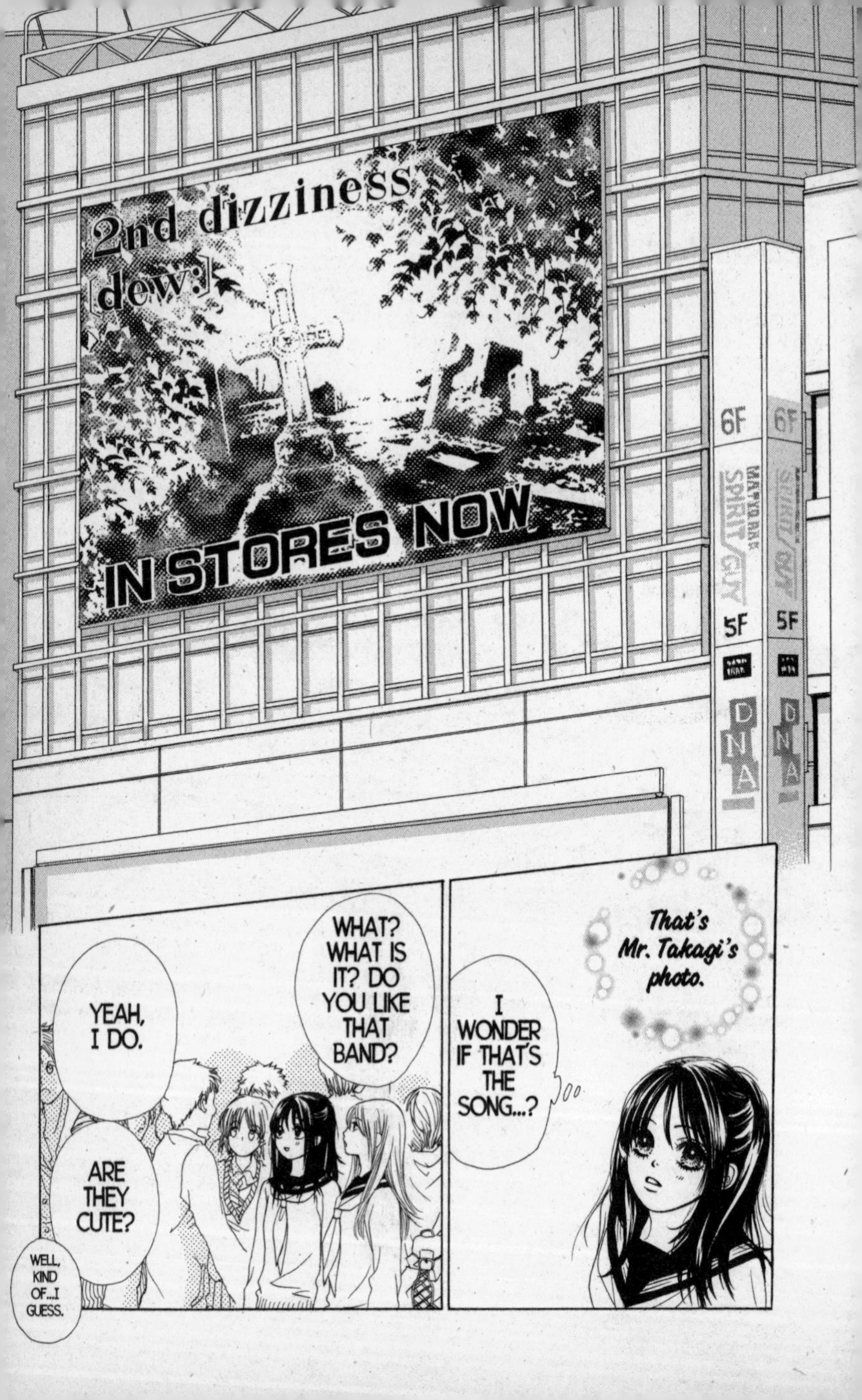
2nd dizziness
[dew:]
IN STORES NOW
6F
SPIRIT GUY
5F
DNA
That's Mr. Takagi's photo.
I WONDER IF THAT'S THE SONG...?
WHAT? WHAT IS IT? DO YOU LIKE THAT BAND?
YEAH, I DO.
ARE THEY CUTE?
WELL, KIND OF...I GUESS.

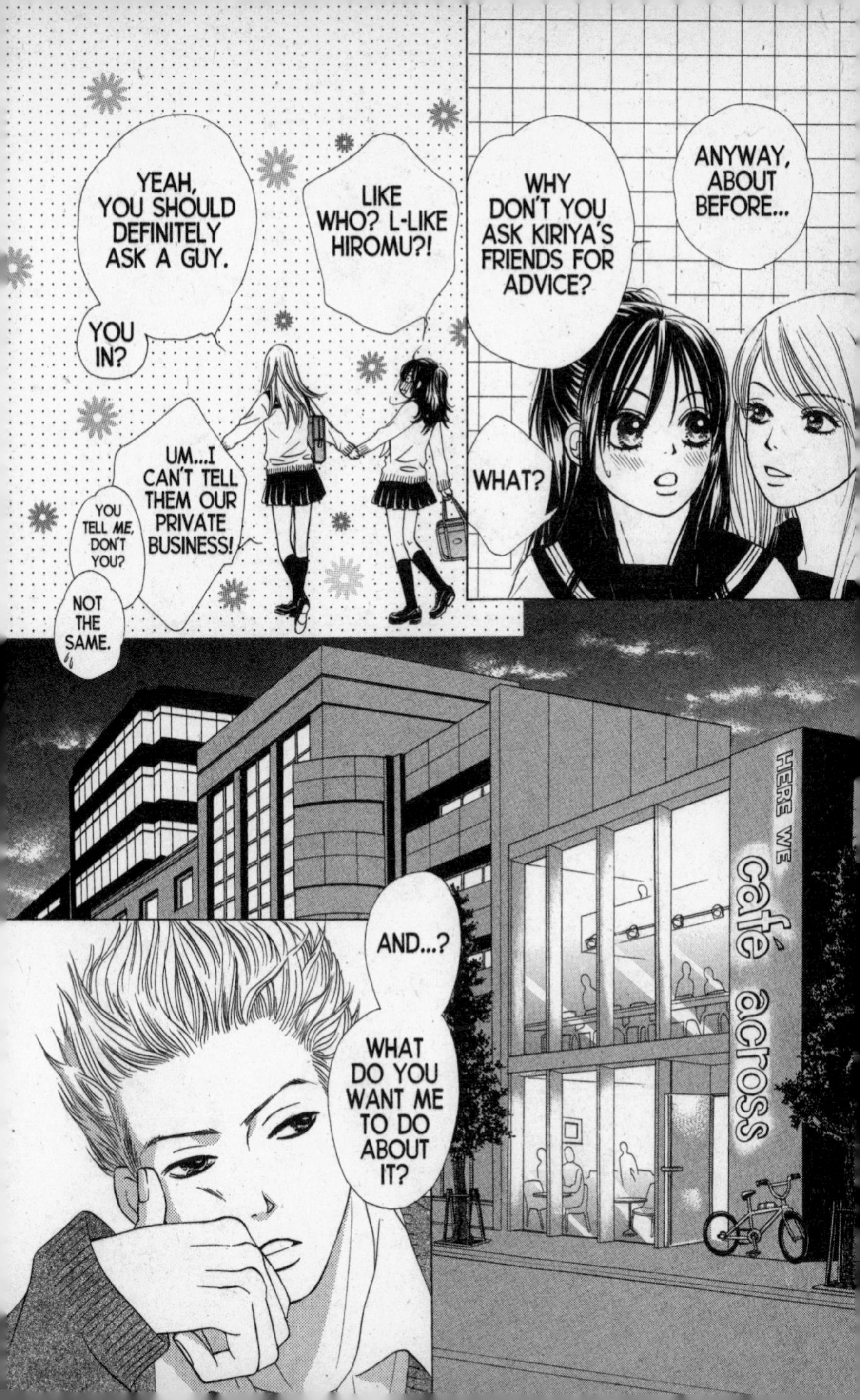
ANYWAY, ABOUT BEFORE...
WHY DON'T YOU ASK KIRIYA'S FRIENDS FOR ADVICE?
WHAT?
LIKE WHO? L-LIKE HIROMU?!
YEAH, YOU SHOULD DEFINITELY ASK A GUY.
YOU IN?
UM...I CAN'T TELL THEM OUR PRIVATE BUSINESS!
YOU TELL *ME*, DON'T YOU?
NOT THE SAME.
HERE WE
café across
AND...?
WHAT DO YOU WANT ME TO DO ABOUT IT?

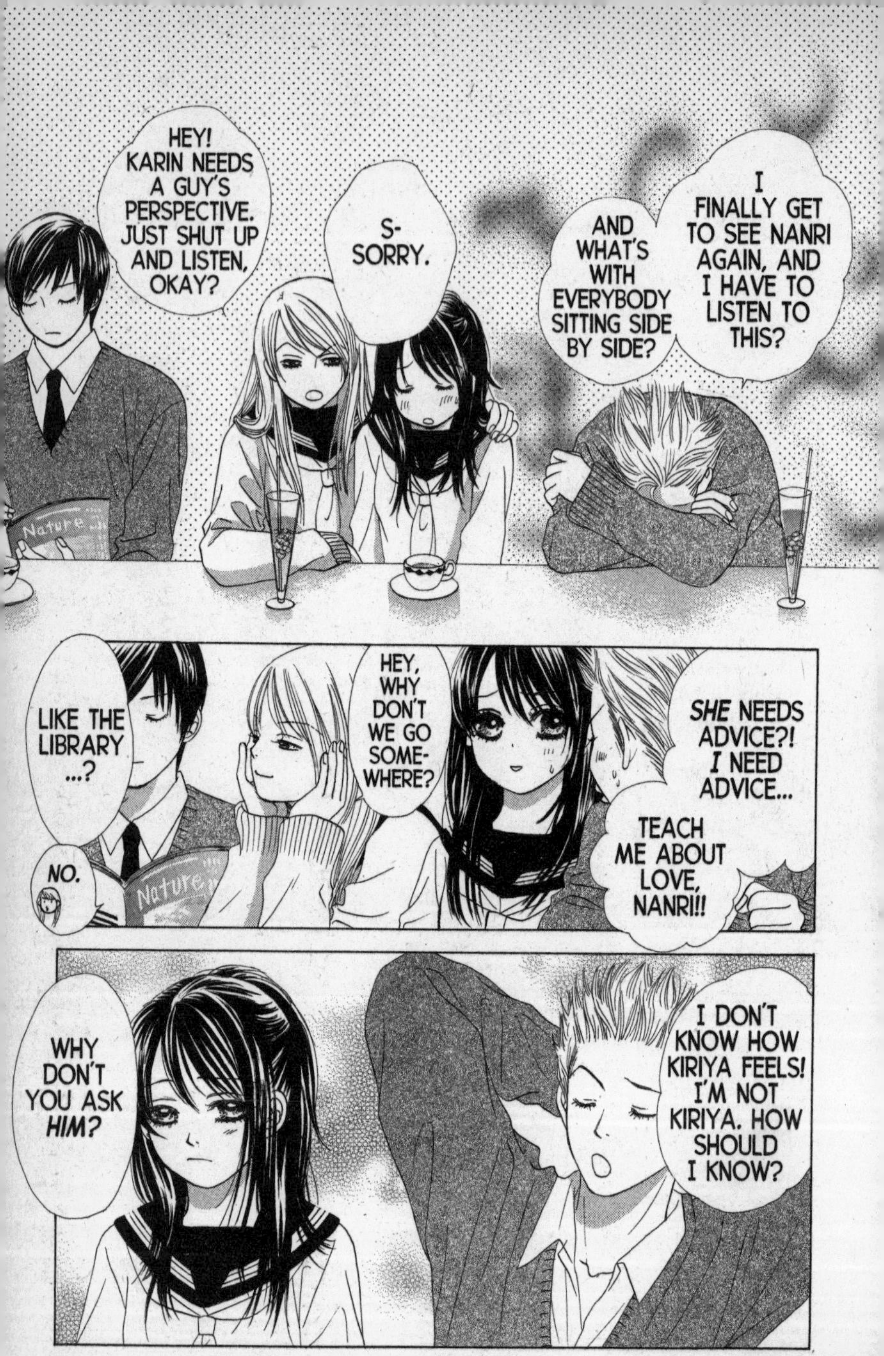
I FINALLY GET TO SEE NANRI AGAIN, AND I HAVE TO LISTEN TO THIS?
AND WHAT'S WITH EVERYBODY SITTING SIDE BY SIDE?
HEY! KARIN NEEDS A GUY'S PERSPECTIVE. JUST SHUT UP AND LISTEN, OKAY?
S- SORRY.
Nature
SHE NEEDS ADVICE?! *I* NEED ADVICE...
TEACH ME ABOUT LOVE, NANRI!!
HEY, WHY DON'T WE GO SOME-WHERE?
LIKE THE LIBRARY ...?
NO.
Nature
I DON'T KNOW HOW KIRIYA FEELS! I'M NOT KIRIYA. HOW SHOULD I KNOW?
WHY DON'T YOU ASK *HIM*?

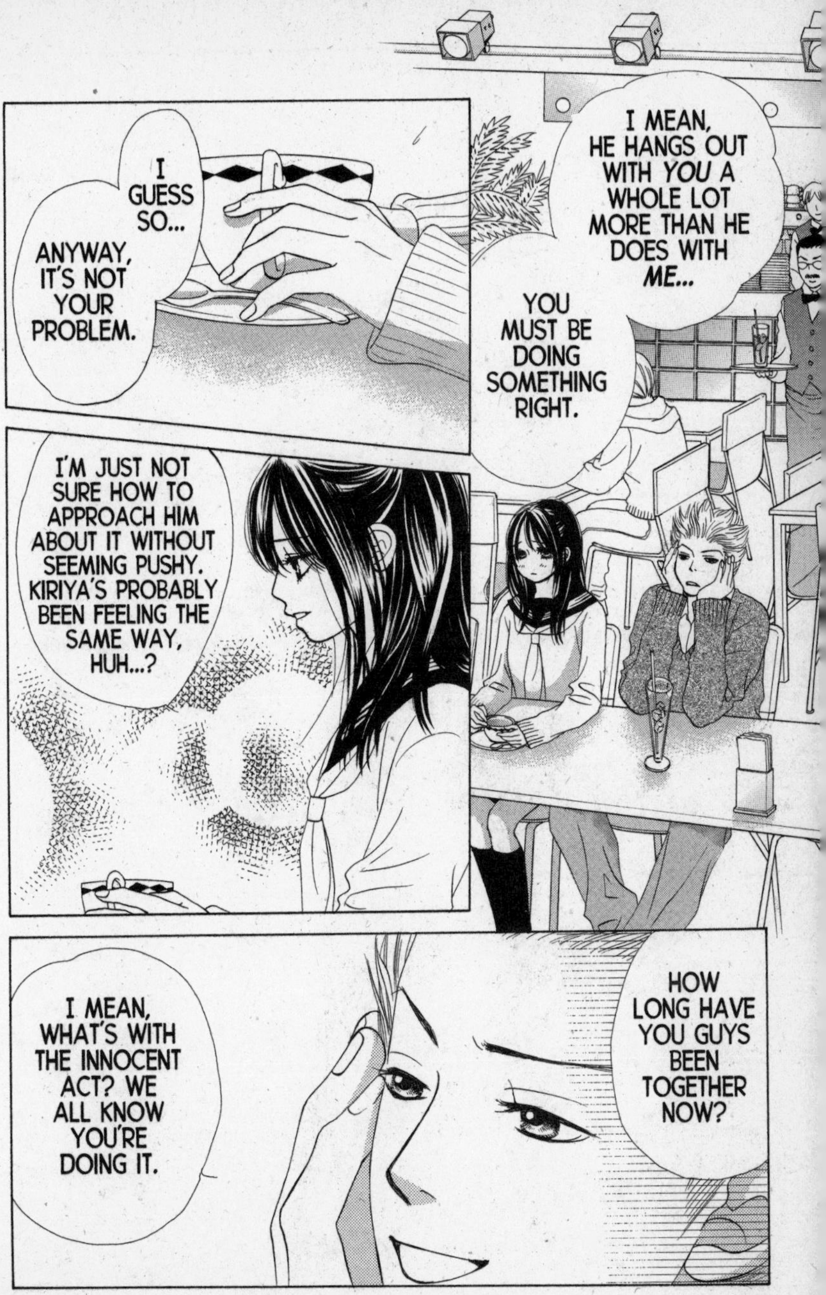
I MEAN, HE HANGS OUT WITH *YOU* A WHOLE LOT MORE THAN HE DOES WITH *ME*...
YOU MUST BE DOING SOMETHING RIGHT.
I GUESS SO...
ANYWAY, IT'S NOT YOUR PROBLEM.
I'M JUST NOT SURE HOW TO APPROACH HIM ABOUT IT WITHOUT SEEMING PUSHY. KIRIYA'S PROBABLY BEEN FEELING THE SAME WAY, HUH...?
HOW LONG HAVE YOU GUYS BEEN TOGETHER NOW?
I MEAN, WHAT'S WITH THE INNOCENT ACT? WE ALL KNOW YOU'RE DOING IT.

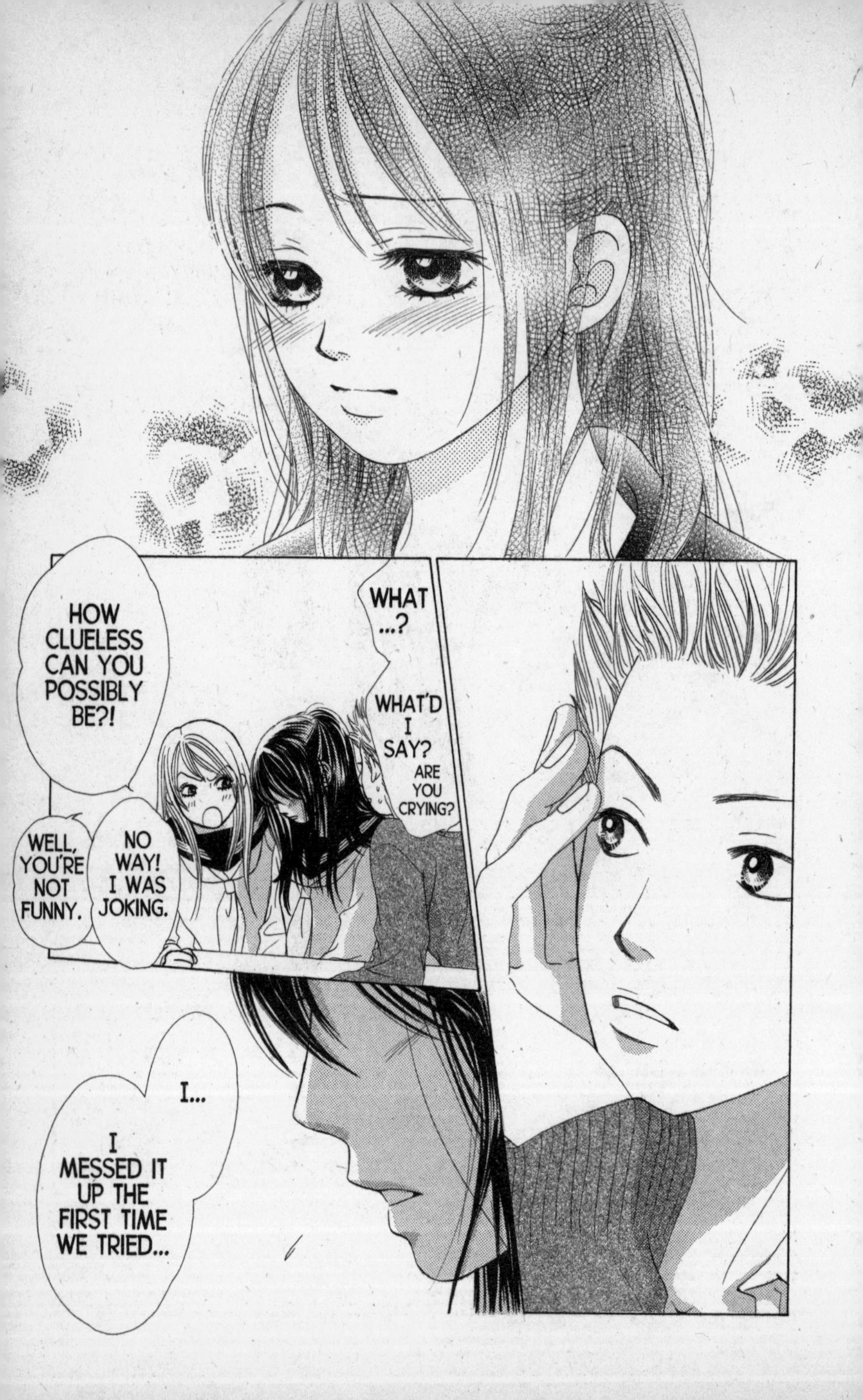
WHAT ...?
WHAT'D I SAY?
ARE YOU CRYING?
HOW CLUELESS CAN YOU POSSIBLY BE?!
NO WAY! I WAS JOKING.
WELL, YOU'RE NOT FUNNY.
I...
I MESSED IT UP THE FIRST TIME WE TRIED...

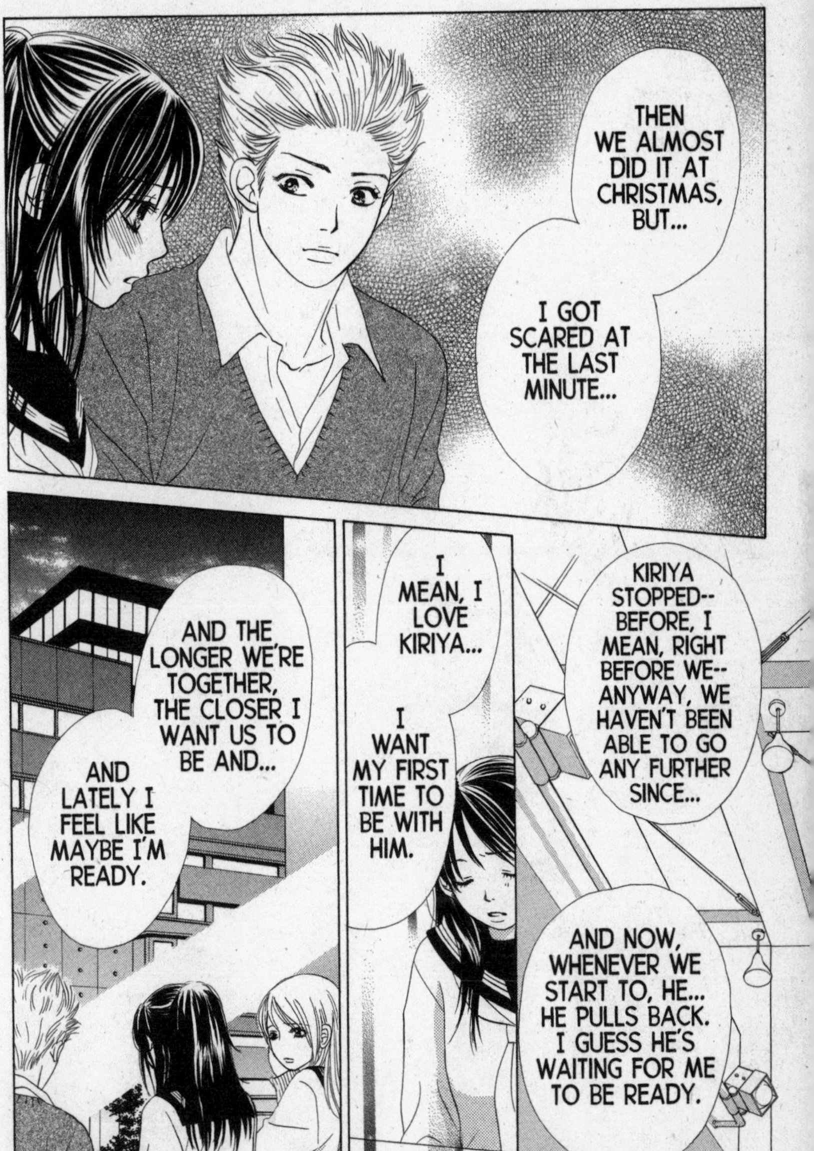
THEN WE ALMOST DID IT AT CHRISTMAS, BUT...
I GOT SCARED AT THE LAST MINUTE...
KIRIYA STOPPED-- BEFORE, I MEAN, RIGHT BEFORE WE-- ANYWAY, WE HAVEN'T BEEN ABLE TO GO ANY FURTHER SINCE...
AND NOW, WHENEVER WE START TO, HE... HE PULLS BACK. I GUESS HE'S WAITING FOR ME TO BE READY.
I MEAN, I LOVE KIRIYA...
I WANT MY FIRST TIME TO BE WITH HIM.
AND THE LONGER WE'RE TOGETHER, THE CLOSER I WANT US TO BE AND...
AND LATELY I FEEL LIKE MAYBE I'M READY.

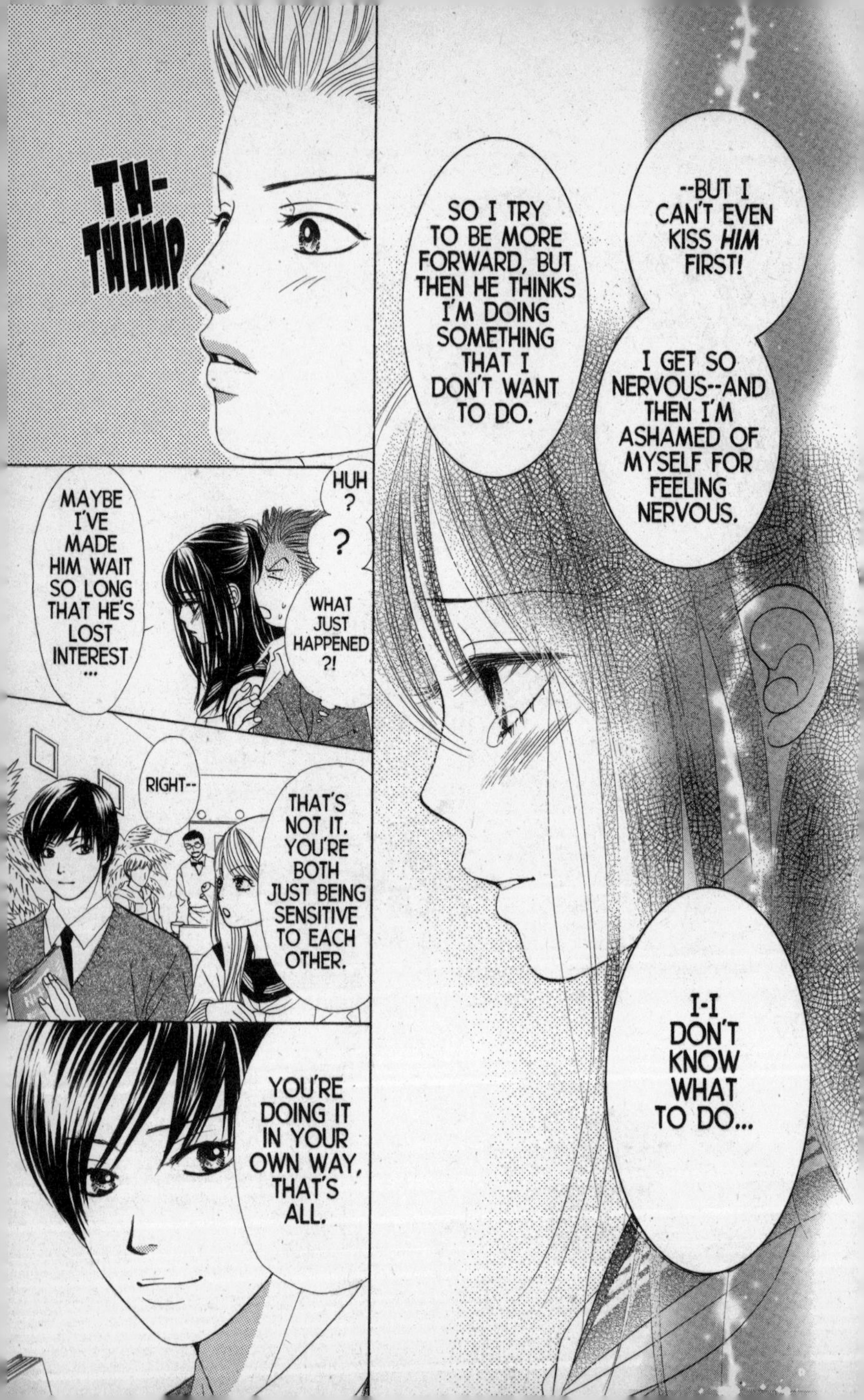
--BUT I CAN'T EVEN KISS *HIM* FIRST!
I GET SO NERVOUS--AND THEN I'M ASHAMED OF MYSELF FOR FEELING NERVOUS.
SO I TRY TO BE MORE FORWARD, BUT THEN HE THINKS I'M DOING SOMETHING THAT I DON'T WANT TO DO.
I-I DON'T KNOW WHAT TO DO...
TH-THUMP
HUH?
?
WHAT JUST HAPPENED?!
MAYBE I'VE MADE HIM WAIT SO LONG THAT HE'S LOST INTEREST...
RIGHT--
THAT'S NOT IT. YOU'RE BOTH JUST BEING SENSITIVE TO EACH OTHER.
YOU'RE DOING IT IN YOUR OWN WAY, THAT'S ALL.

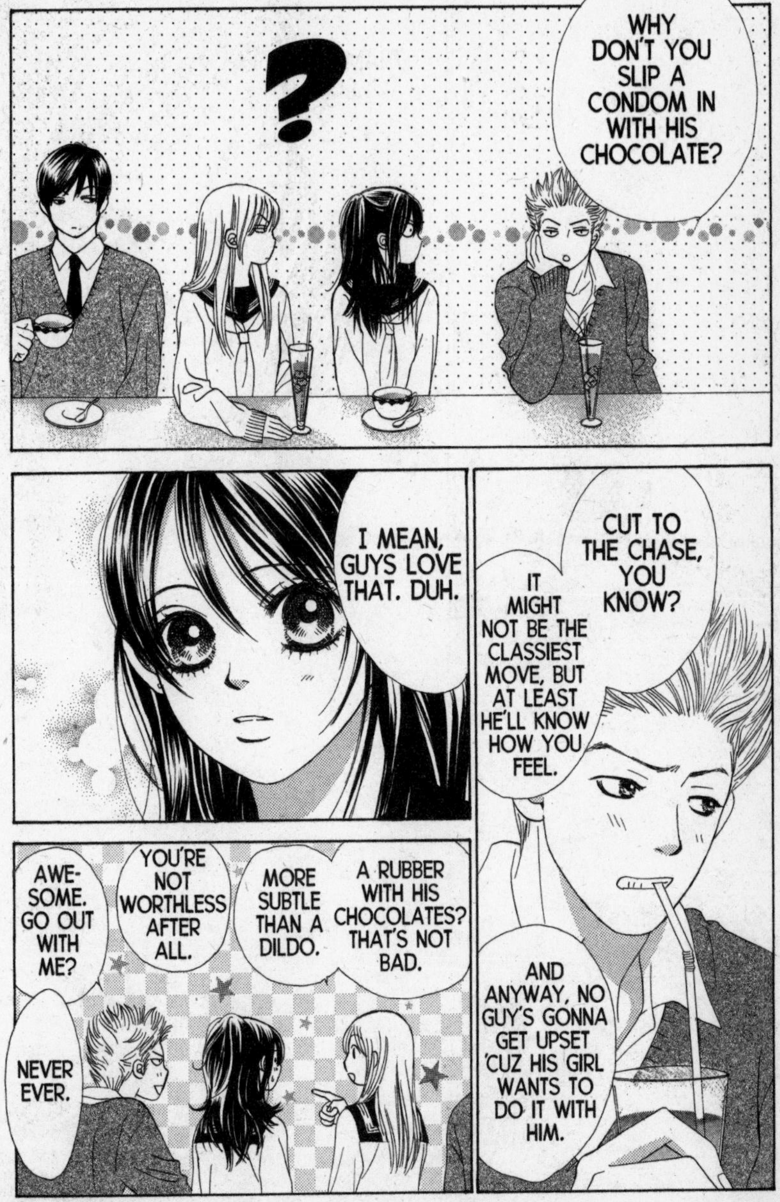
?
WHY DON'T YOU SLIP A CONDOM IN WITH HIS CHOCOLATE?
CUT TO THE CHASE, YOU KNOW?
IT MIGHT NOT BE THE CLASSIEST MOVE, BUT AT LEAST HE'LL KNOW HOW YOU FEEL.
AND ANYWAY, NO GUY'S GONNA GET UPSET 'CUZ HIS GIRL WANTS TO DO IT WITH HIM.
I MEAN, GUYS LOVE THAT. DUH.
A RUBBER WITH HIS CHOCOLATES? THAT'S NOT BAD.
MORE SUBTLE THAN A DILDO.
YOU'RE NOT WORTHLESS AFTER ALL.
AWE-SOME. GO OUT WITH ME?
NEVER EVER.

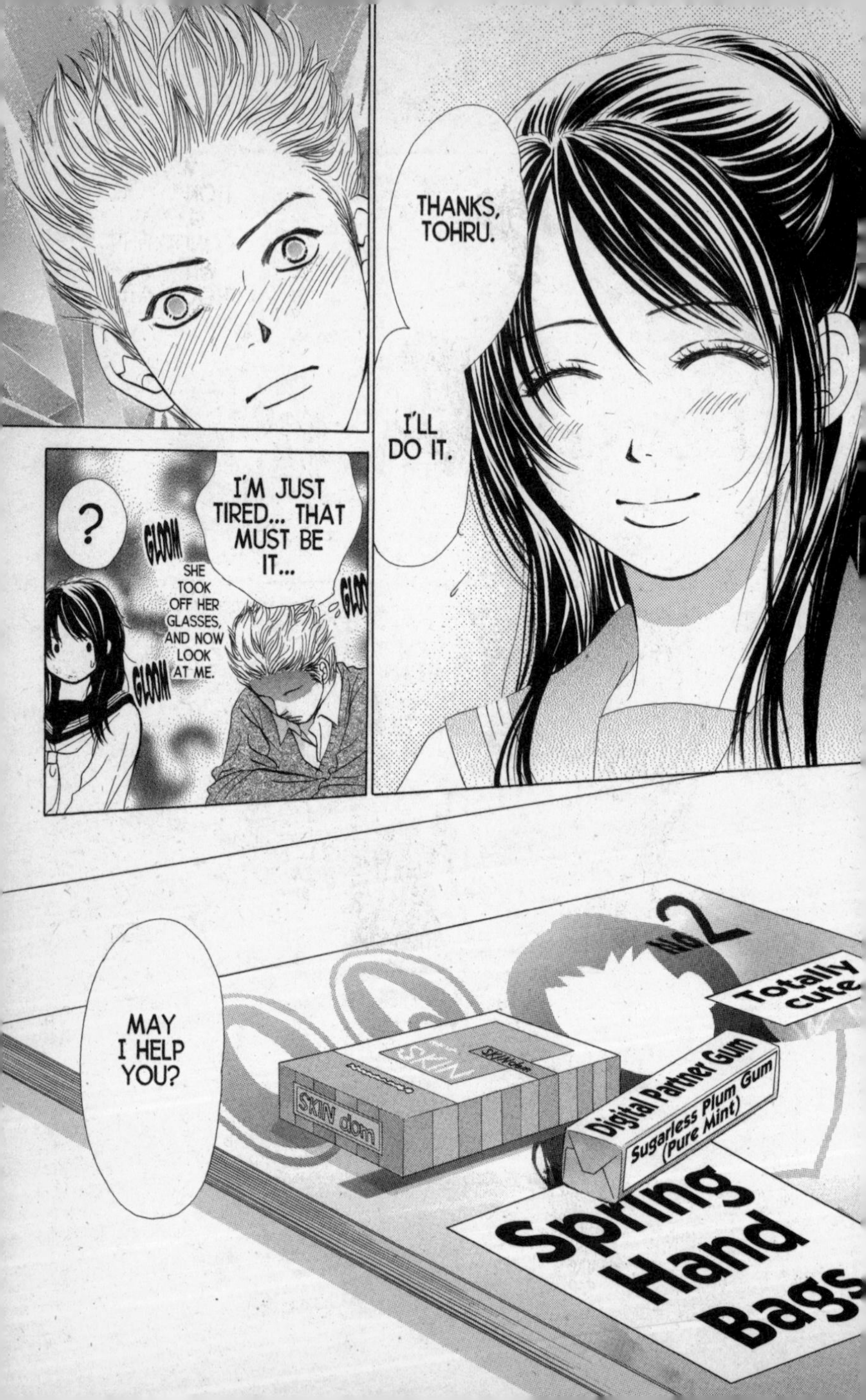
THANKS, TOHRU.
I'LL DO IT.
I'M JUST TIRED... THAT MUST BE IT...
GLOOM
SHE TOOK OFF HER GLASSES, AND NOW LOOK AT ME.
GLOOM
?
GLOOM
MAY I HELP YOU?
No 2
Totally cute
SKIN
SKIN dom
Digital Partner Gum
Sugarless Plum Gum (Pure Mint)
Spring Hand Bags

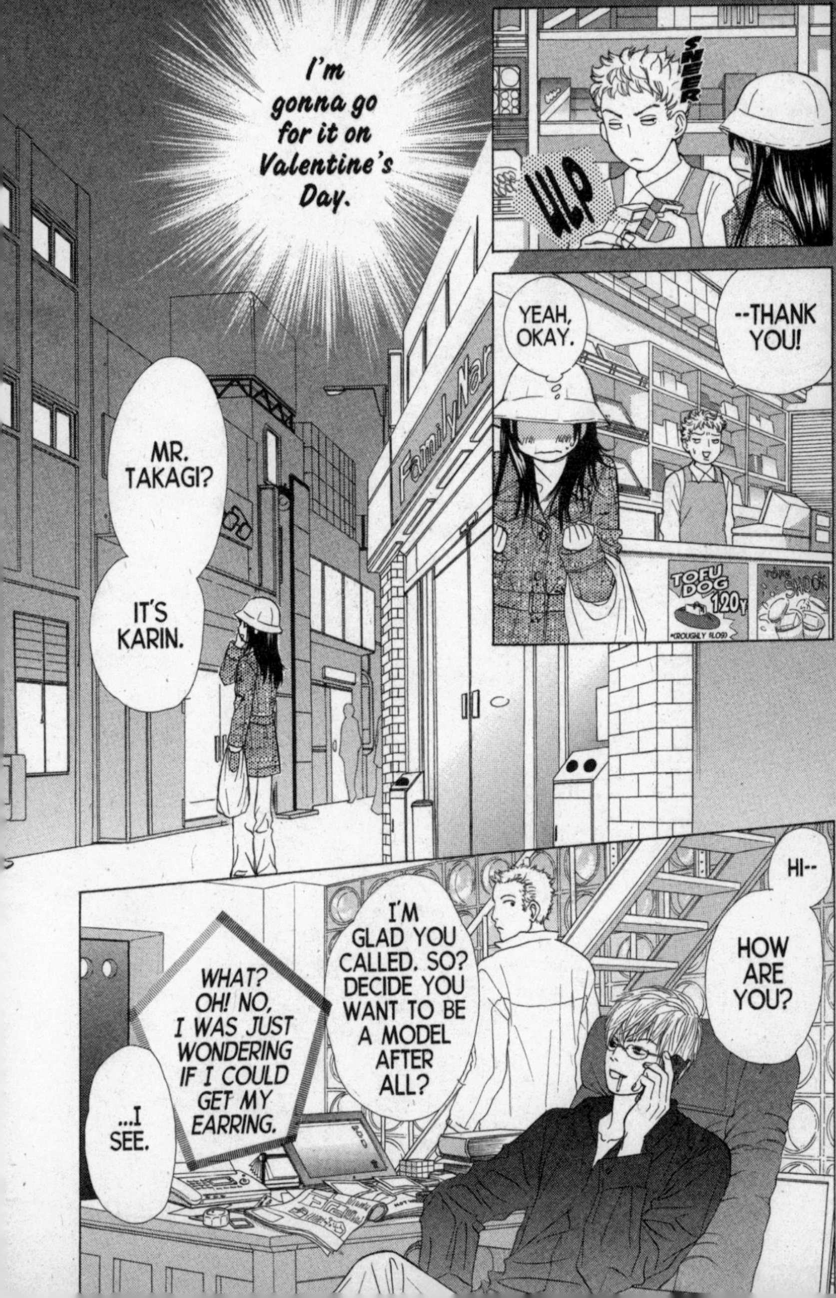
SNEER
ULP
--THANK YOU!
YEAH, OKAY.
TOFU DOG 120¥
*(ROUGHLY $1.09)
I'm gonna go for it on Valentine's Day.
MR. TAKAGI?
IT'S JUST KARIN.
HI--
HOW ARE YOU?
I'M GLAD YOU CALLED. SO? DECIDE YOU WANT TO BE A MODEL AFTER ALL?
WHAT? OH! NO, I WAS JUST WONDERING IF I COULD GET MY EARRING.
...I SEE.

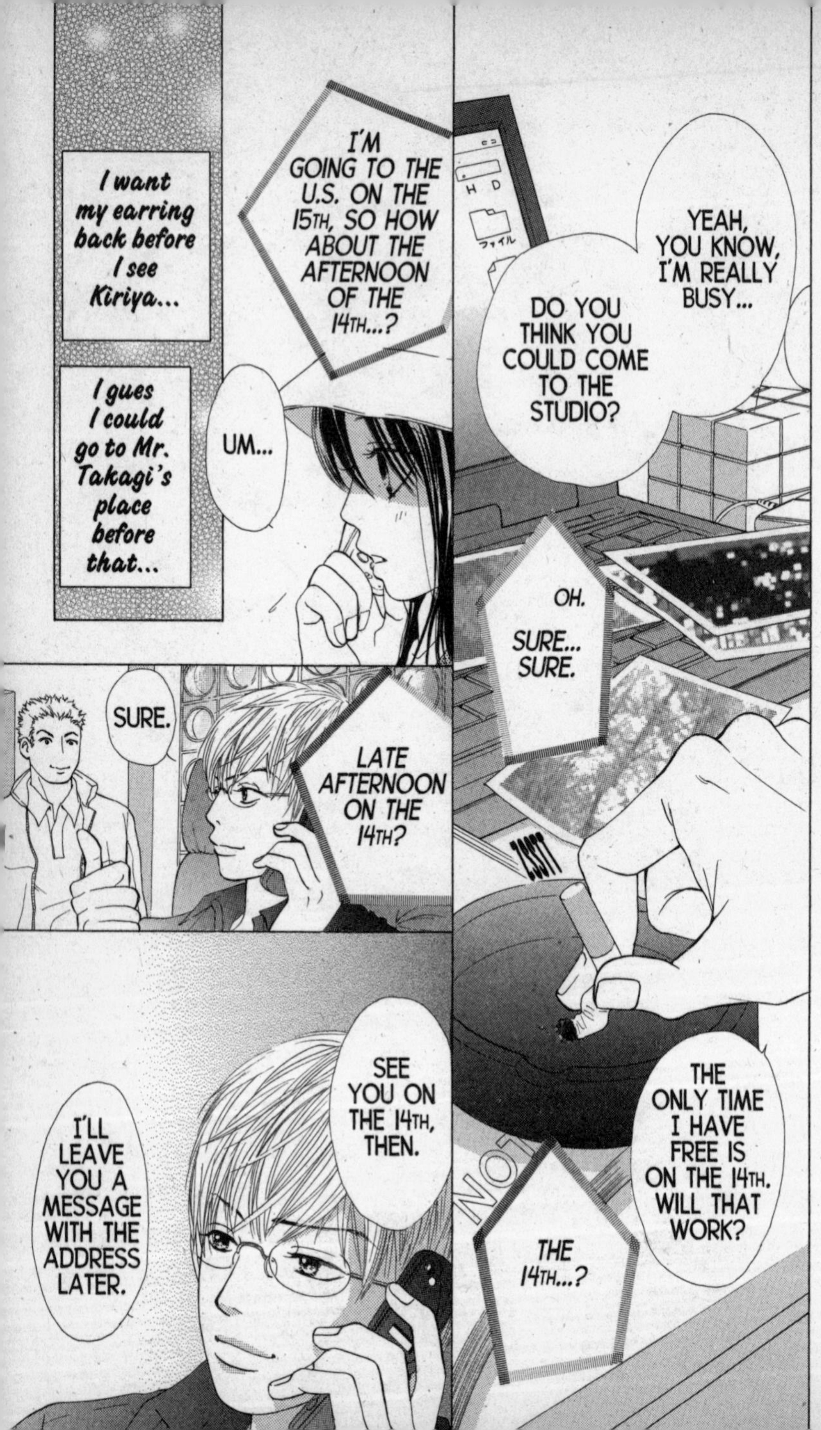
YEAH, YOU KNOW, I'M REALLY BUSY...
DO YOU THINK YOU COULD COME TO THE STUDIO?
OH. SURE... SURE.
THE ONLY TIME I HAVE FREE IS ON THE 14TH. WILL THAT WORK?
THE 14TH...?
I'M GOING TO THE U.S. ON THE 15TH, SO HOW ABOUT THE AFTERNOON OF THE 14TH...?
UM...
I want my earring back before I see Kiriya...
I gues I could go to Mr. Takagi's place before that...
LATE AFTERNOON ON THE 14TH?
SURE.
SEE YOU ON THE 14TH, THEN.
I'LL LEAVE YOU A MESSAGE WITH THE ADDRESS LATER.

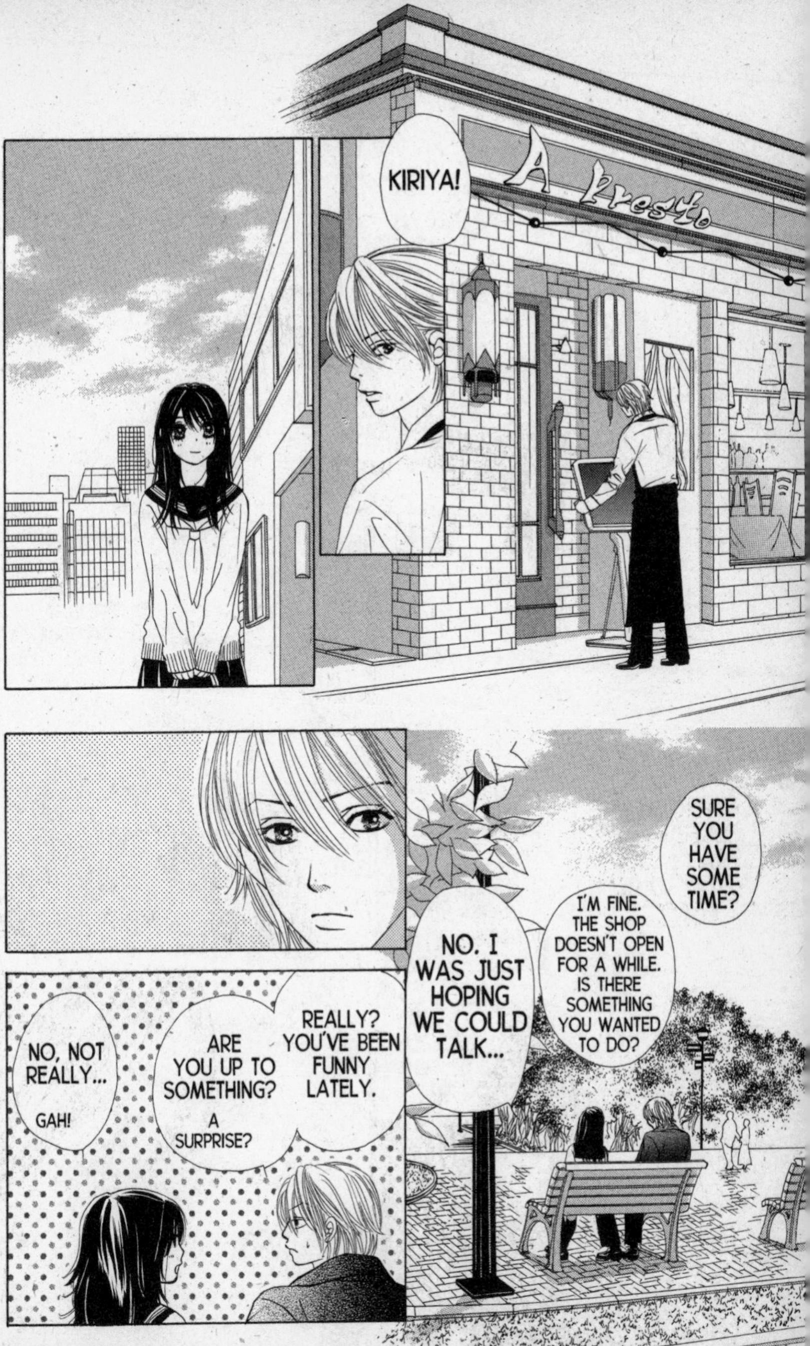
KIRIYA!
A Presto
SURE YOU HAVE SOME TIME?
I'M FINE. THE SHOP DOESN'T OPEN FOR A WHILE. IS THERE SOMETHING YOU WANTED TO DO?
NO. I WAS JUST HOPING WE COULD TALK...
REALLY? YOU'VE BEEN FUNNY LATELY.
ARE YOU UP TO SOMETHING?
A SURPRISE?
NO, NOT REALLY...
GAH!

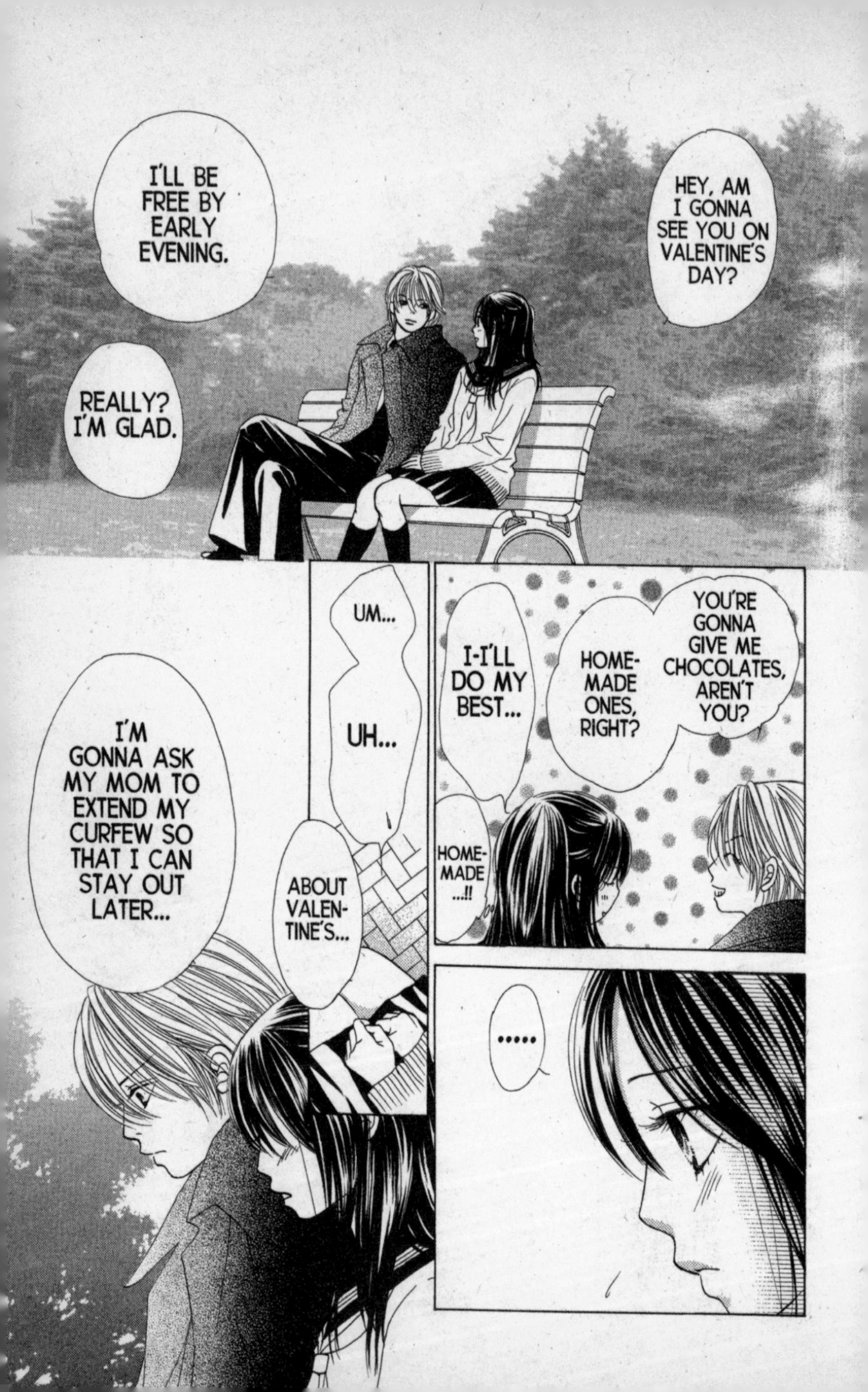
HEY, AM I GONNA SEE YOU ON VALENTINE'S DAY?
I'LL BE FREE BY EARLY EVENING.
REALLY? I'M GLAD.
YOU'RE GONNA GIVE ME CHOCOLATES, AREN'T YOU?
HOME-MADE ONES, RIGHT?
I-I'LL DO MY BEST...
HOME-MADE ...!!
......
UM...
UH...
ABOUT VALEN-TINE'S...
I'M GONNA ASK MY MOM TO EXTEND MY CURFEW SO THAT I CAN STAY OUT LATER...

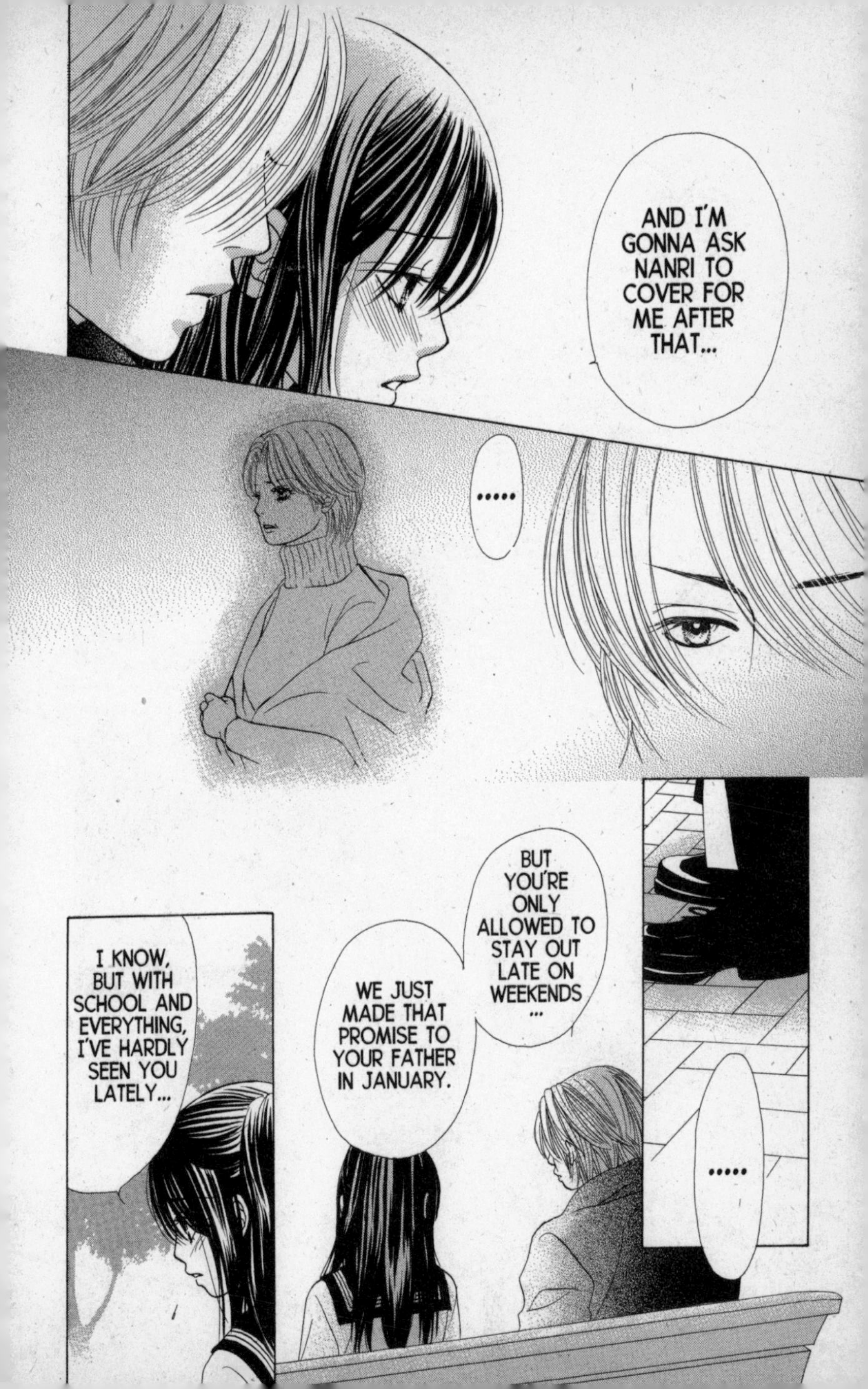
AND I'M GONNA ASK NANRI TO COVER FOR ME AFTER THAT...
......
BUT YOU'RE ONLY ALLOWED TO STAY OUT LATE ON WEEKENDS ...
WE JUST MADE THAT PROMISE TO YOUR FATHER IN JANUARY.
I KNOW, BUT WITH SCHOOL AND EVERYTHING, I'VE HARDLY SEEN YOU LATELY...
......

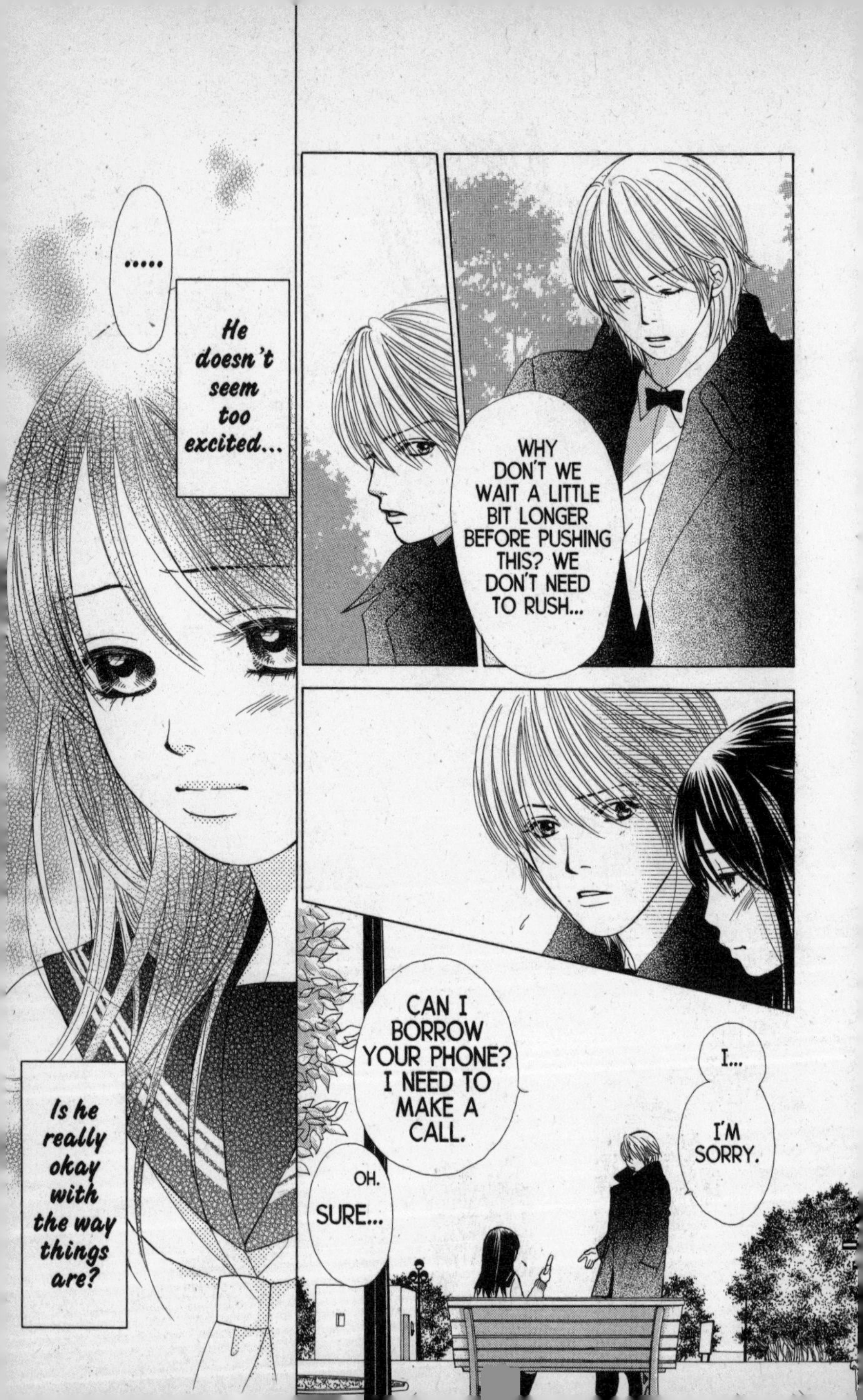
WHY DON'T WE WAIT A LITTLE BIT LONGER BEFORE PUSHING THIS? WE DON'T NEED TO RUSH...
I... I'M SORRY.
CAN I BORROW YOUR PHONE? I NEED TO MAKE A CALL.
OH. SURE...
.....
He doesn't seem too excited...
Is he really okay with the way things are?

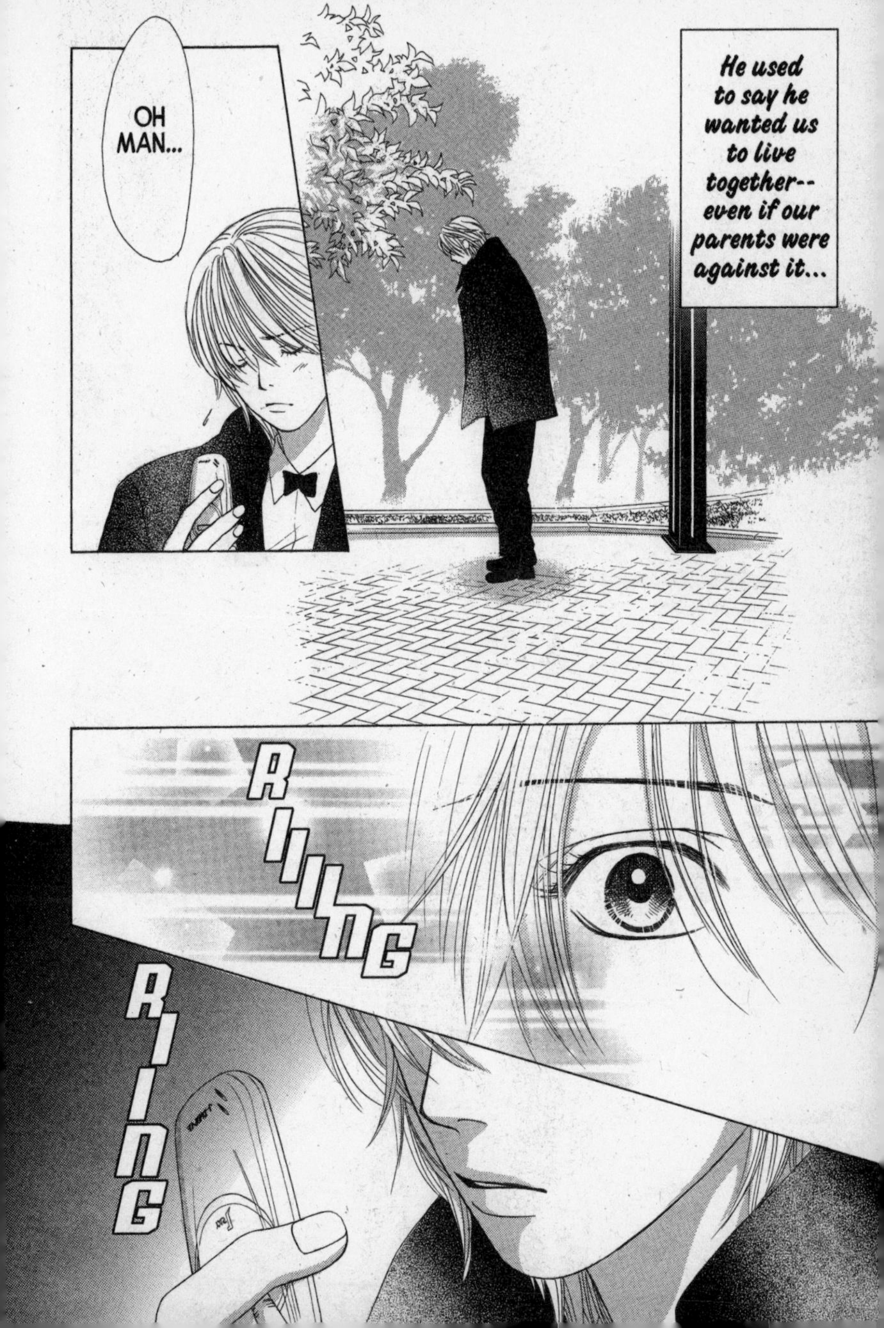
He used to say he wanted us to live together--even if our parents were against it...
OH MAN...
RIIING
RIING

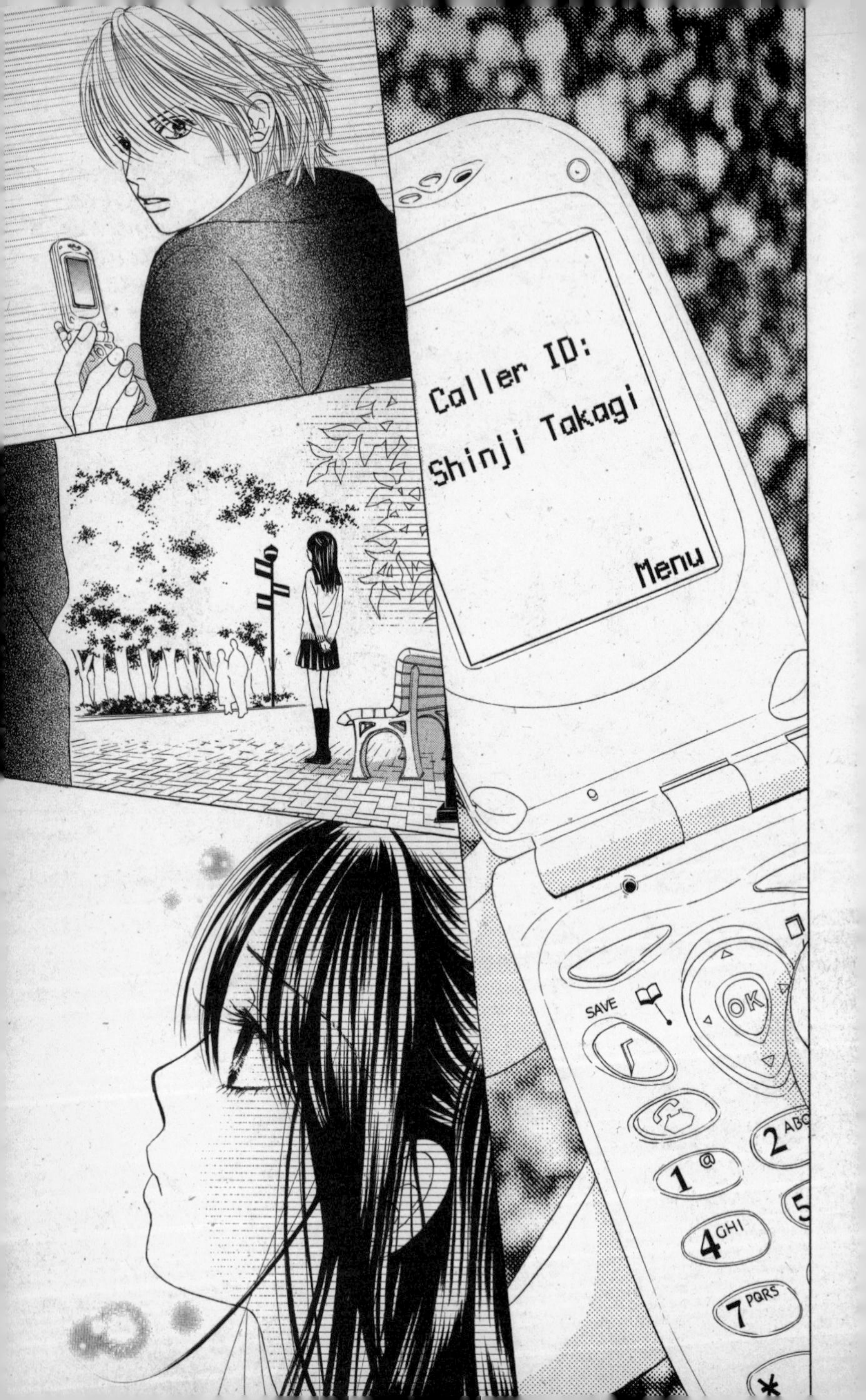
Caller ID:
Shinji Takagi
Menu
SAVE
OK

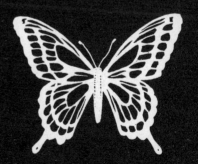

彼 *KARE*
First Love

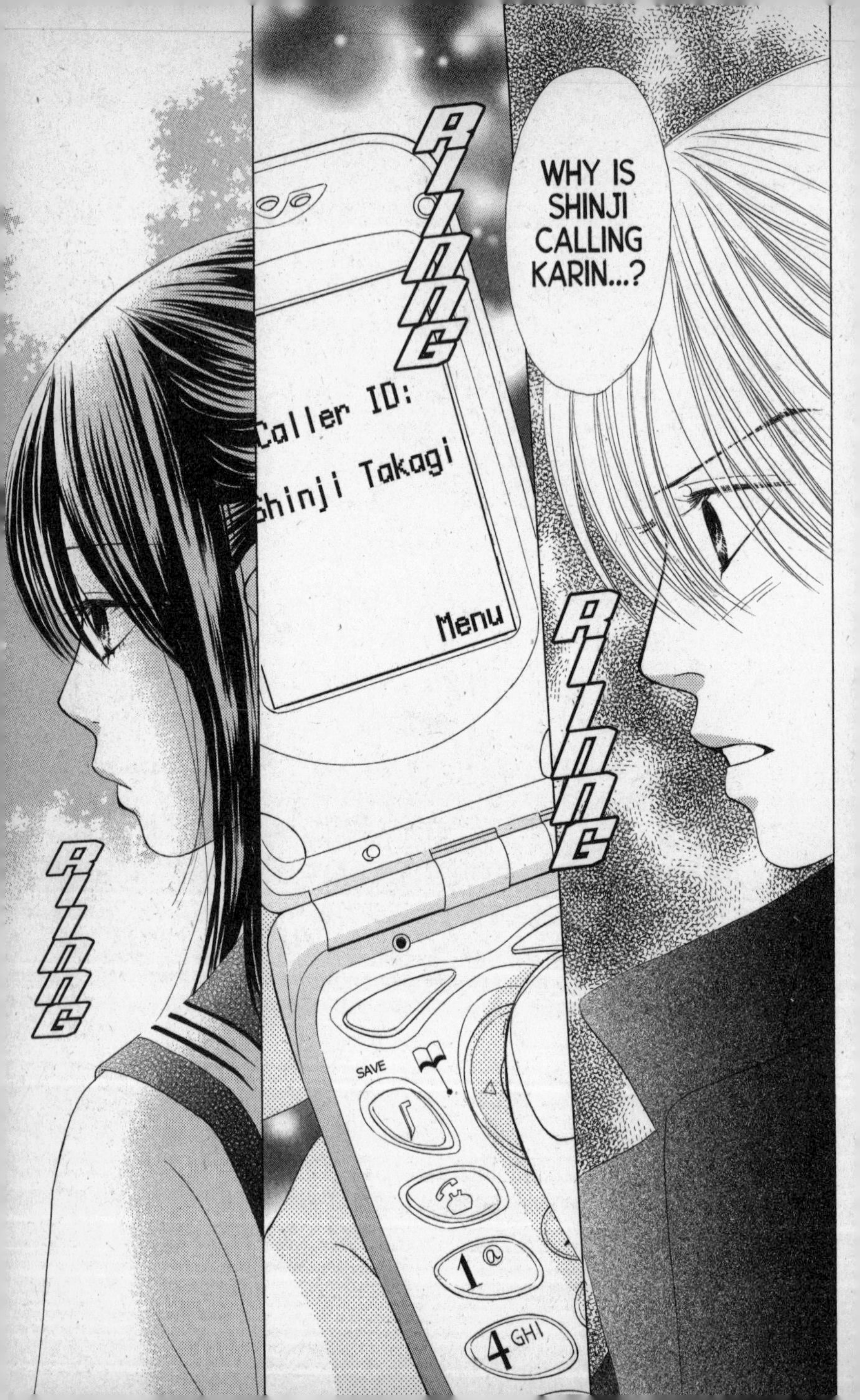
WHY IS SHINJI CALLING KARIN...?
RING
RING
Caller ID:
Shinji Takagi
Menu
SAVE
1
4 GHI
RING

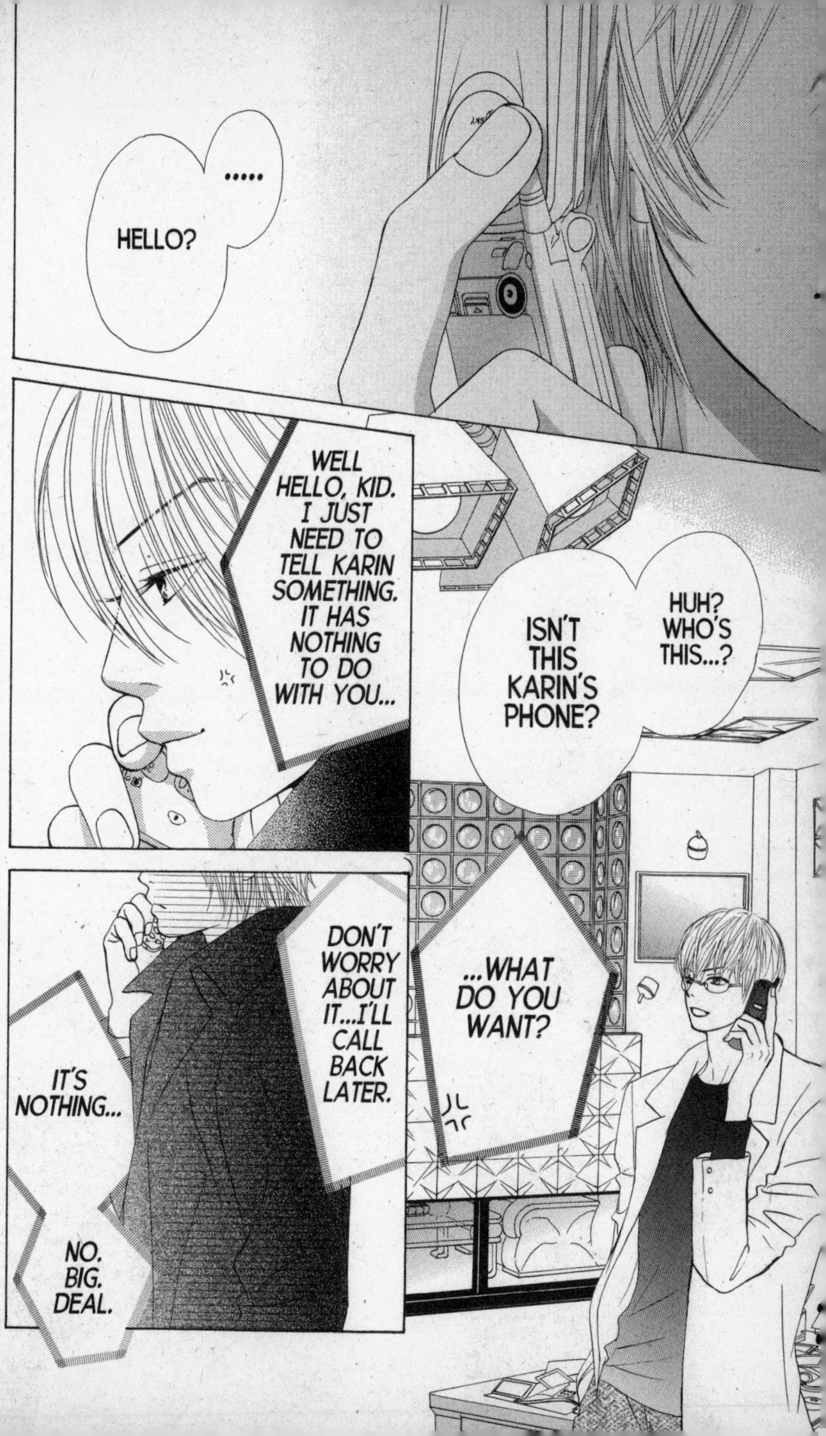
.....
HELLO?
HUH? WHO'S THIS...?
ISN'T THIS KARIN'S PHONE?
WELL HELLO, KID. I JUST NEED TO TELL KARIN SOMETHING. IT HAS NOTHING TO DO WITH YOU...
...WHAT DO YOU WANT?
DON'T WORRY ABOUT IT...I'LL CALL BACK LATER.
IT'S NOTHING...
NO. BIG. DEAL.

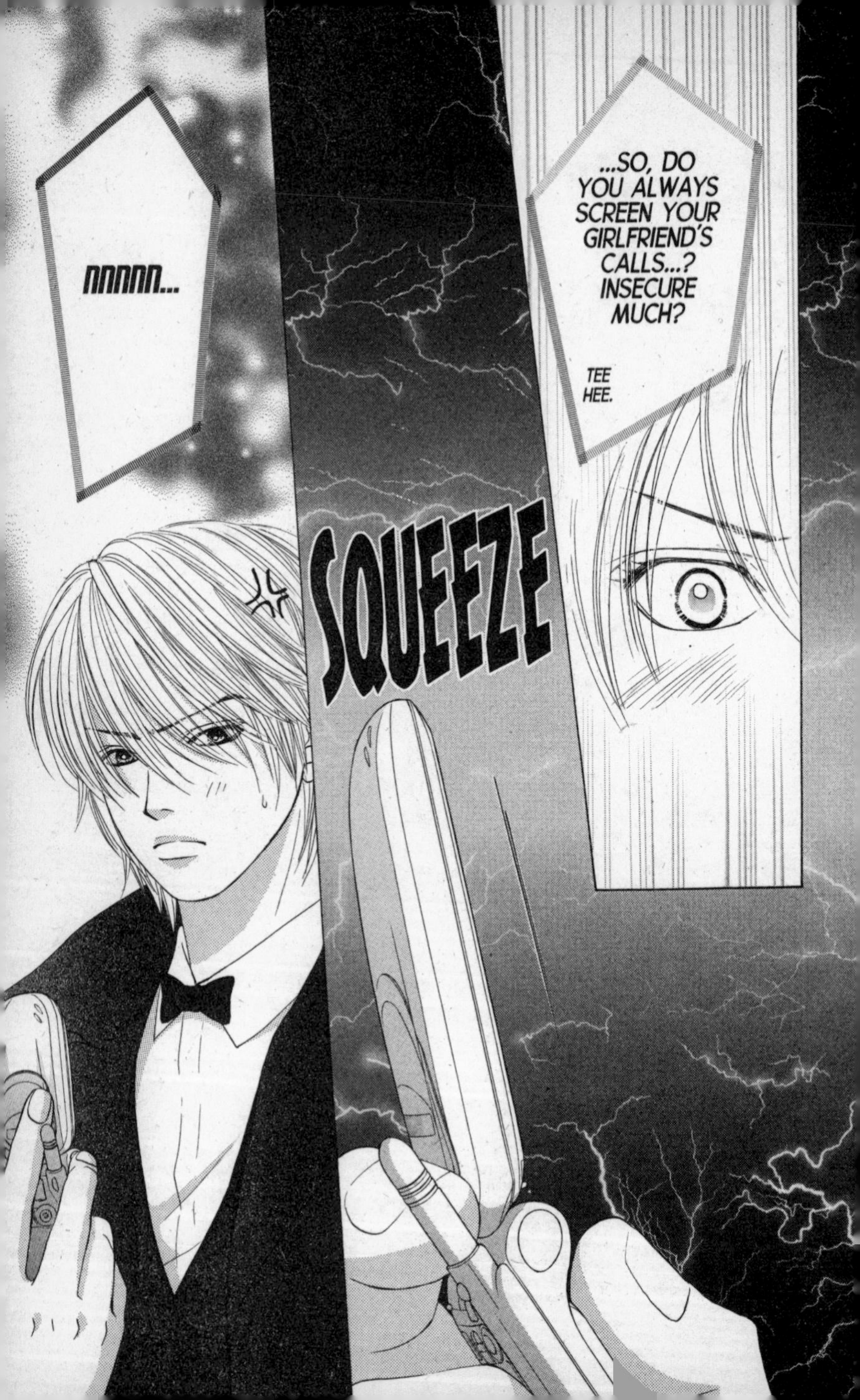
...SO, DO YOU ALWAYS SCREEN YOUR GIRLFRIEND'S CALLS...? INSECURE MUCH?
TEE HEE.
SQUEEZE
nnnnn...

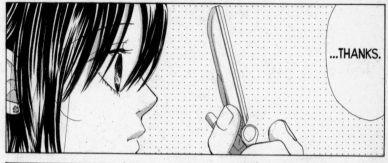

...THANKS.

•••••

ARE YOU DONE WITH IT?

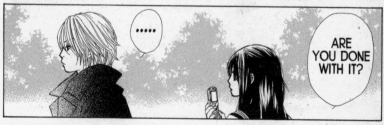

YOU HAD A CRANK CALL.

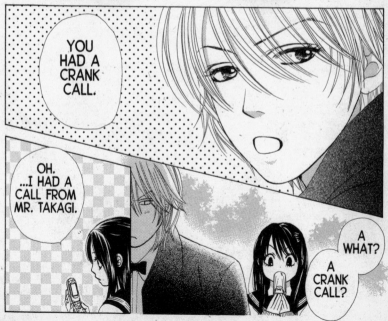

OH. ...I HAD A CALL FROM MR. TAKAGI.

A WHAT?

A CRANK CALL?

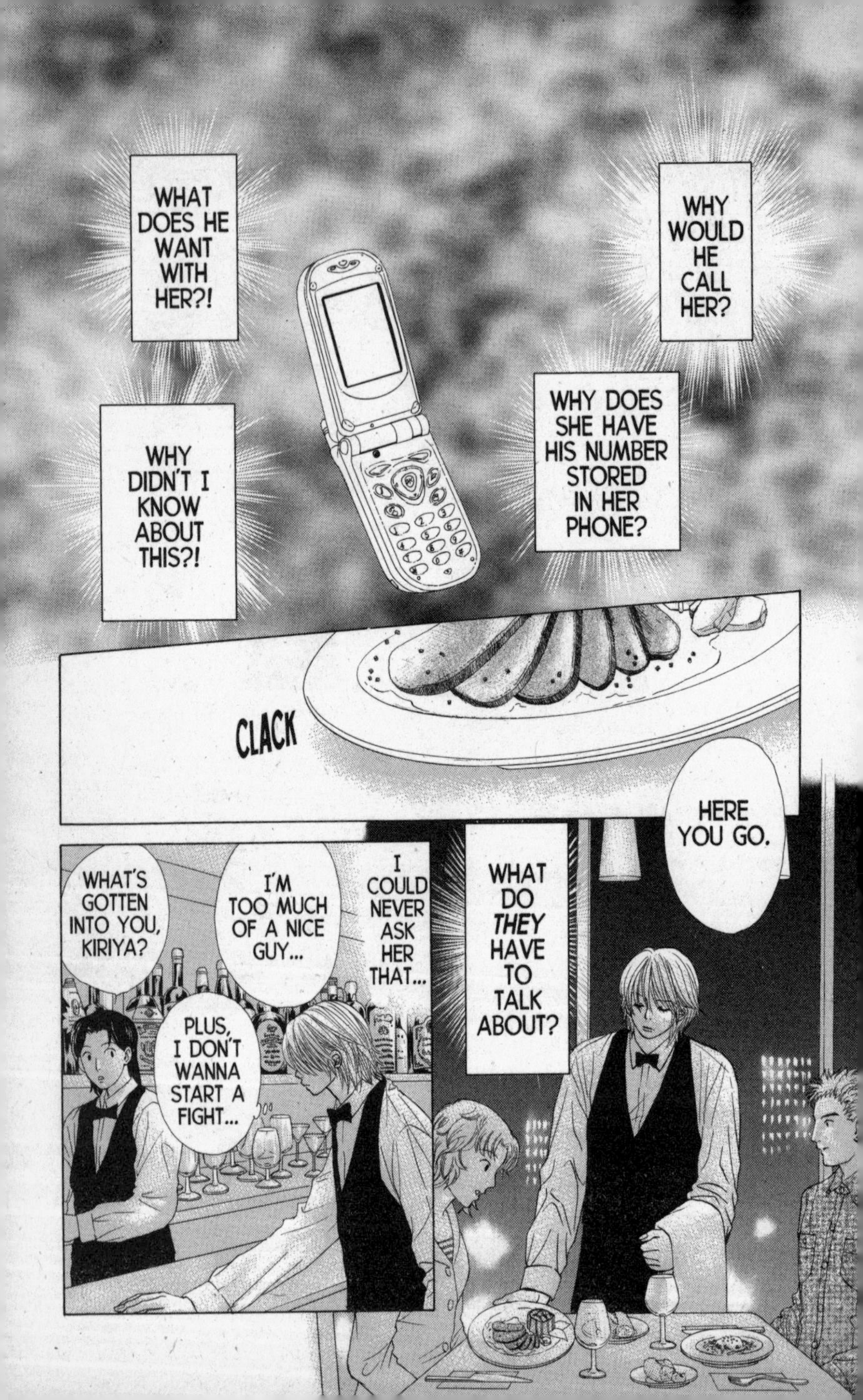

WHY WOULD HE CALL HER?
WHAT DOES HE WANT WITH HER?!
WHY DOES SHE HAVE HIS NUMBER STORED IN HER PHONE?
WHY DIDN'T I KNOW ABOUT THIS?!
CLACK
HERE YOU GO.
WHAT DO *THEY* HAVE TO TALK ABOUT?
I COULD NEVER ASK HER THAT...
I'M TOO MUCH OF A NICE GUY...
PLUS, I DON'T WANNA START A FIGHT...
WHAT'S GOTTEN INTO YOU, KIRIYA?

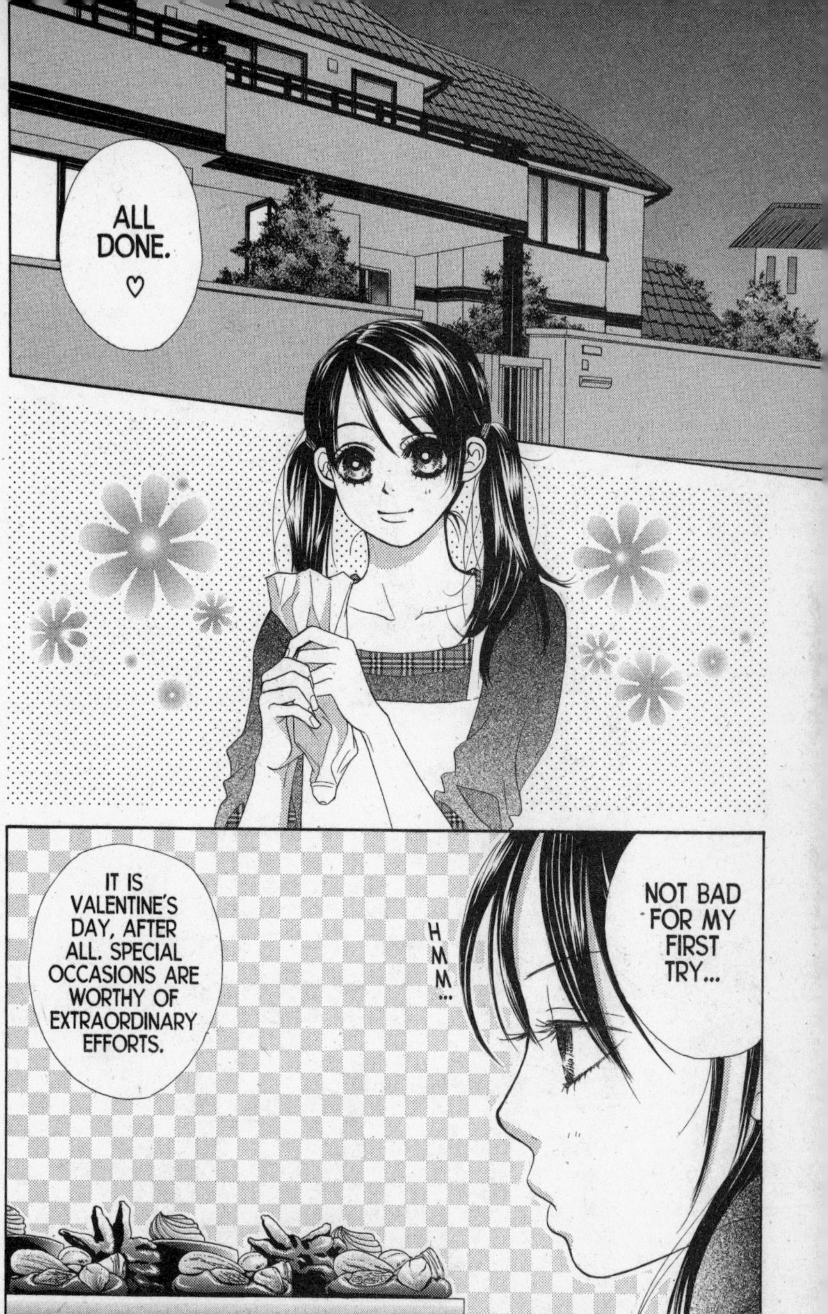
ALL DONE. ♡
NOT BAD FOR MY FIRST TRY...
HMM...
IT IS VALENTINE'S DAY, AFTER ALL. SPECIAL OCCASIONS ARE WORTHY OF EXTRAORDINARY EFFORTS.

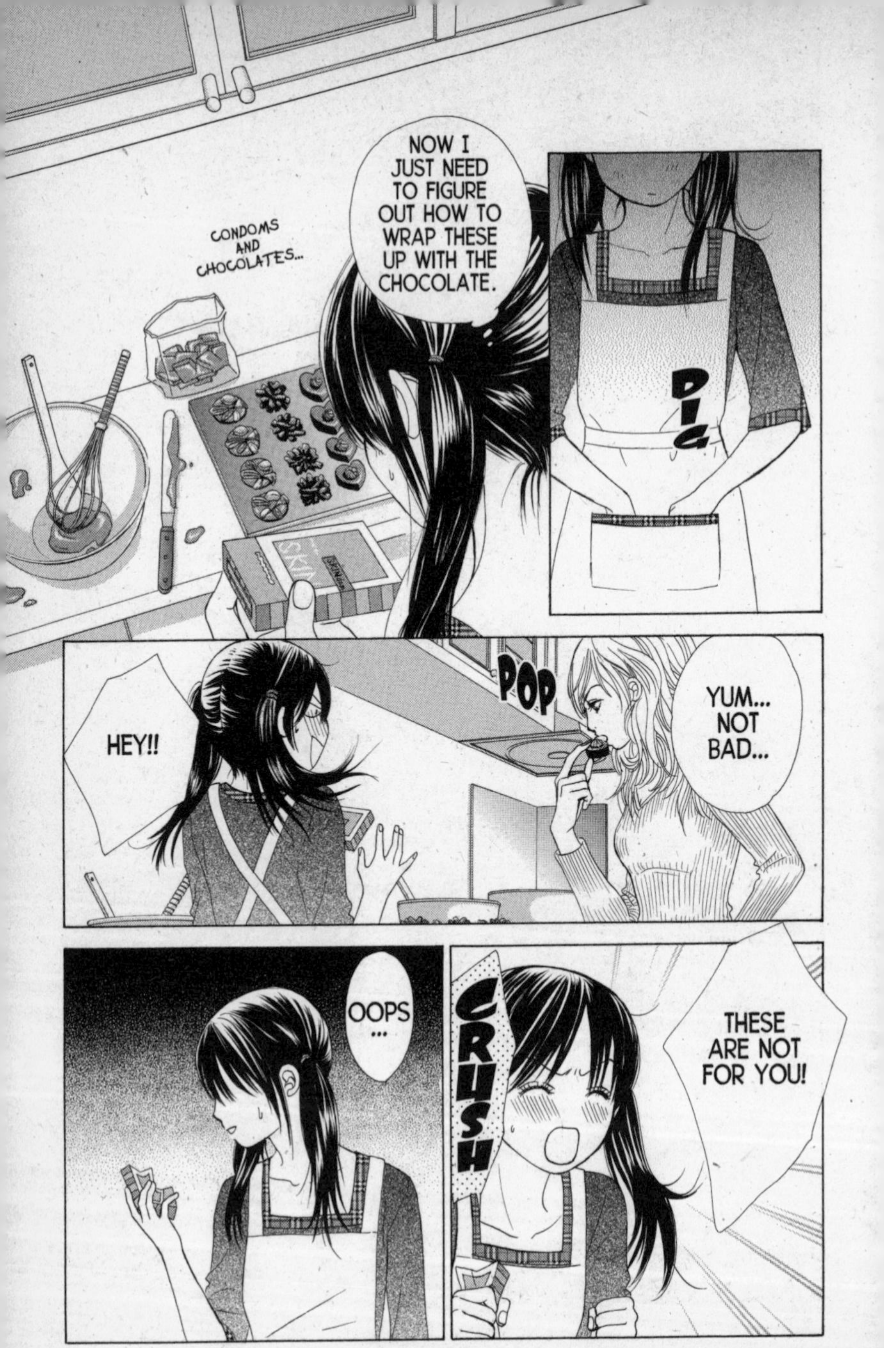
NOW I JUST NEED TO FIGURE OUT HOW TO WRAP THESE UP WITH THE CHOCOLATE.
CONDOMS AND CHOCOLATES...
DIG
YUM... NOT BAD...
POP
HEY!!
THESE ARE NOT FOR YOU!
CRUSH
OOPS...

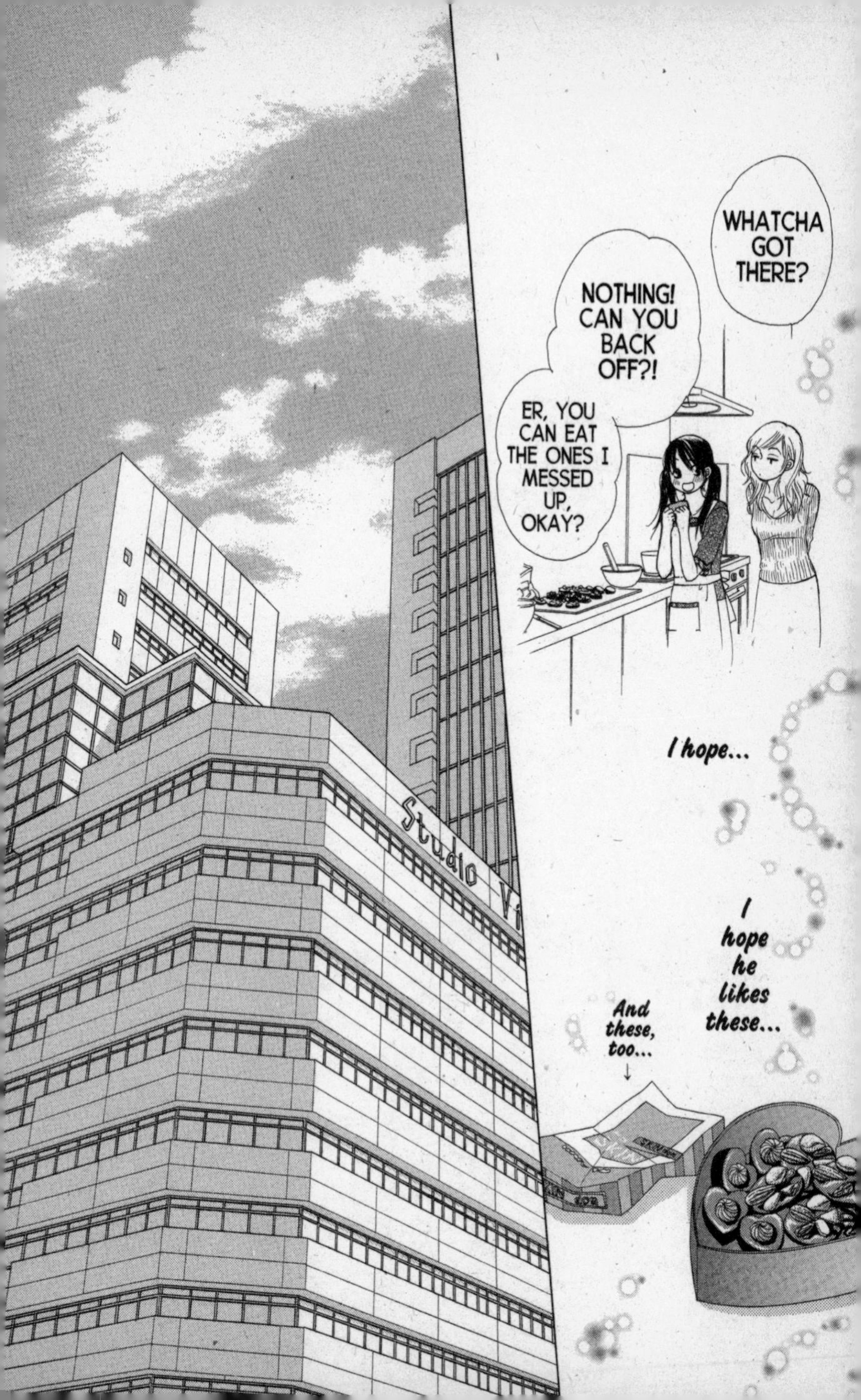
WHATCHA GOT THERE?
NOTHING! CAN YOU BACK OFF?!
ER, YOU CAN EAT THE ONES I MESSED UP, OKAY?
I hope...
I hope he likes these...
And these, too...
Studio

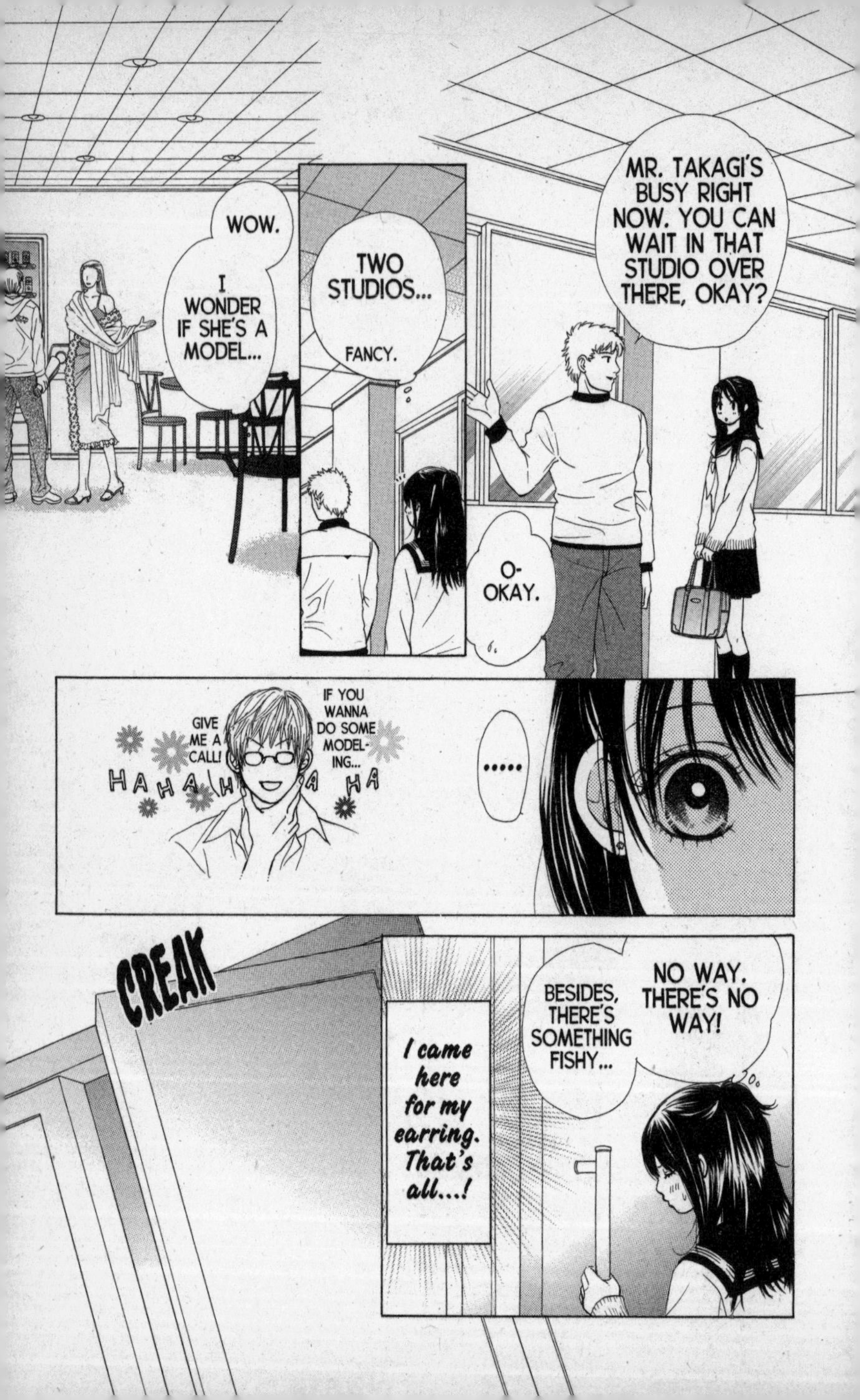
MR. TAKAGI'S BUSY RIGHT NOW. YOU CAN WAIT IN THAT STUDIO OVER THERE, OKAY?
O-OKAY.
TWO STUDIOS...
FANCY.
WOW.
I WONDER IF SHE'S A MODEL...
......
IF YOU WANNA DO SOME MODELING...
GIVE ME A CALL!
HAHAHAHAHA
NO WAY. THERE'S NO WAY!
BESIDES, THERE'S SOMETHING FISHY...
I came here for my earring. That's all...!
CREAK

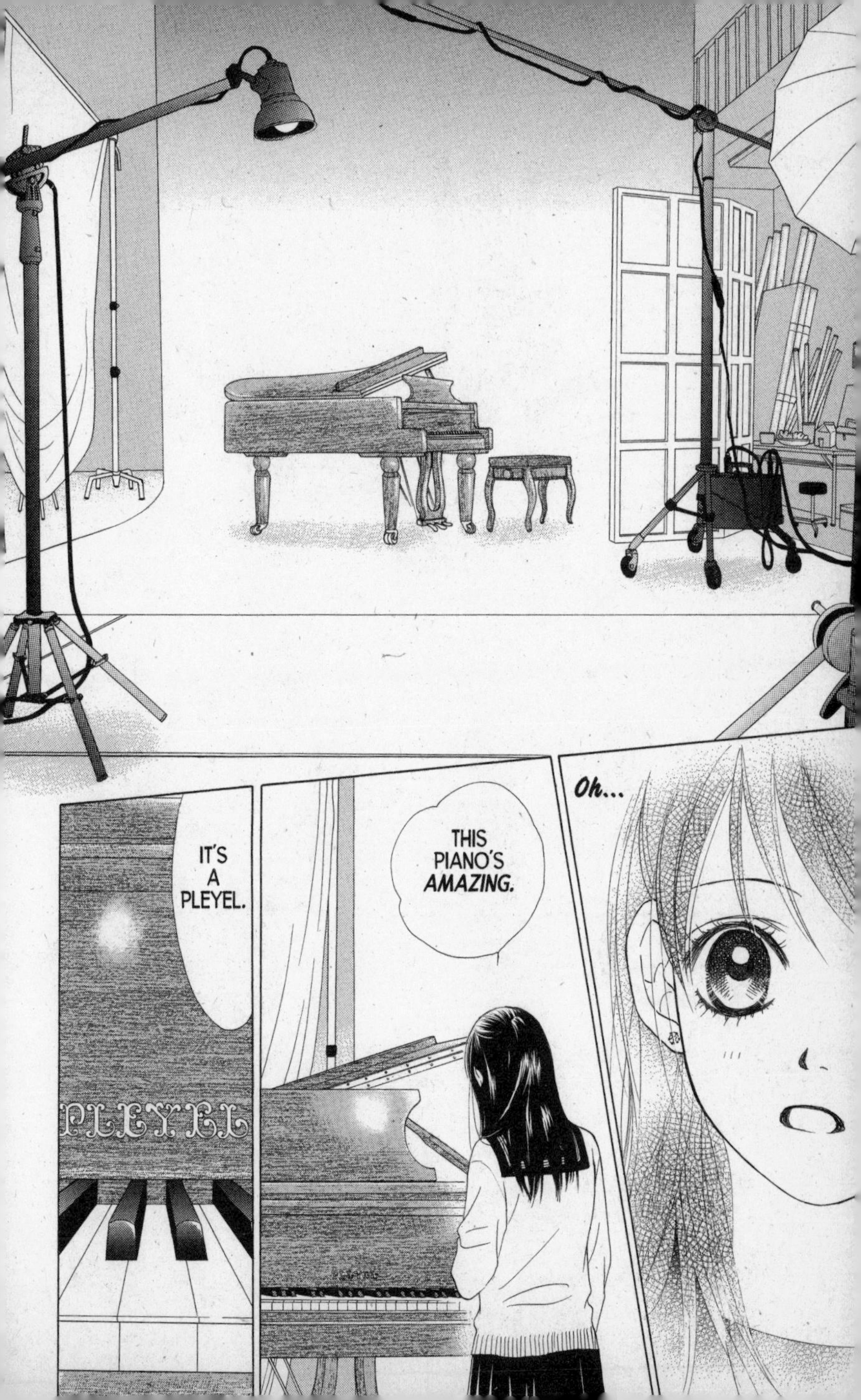
Oh...
THIS PIANO'S *AMAZING.*
IT'S A PLEYEL.
PLEYEL

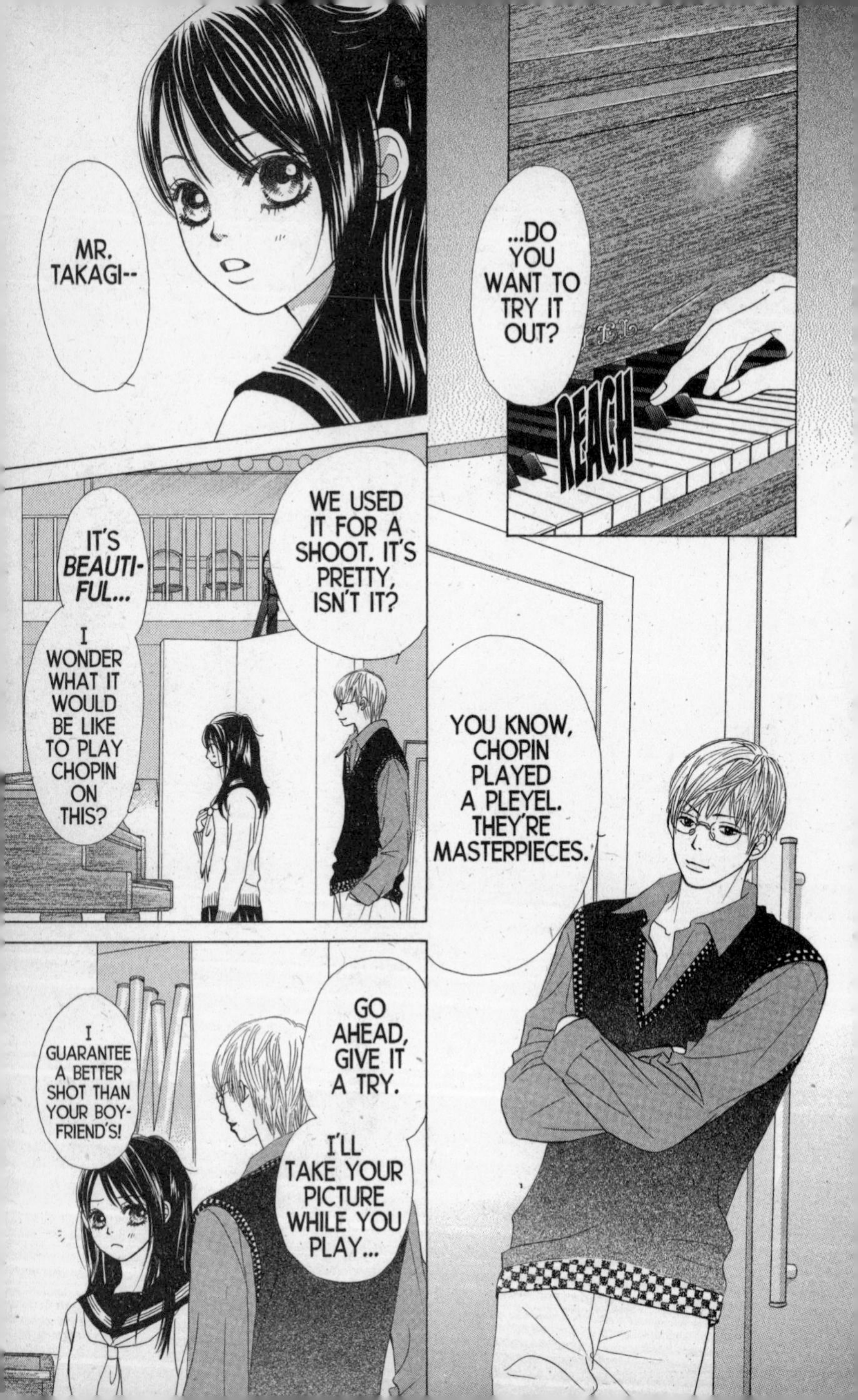
...DO YOU WANT TO TRY IT OUT?
REACH
MR. TAKAGI--
YOU KNOW, CHOPIN PLAYED A PLEYEL. THEY'RE MASTERPIECES.
WE USED IT FOR A SHOOT. IT'S PRETTY, ISN'T IT?
IT'S *BEAUTIFUL...*
I WONDER WHAT IT WOULD BE LIKE TO PLAY CHOPIN ON THIS?
GO AHEAD, GIVE IT A TRY.
I'LL TAKE YOUR PICTURE WHILE YOU PLAY...
I GUARANTEE A BETTER SHOT THAN YOUR BOY-FRIEND'S!

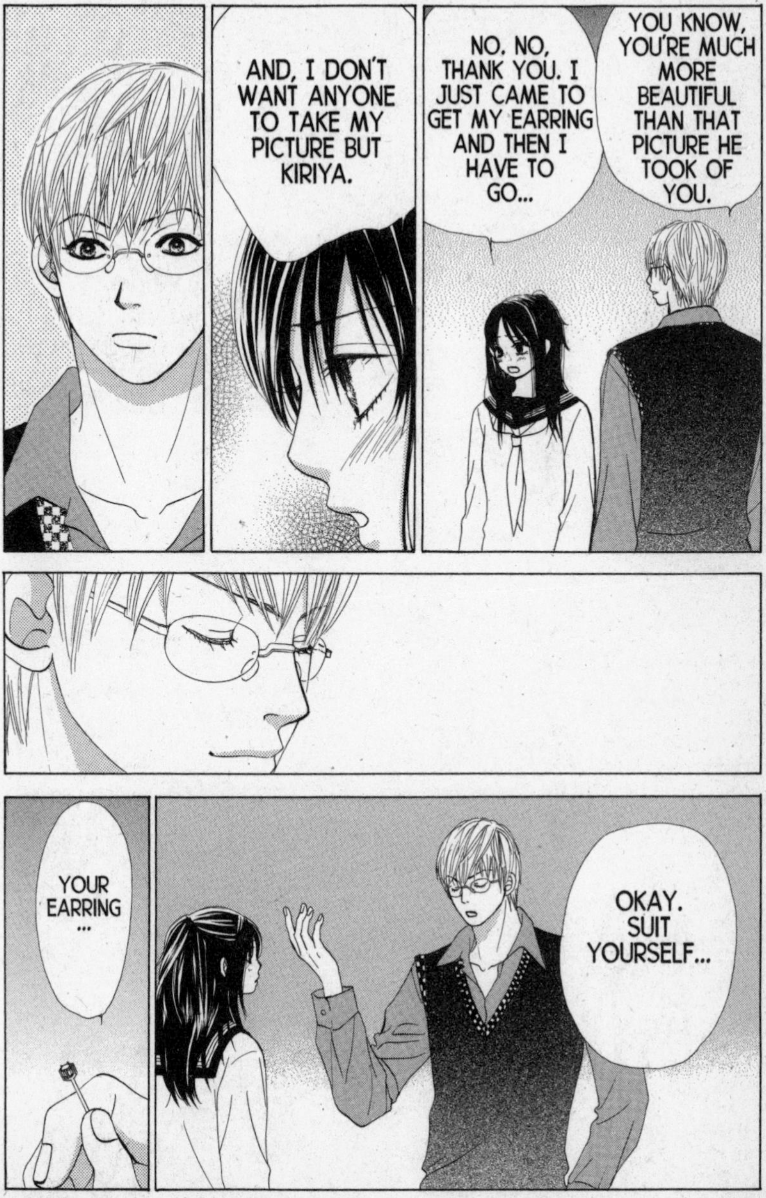
YOU KNOW, YOU'RE MUCH MORE BEAUTIFUL THAN THAT PICTURE HE TOOK OF YOU.
NO. NO, THANK YOU. I JUST CAME TO GET MY EARRING AND THEN I HAVE TO GO...
AND, I DON'T WANT ANYONE TO TAKE MY PICTURE BUT KIRIYA.
OKAY. SUIT YOURSELF...
YOUR EARRING ...

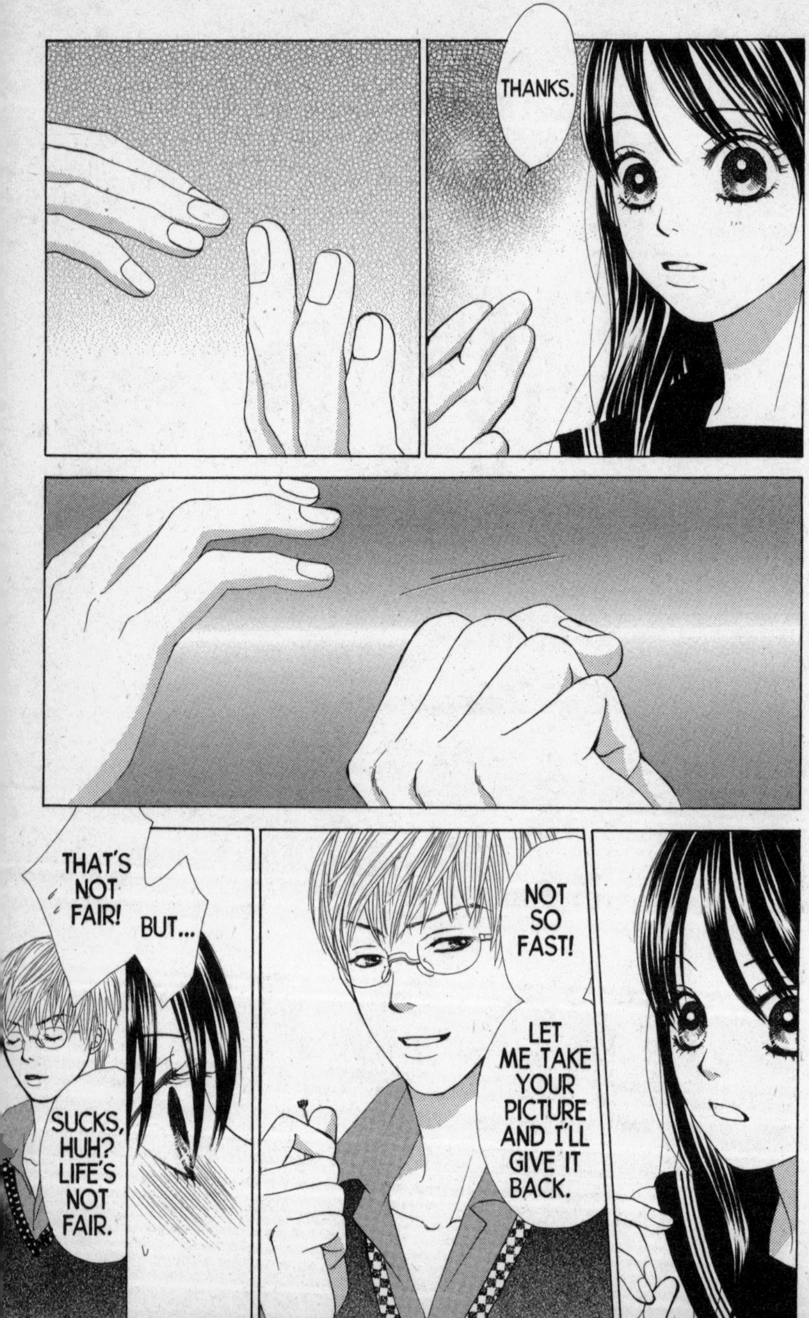
THANKS.
NOT SO FAST!
LET ME TAKE YOUR PICTURE AND I'LL GIVE IT BACK.
THAT'S NOT FAIR!
BUT...
SUCKS, HUH? LIFE'S NOT FAIR.

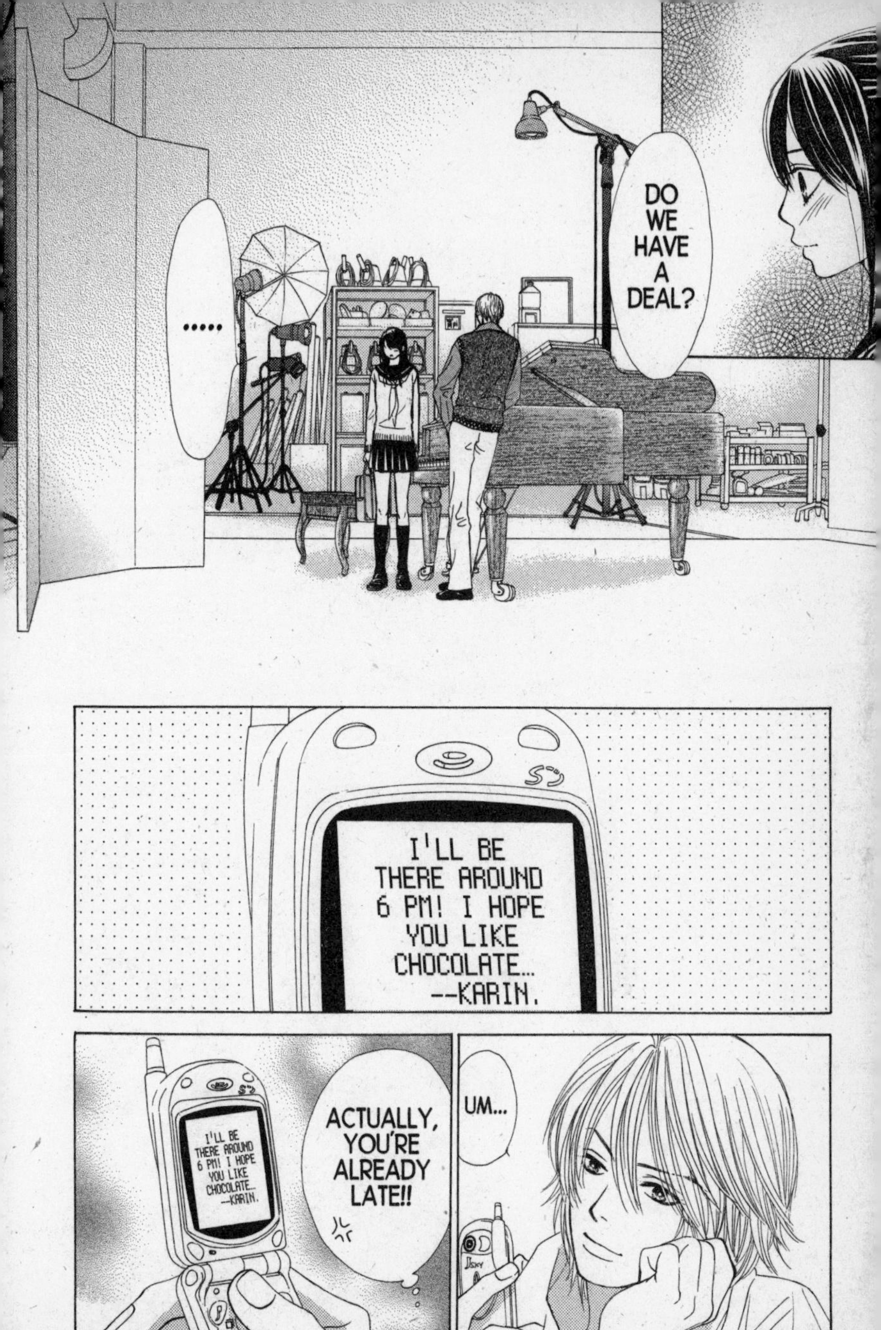
DO WE HAVE A DEAL?
.....
I'LL BE THERE AROUND 6 PM! I HOPE YOU LIKE CHOCOLATE... --KARIN.
UM...
I'LL BE THERE AROUND 6 PM! I HOPE YOU LIKE CHOCOLATE... --KARIN.
ACTUALLY, YOU'RE ALREADY LATE!!

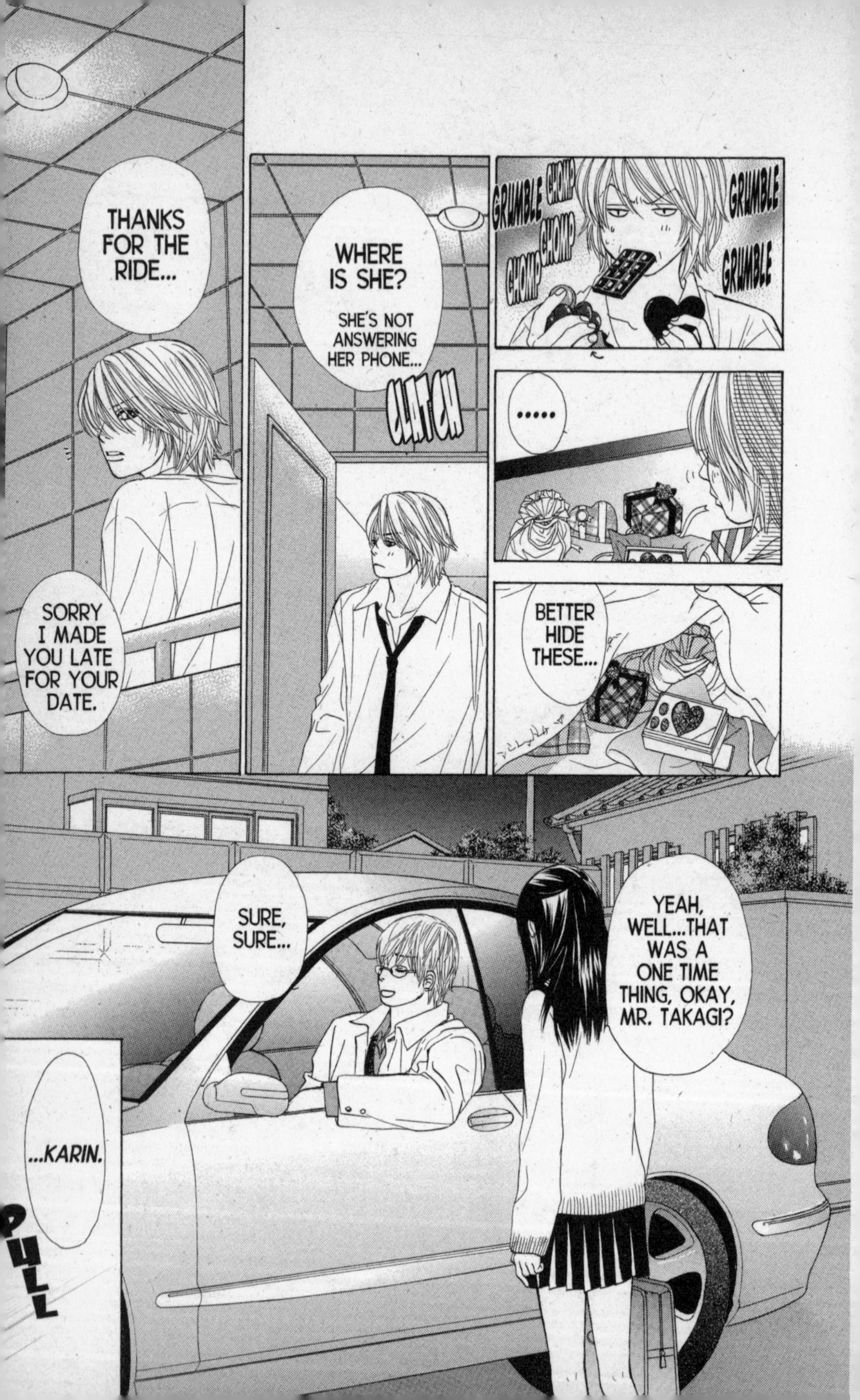
GRUMBLE GRUMBLE
GRUMBLE CHOMP CHOMP CHOMP
......
BETTER HIDE THESE...
WHERE IS SHE?
SHE'S NOT ANSWERING HER PHONE...
CLUTCH
THANKS FOR THE RIDE...
SORRY I MADE YOU LATE FOR YOUR DATE.
YEAH, WELL...THAT WAS A ONE TIME THING, OKAY, MR. TAKAGI?
SURE, SURE...
...KARIN.
PULL

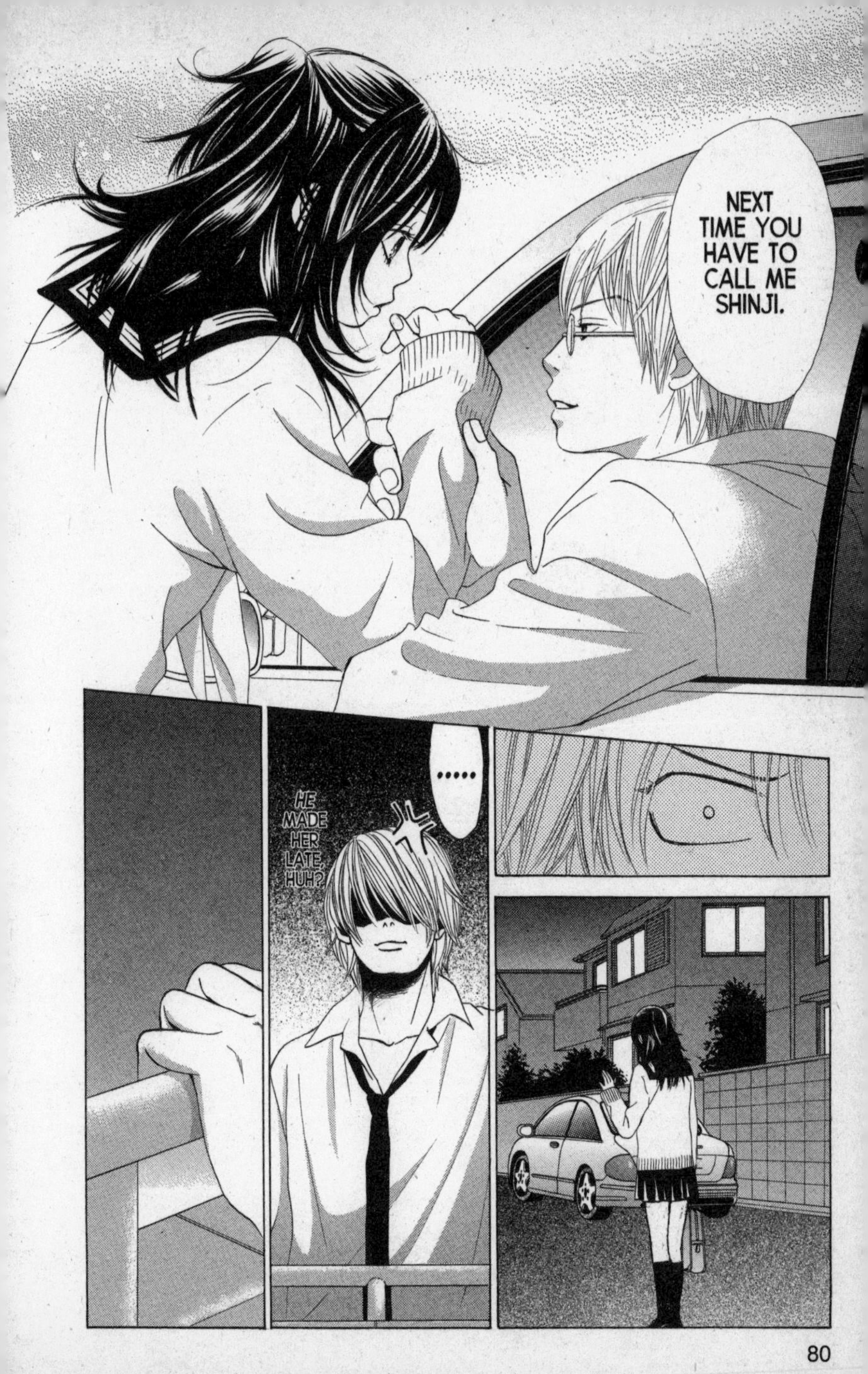
NEXT TIME YOU HAVE TO CALL ME SHINJI.
.....
HE MADE HER LATE, HUH?

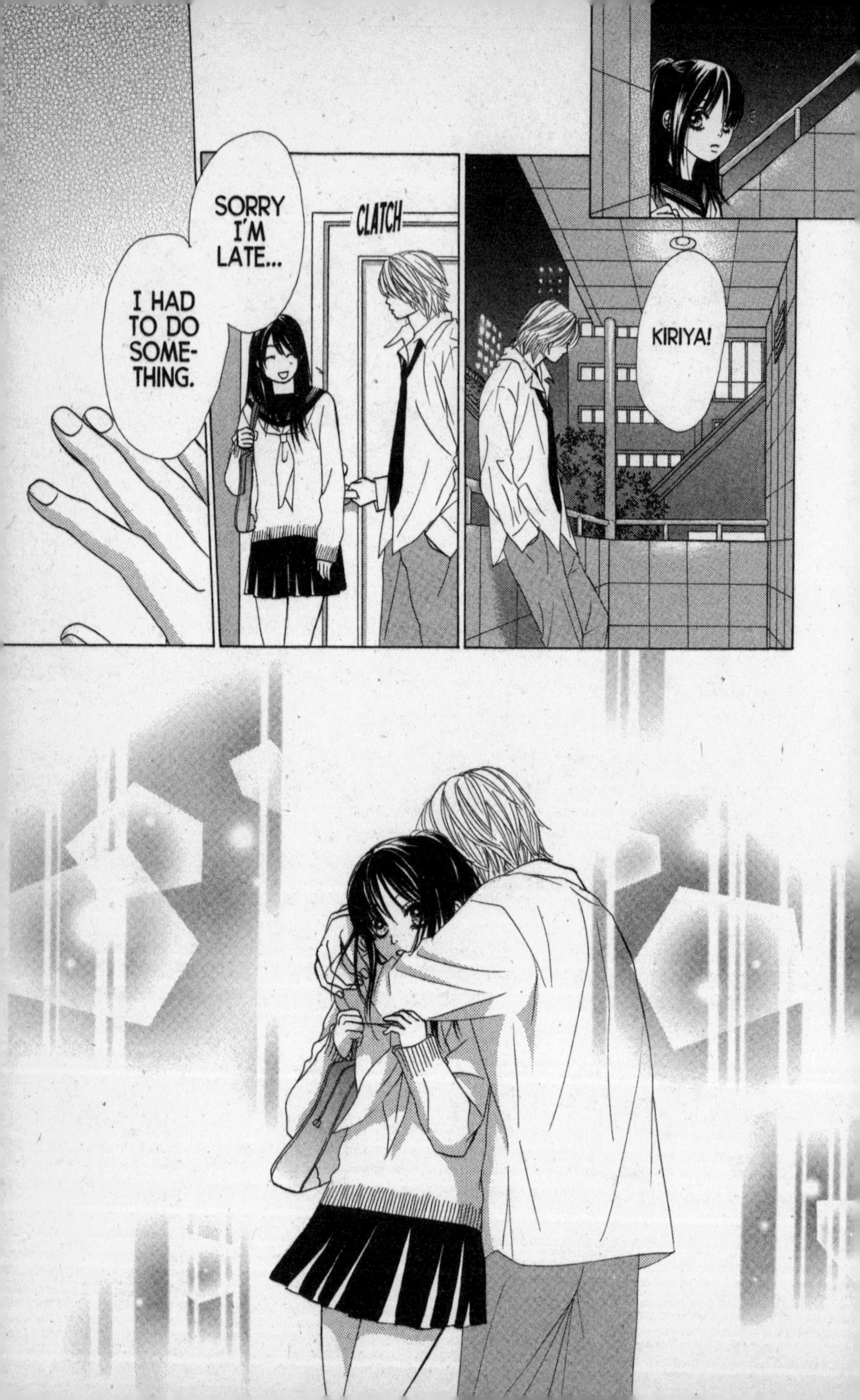
KIRIYA!
CLATCH
SORRY I'M LATE...
I HAD TO DO SOME-THING.

KI...
KIRIYA...
TH-THUMP
ANYTHING YOU WANT TO TELL ME?
HUH?
LIKE WHY YOU'RE LATE...?
WHAT?
Did he know...
...about my earring?
OH... UM...
WELL...
I...I HAD TO MEET SOMEBODY...
Somebody?
!

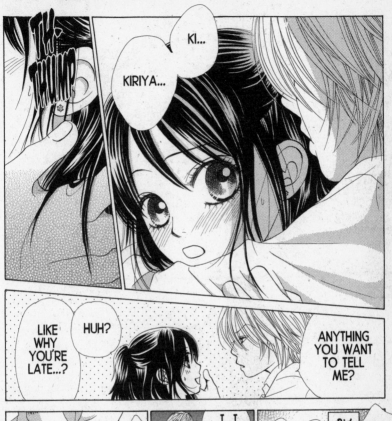

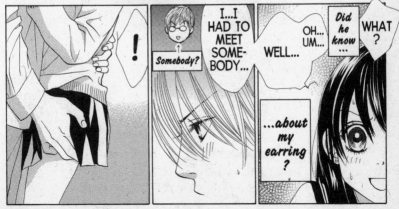

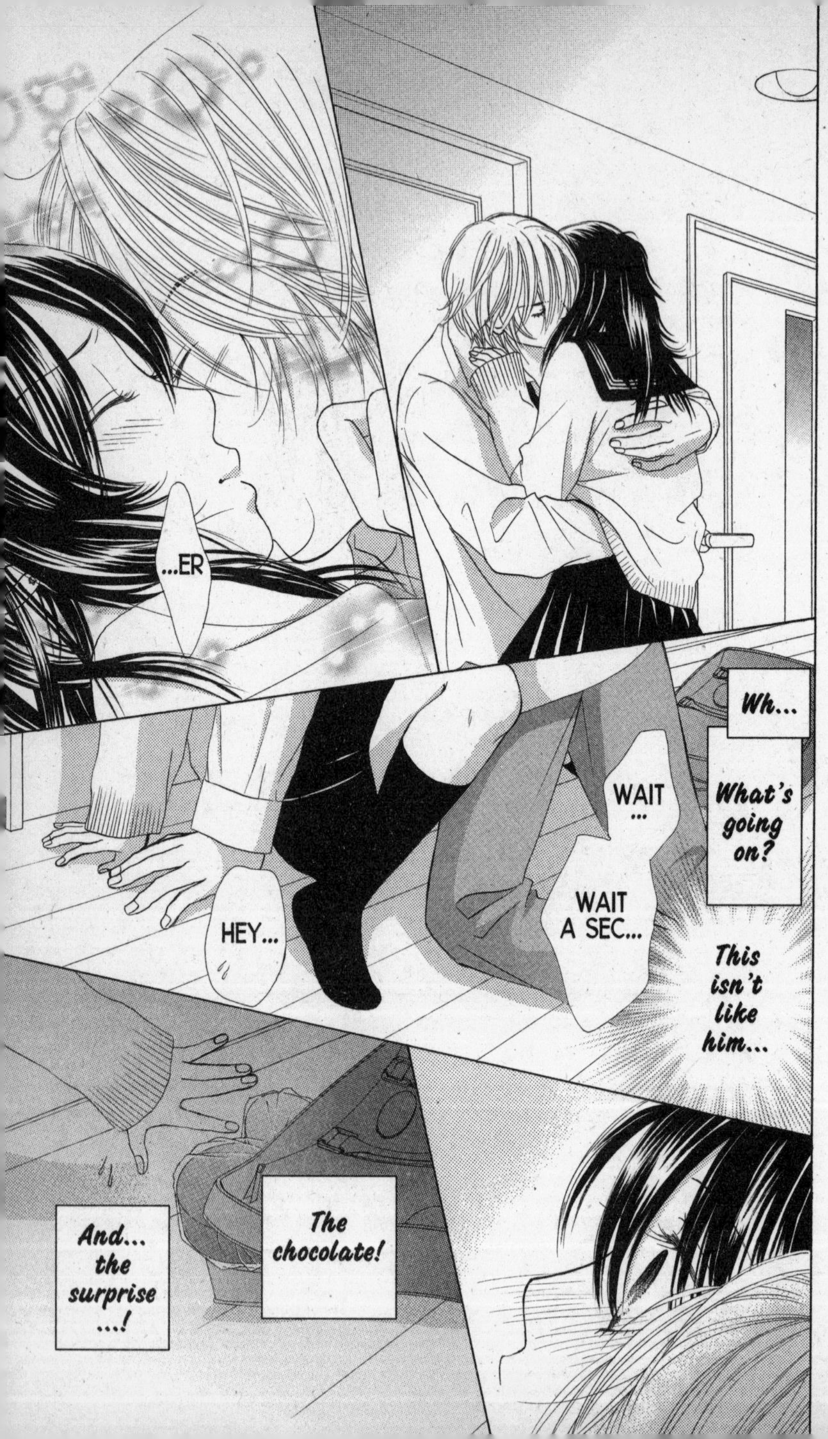
...ER
Wh...
What's going on?
WAIT ...
WAIT A SEC...
This isn't like him...
HEY...
The chocolate!
And... the surprise ...!

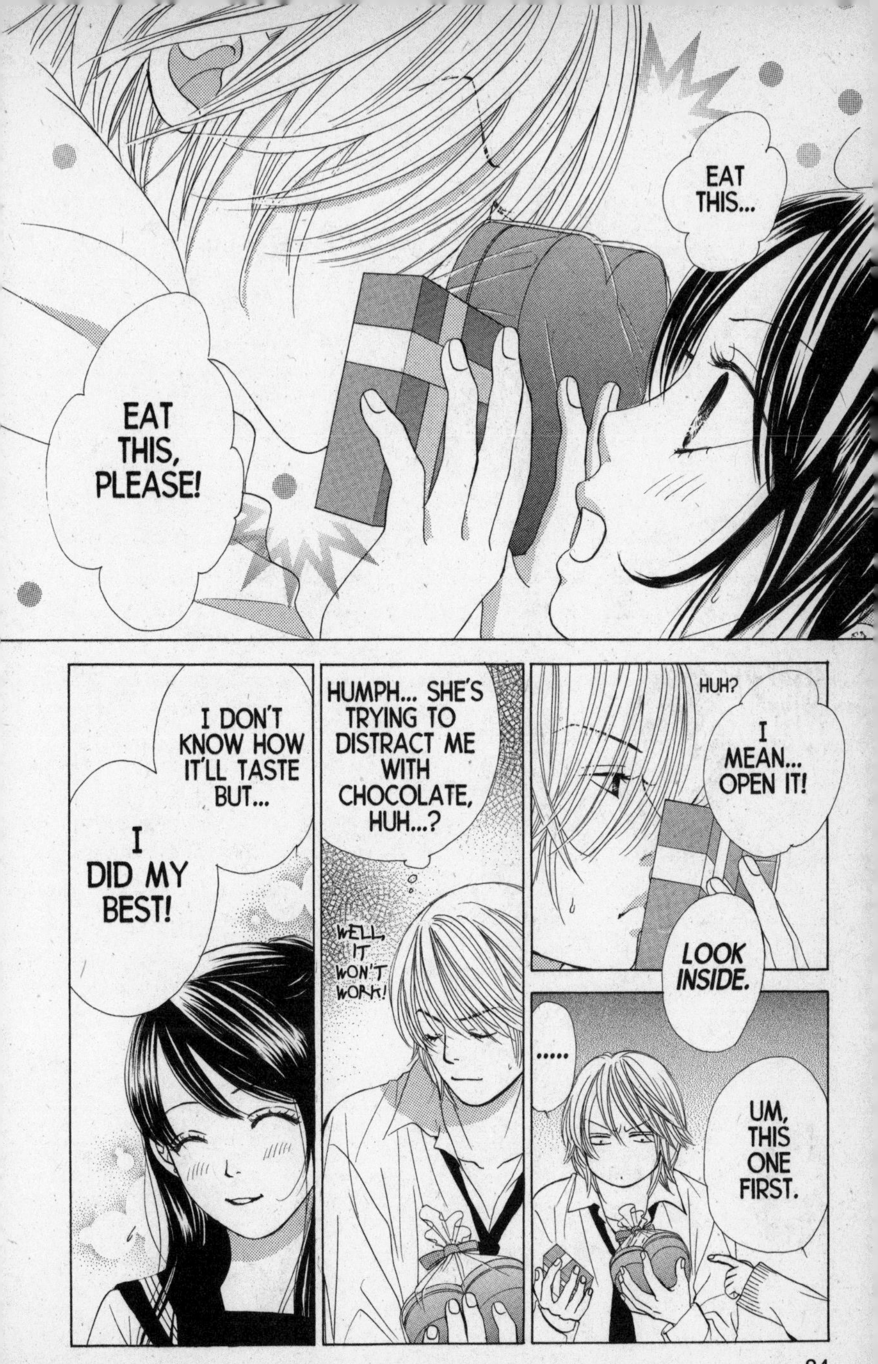
EAT THIS...
EAT THIS, PLEASE!
HUH?
I MEAN... OPEN IT!
LOOK INSIDE.
UM, THIS ONE FIRST.
.....
HUMPH... SHE'S TRYING TO DISTRACT ME WITH CHOCOLATE, HUH...?
WELL, IT WON'T WORK!
I DON'T KNOW HOW IT'LL TASTE BUT...
I DID MY BEST!

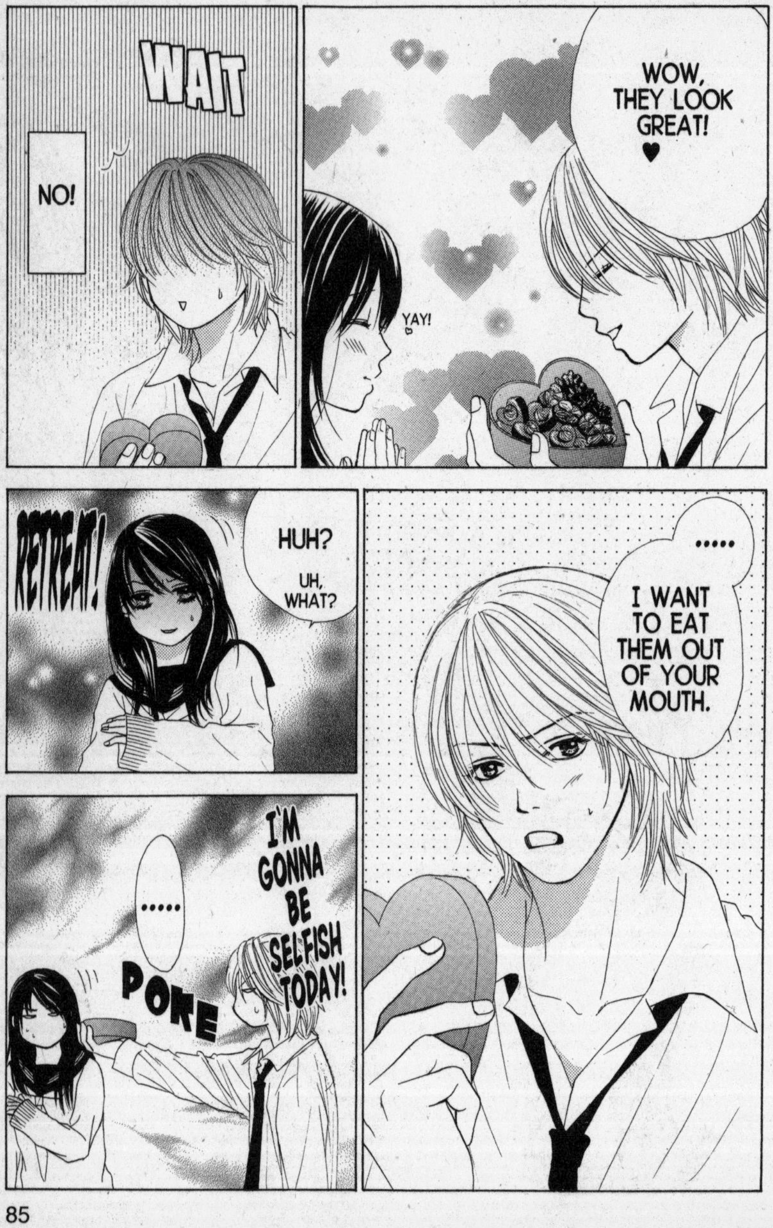
WOW, THEY LOOK GREAT! ♥
YAY! ♥
WAIT
NO!
.....
I WANT TO EAT THEM OUT OF YOUR MOUTH.
HUH?
UH, WHAT?
RETREAT!
I'M GONNA BE SELFISH TODAY!
.....
POKE

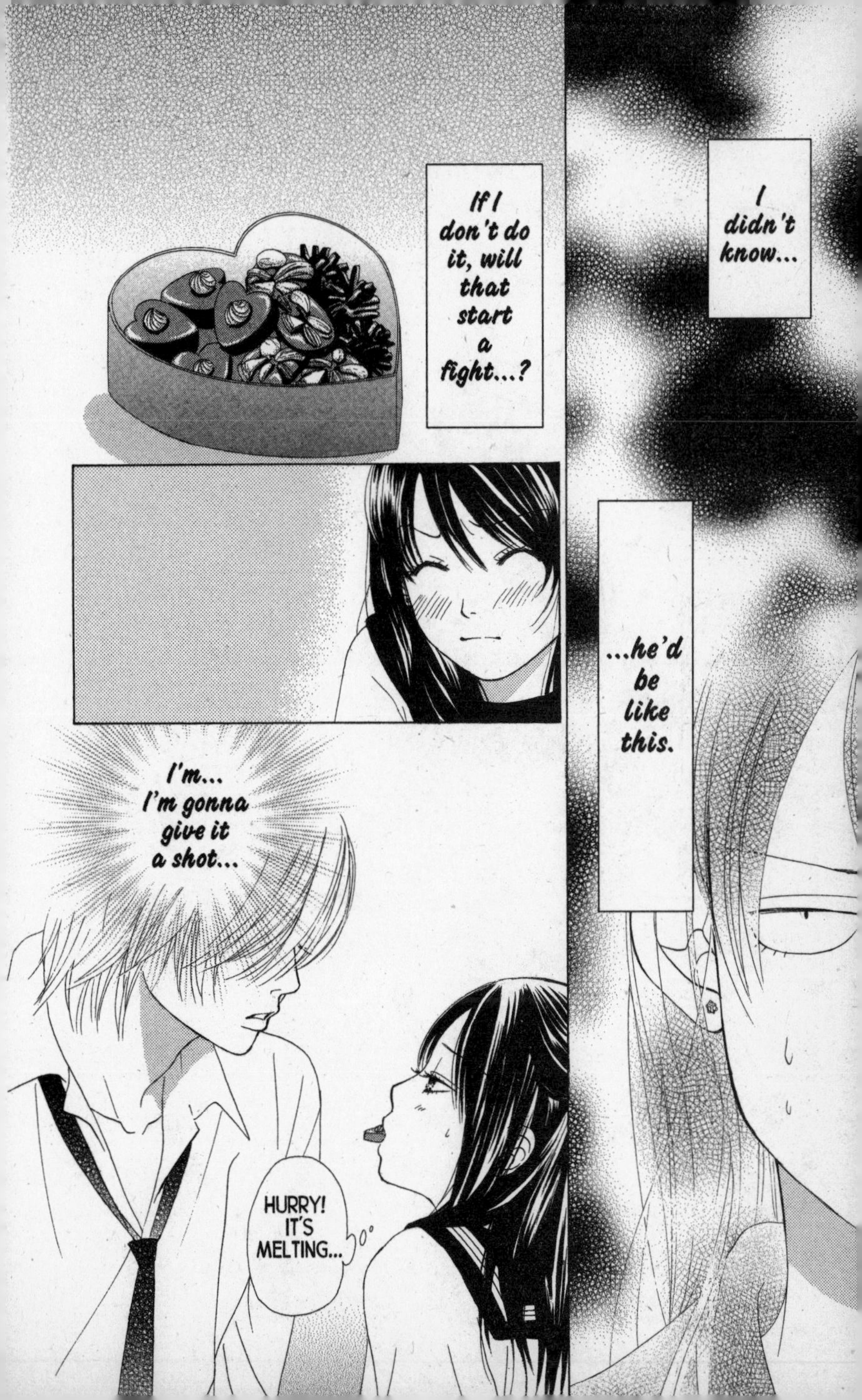
I didn't know...
...he'd be like this.
If I don't do it, will that start a fight...?
I'm... I'm gonna give it a shot...
HURRY! IT'S MELTING...

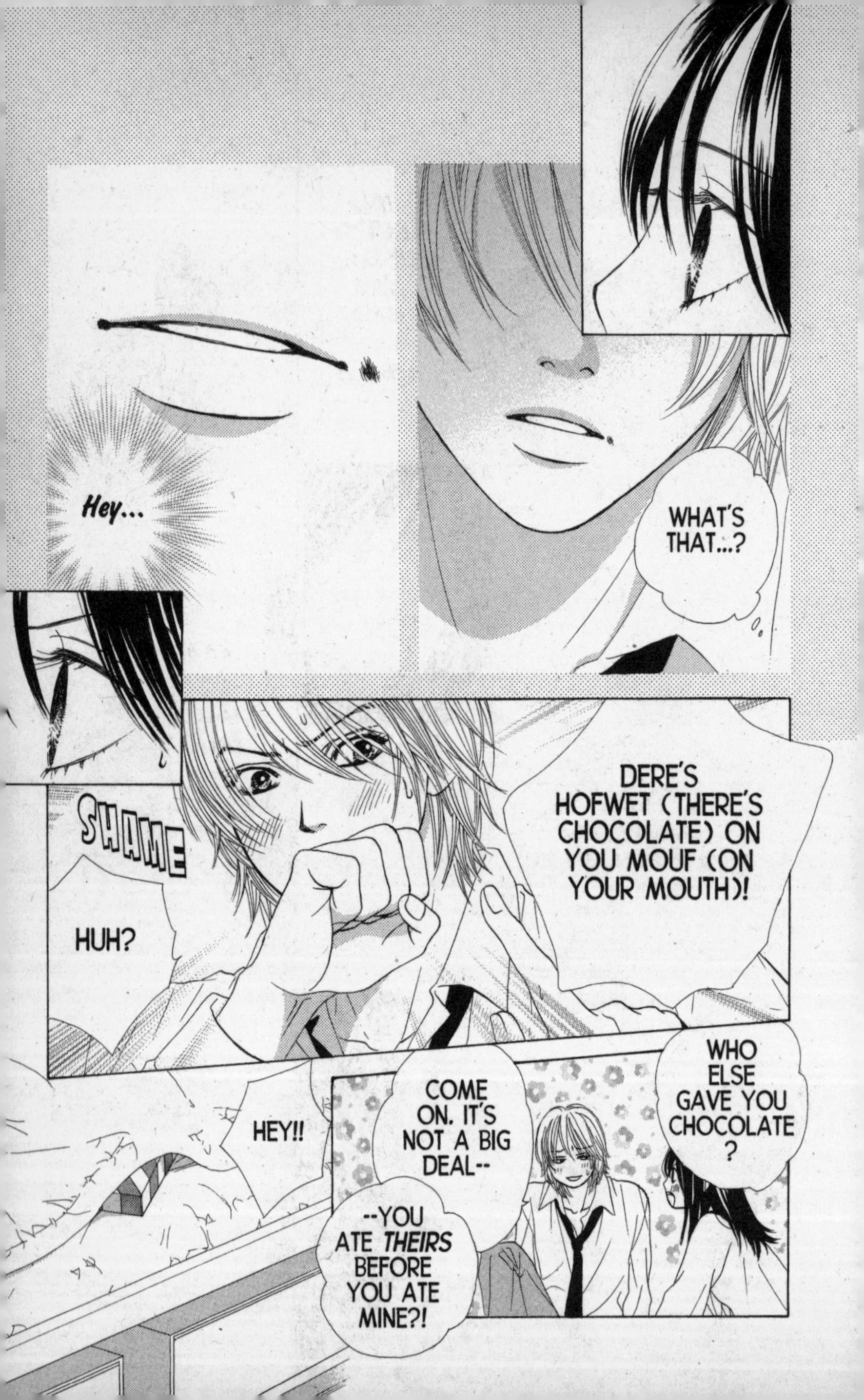
WHAT'S THAT...?
Hey...
DERE'S HOFWET (THERE'S CHOCOLATE) ON YOU MOUF (ON YOUR MOUTH)!
SHAME
HUH?
WHO ELSE GAVE YOU CHOCOLATE?
COME ON. IT'S NOT A BIG DEAL--
--YOU ATE *THEIRS* BEFORE YOU ATE MINE?!
HEY!!

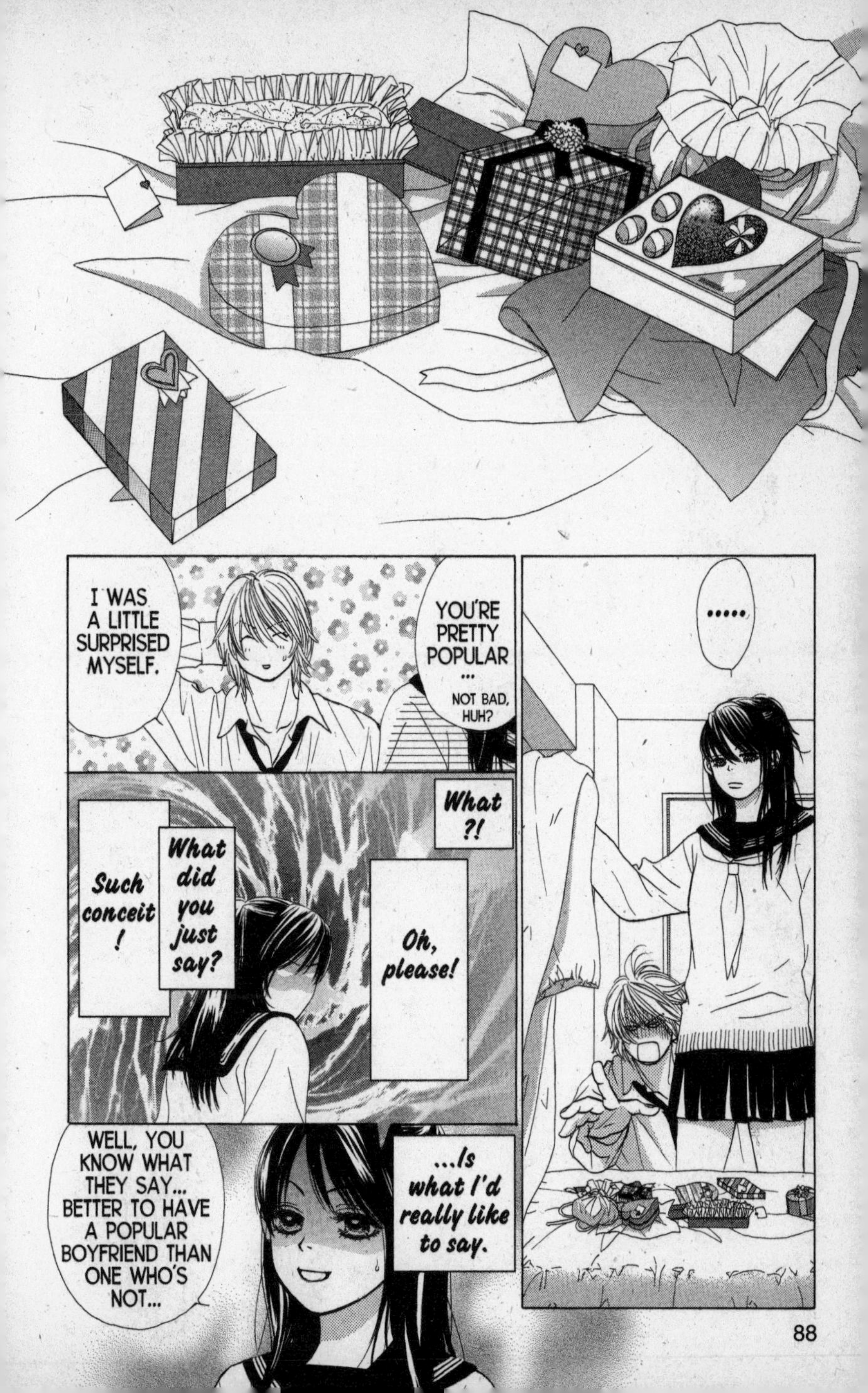
......
YOU'RE PRETTY POPULAR ... NOT BAD, HUH?
I WAS A LITTLE SURPRISED MYSELF.
What ?!
Oh, please!
What did you just say?
Such conceit !
...Is what I'd really like to say.
WELL, YOU KNOW WHAT THEY SAY... BETTER TO HAVE A POPULAR BOYFRIEND THAN ONE WHO'S NOT...

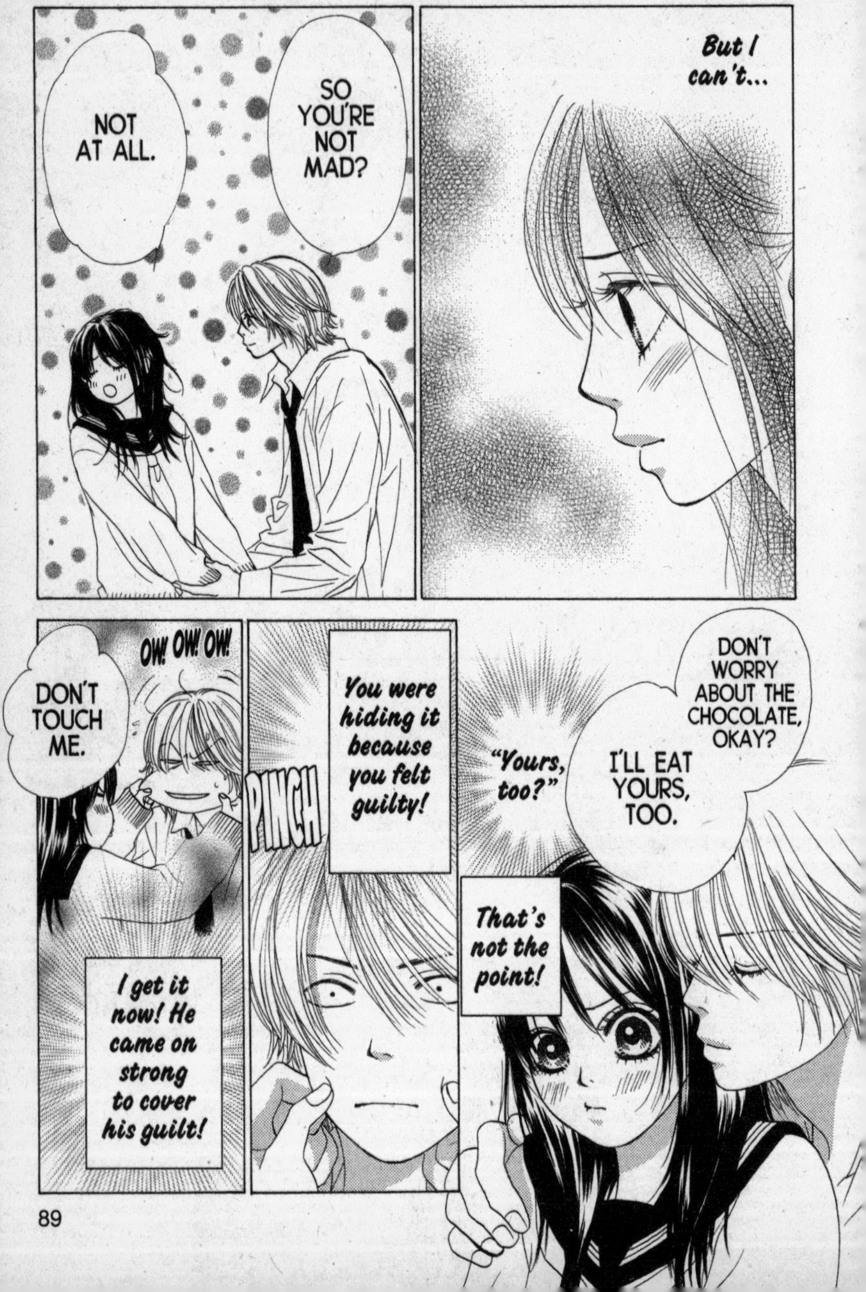

But I can't...
SO YOU'RE NOT MAD?
NOT AT ALL.
DON'T WORRY ABOUT THE CHOCOLATE, OKAY?
I'LL EAT YOURS, TOO.
"Yours, too?"
That's not the point!
You were hiding it because you felt guilty!
PINCH
OW! OW! OW!
DON'T TOUCH ME.
I get it now! He came on strong to cover his guilt!

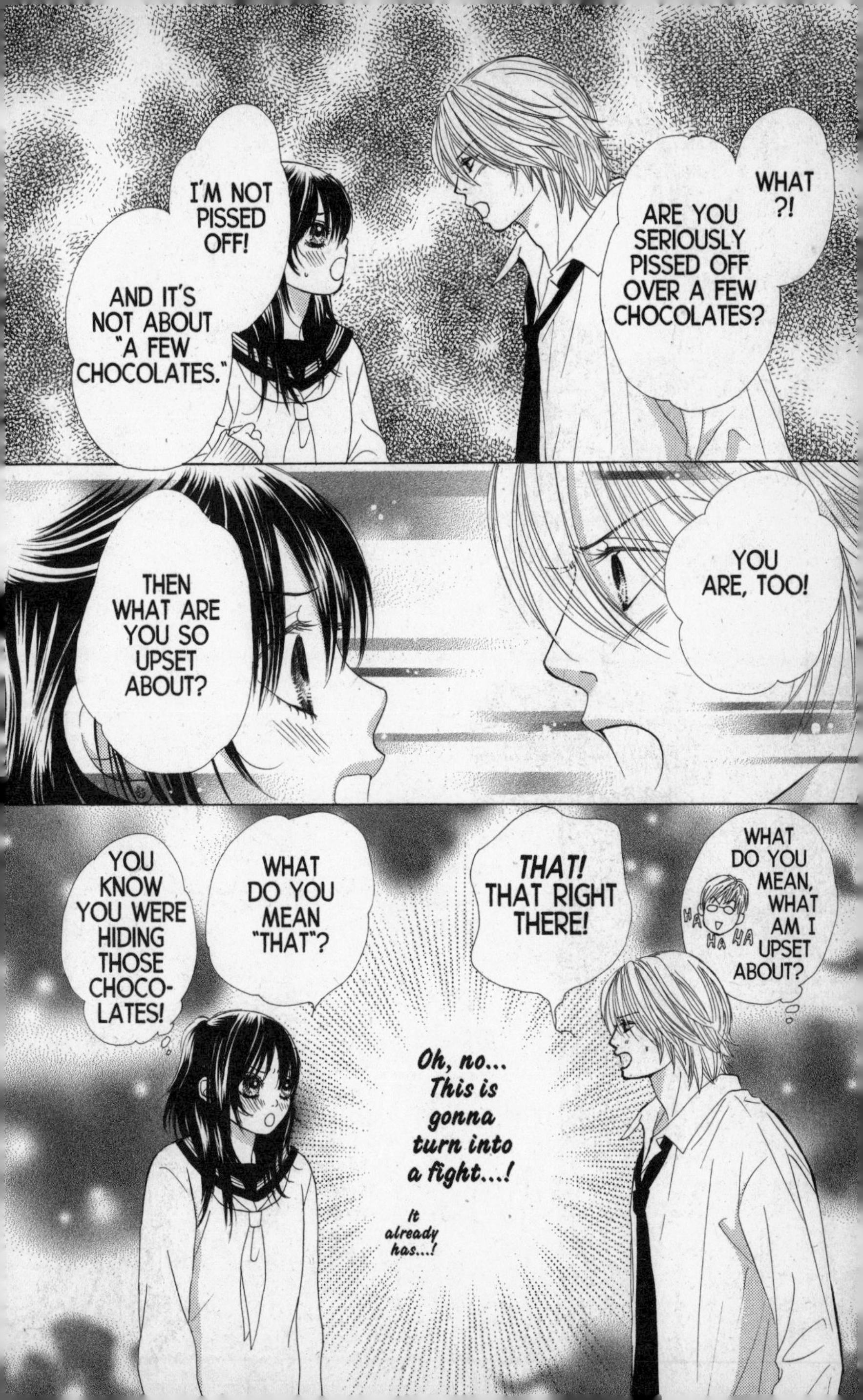
WHAT ?!
ARE YOU SERIOUSLY PISSED OFF OVER A FEW CHOCOLATES?
I'M NOT PISSED OFF!
AND IT'S NOT ABOUT "A FEW CHOCOLATES."
YOU ARE, TOO!
THEN WHAT ARE YOU SO UPSET ABOUT?
WHAT DO YOU MEAN, WHAT AM I UPSET ABOUT?
HA HA HA HA
THAT! THAT RIGHT THERE!
WHAT DO YOU MEAN "THAT"?
YOU KNOW YOU WERE HIDING THOSE CHOCO-LATES!
Oh, no... This is gonna turn into a fight...!
It already has...!

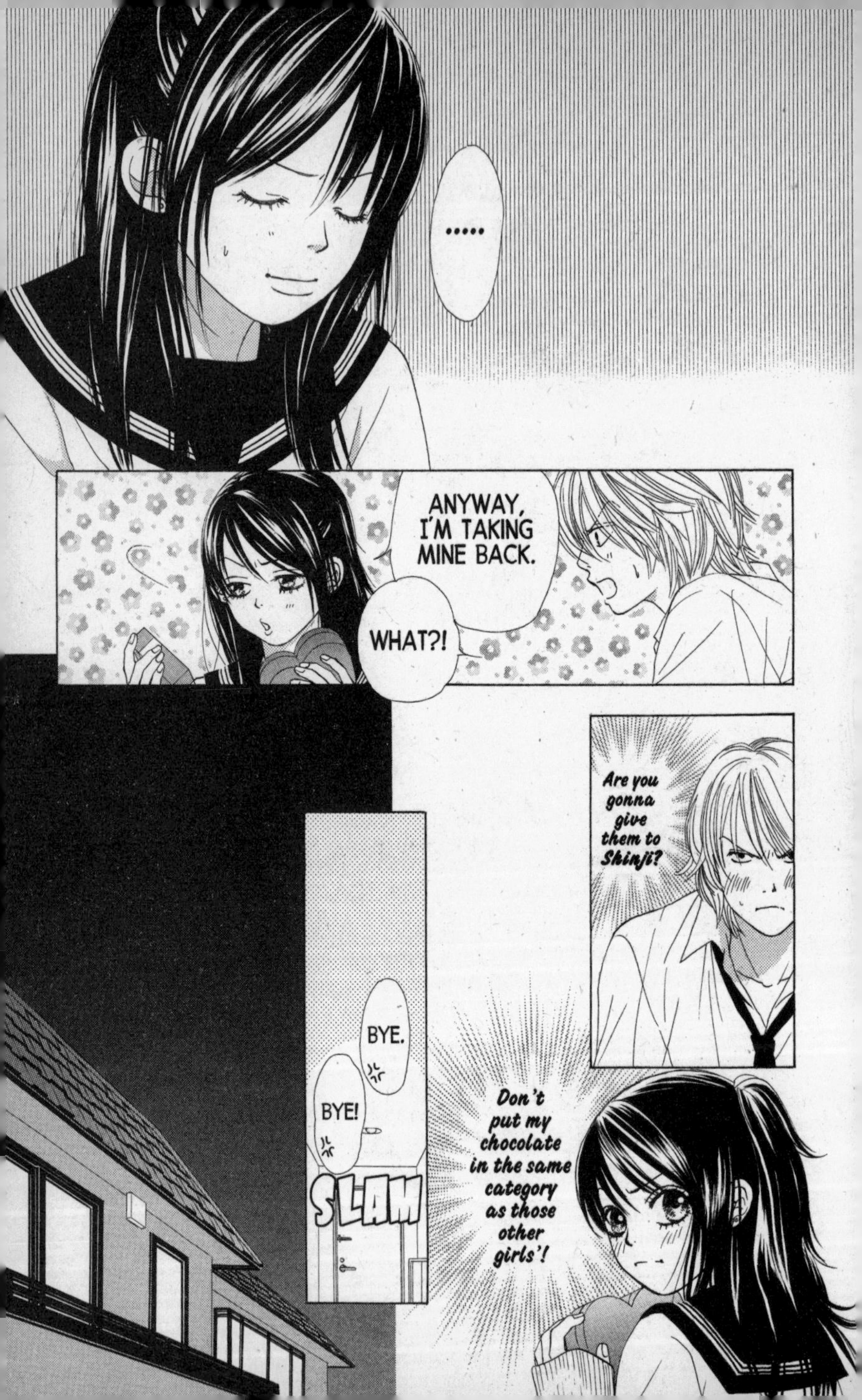
......
ANYWAY, I'M TAKING MINE BACK.
WHAT?!
Are you gonna give them to Shinji?
Don't put my chocolate in the same category as those other girls'!
BYE.
BYE!
SLAM

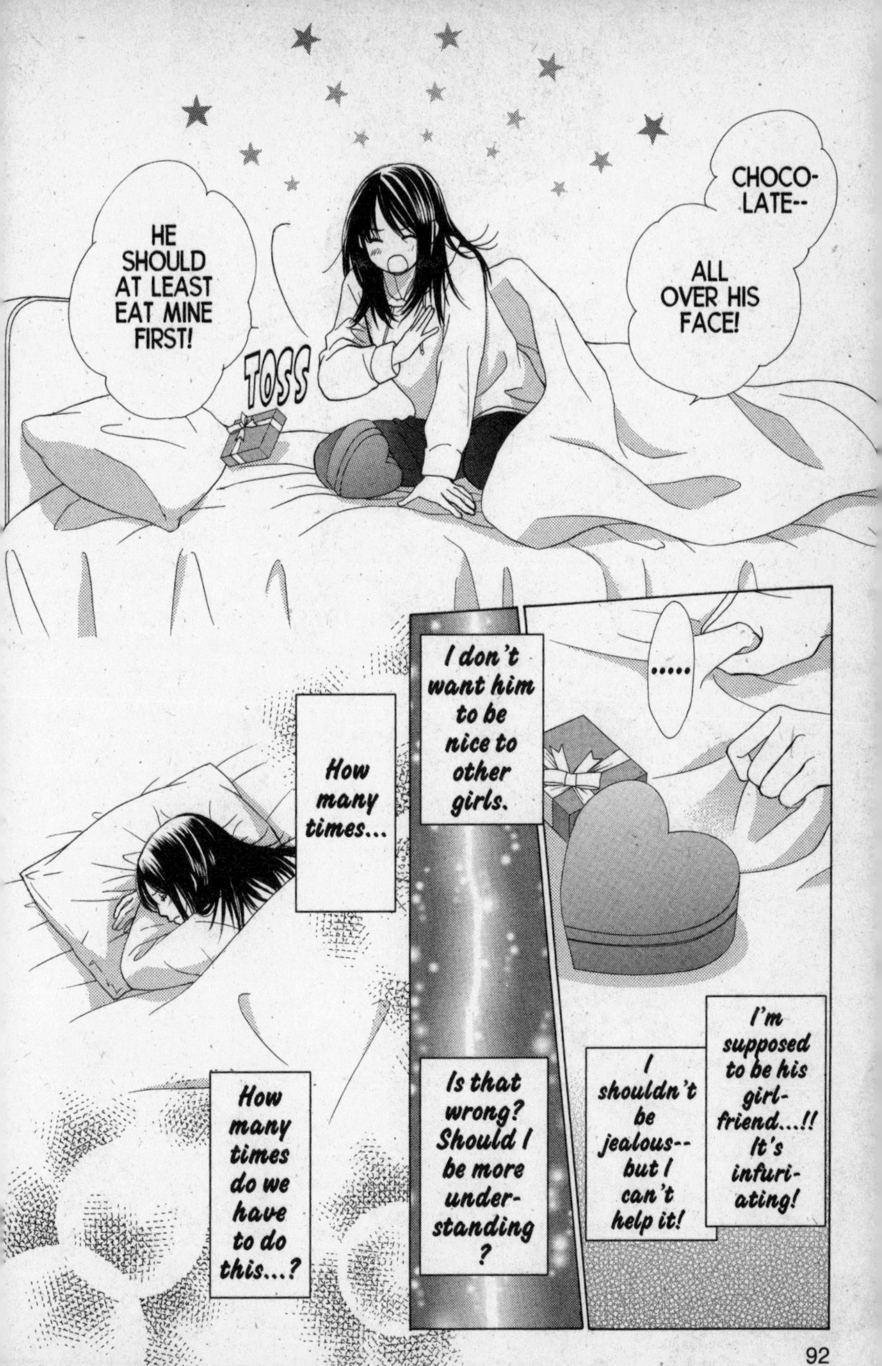
CHOCO-LATE--
ALL OVER HIS FACE!
HE SHOULD AT LEAST EAT MINE FIRST!
TOSS
.....
I'm supposed to be his girl-friend...!! It's infuri-ating!
I shouldn't be jealous--but I can't help it!
I don't want him to be nice to other girls.
Is that wrong? Should I be more under-standing?
How many times...
How many times do we have to do this...?

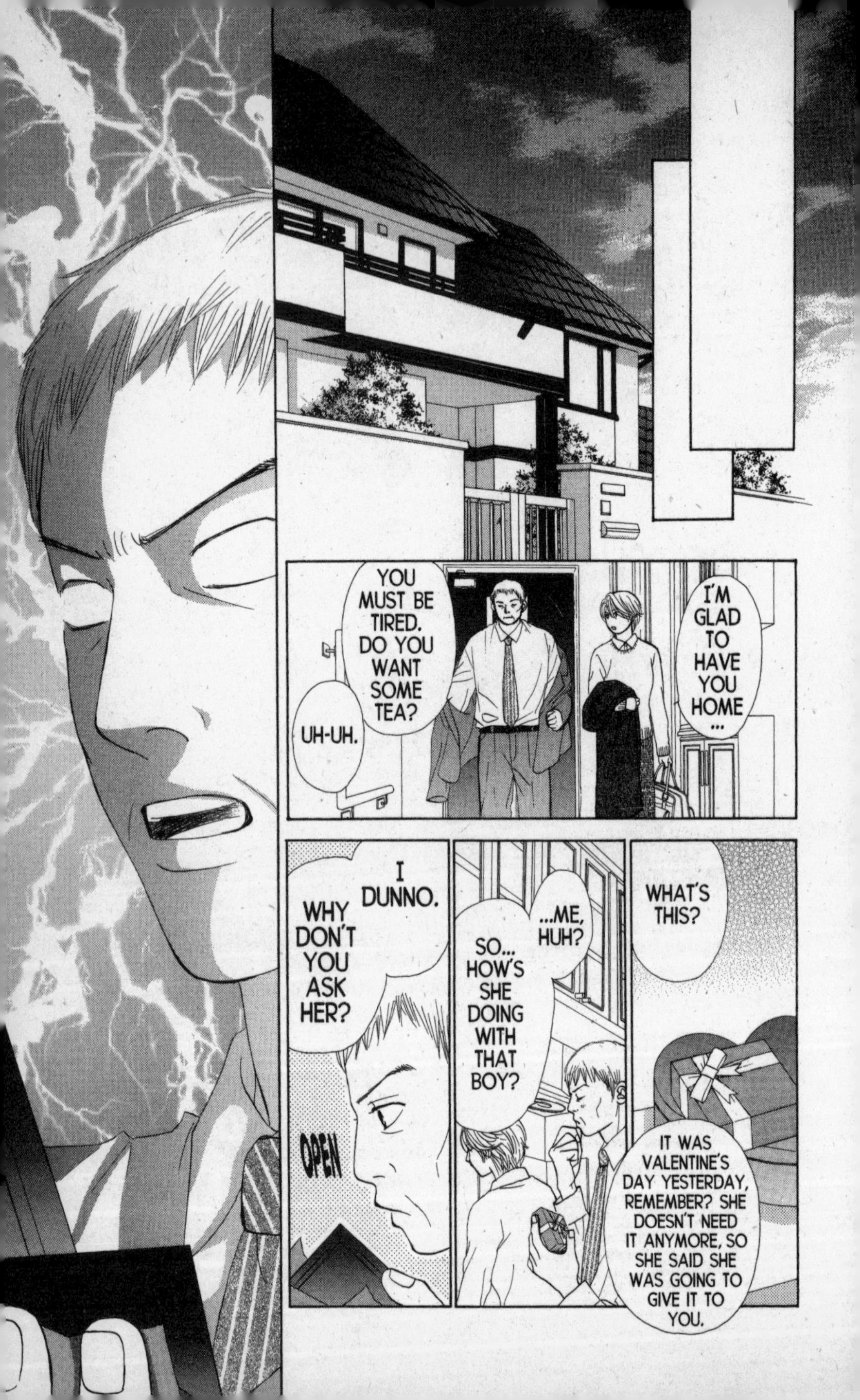
I'M GLAD TO HAVE YOU HOME...
YOU MUST BE TIRED. DO YOU WANT SOME TEA?
UH-UH.
WHAT'S THIS?
IT WAS VALENTINE'S DAY YESTERDAY, REMEMBER? SHE DOESN'T NEED IT ANYMORE, SO SHE SAID SHE WAS GOING TO GIVE IT TO YOU.
...ME, HUH?
SO... HOW'S SHE DOING WITH THAT BOY?
I DUNNO.
WHY DON'T YOU ASK HER?
OPEN

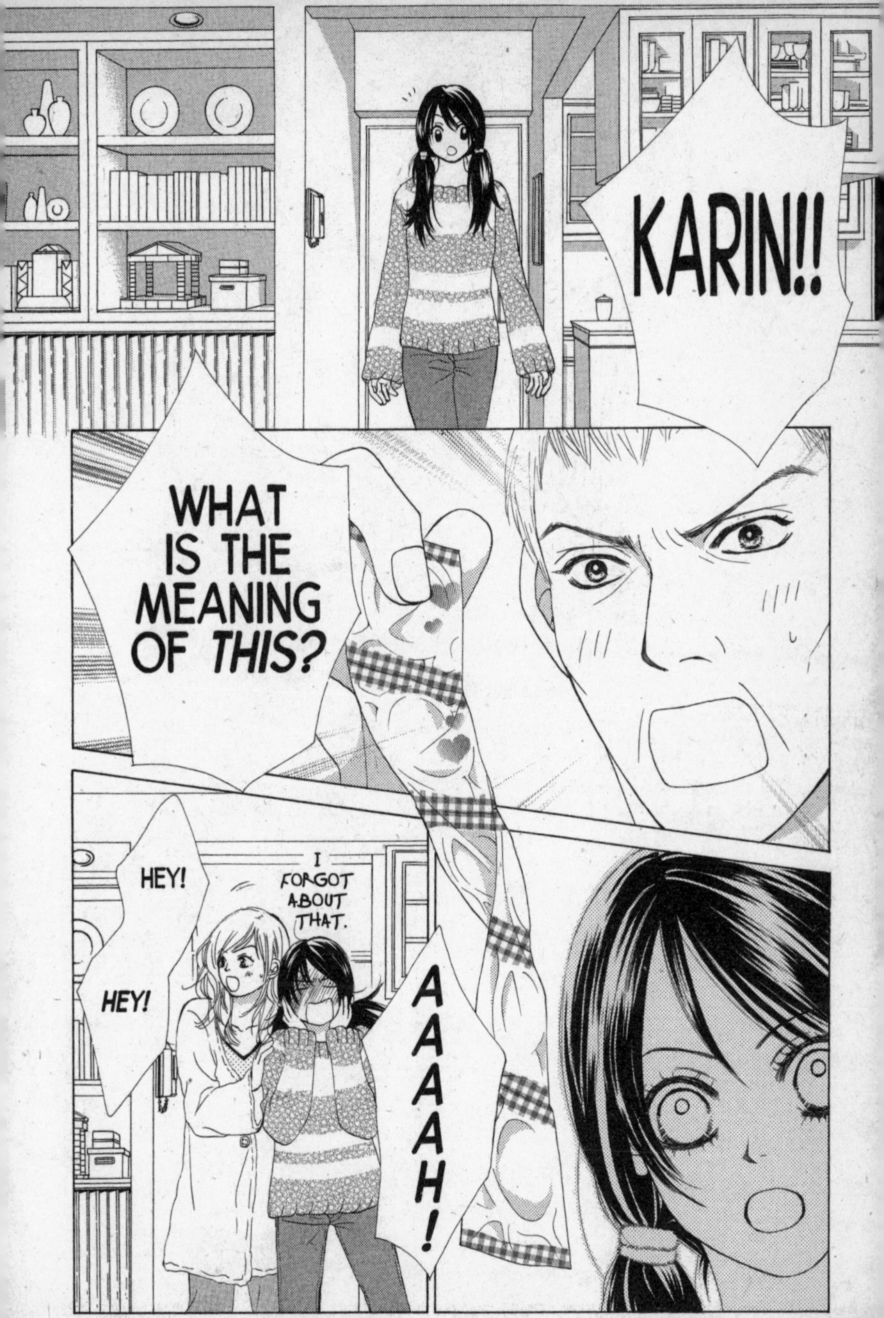
KARIN!!
WHAT IS THE MEANING OF THIS?
AAAAAH!
I FORGOT ABOUT THAT.
HEY!
HEY!

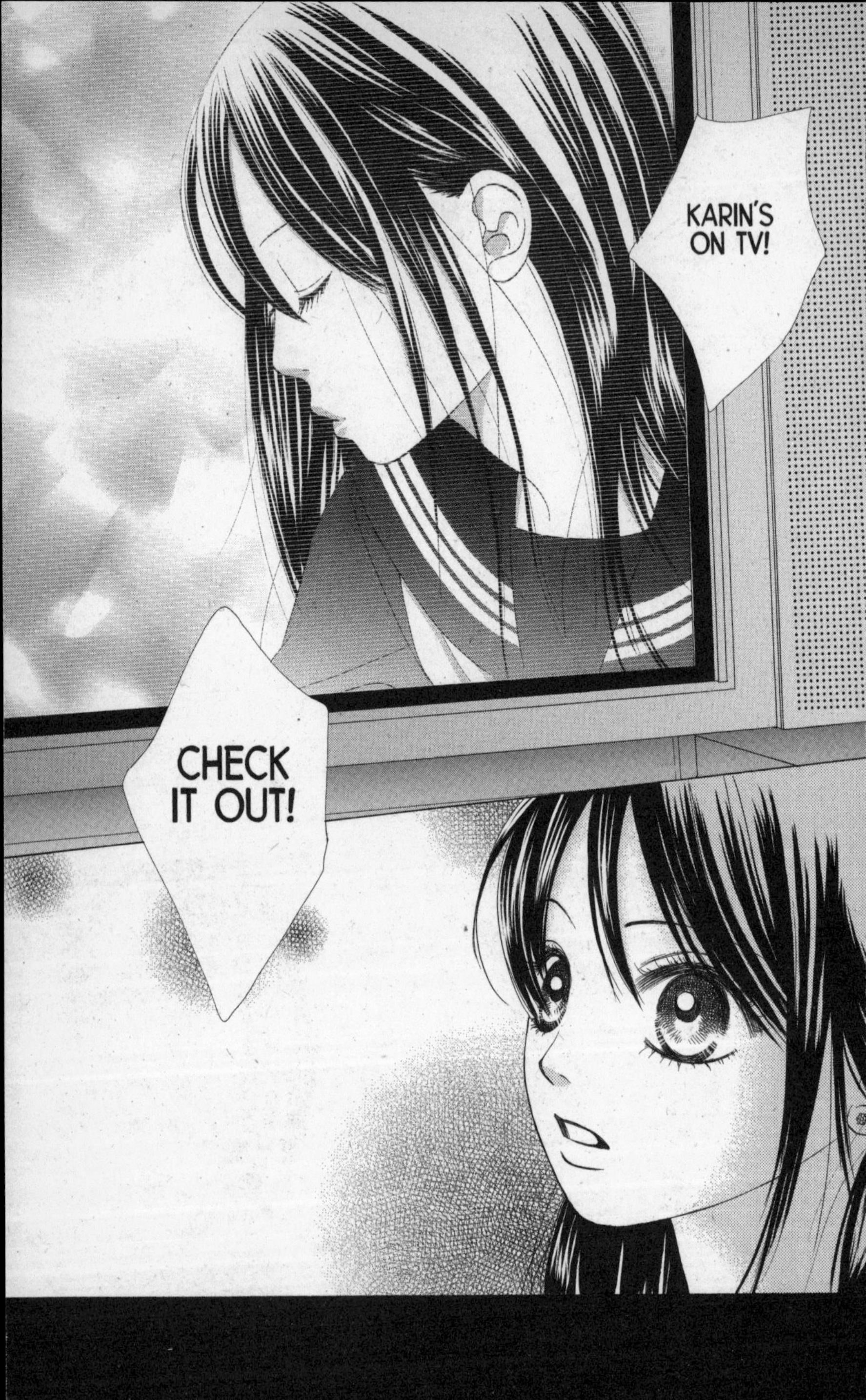
KARIN'S ON TV!
CHECK IT OUT!

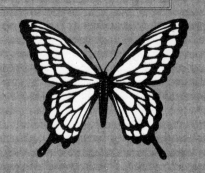
彼 *KARE*
First Love

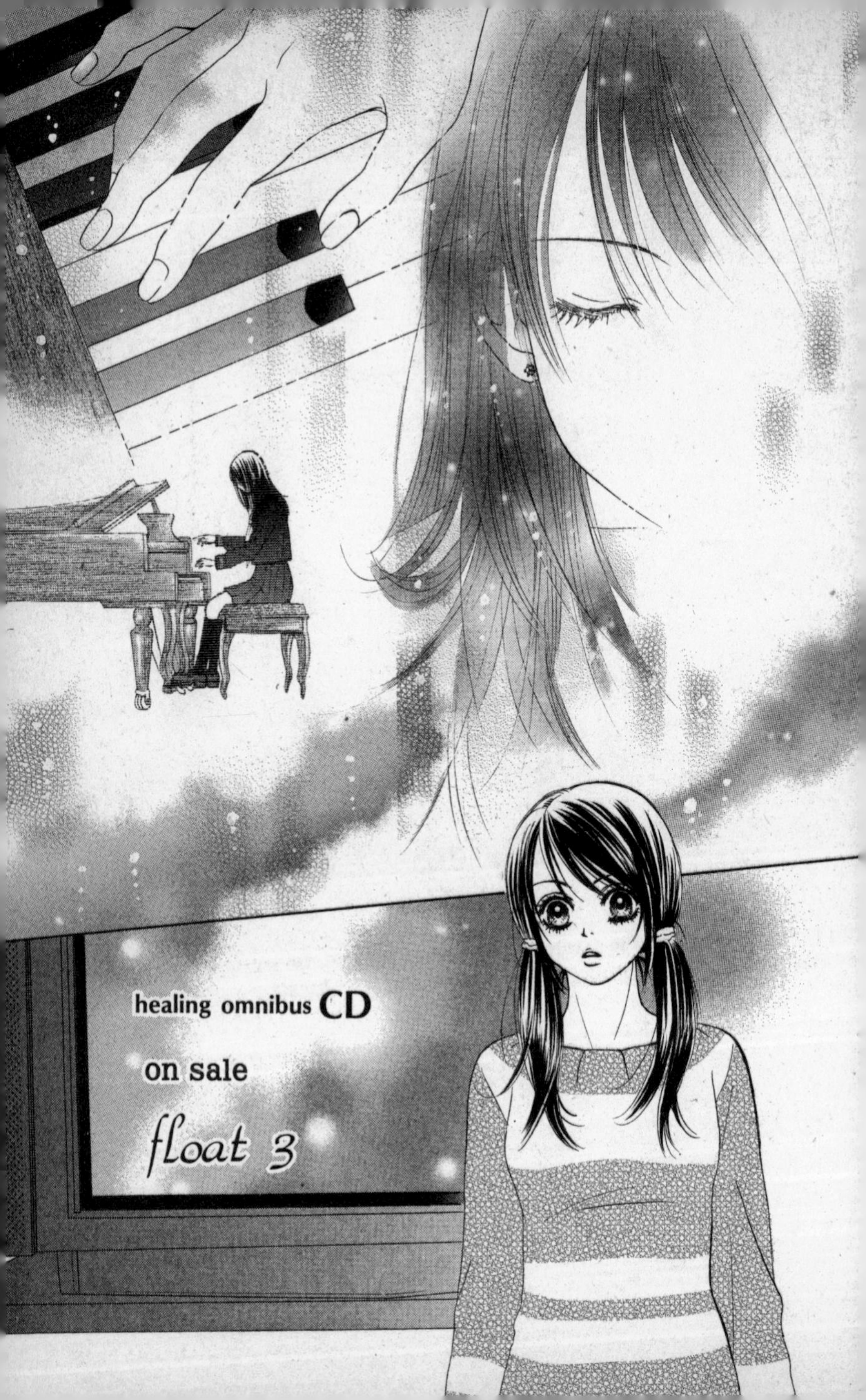
healing omnibus CD
on sale
float 3

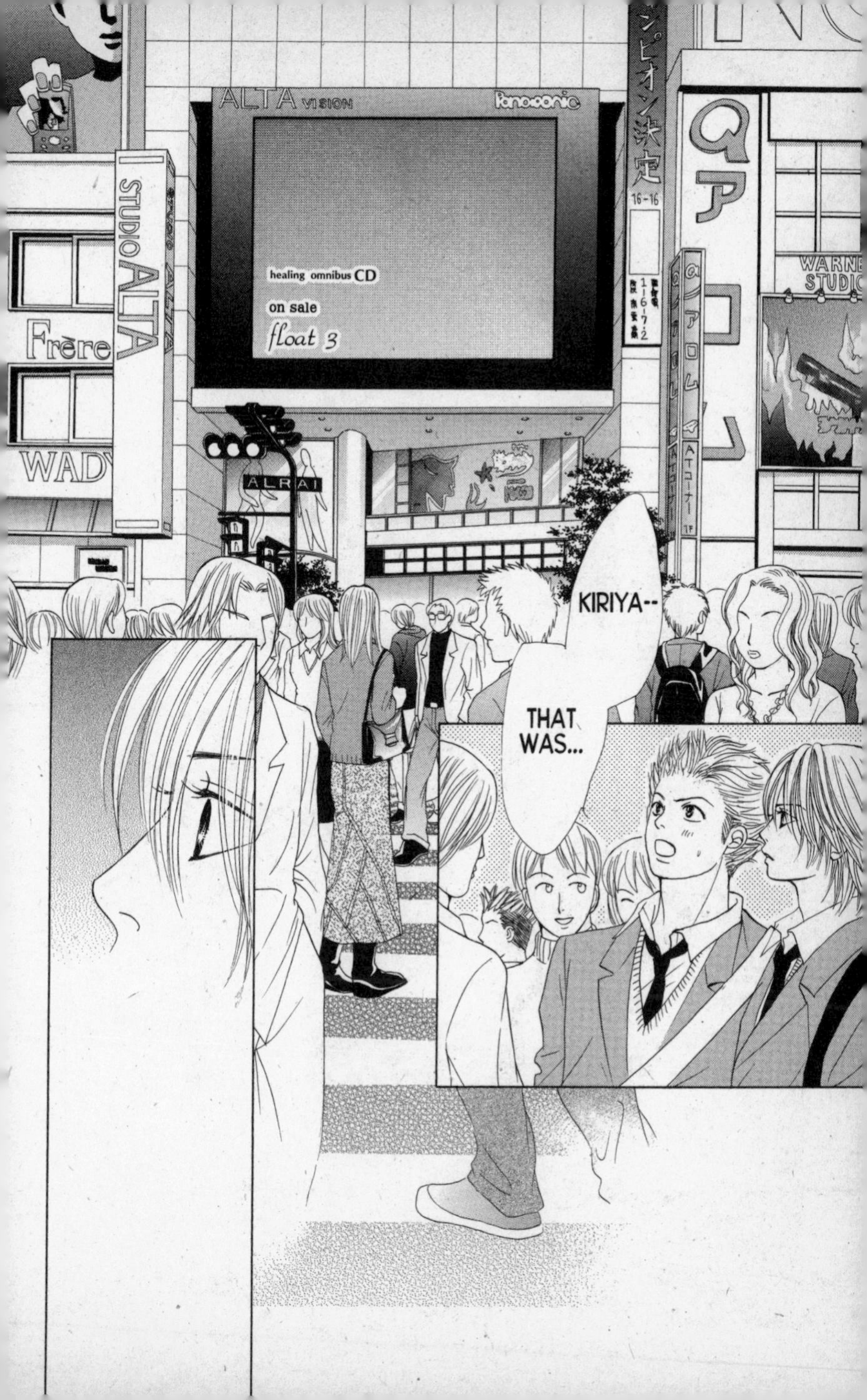
ALTA VISION
healing omnibus CD
on sale
float 3
STUDIO ALTA
Frère
WADY
ALRAI
KIRIYA--
THAT WAS...

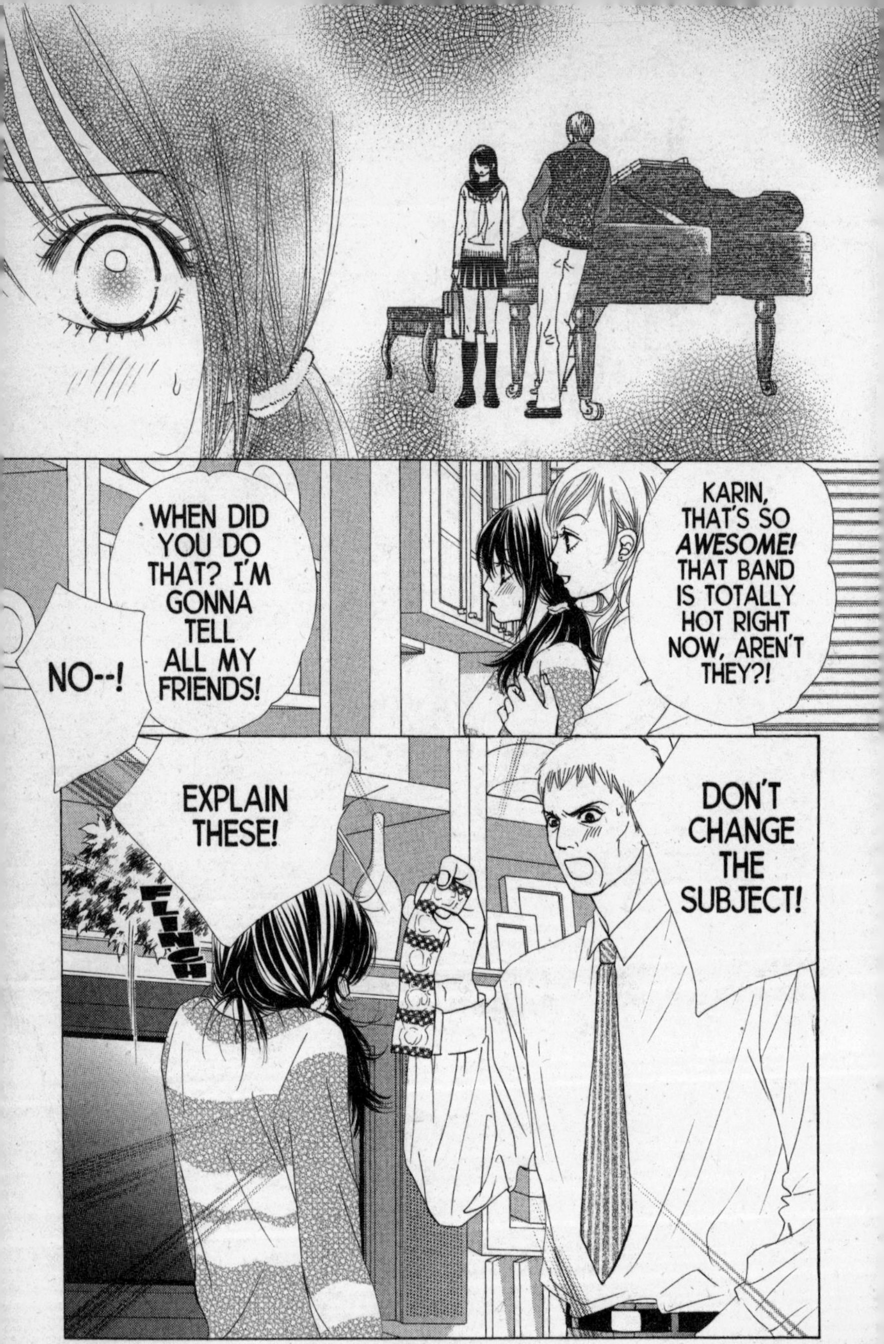
KARIN, THAT'S SO *AWESOME!* THAT BAND IS TOTALLY HOT RIGHT NOW, AREN'T THEY?!
WHEN DID YOU DO THAT? I'M GONNA TELL ALL MY FRIENDS!
NO--!
DON'T CHANGE THE SUBJECT!
EXPLAIN THESE!
FLINCH

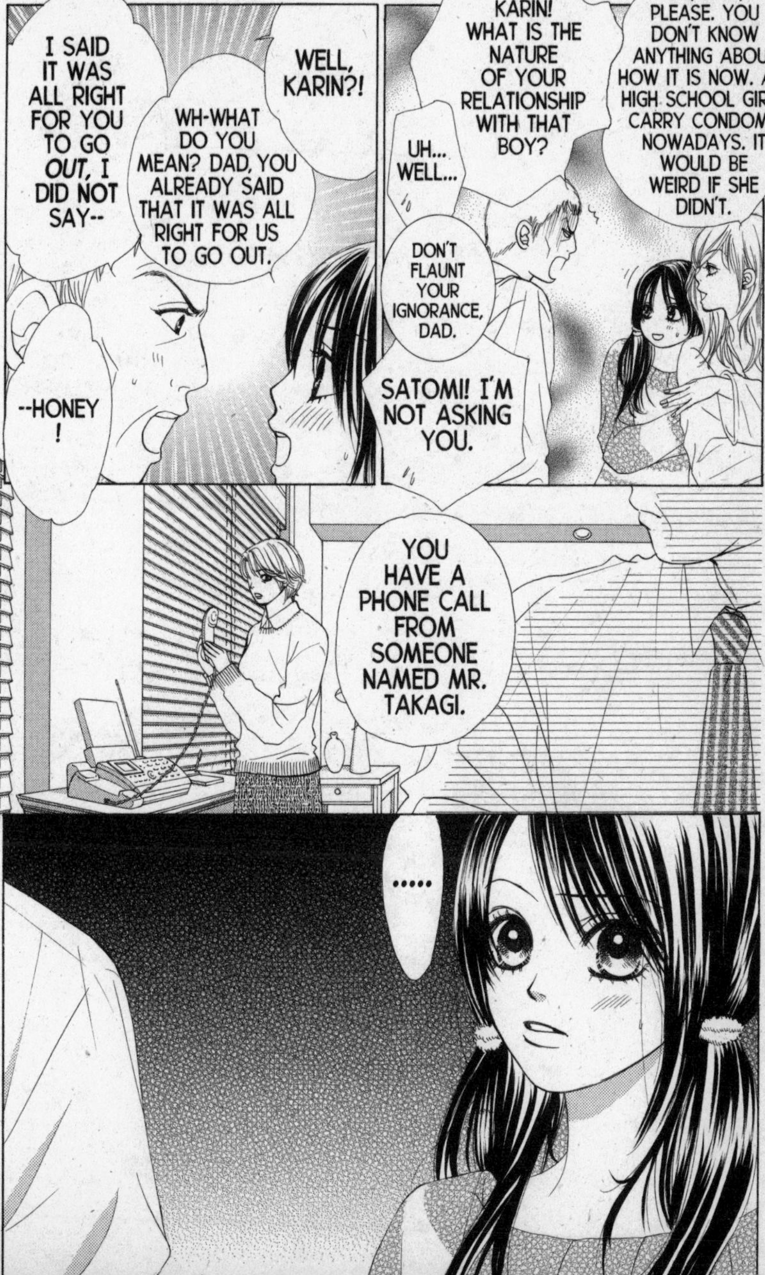
KARIN! WHAT IS THE NATURE OF YOUR RELATIONSHIP WITH THAT BOY?
UH... WELL...
OH, DAD, PLEASE. YOU DON'T KNOW ANYTHING ABOUT HOW IT IS NOW. ALL HIGH SCHOOL GIRLS CARRY CONDOMS NOWADAYS. IT WOULD BE WEIRD IF SHE DIDN'T.
DON'T FLAUNT YOUR IGNORANCE, DAD.
SATOMI! I'M NOT ASKING YOU.
WELL, KARIN?!
WH-WHAT DO YOU MEAN? DAD, YOU ALREADY SAID THAT IT WAS ALL RIGHT FOR US TO GO OUT.
I SAID IT WAS ALL RIGHT FOR YOU TO GO *OUT*, I DID NOT SAY--
--HONEY !
YOU HAVE A PHONE CALL FROM SOMEONE NAMED MR. TAKAGI.
......

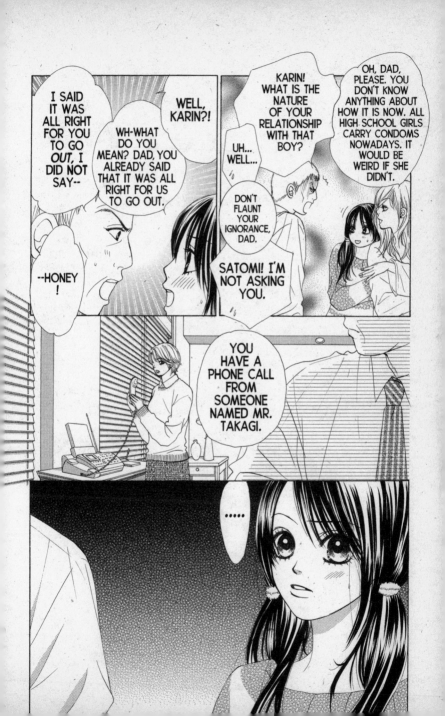

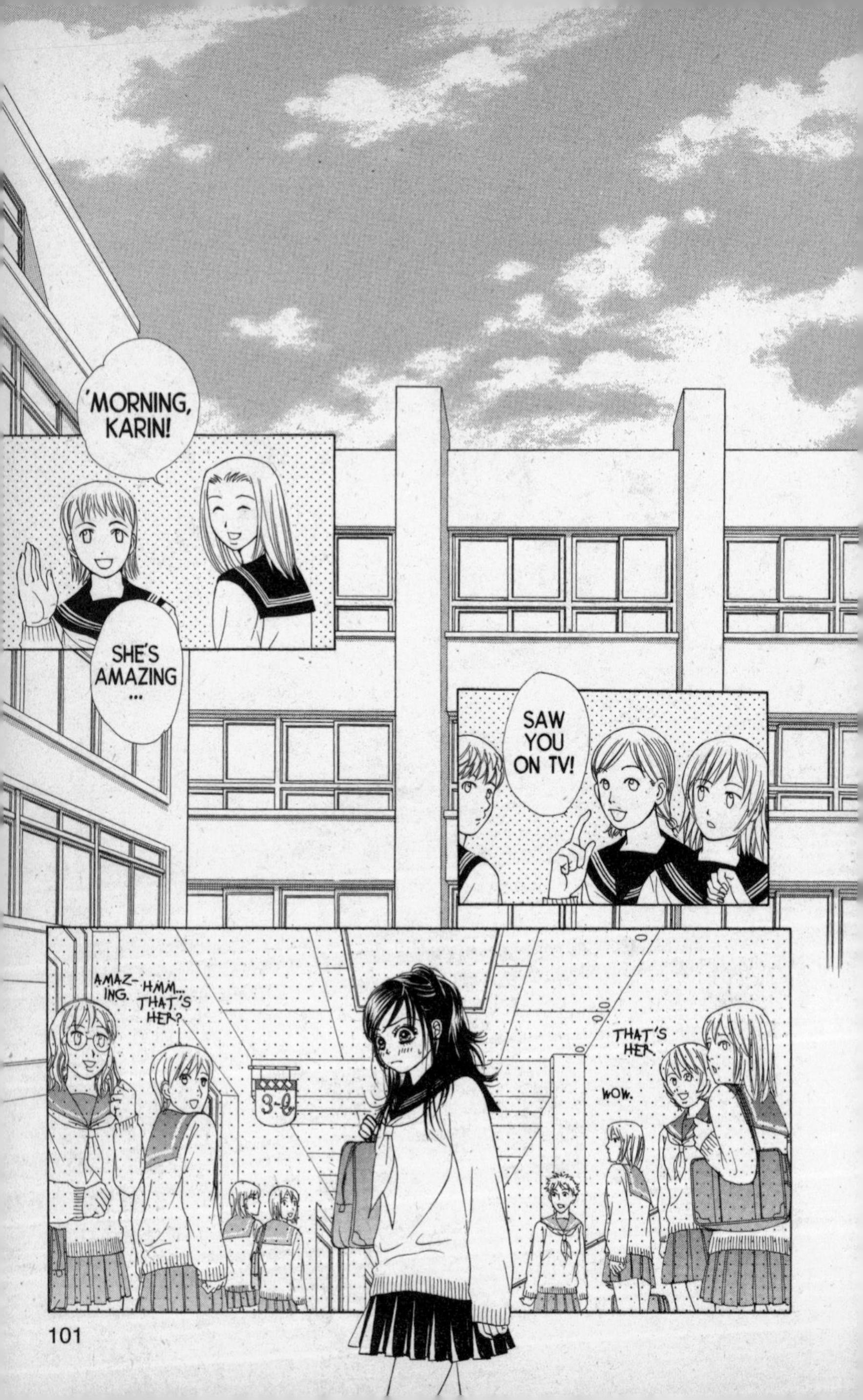
'MORNING, KARIN!
SHE'S AMAZING ...
SAW YOU ON TV!
THAT'S HER.
WOW.
HMM... THAT'S HER?
AMAZ-ING.

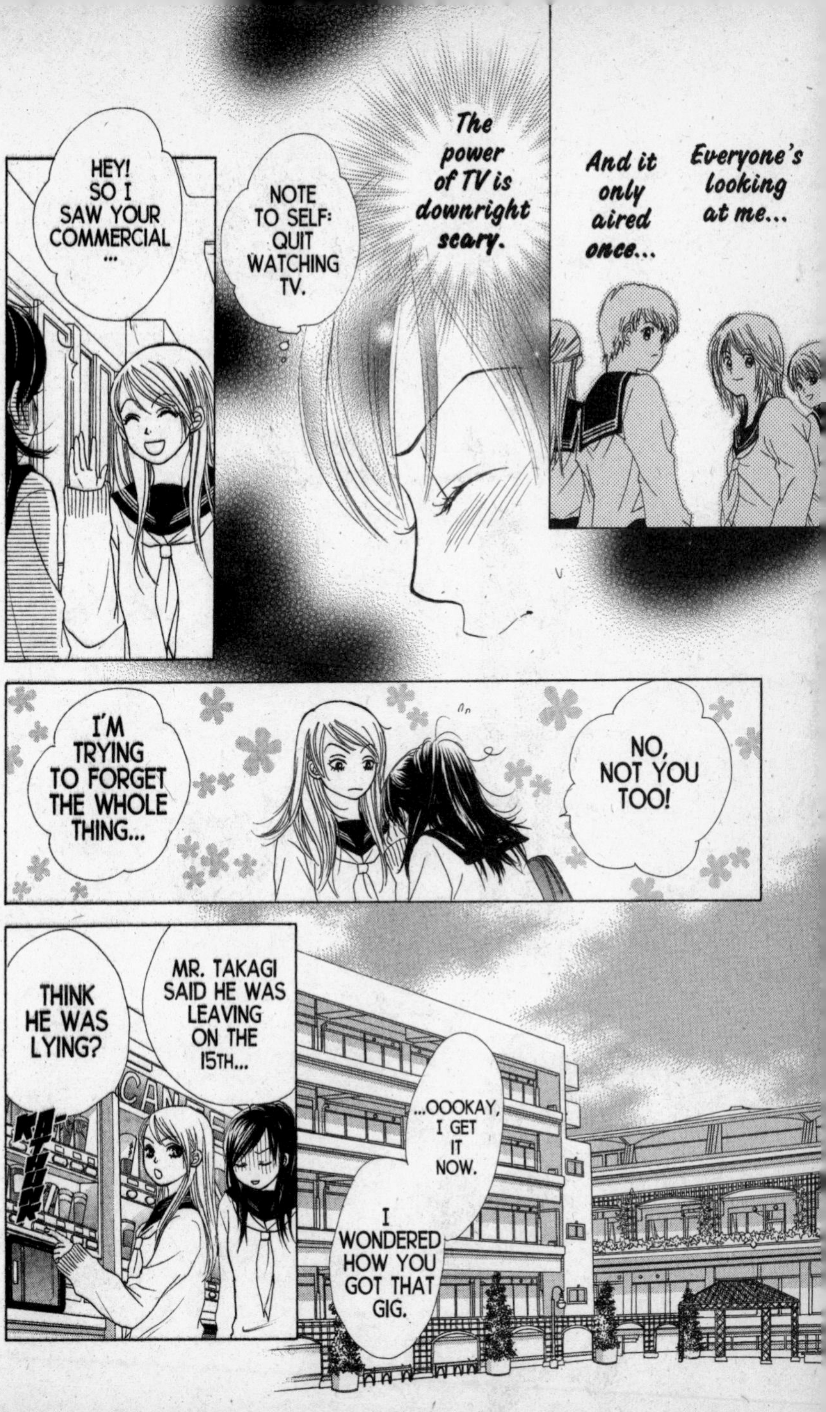
Everyone's looking at me...
And it only aired once...
The power of TV is downright scary.
NOTE TO SELF: QUIT WATCHING TV.
HEY! SO I SAW YOUR COMMERCIAL ...
NO, NOT YOU TOO!
I'M TRYING TO FORGET THE WHOLE THING...
...OOOKAY, I GET IT NOW.
I WONDERED HOW YOU GOT THAT GIG.
MR. TAKAGI SAID HE WAS LEAVING ON THE 15TH...
THINK HE WAS LYING?
KA-CHUNK

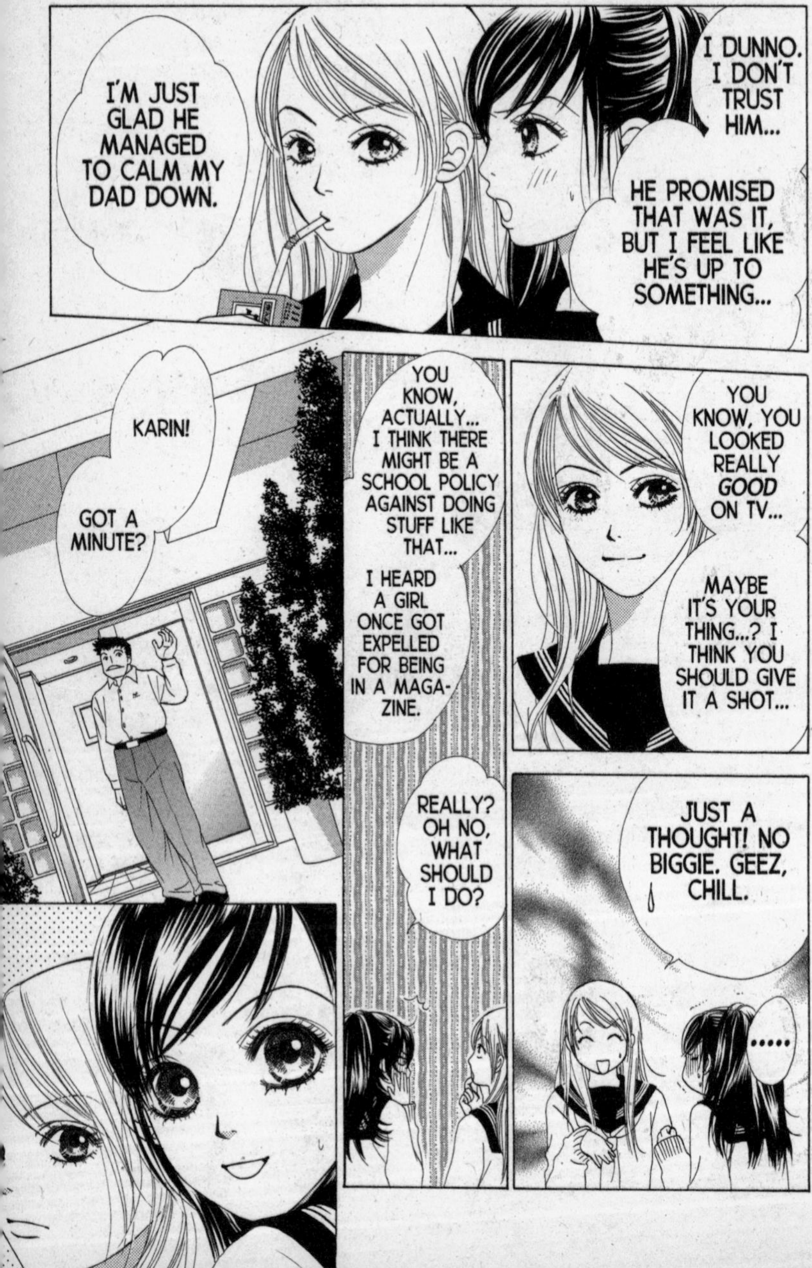
I DUNNO. I DON'T TRUST HIM...
HE PROMISED THAT WAS IT, BUT I FEEL LIKE HE'S UP TO SOMETHING...
I'M JUST GLAD HE MANAGED TO CALM MY DAD DOWN.
YOU KNOW, YOU LOOKED REALLY *GOOD* ON TV...
MAYBE IT'S YOUR THING...? I THINK YOU SHOULD GIVE IT A SHOT...
JUST A THOUGHT! NO BIGGIE. GEEZ, CHILL.
......
YOU KNOW, ACTUALLY... I THINK THERE MIGHT BE A SCHOOL POLICY AGAINST DOING STUFF LIKE THAT...
I HEARD A GIRL ONCE GOT EXPELLED FOR BEING IN A MAGA-ZINE.
REALLY? OH NO, WHAT SHOULD I DO?
KARIN!
GOT A MINUTE?

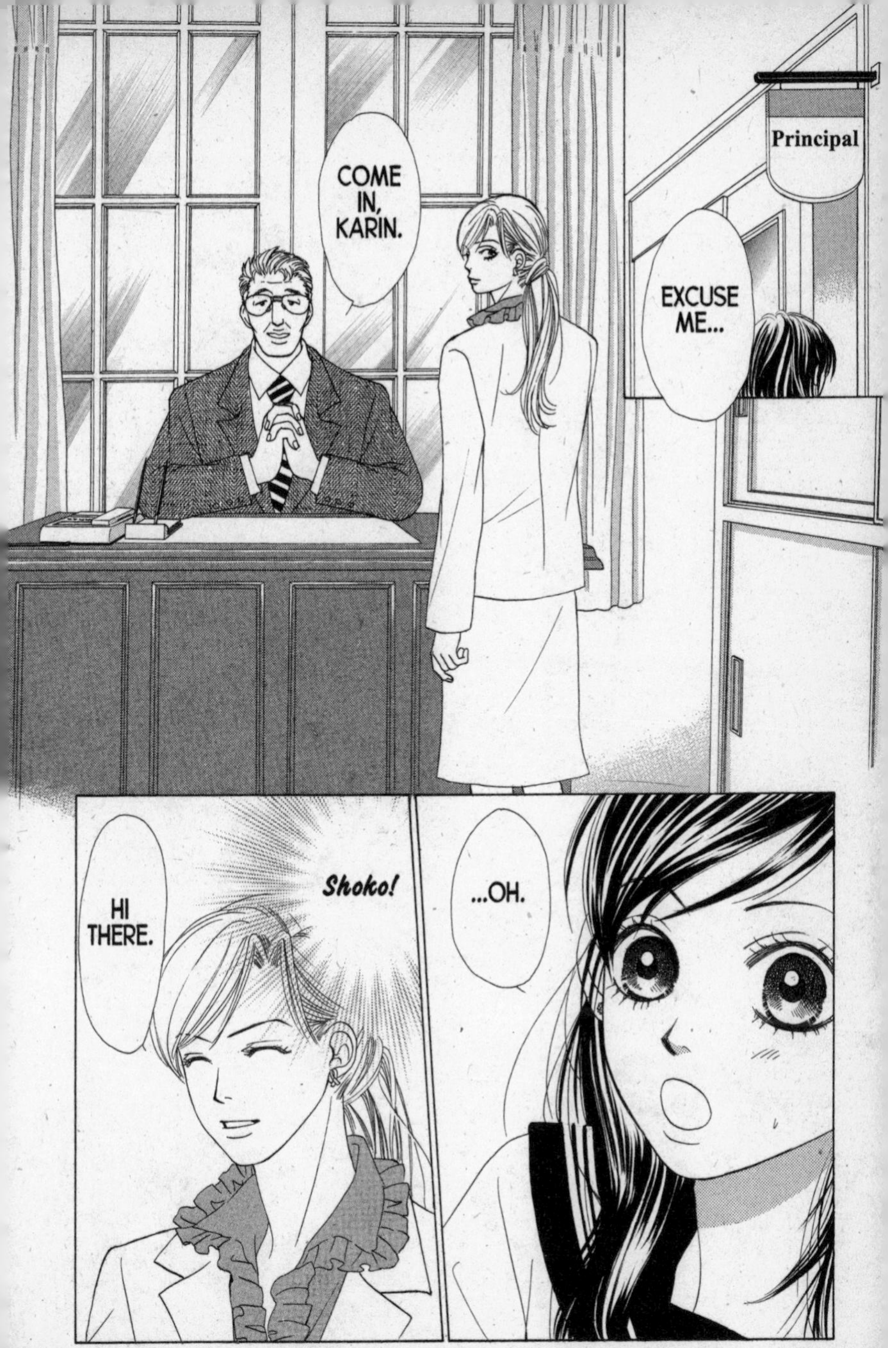
Principal
EXCUSE ME...
COME IN, KARIN.
...OH.
Shoko!
HI THERE.

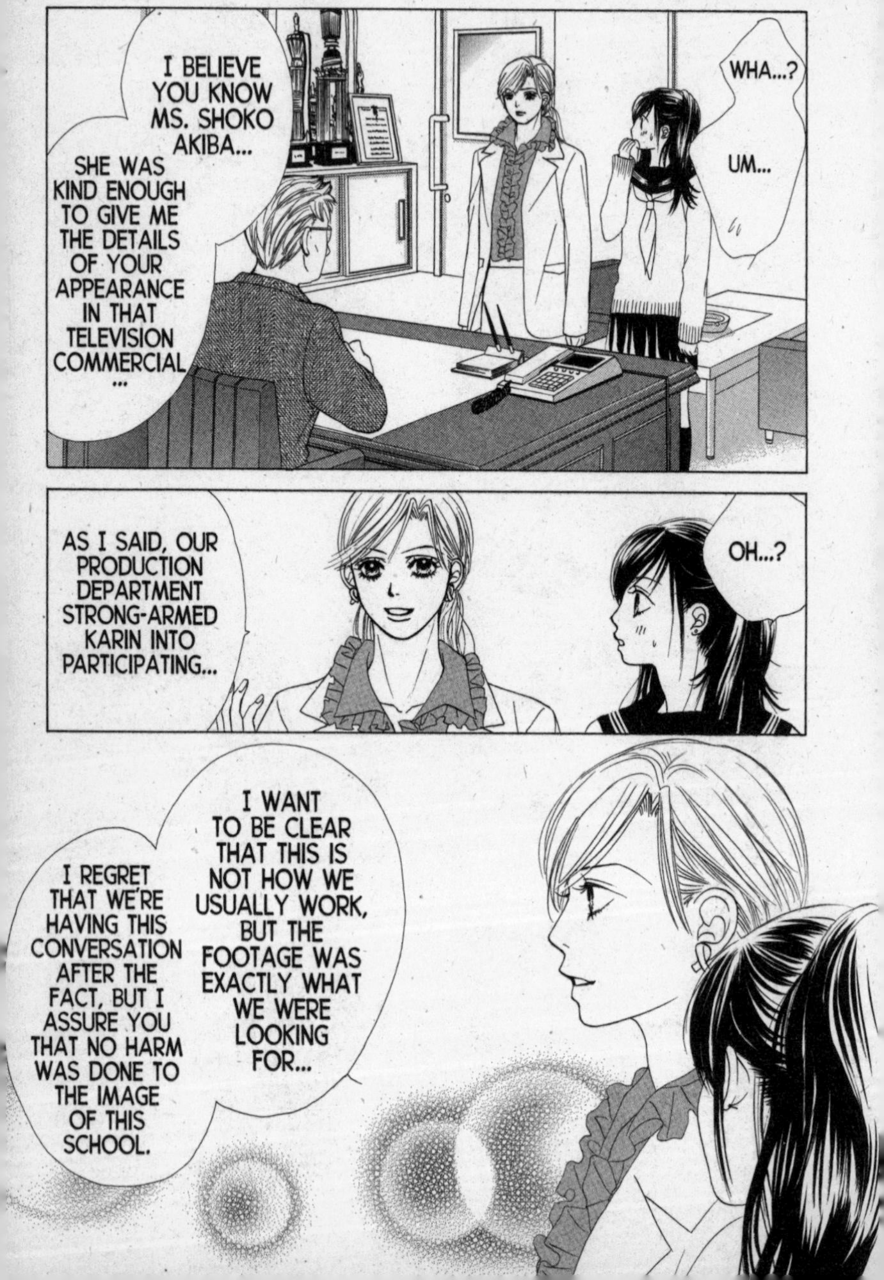
WHA...? UM...
I BELIEVE YOU KNOW MS. SHOKO AKIBA...
SHE WAS KIND ENOUGH TO GIVE ME THE DETAILS OF YOUR APPEARANCE IN THAT TELEVISION COMMERCIAL...
OH...?
AS I SAID, OUR PRODUCTION DEPARTMENT STRONG-ARMED KARIN INTO PARTICIPATING...
I WANT TO BE CLEAR THAT THIS IS NOT HOW WE USUALLY WORK, BUT THE FOOTAGE WAS EXACTLY WHAT WE WERE LOOKING FOR...
I REGRET THAT WE'RE HAVING THIS CONVERSATION AFTER THE FACT, BUT I ASSURE YOU THAT NO HARM WAS DONE TO THE IMAGE OF THIS SCHOOL.

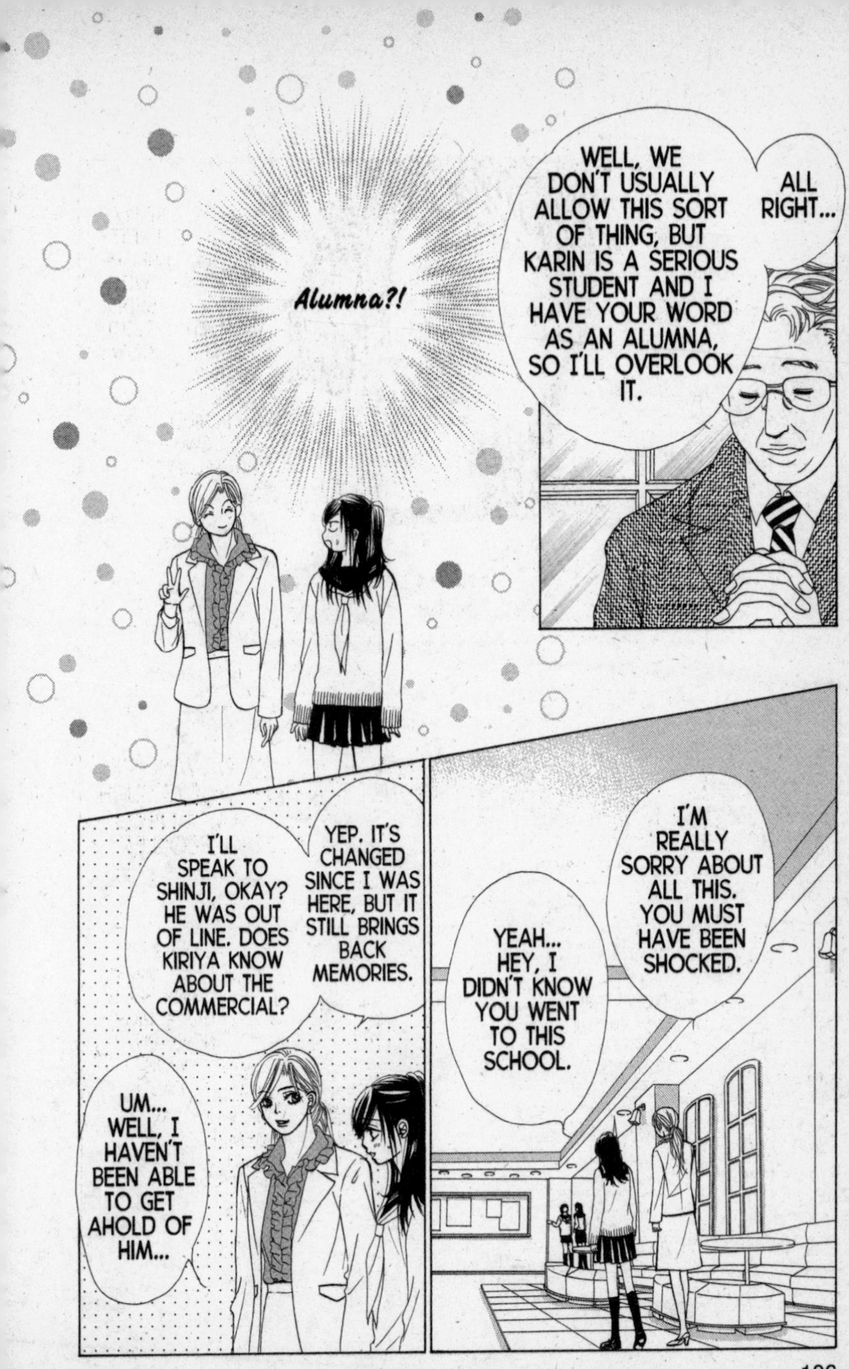
ALL RIGHT...
WELL, WE DON'T USUALLY ALLOW THIS SORT OF THING, BUT KARIN IS A SERIOUS STUDENT AND I HAVE YOUR WORD AS AN ALUMNA, SO I'LL OVERLOOK IT.
Alumna?!
I'M REALLY SORRY ABOUT ALL THIS. YOU MUST HAVE BEEN SHOCKED.
YEAH... HEY, I DIDN'T KNOW YOU WENT TO THIS SCHOOL.
YEP. IT'S CHANGED SINCE I WAS HERE, BUT IT STILL BRINGS BACK MEMORIES.
I'LL SPEAK TO SHINJI, OKAY? HE WAS OUT OF LINE. DOES KIRIYA KNOW ABOUT THE COMMERCIAL?
UM... WELL, I HAVEN'T BEEN ABLE TO GET AHOLD OF HIM...

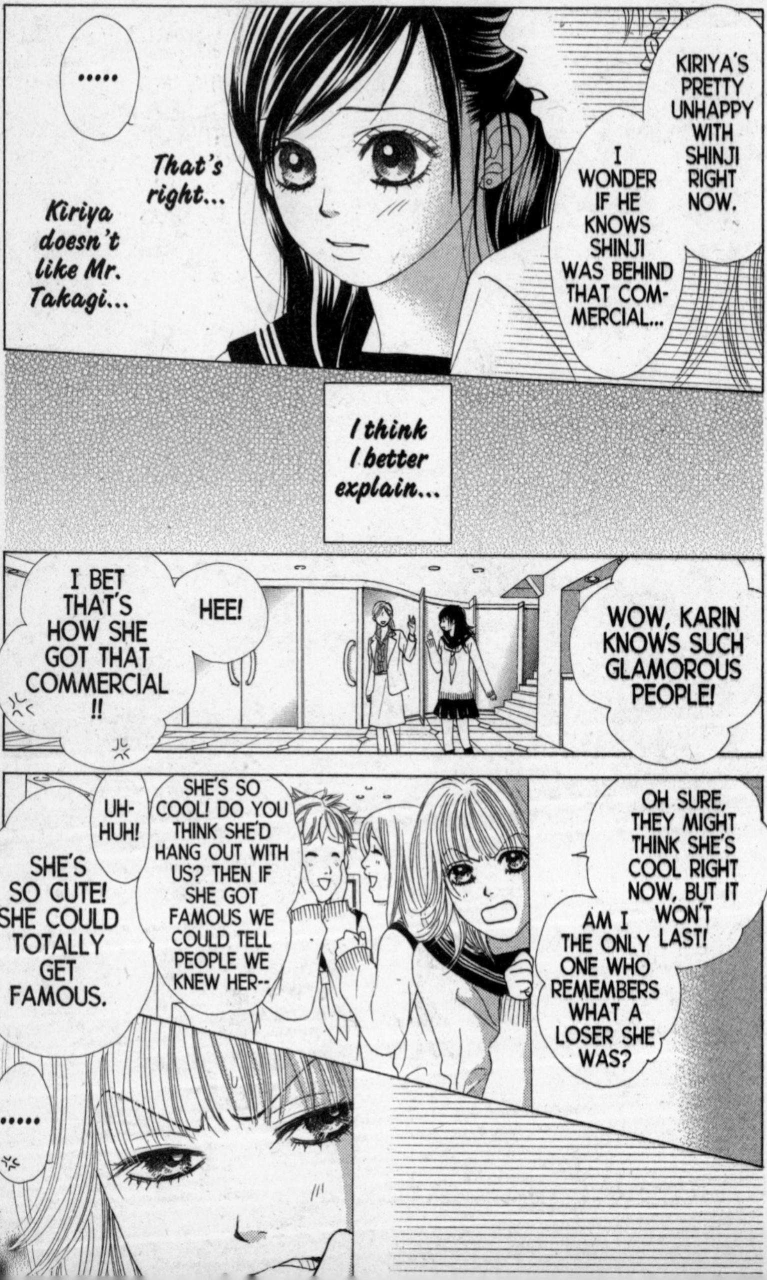

KIRIYA'S PRETTY UNHAPPY WITH SHINJI RIGHT NOW.
I WONDER IF HE KNOWS SHINJI WAS BEHIND THAT COMMERCIAL...
That's right...
.....
Kiriya doesn't like Mr. Takagi...
I think I better explain...
WOW, KARIN KNOWS SUCH GLAMOROUS PEOPLE!
HEE!
I BET THAT'S HOW SHE GOT THAT COMMERCIAL !!
OH SURE, THEY MIGHT THINK SHE'S COOL RIGHT NOW, BUT IT WON'T LAST!
AM I THE ONLY ONE WHO REMEMBERS WHAT A LOSER SHE WAS?
SHE'S SO COOL! DO YOU THINK SHE'D HANG OUT WITH US? THEN IF SHE GOT FAMOUS WE COULD TELL PEOPLE WE KNEW HER--
UH-HUH!
SHE'S SO CUTE! SHE COULD TOTALLY GET FAMOUS.
.....

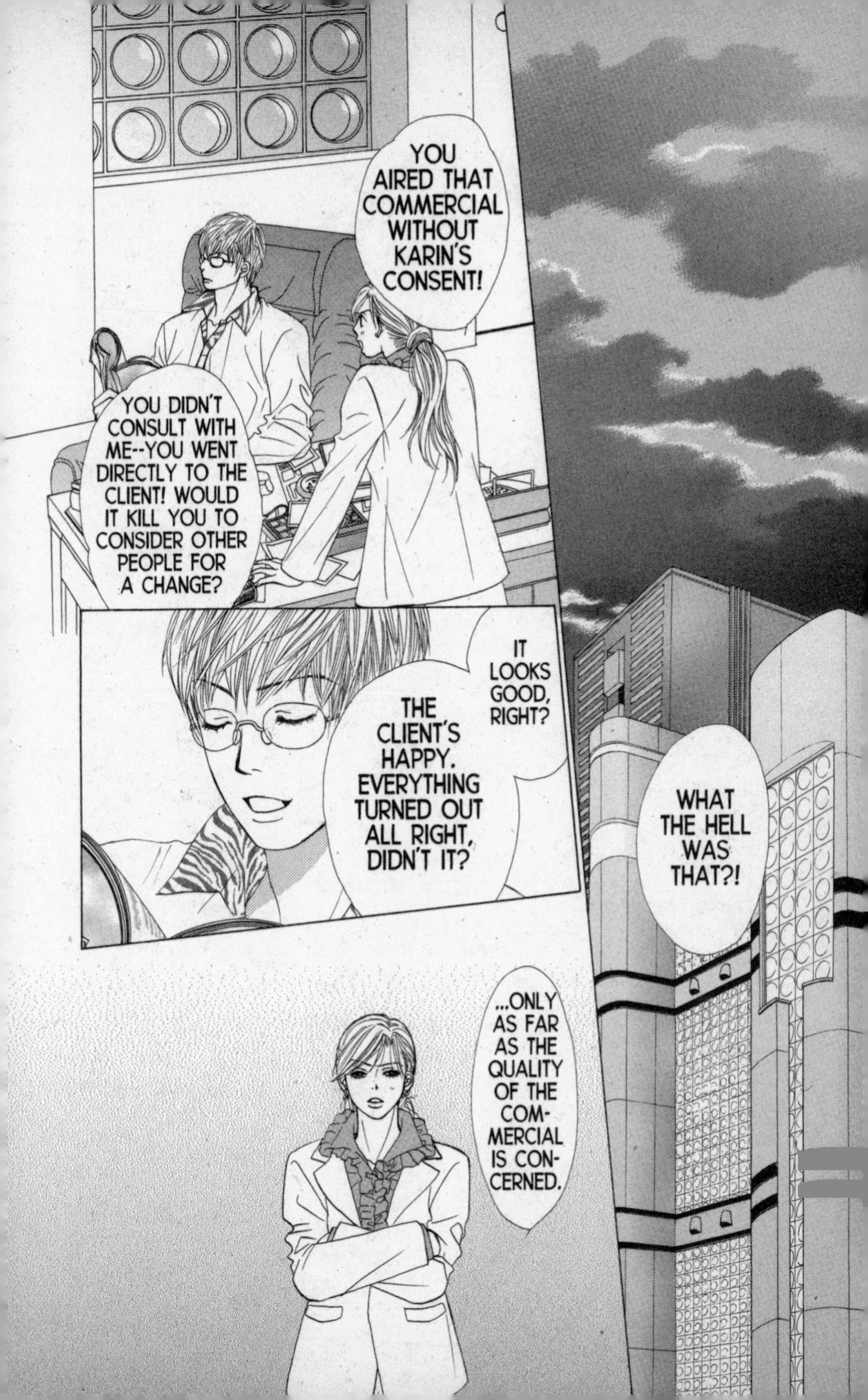
WHAT THE HELL WAS THAT?!
YOU AIRED THAT COMMERCIAL WITHOUT KARIN'S CONSENT!
YOU DIDN'T CONSULT WITH ME--YOU WENT DIRECTLY TO THE CLIENT! WOULD IT KILL YOU TO CONSIDER OTHER PEOPLE FOR A CHANGE?
IT LOOKS GOOD, RIGHT?
THE CLIENT'S HAPPY. EVERYTHING TURNED OUT ALL RIGHT, DIDN'T IT?
...ONLY AS FAR AS THE QUALITY OF THE COM-MERCIAL IS CON-CERNED.

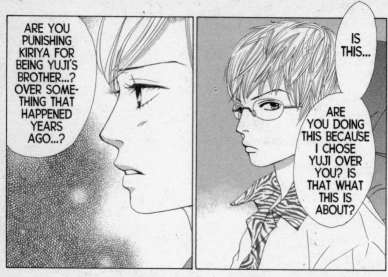

IS THIS...
ARE YOU DOING THIS BECAUSE I CHOSE YUJI OVER YOU? IS THAT WHAT THIS IS ABOUT?
ARE YOU PUNISHING KIRIYA FOR BEING YUJI'S BROTHER...? OVER SOME-THING THAT HAPPENED YEARS AGO...?
YUP.
GOT YOUR ATTENTION, DIDN'T I?
!
I'M KIDDING. PISSED YOU OFF THOUGH, HUH?

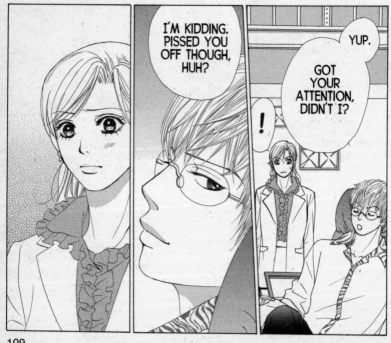

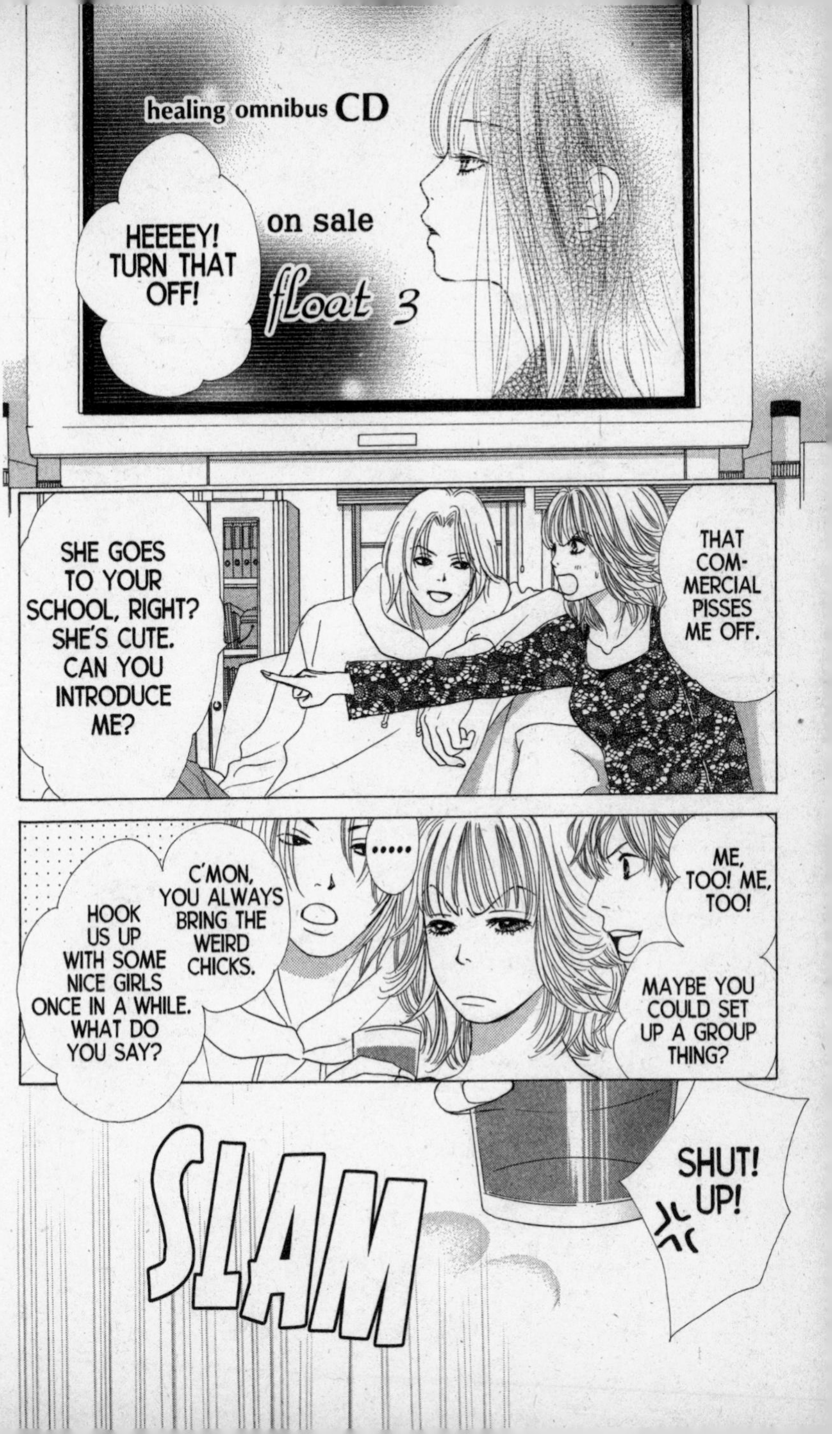
healing omnibus CD
on sale
float 3
HEEEEY! TURN THAT OFF!
THAT COMMERCIAL PISSES ME OFF.
SHE GOES TO YOUR SCHOOL, RIGHT? SHE'S CUTE. CAN YOU INTRODUCE ME?
ME, TOO! ME, TOO!
MAYBE YOU COULD SET UP A GROUP THING?
......
C'MON, YOU ALWAYS BRING THE WEIRD CHICKS.
HOOK US UP WITH SOME NICE GIRLS ONCE IN A WHILE. WHAT DO YOU SAY?
SHUT! UP!
SLAM

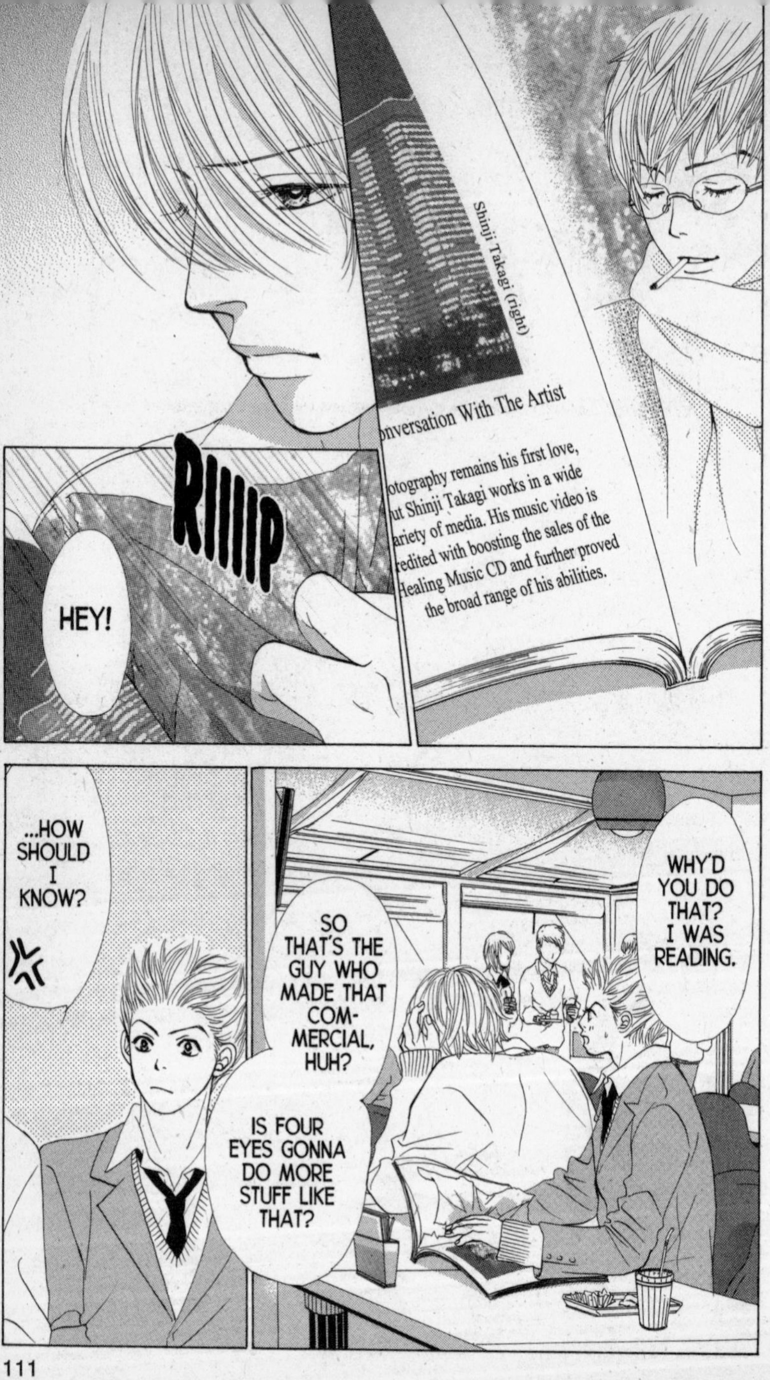
Shinji Takagi (right)
onversation With The Artist
otography remains his first love,
ut Shinji Takagi works in a wide
ariety of media. His music video is
redited with boosting the sales of the
Healing Music CD and further proved
the broad range of his abilities.
RIIIP
HEY!
WHY'D YOU DO THAT? I WAS READING.
SO THAT'S THE GUY WHO MADE THAT COM-MERCIAL, HUH?
IS FOUR EYES GONNA DO MORE STUFF LIKE THAT?
...HOW SHOULD I KNOW?

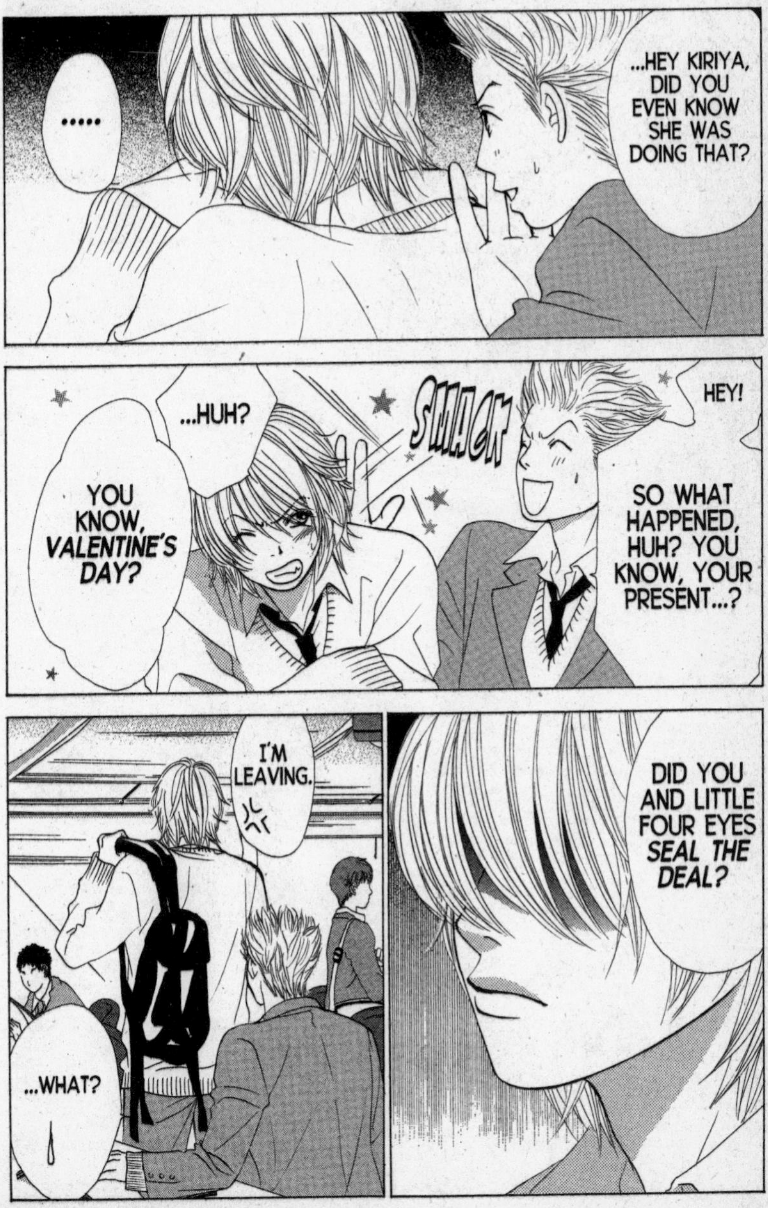
...HEY KIRIYA, DID YOU EVEN KNOW SHE WAS DOING THAT?
......
HEY!
SO WHAT HAPPENED, HUH? YOU KNOW, YOUR PRESENT...?
SMACK
...HUH?
YOU KNOW, VALENTINE'S DAY?
DID YOU AND LITTLE FOUR EYES SEAL THE DEAL?
I'M LEAVING.
...WHAT?

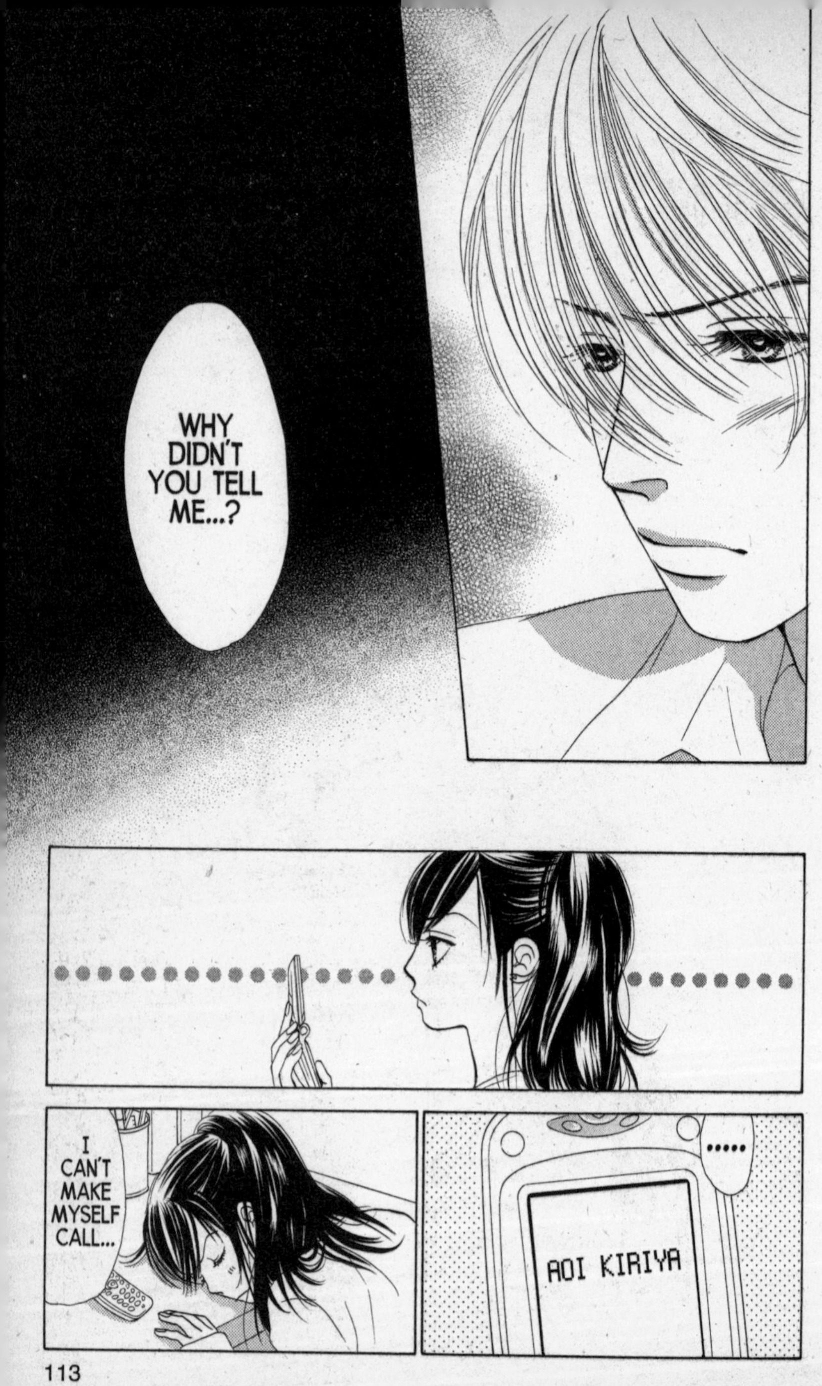
WHY DIDN'T YOU TELL ME...?
......
AOI KIRIYA
I CAN'T MAKE MYSELF CALL...

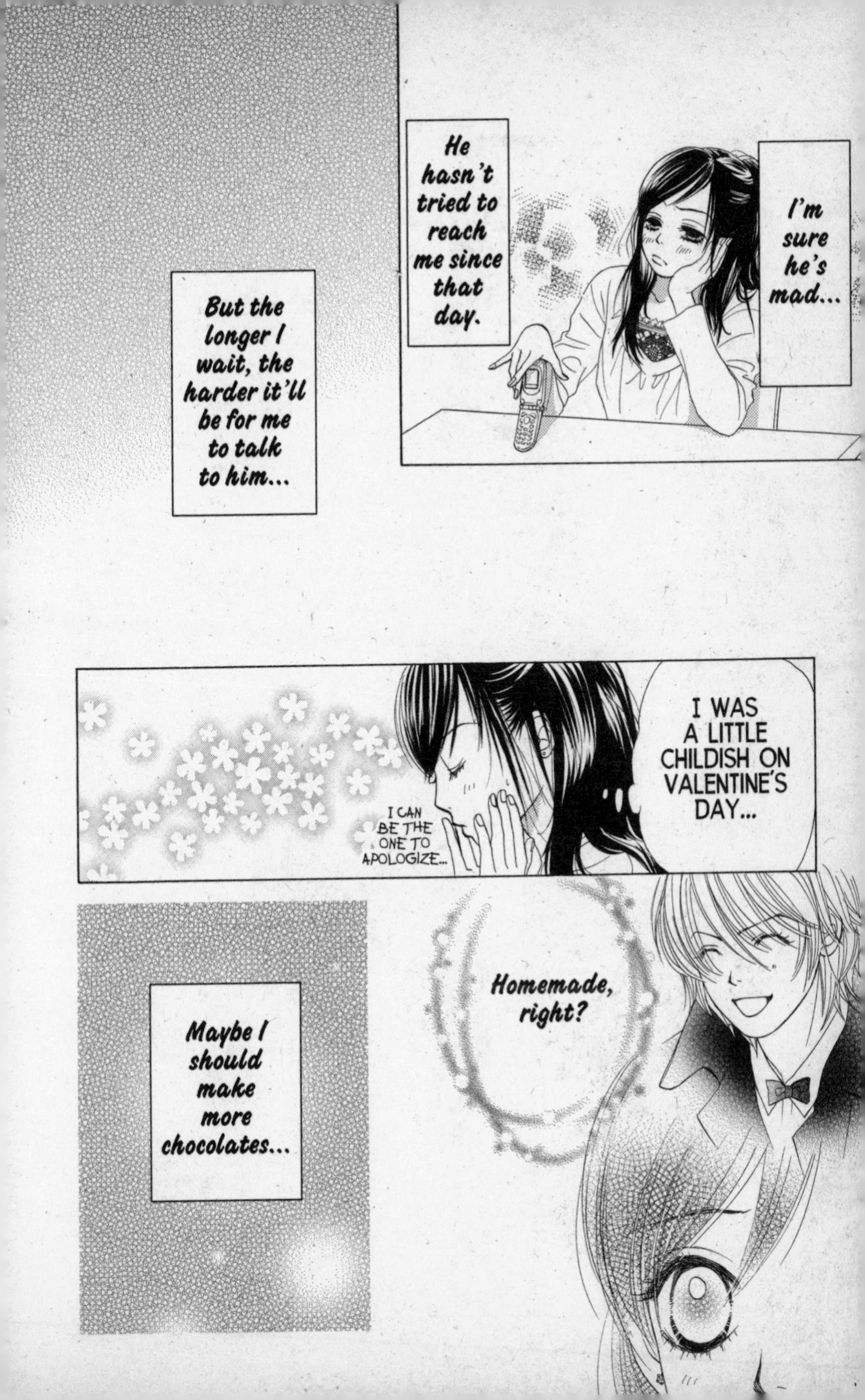
I'm sure he's mad...
He hasn't tried to reach me since that day.
But the longer I wait, the harder it'll be for me to talk to him...
I WAS A LITTLE CHILDISH ON VALENTINE'S DAY...
I CAN BE THE ONE TO APOLOGIZE...
Homemade, right?
Maybe I should make more chocolates...

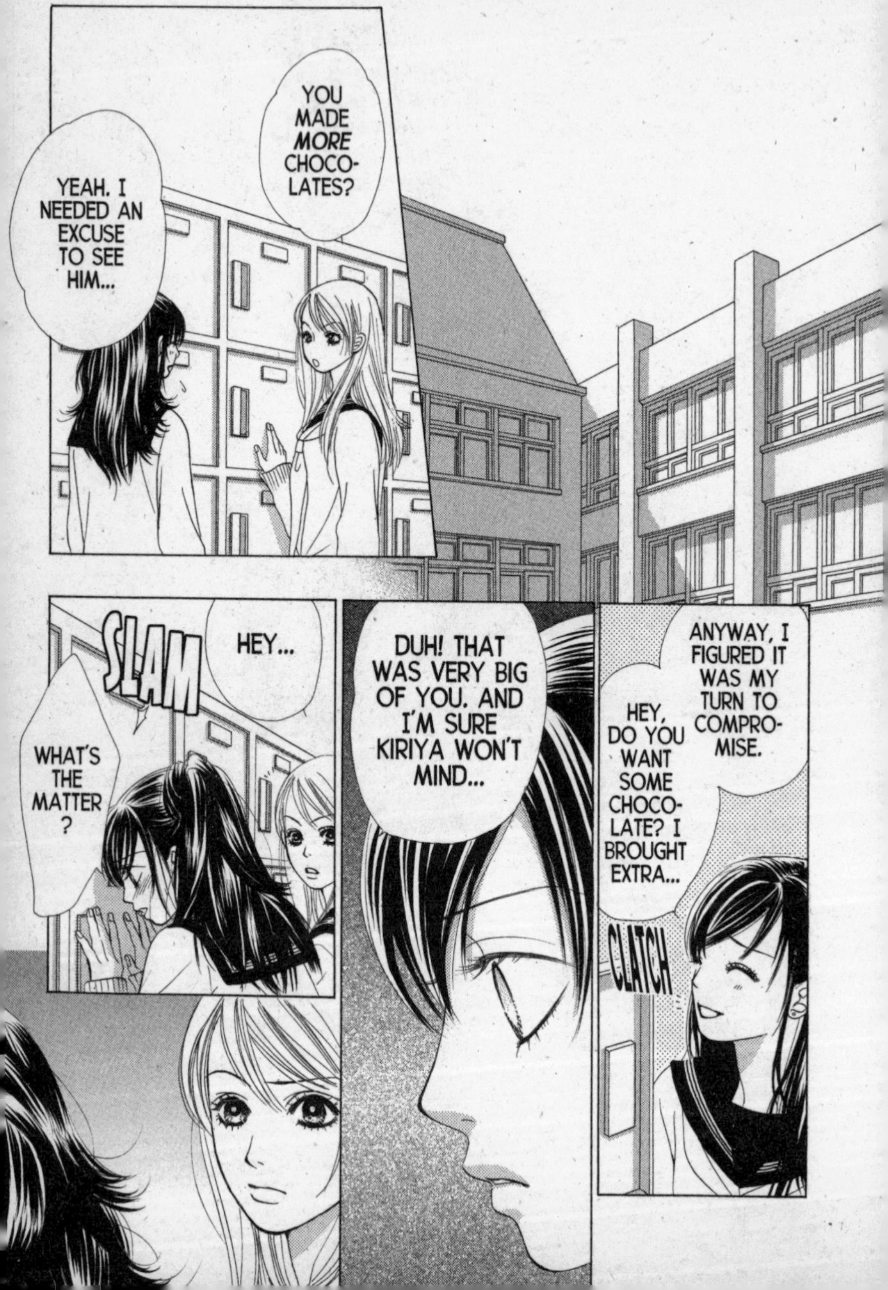
YOU MADE *MORE* CHOCOLATES?
YEAH. I NEEDED AN EXCUSE TO SEE HIM...
ANYWAY, I FIGURED IT WAS MY TURN TO COMPROMISE.
HEY, DO YOU WANT SOME CHOCOLATE? I BROUGHT EXTRA...
CLATCH
DUH! THAT WAS VERY BIG OF YOU. AND I'M SURE KIRIYA WON'T MIND...
HEY...
SLAM
WHAT'S THE MATTER?

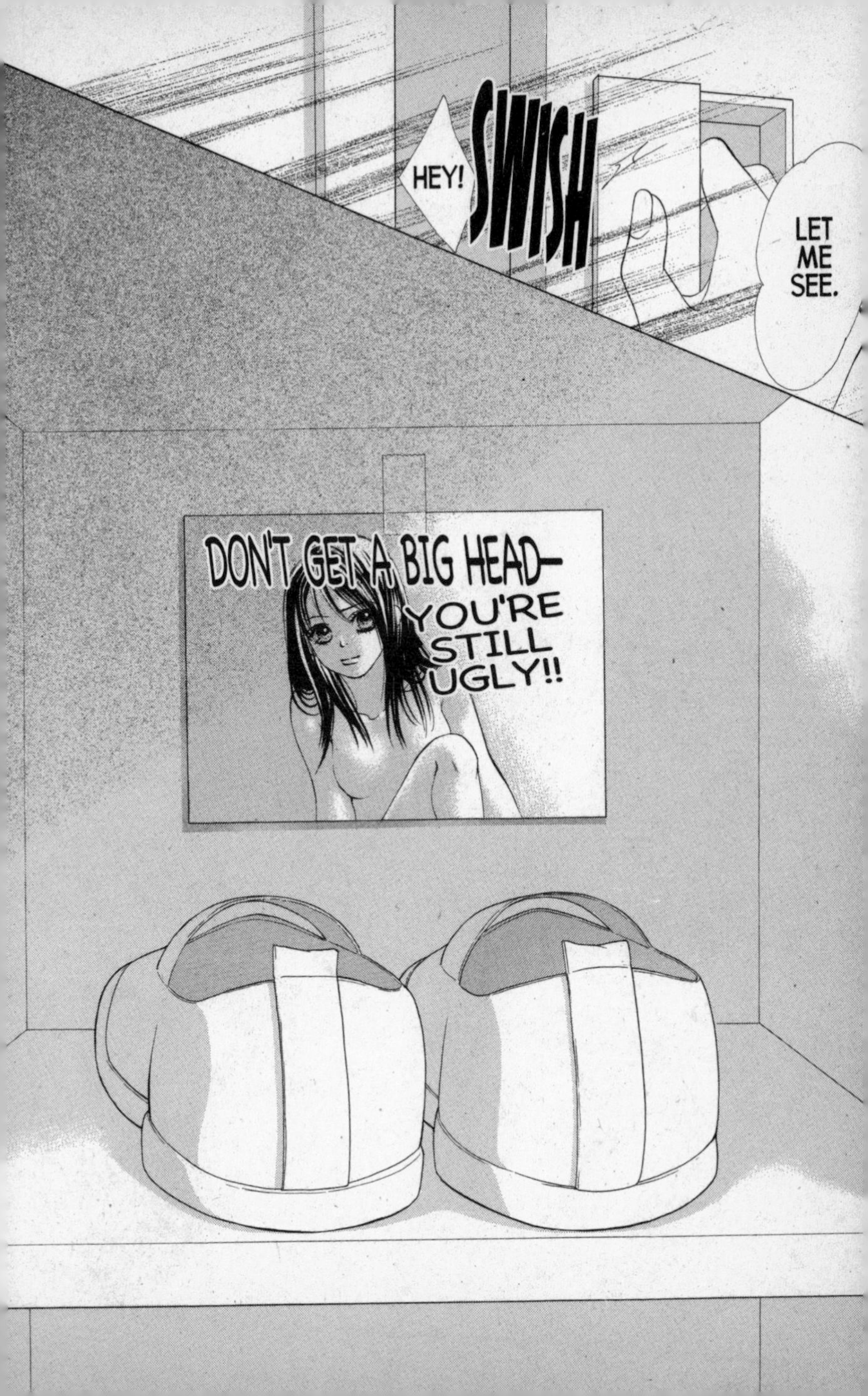
LET ME SEE.
SWISH
HEY!
DON'T GET A BIG HEAD—
YOU'RE STILL UGLY!!

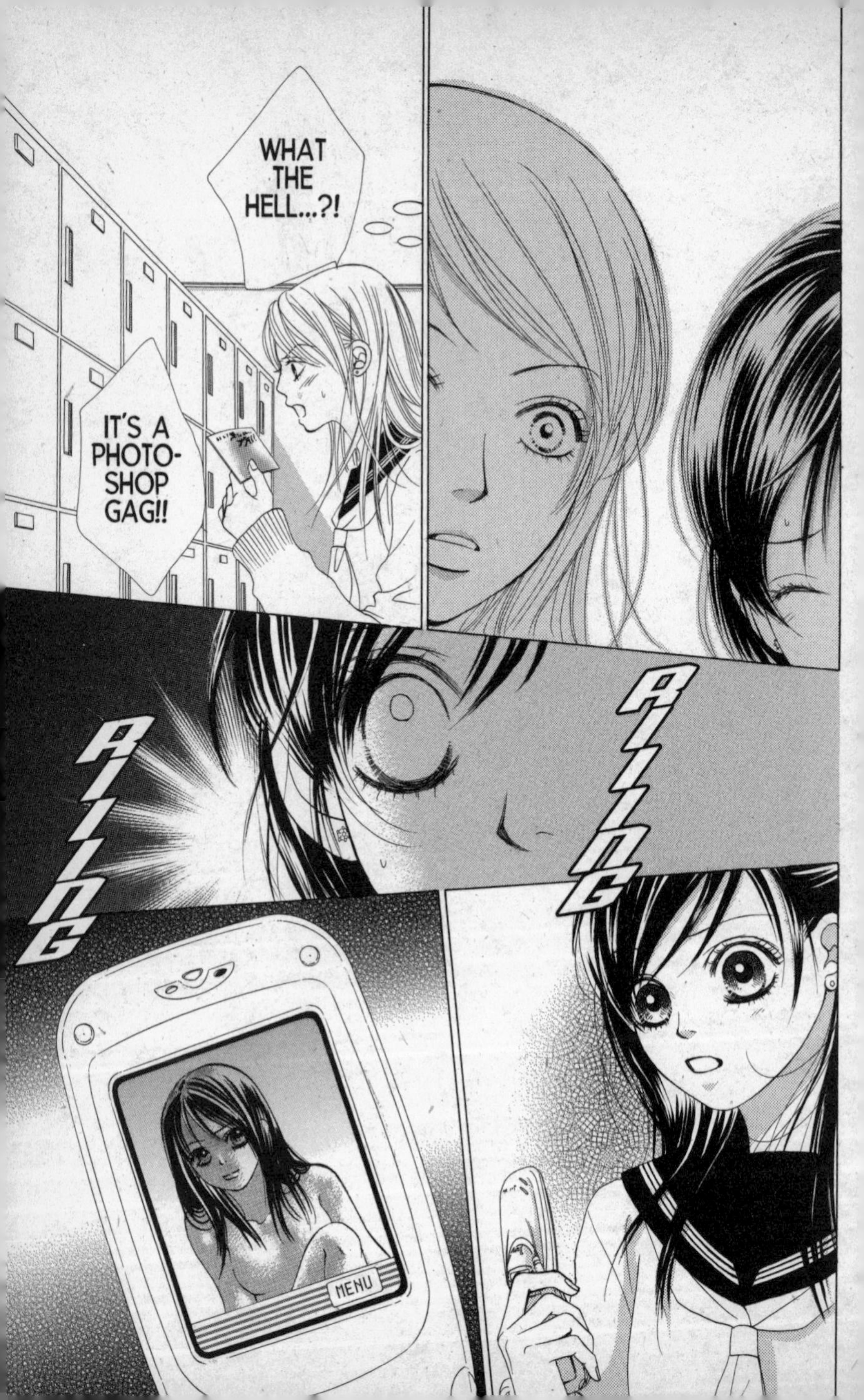
WHAT THE HELL...?!
IT'S A PHOTO-SHOP GAG!!
RIING
RIING
MENU

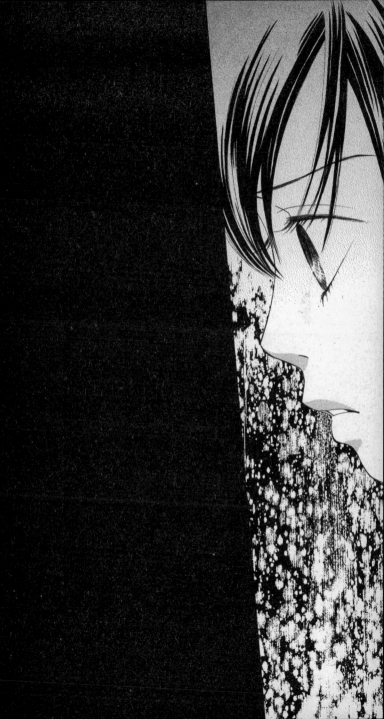

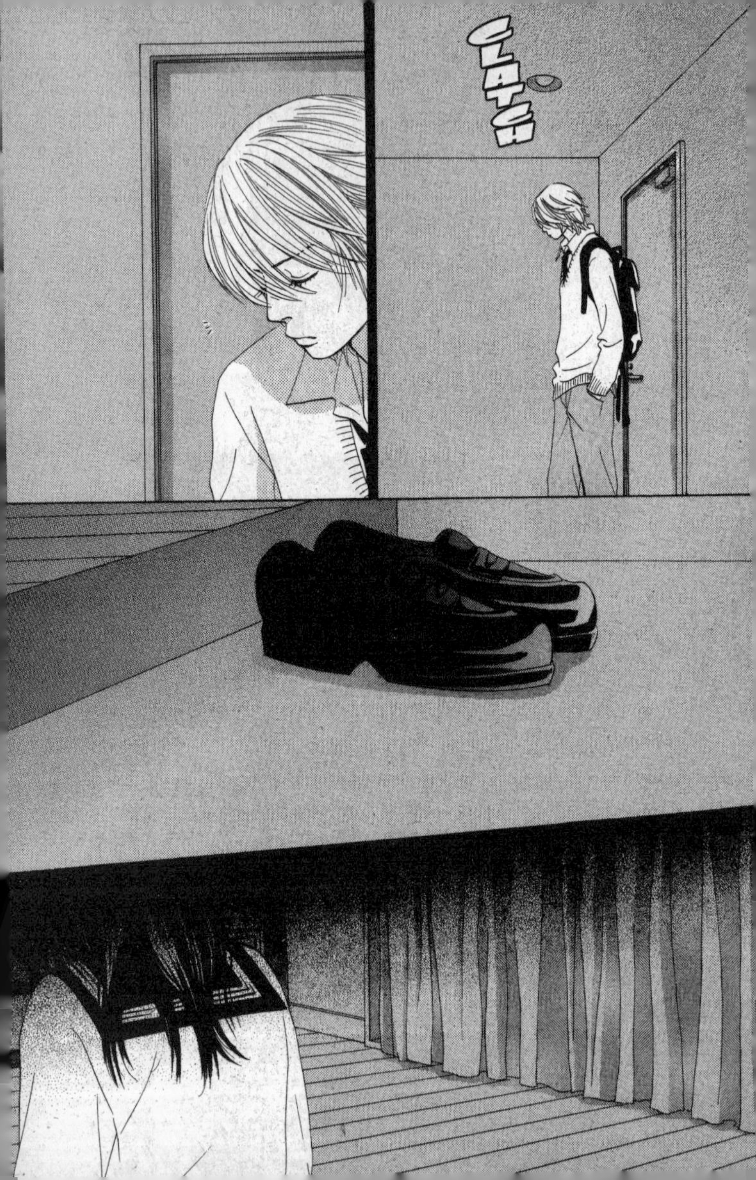
CLATCH

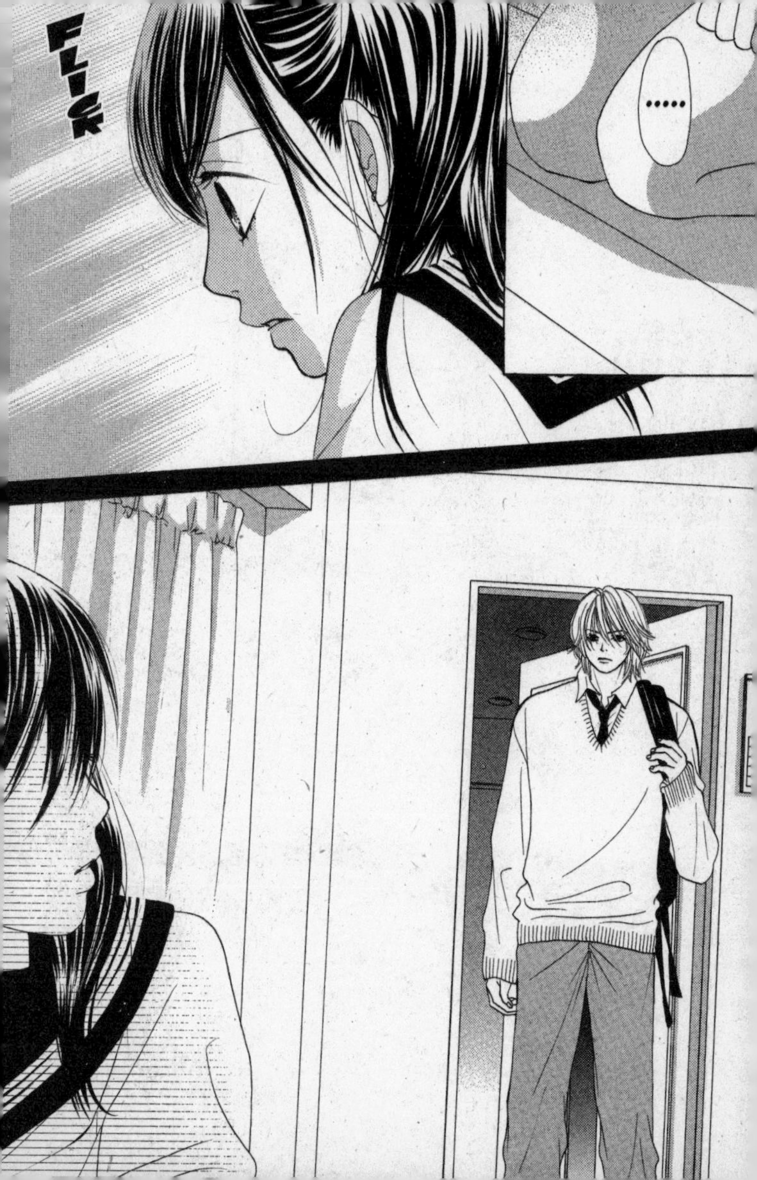
......
FLICK

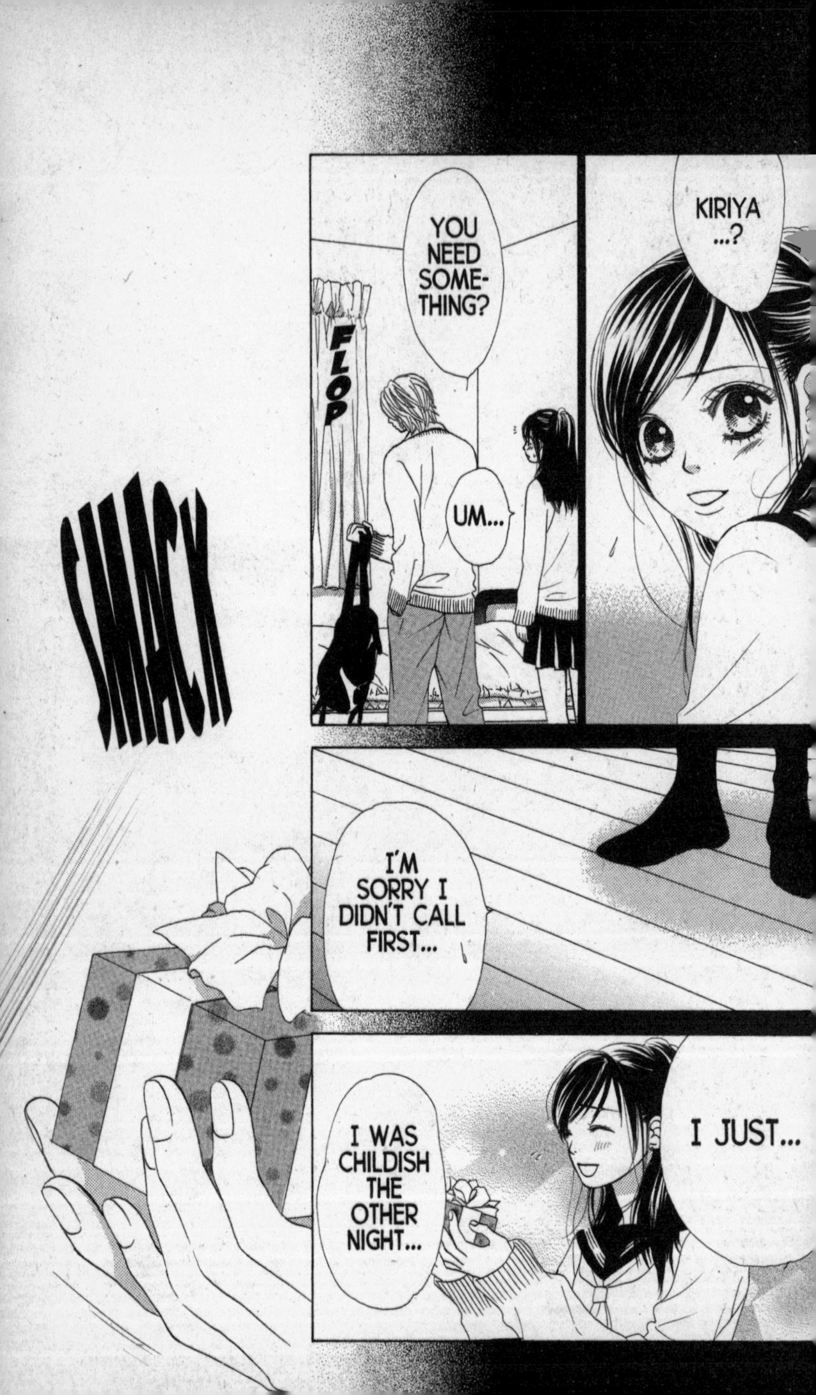
KIRIYA ...?
YOU NEED SOME-THING?
FLOP
UM...
I'M SORRY I DIDN'T CALL FIRST...
I JUST...
I WAS CHILDISH THE OTHER NIGHT...
SMACK

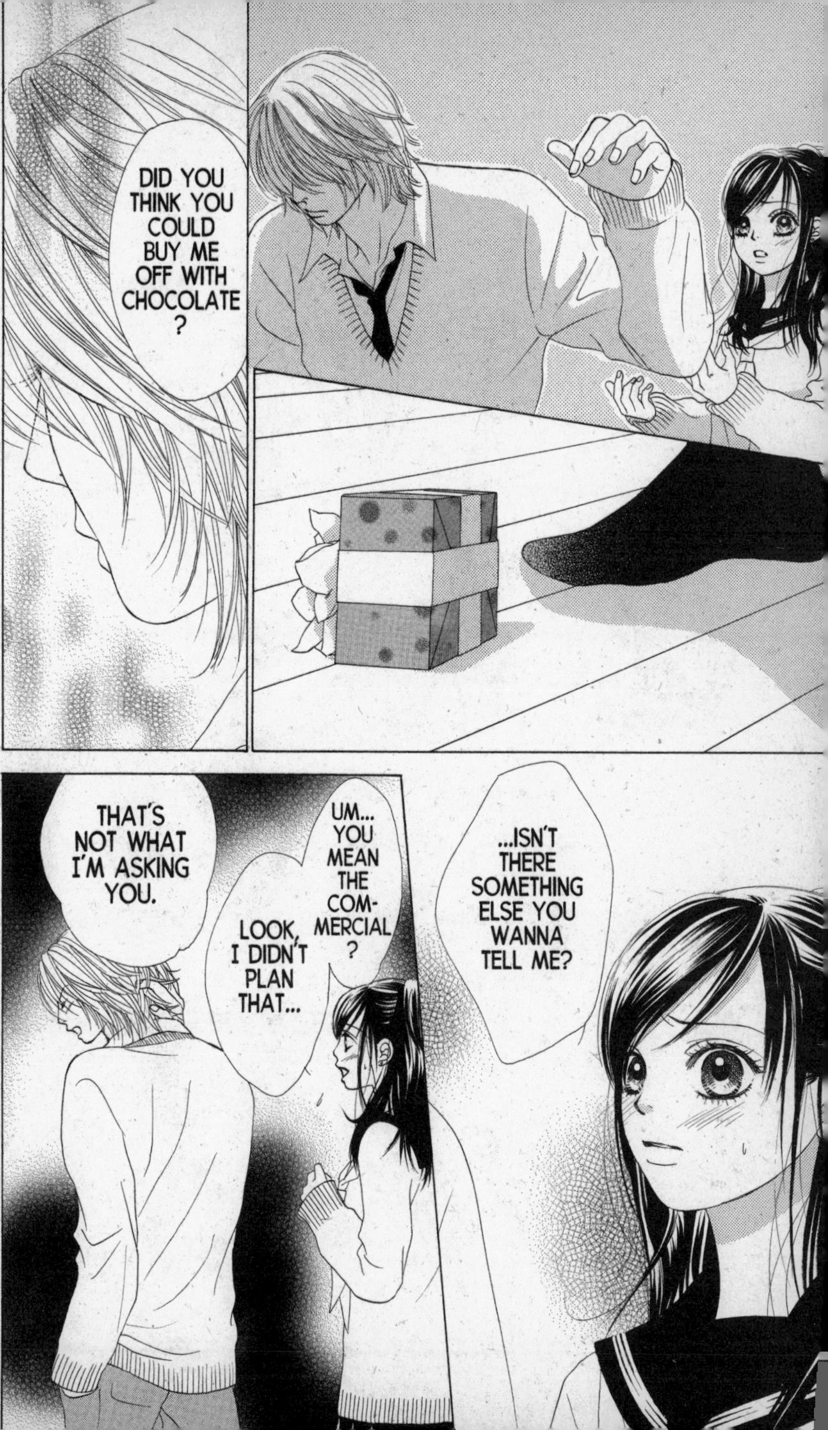
DID YOU THINK YOU COULD BUY ME OFF WITH CHOCOLATE?
...ISN'T THERE SOMETHING ELSE YOU WANNA TELL ME?
UM... YOU MEAN THE COMMERCIAL?
LOOK, I DIDN'T PLAN THAT...
THAT'S NOT WHAT I'M ASKING YOU.

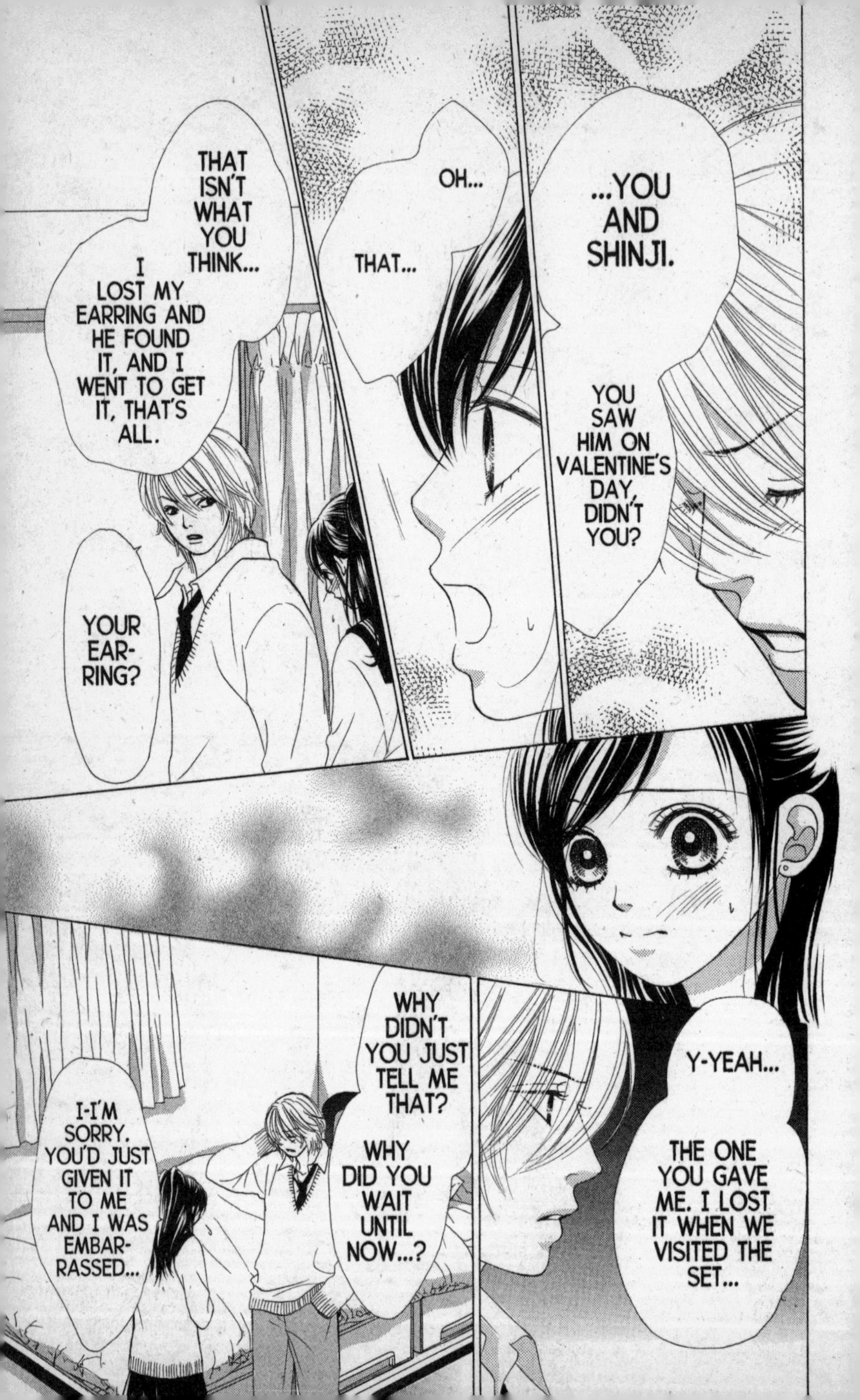
...YOU AND SHINJI.
YOU SAW HIM ON VALENTINE'S DAY, DIDN'T YOU?
OH...
THAT...
THAT ISN'T WHAT YOU THINK...
I LOST MY EARRING AND HE FOUND IT, AND I WENT TO GET IT, THAT'S ALL.
YOUR EAR-RING?
Y-YEAH...
THE ONE YOU GAVE ME. I LOST IT WHEN WE VISITED THE SET...
WHY DIDN'T YOU JUST TELL ME THAT?
WHY DID YOU WAIT UNTIL NOW...?
I-I'M SORRY. YOU'D JUST GIVEN IT TO ME AND I WAS EMBAR-RASSED...

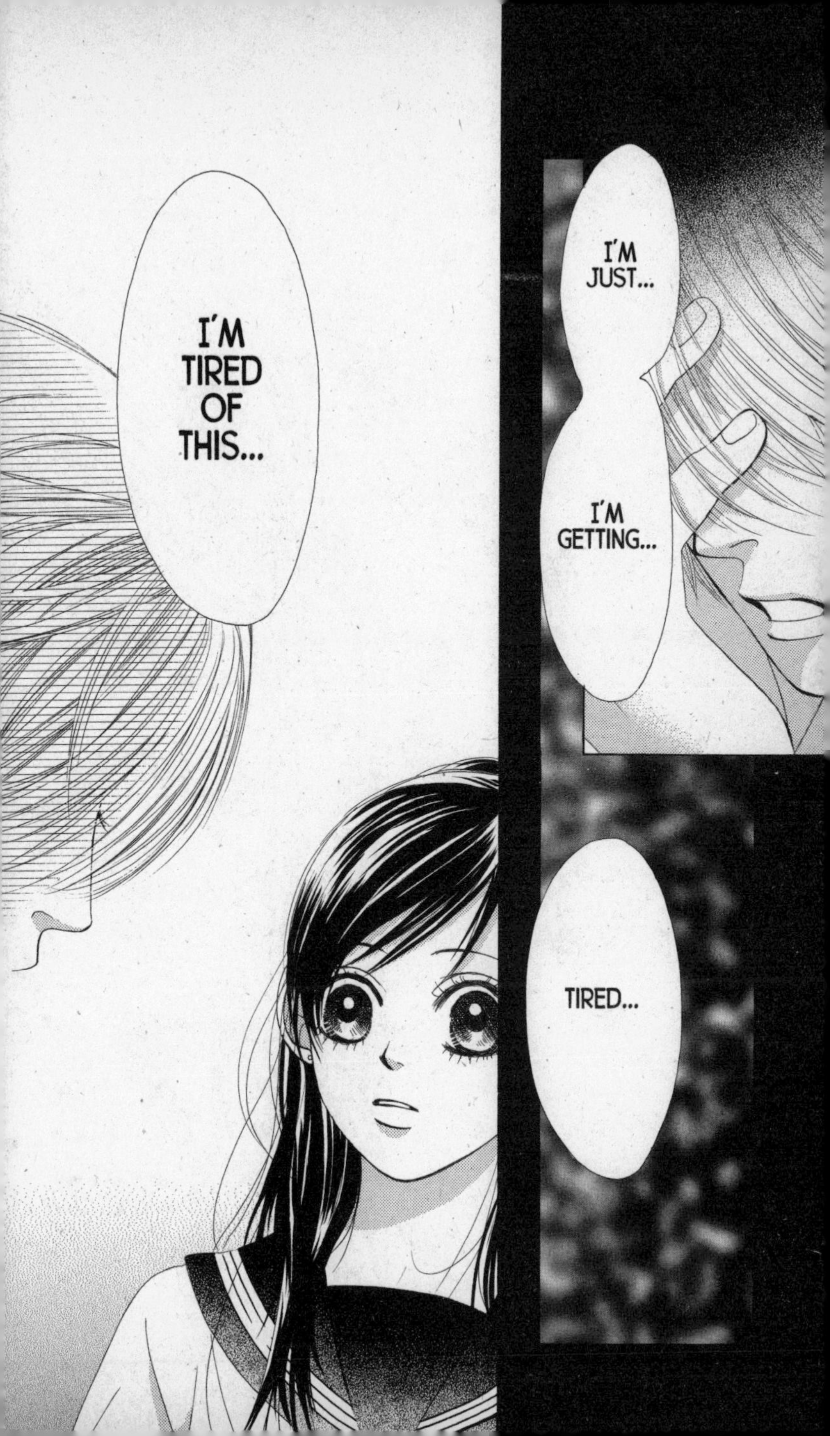
I'M JUST...
I'M GETTING...
TIRED...
I'M TIRED OF THIS...

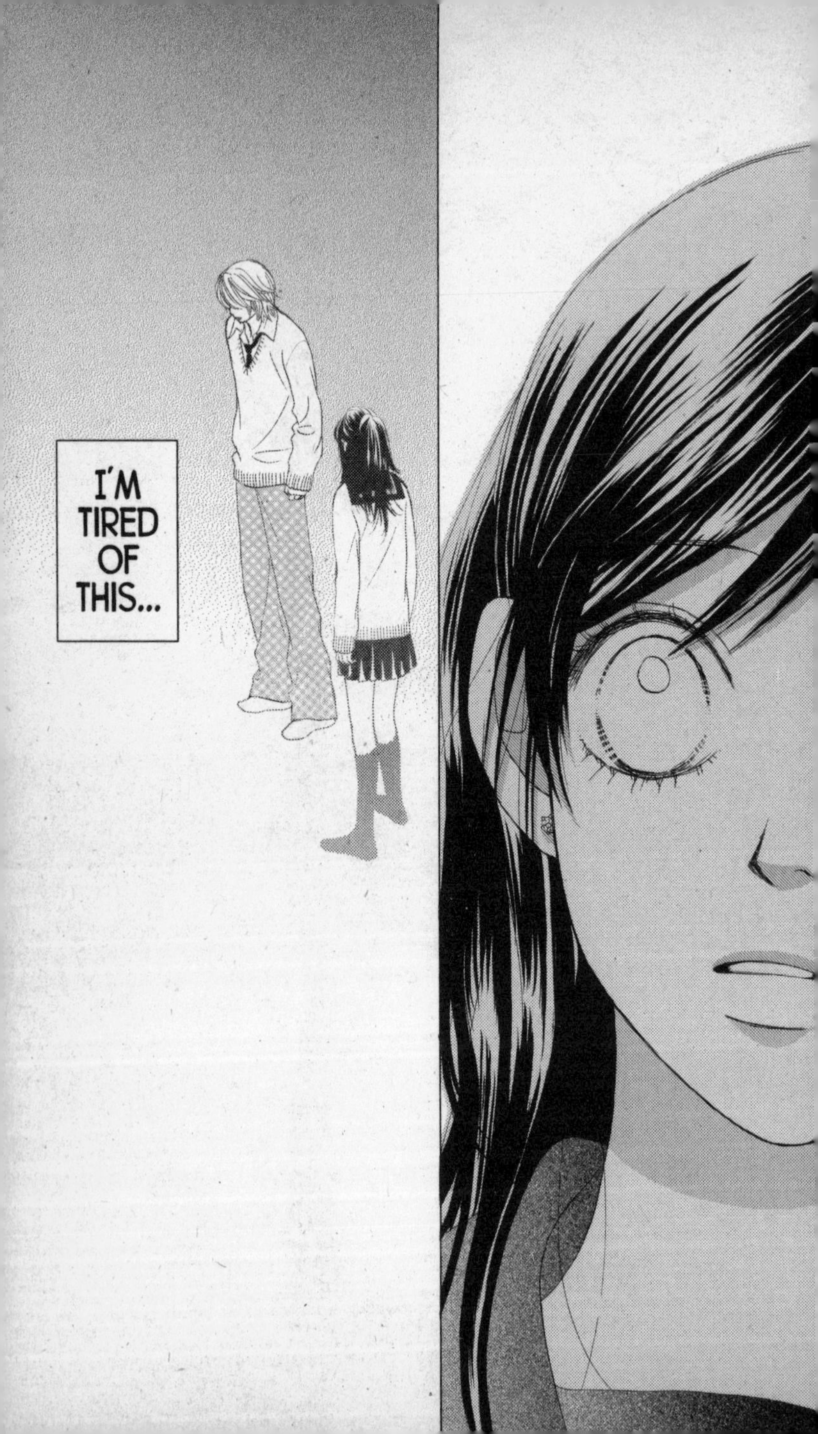
I'M TIRED OF THIS...

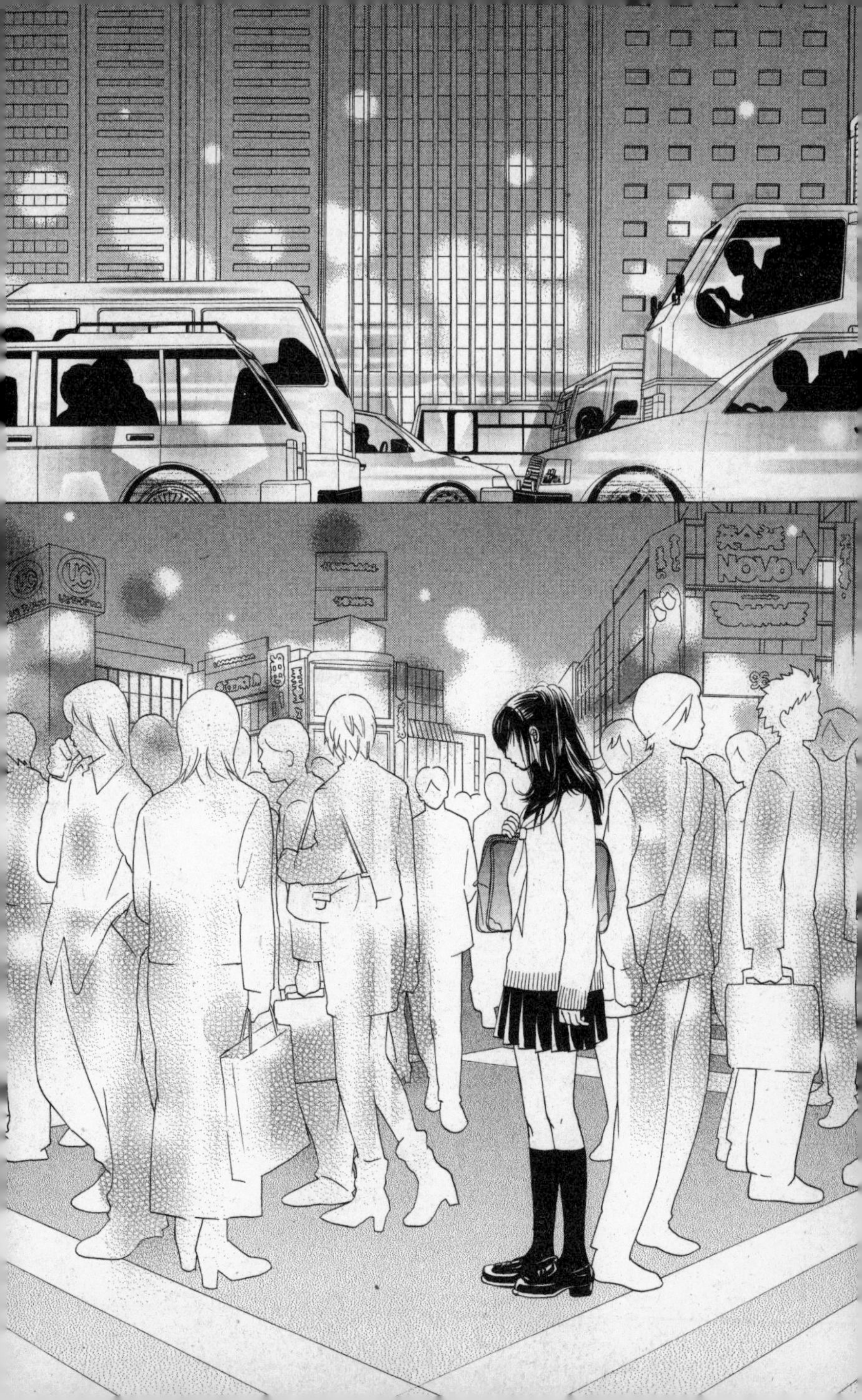
NOVO
UC

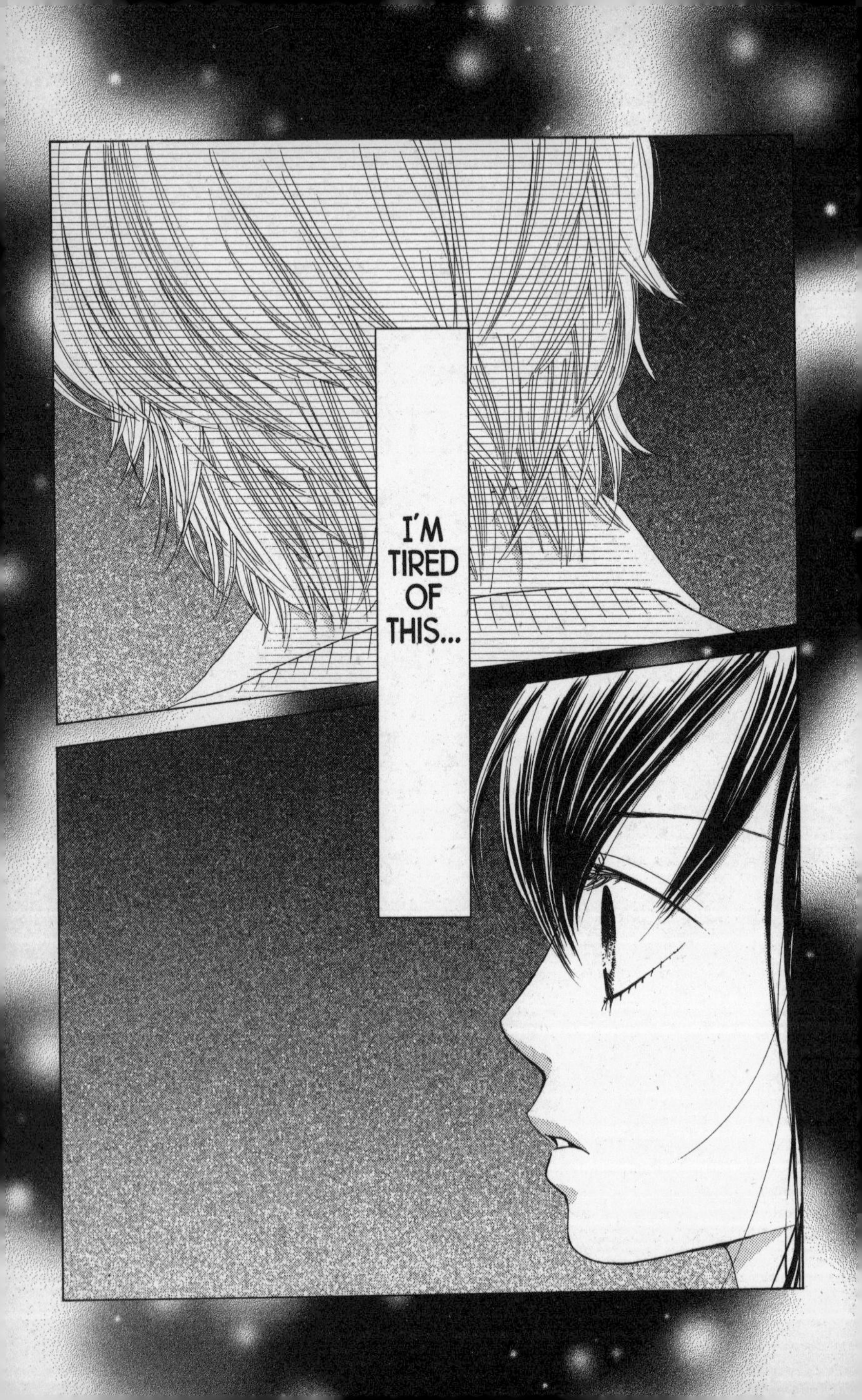
I'M TIRED OF THIS...

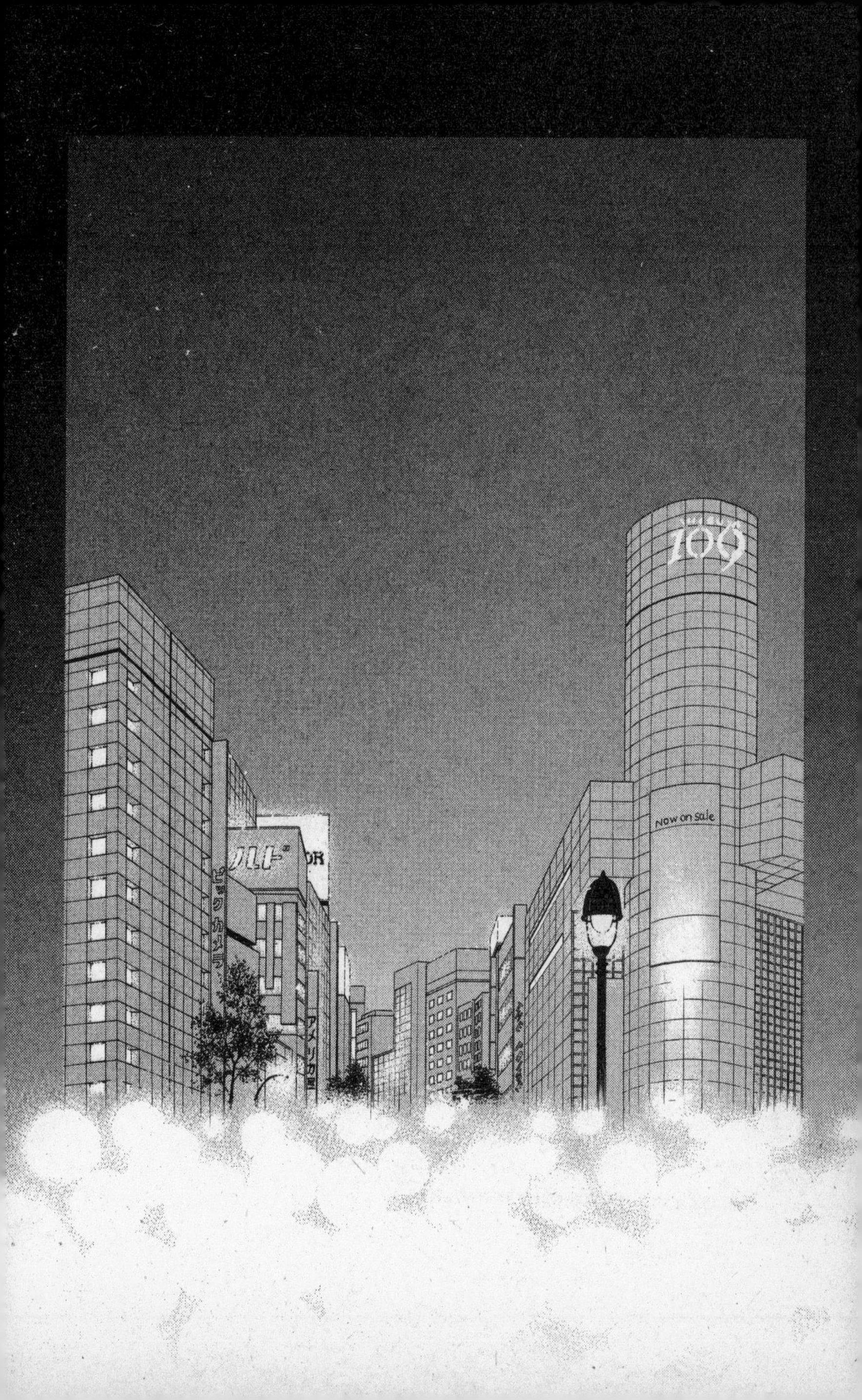
109
Now on sale
ビックカメラ

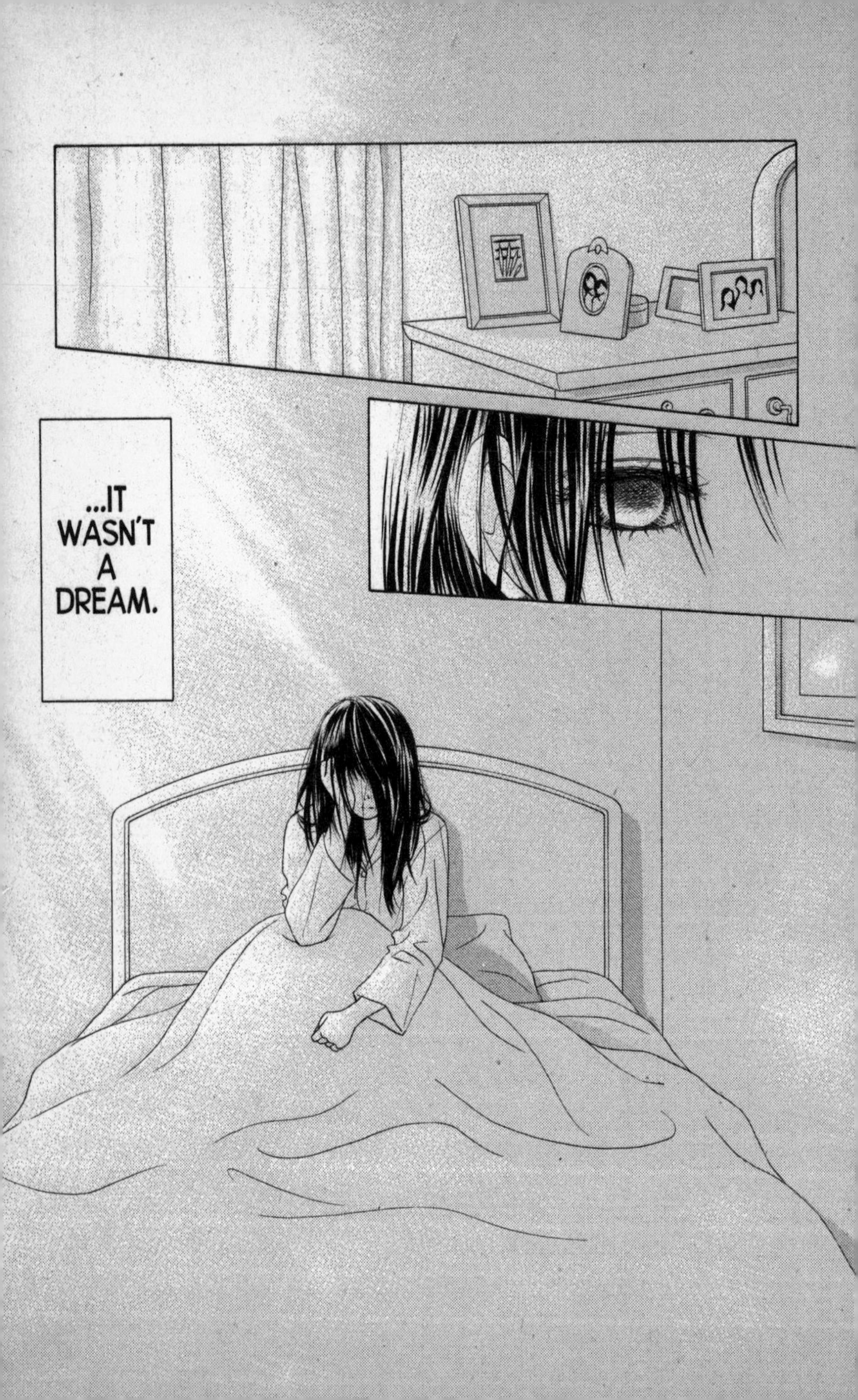
...IT WASN'T A DREAM.

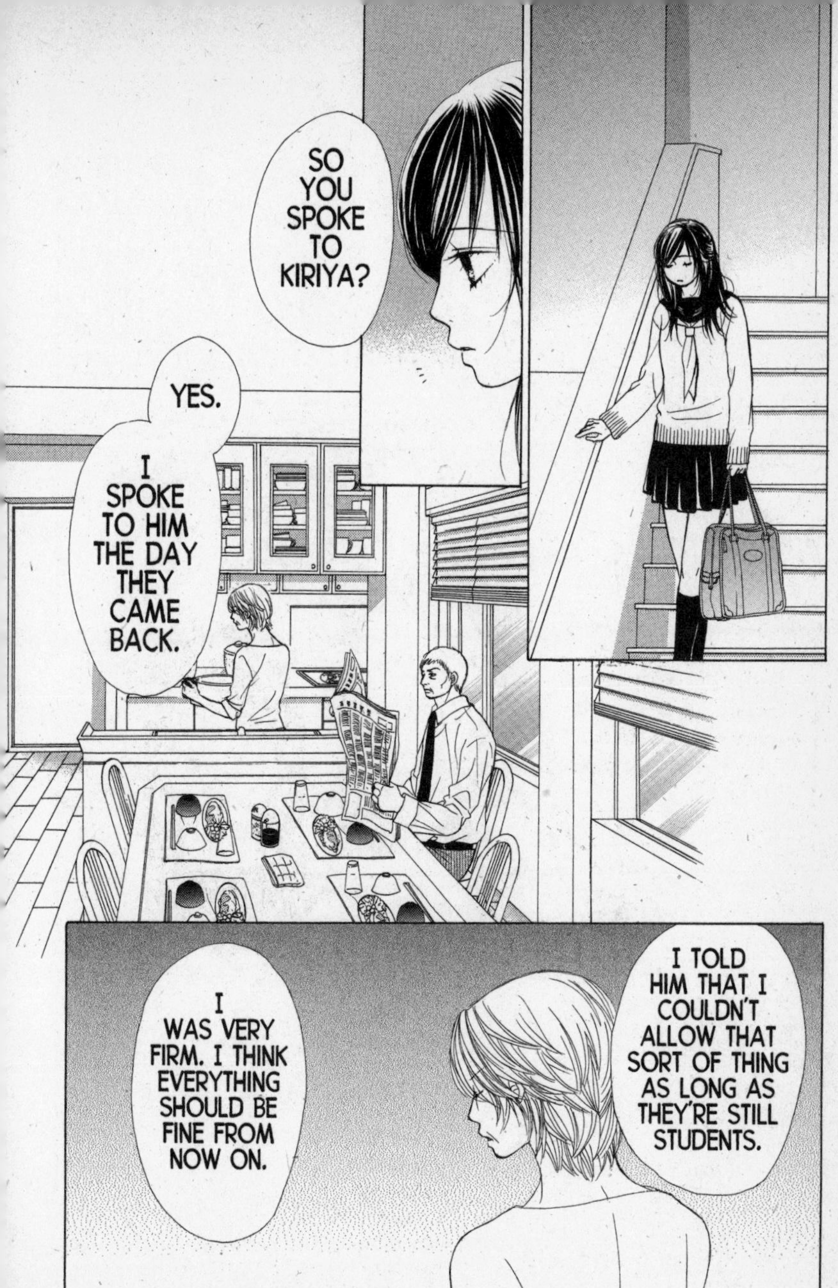
SO YOU SPOKE TO KIRIYA?
YES.
I SPOKE TO HIM THE DAY THEY CAME BACK.
I TOLD HIM THAT I COULDN'T ALLOW THAT SORT OF THING AS LONG AS THEY'RE STILL STUDENTS.
I WAS VERY FIRM. I THINK EVERYTHING SHOULD BE FINE FROM NOW ON.

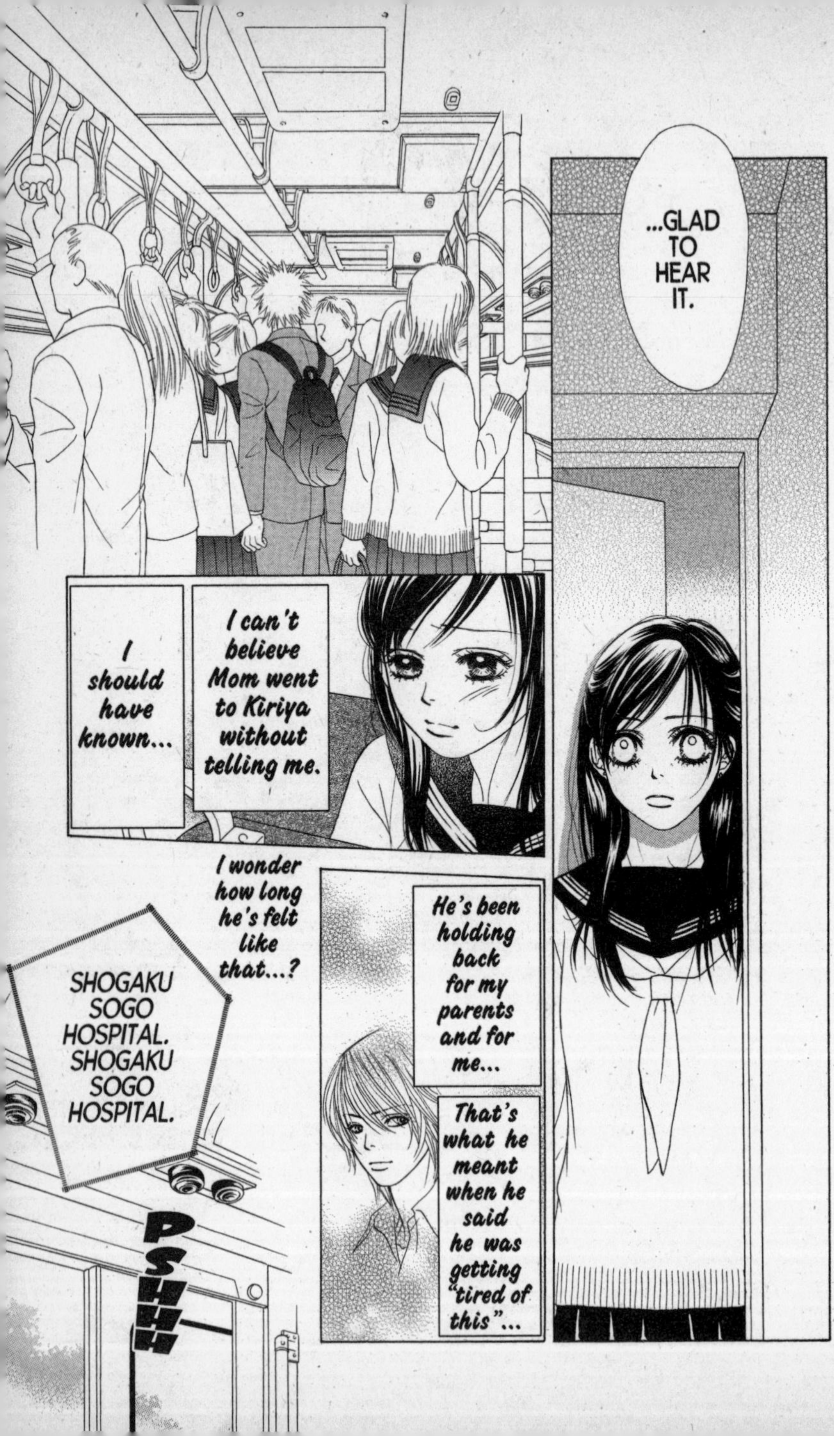
...GLAD TO HEAR IT.
I can't believe Mom went to Kiriya without telling me.
I should have known...
I wonder how long he's felt like that...?
He's been holding back for my parents and for me...
That's what he meant when he said he was getting "tired of this"...
SHOGAKU SOGO HOSPITAL. SHOGAKU SOGO HOSPITAL.
PSHHH

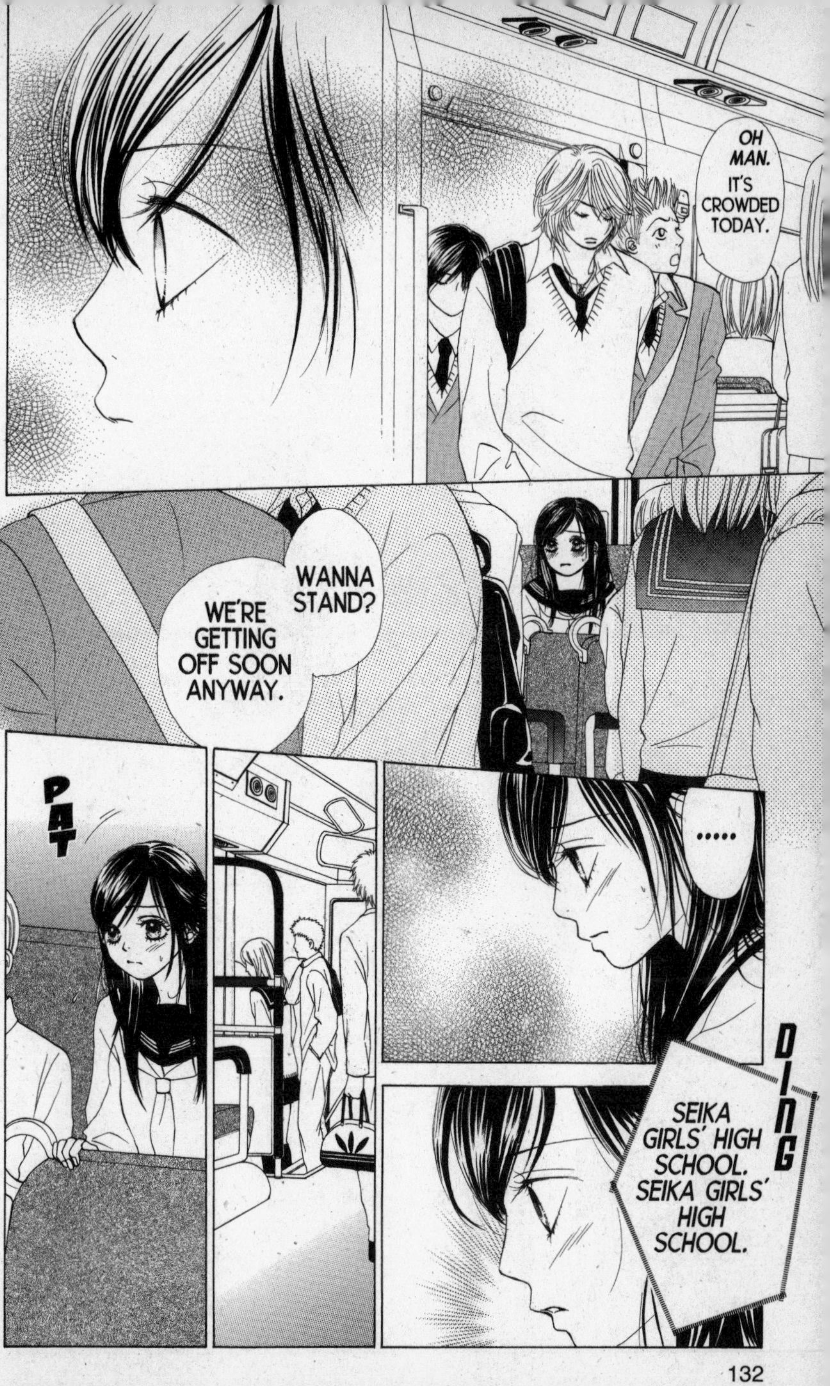
OH MAN. IT'S CROWDED TODAY.
WANNA STAND?
WE'RE GETTING OFF SOON ANYWAY.
.....
DING
SEIKA GIRLS' HIGH SCHOOL. SEIKA GIRLS' HIGH SCHOOL.
PAT

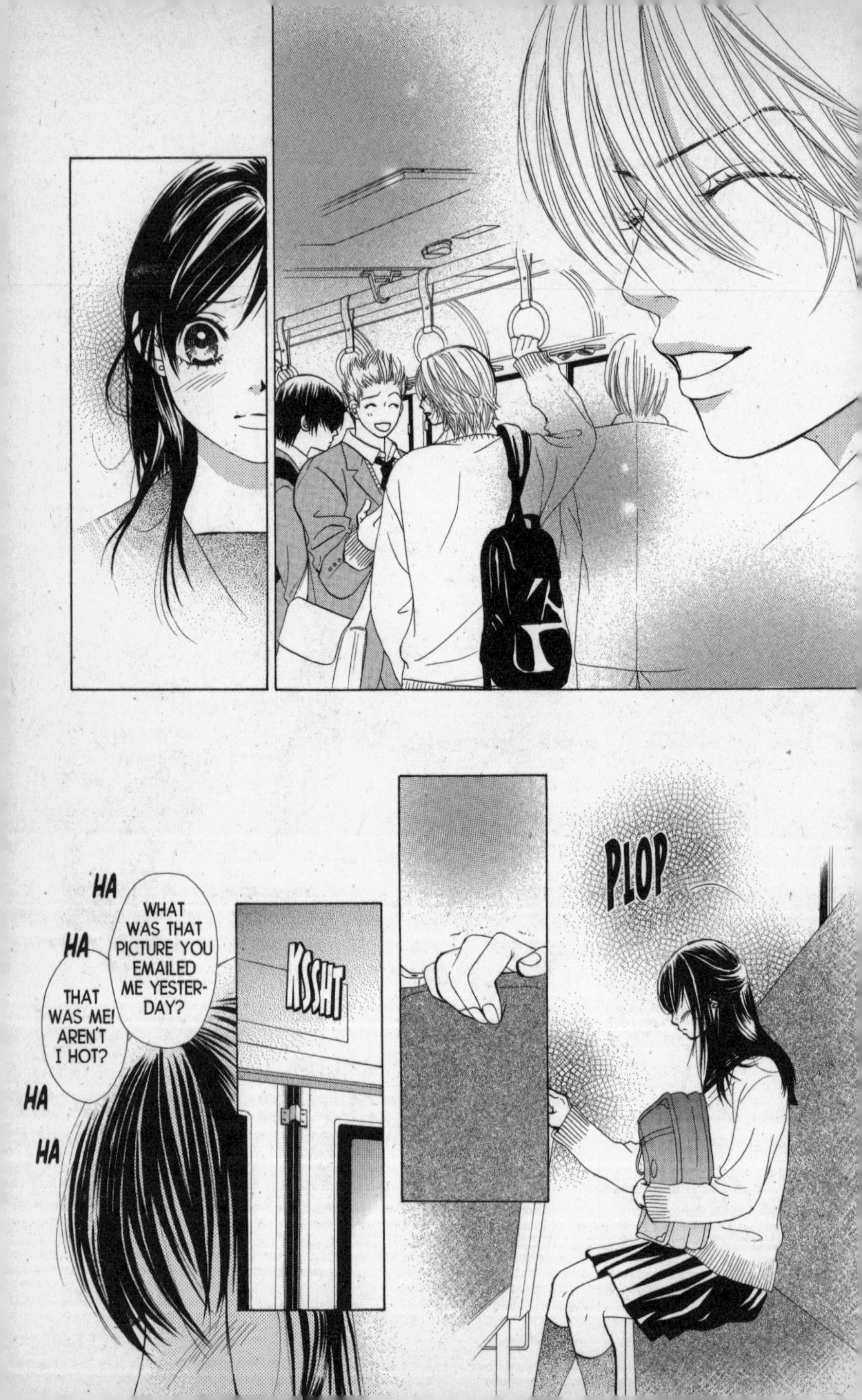
PLOP
KSSHT
WHAT WAS THAT PICTURE YOU EMAILED ME YESTER-DAY?
THAT WAS ME! AREN'T I HOT?
HA
HA
HA
HA

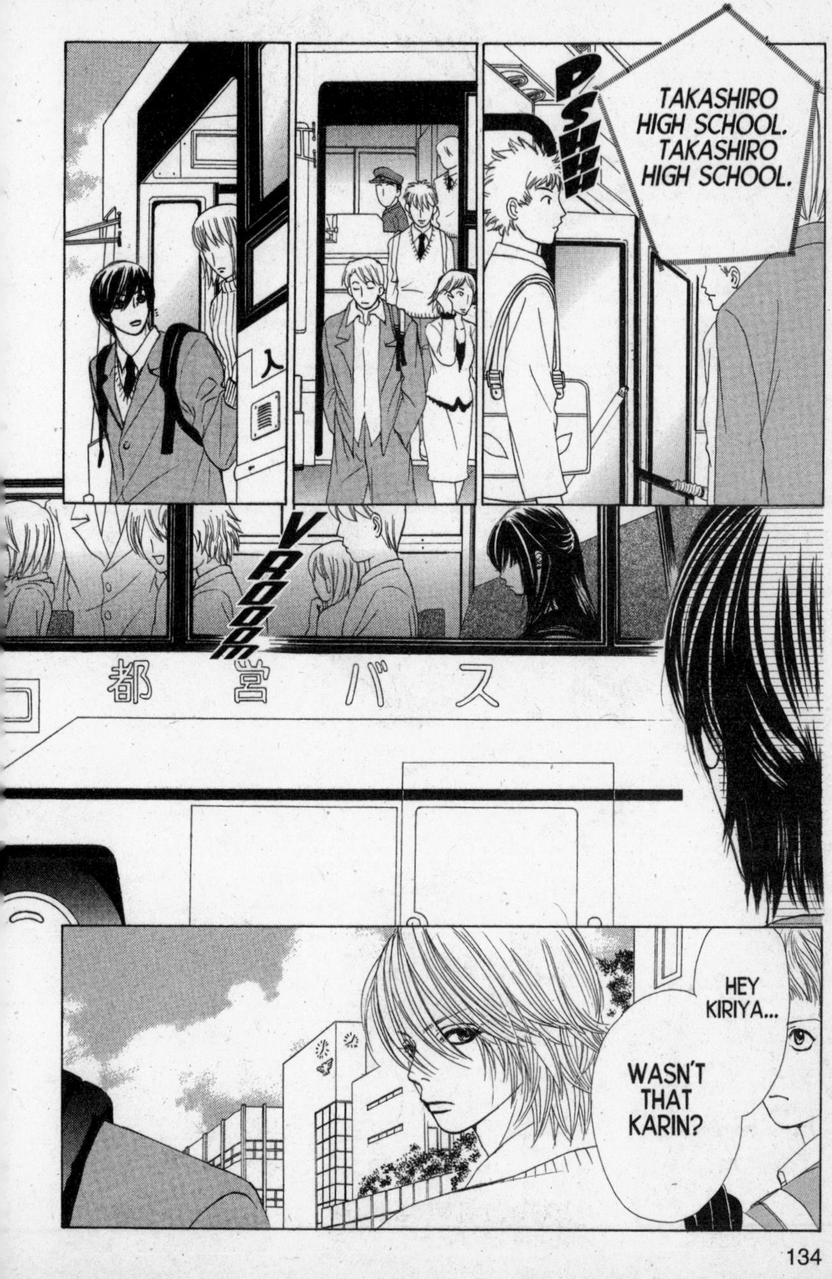
PSHHH
TAKASHIRO HIGH SCHOOL. TAKASHIRO HIGH SCHOOL.
VROOOM
都営バス
HEY KIRIYA...
WASN'T THAT KARIN?

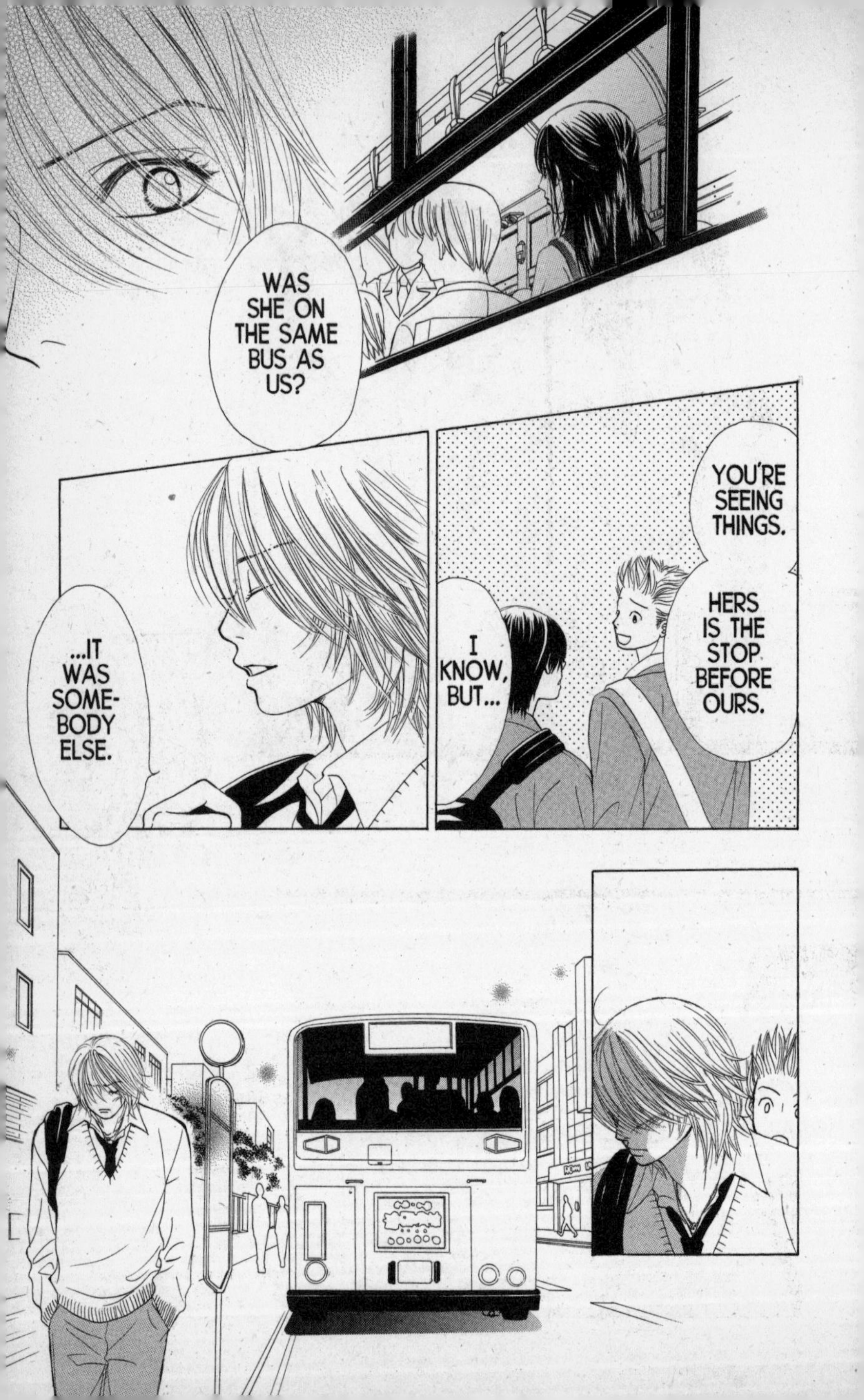
WAS SHE ON THE SAME BUS AS US?
YOU'RE SEEING THINGS.
HERS IS THE STOP BEFORE OURS.
I KNOW, BUT...
...IT WAS SOMEBODY ELSE.

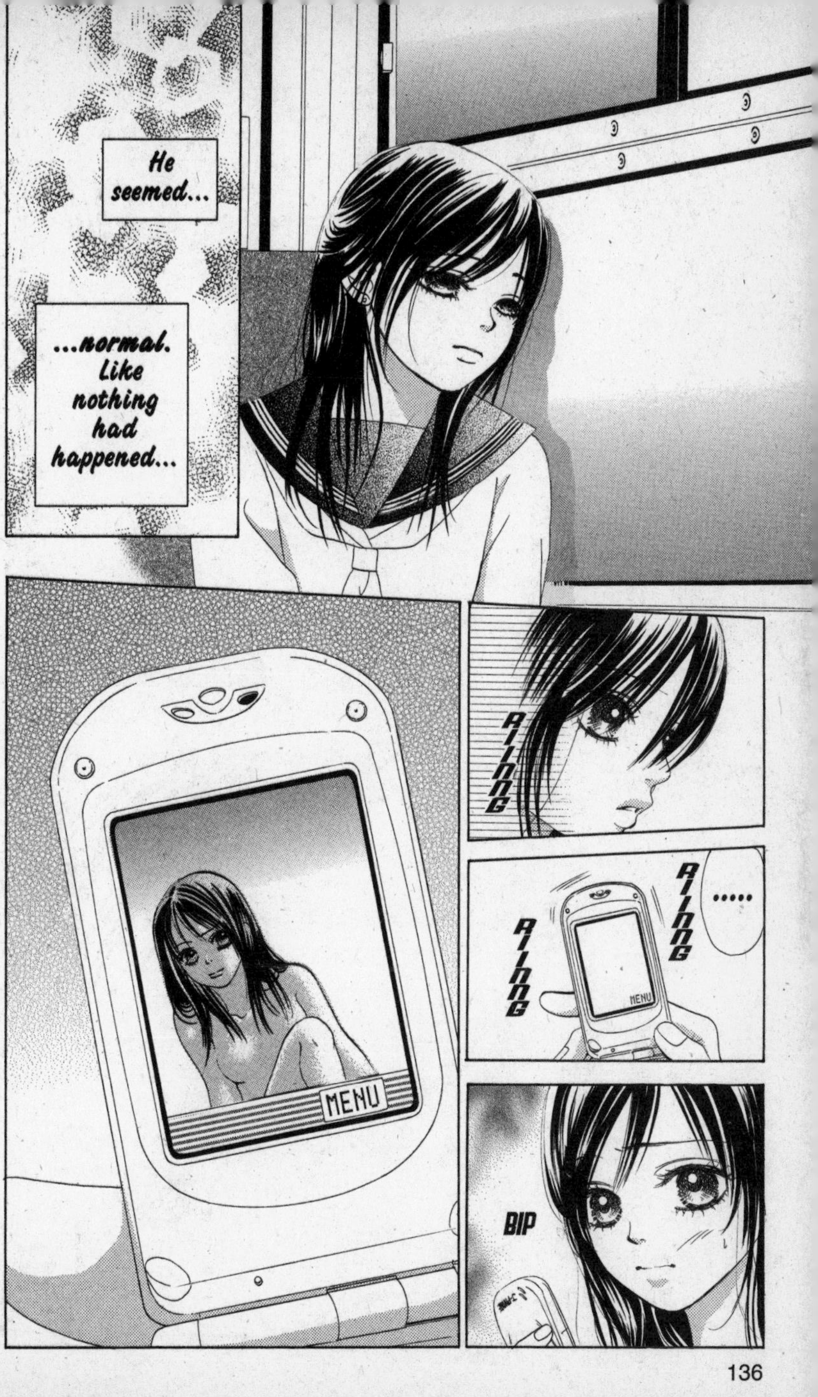
He seemed...
...normal. Like nothing had happened...
RIINNG
RIINNG
RIINNG
......
MENU
BIP
MENU

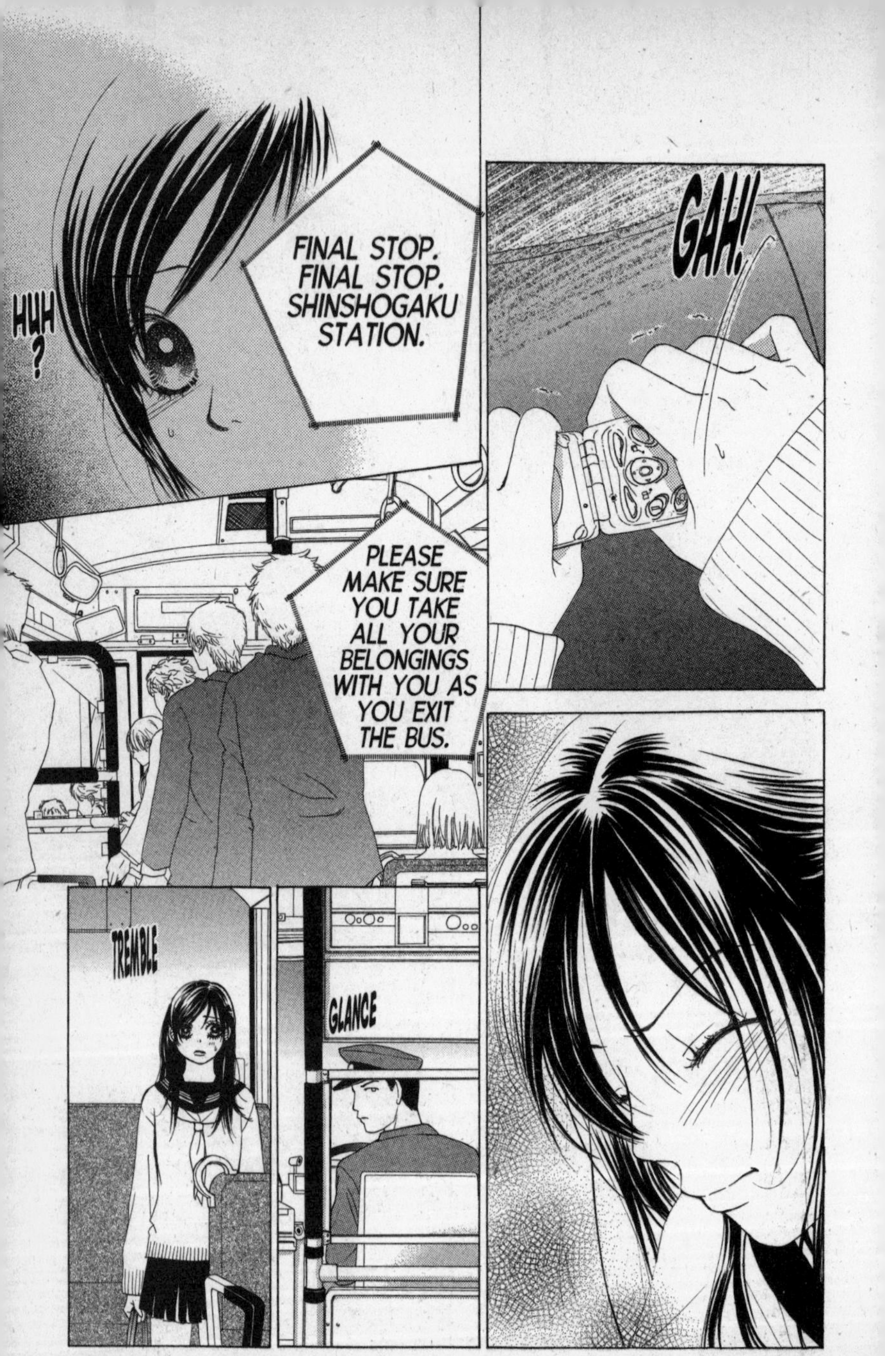
GAH!
HUH?
FINAL STOP. FINAL STOP. SHINSHOGAKU STATION.
PLEASE MAKE SURE YOU TAKE ALL YOUR BELONGINGS WITH YOU AS YOU EXIT THE BUS.
GLANCE
TREMBLE

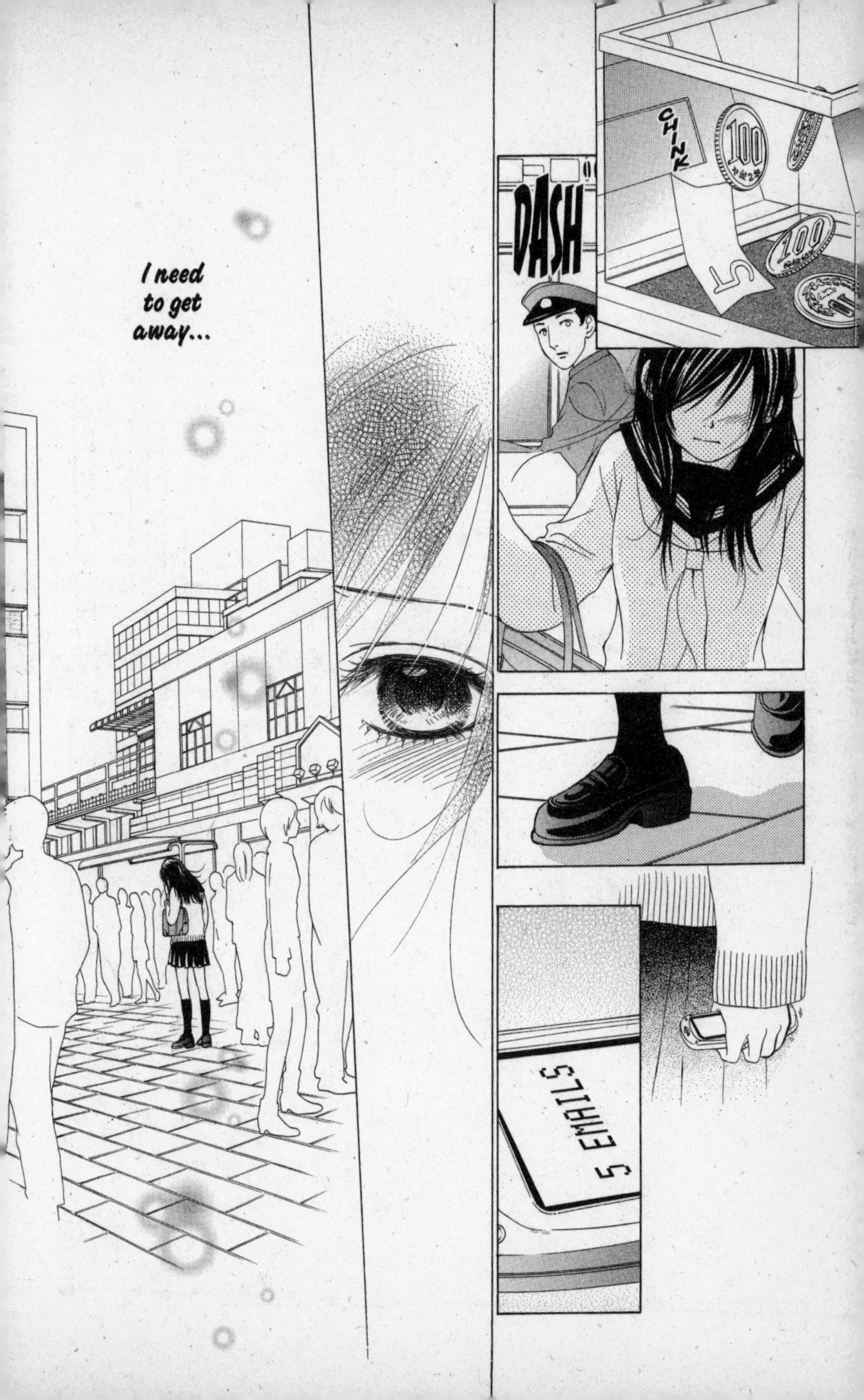
CHINK
DASH
5 EMAILS
I need to get away...

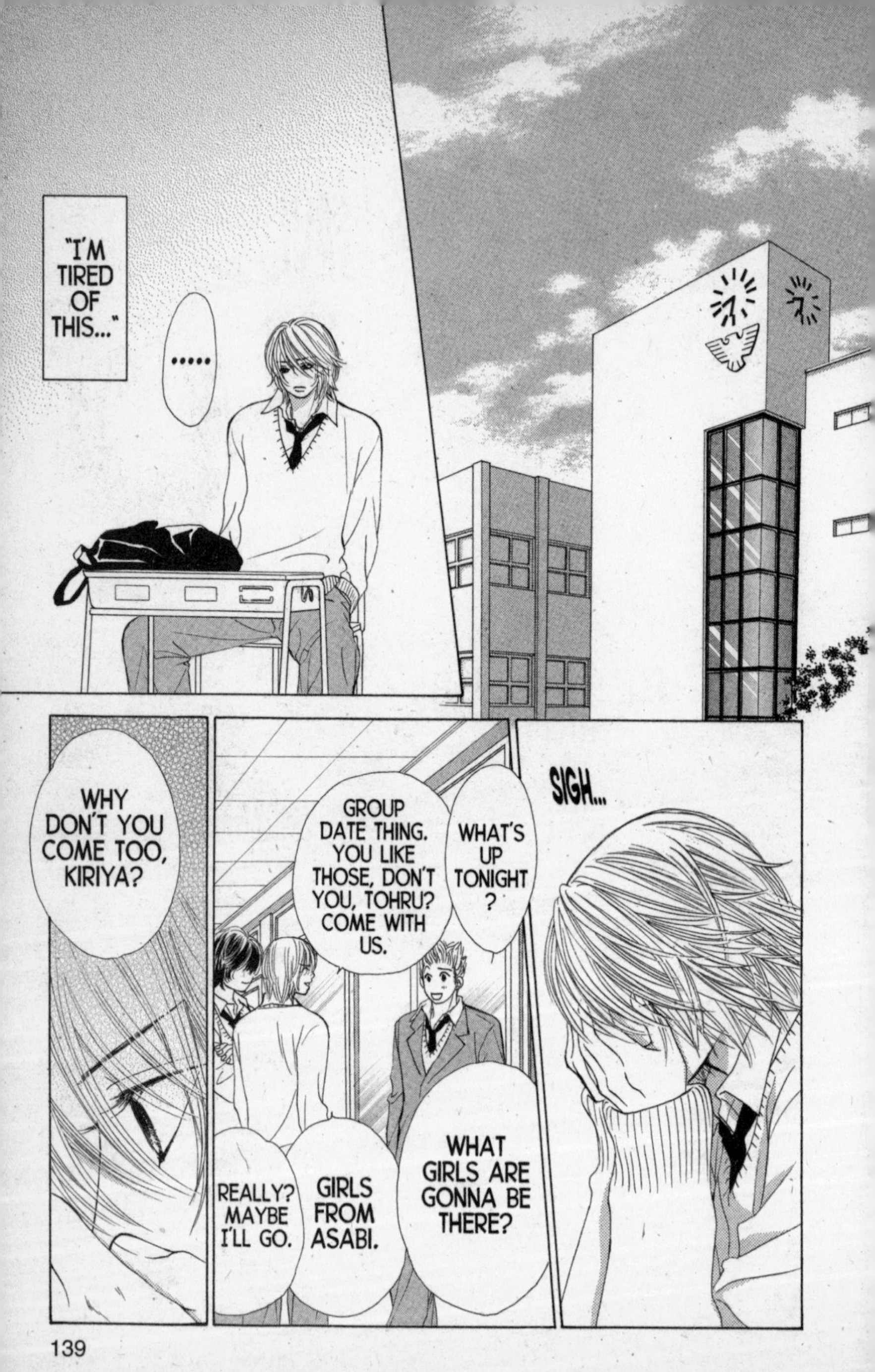
......
"I'M TIRED OF THIS..."
SIGH...
WHAT'S UP TONIGHT?
GROUP DATE THING. YOU LIKE THOSE, DON'T YOU, TOHRU? COME WITH US.
WHAT GIRLS ARE GONNA BE THERE?
GIRLS FROM ASABI.
REALLY? MAYBE I'LL GO.
WHY DON'T YOU COME TOO, KIRIYA?

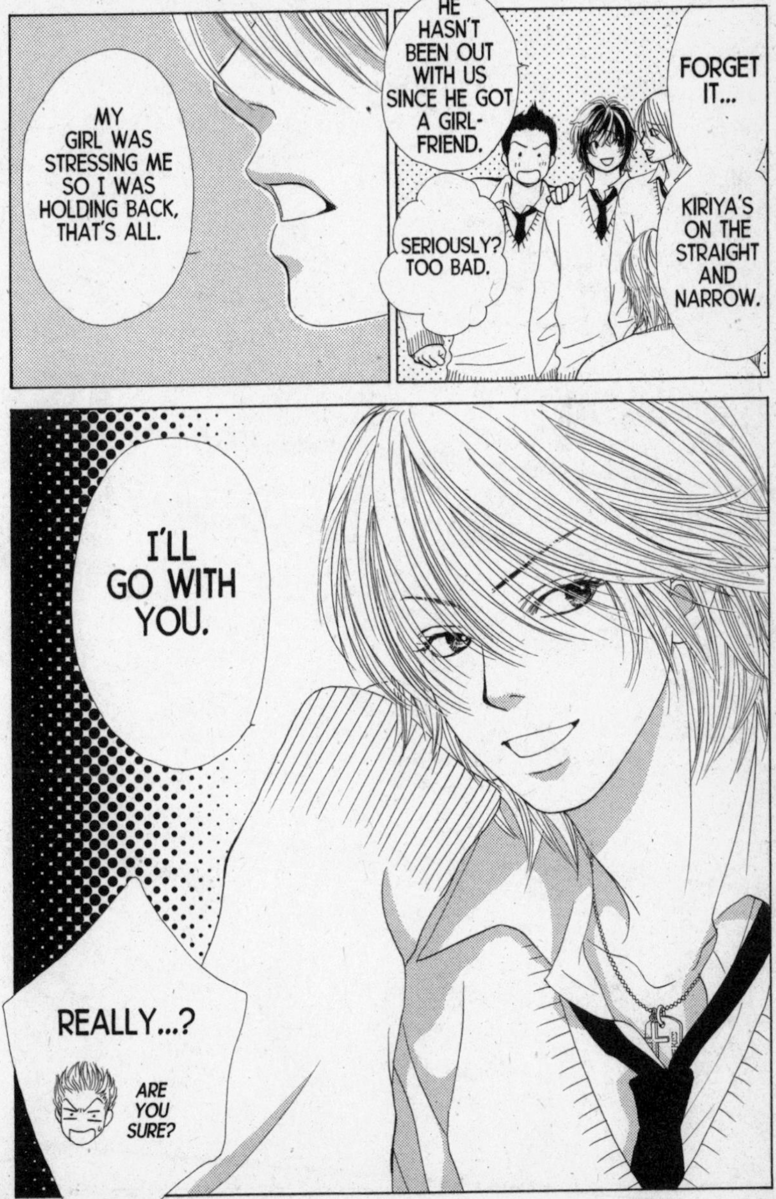
FORGET IT...
KIRIYA'S ON THE STRAIGHT AND NARROW.
HE HASN'T BEEN OUT WITH US SINCE HE GOT A GIRL-FRIEND.
SERIOUSLY? TOO BAD.
MY GIRL WAS STRESSING ME SO I WAS HOLDING BACK, THAT'S ALL.
I'LL GO WITH YOU.
REALLY...?
ARE YOU SURE?

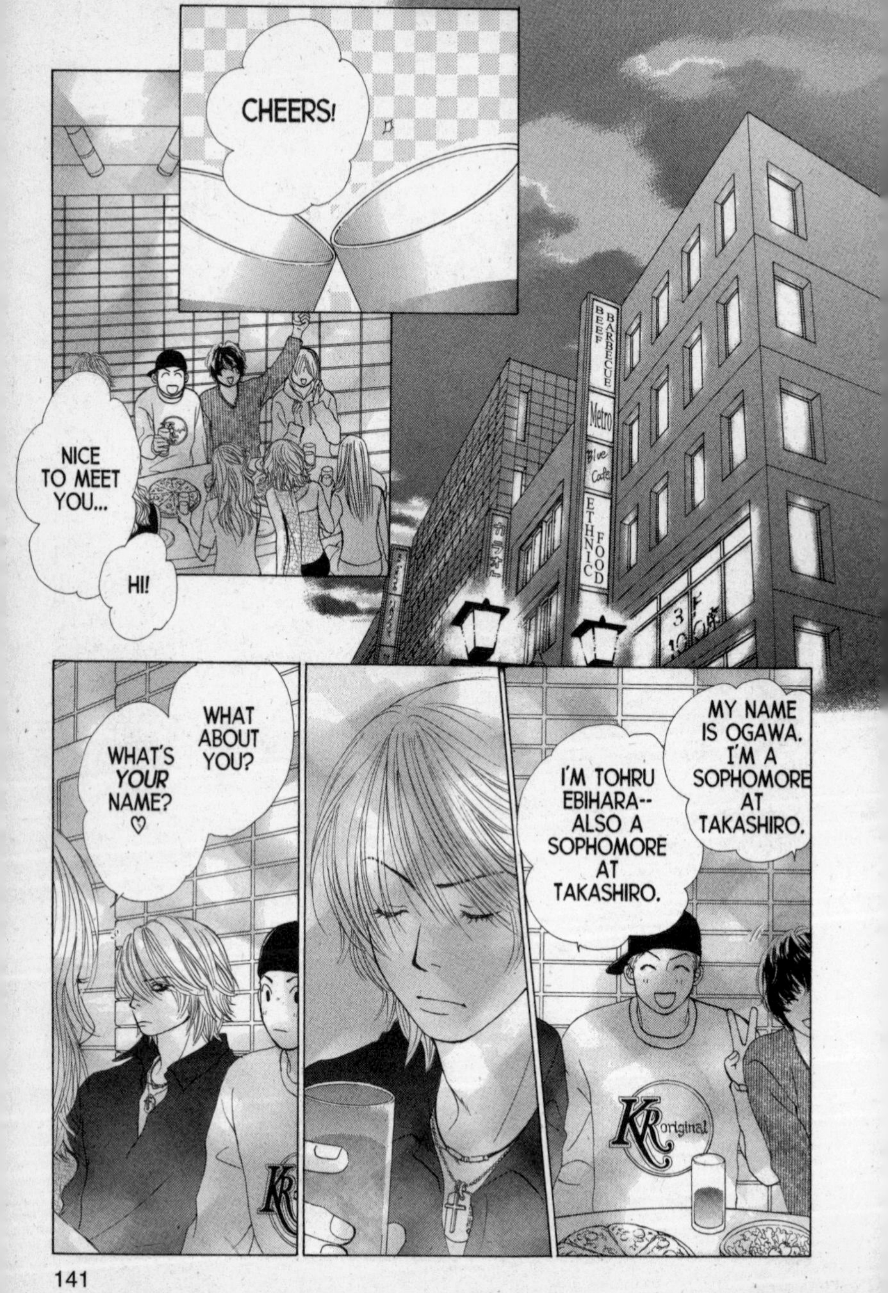
BEEF BARBECUE
Metro
Blue Cafe
ETHNIC FOOD
CHEERS!
NICE TO MEET YOU...
HI!
MY NAME IS OGAWA. I'M A SOPHOMORE AT TAKASHIRO.
I'M TOHRU EBIHARA-- ALSO A SOPHOMORE AT TAKASHIRO.
KR original
WHAT ABOUT YOU?
WHAT'S *YOUR* NAME? ♡

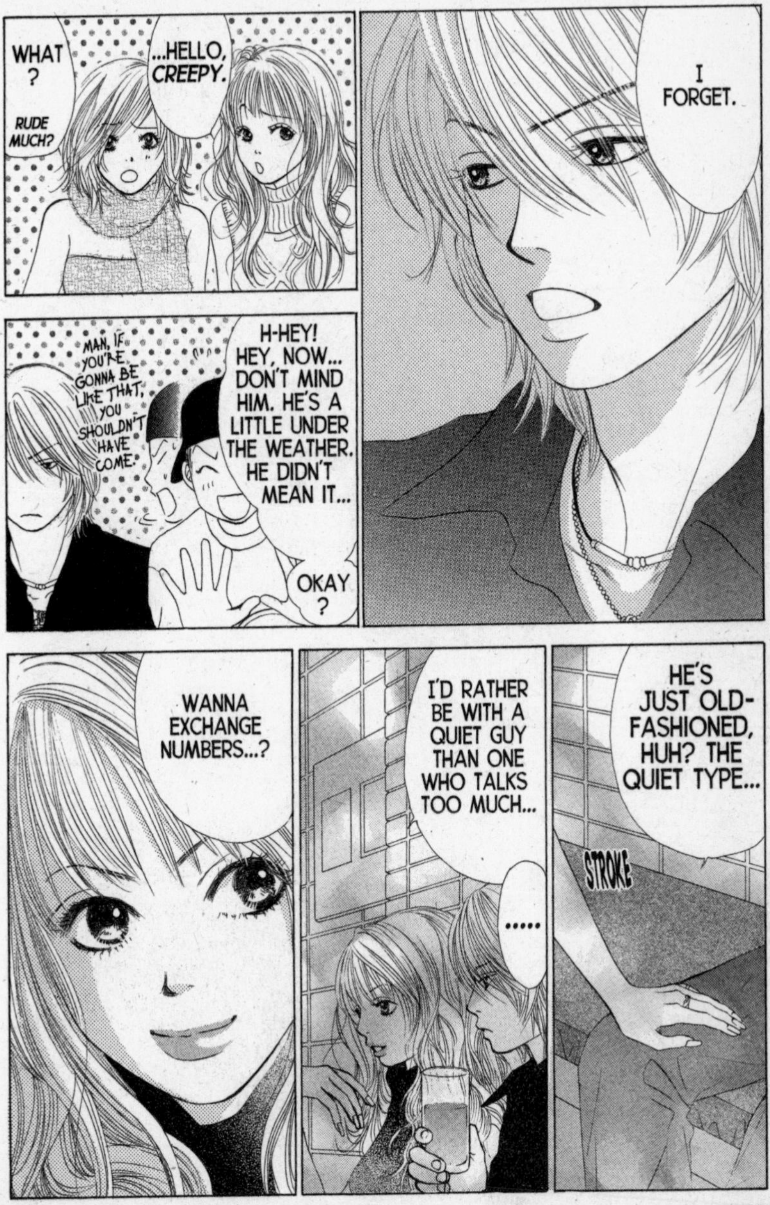
I FORGET.
...HELLO, CREEPY.
WHAT?
RUDE MUCH?
H-HEY! HEY, NOW... DON'T MIND HIM. HE'S A LITTLE UNDER THE WEATHER. HE DIDN'T MEAN IT...
MAN, IF YOU'RE GONNA BE LIKE THAT, YOU SHOULDN'T HAVE COME.
OKAY?
HE'S JUST OLD-FASHIONED, HUH? THE QUIET TYPE...
STROKE
I'D RATHER BE WITH A QUIET GUY THAN ONE WHO TALKS TOO MUCH...
.....
WANNA EXCHANGE NUMBERS...?

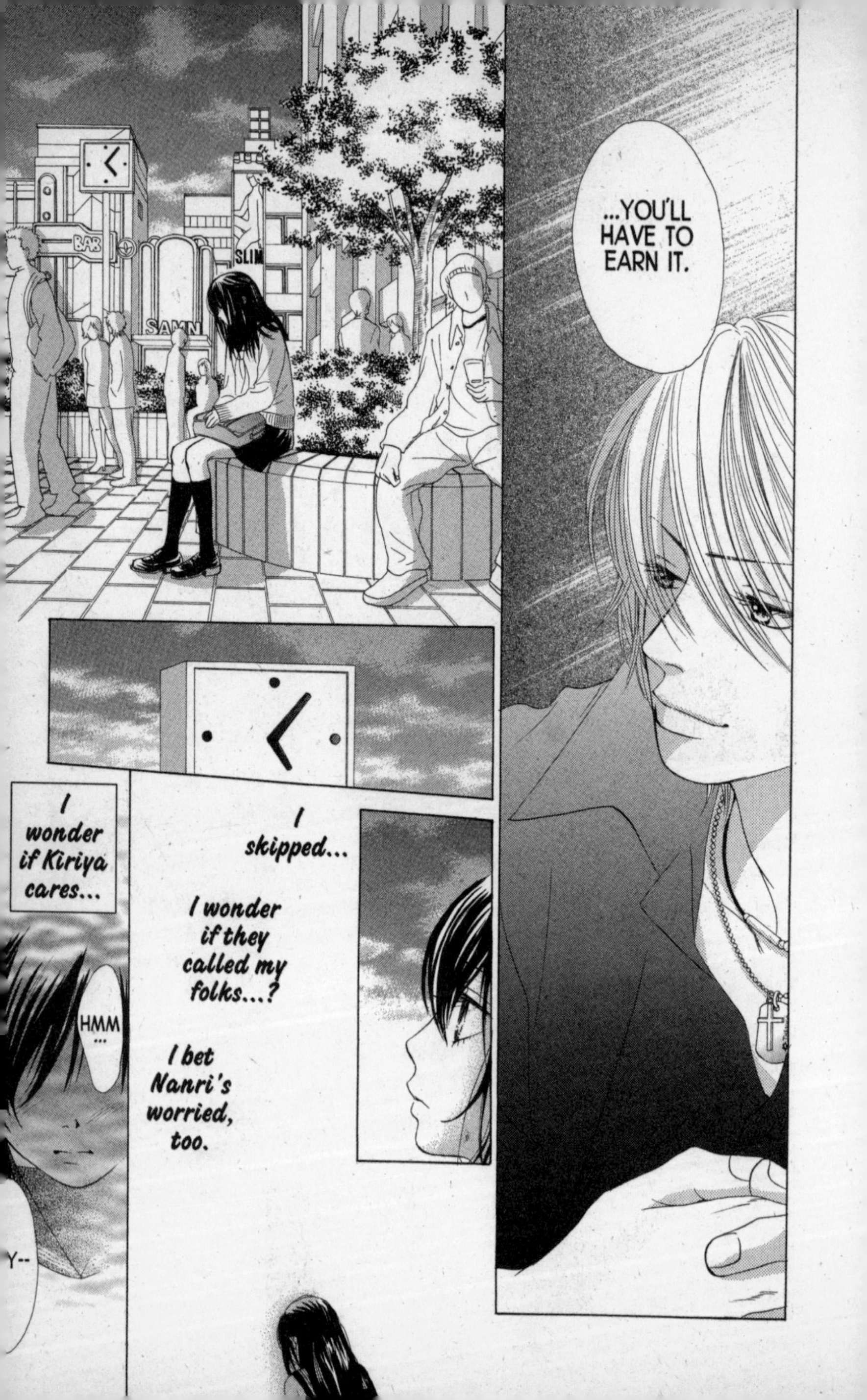
...YOU'LL HAVE TO EARN IT.
I skipped...
I wonder if they called my folks...?
I bet Nanri's worried, too.
I wonder if Kiriya cares...
HMM...
Y--

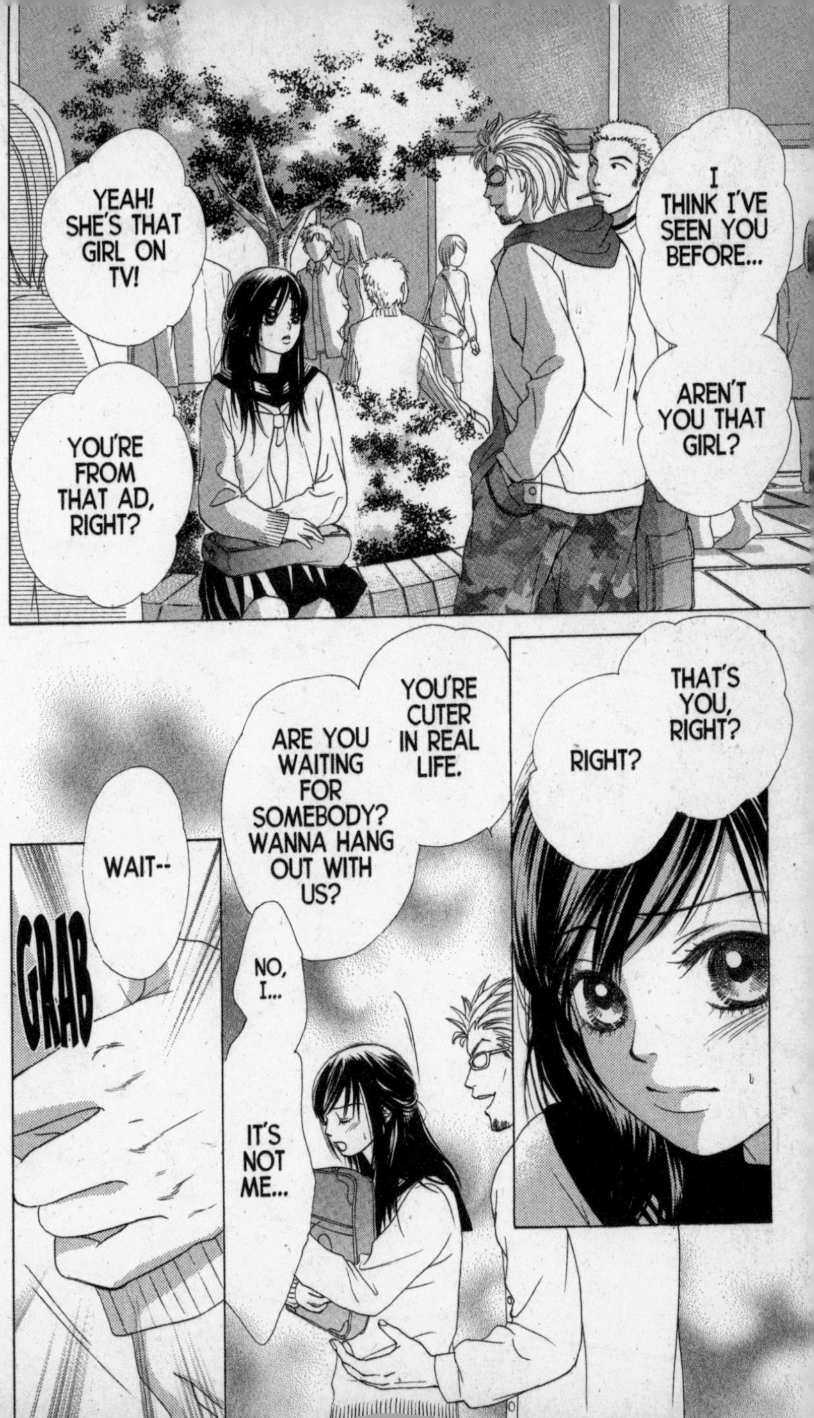
I THINK I'VE SEEN YOU BEFORE...
AREN'T YOU THAT GIRL?
YEAH! SHE'S THAT GIRL ON TV!
YOU'RE FROM THAT AD, RIGHT?
THAT'S YOU, RIGHT?
RIGHT?
YOU'RE CUTER IN REAL LIFE.
ARE YOU WAITING FOR SOMEBODY? WANNA HANG OUT WITH US?
NO, I...
IT'S NOT ME...
WAIT--
GRAB

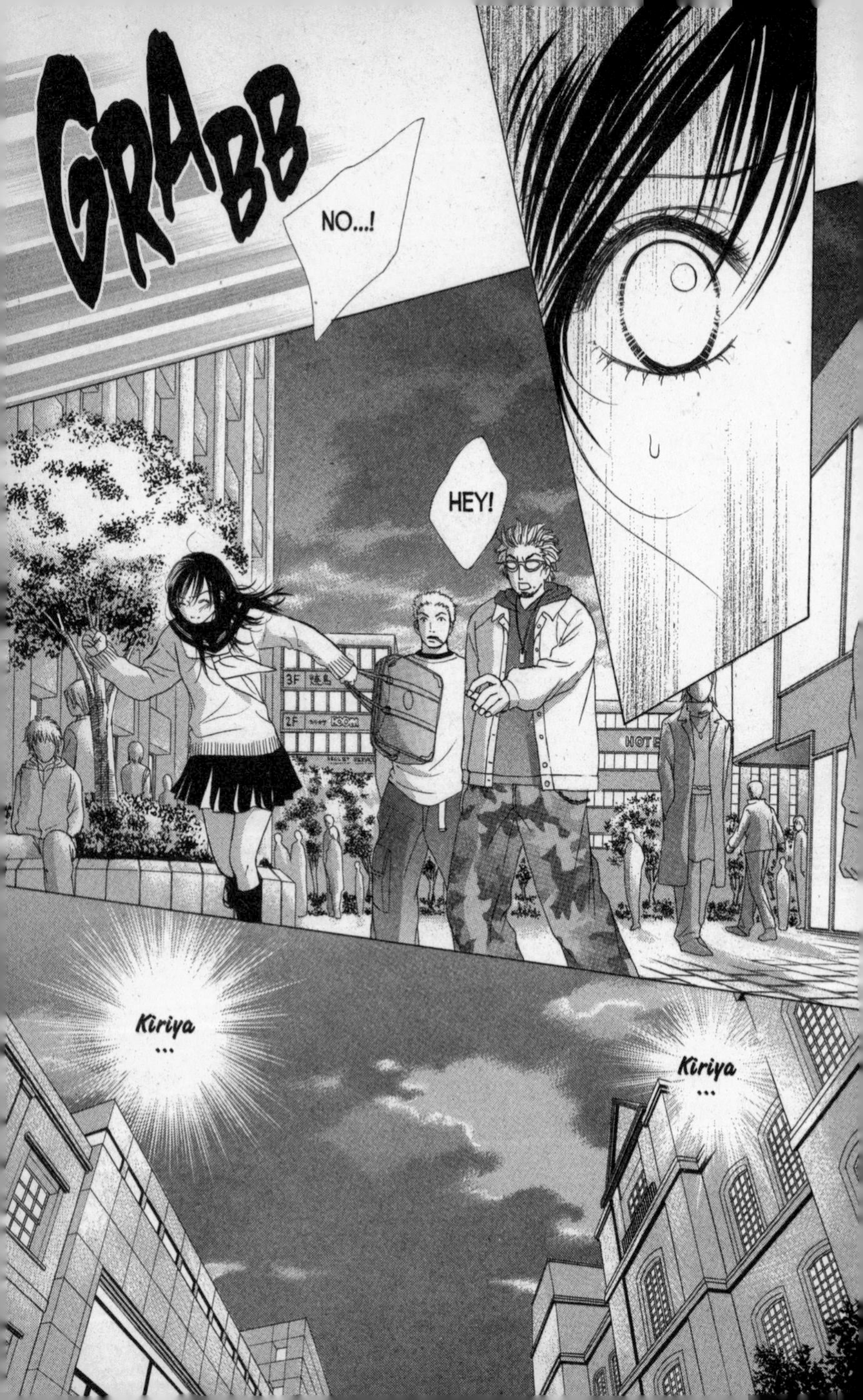
NO...!
GRABB
HEY!
Kiriya
...
Kiriya
...

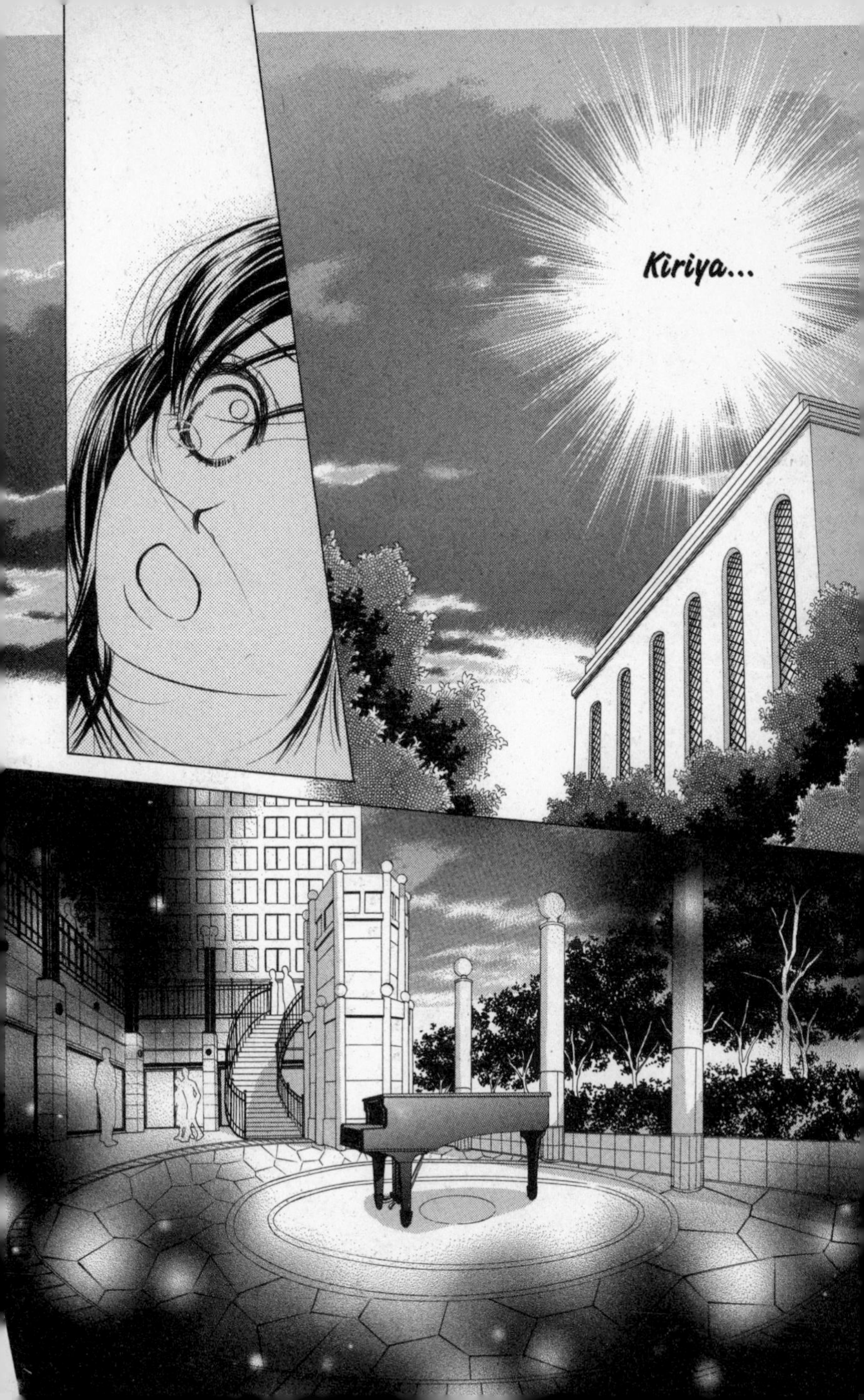
Kiriya...

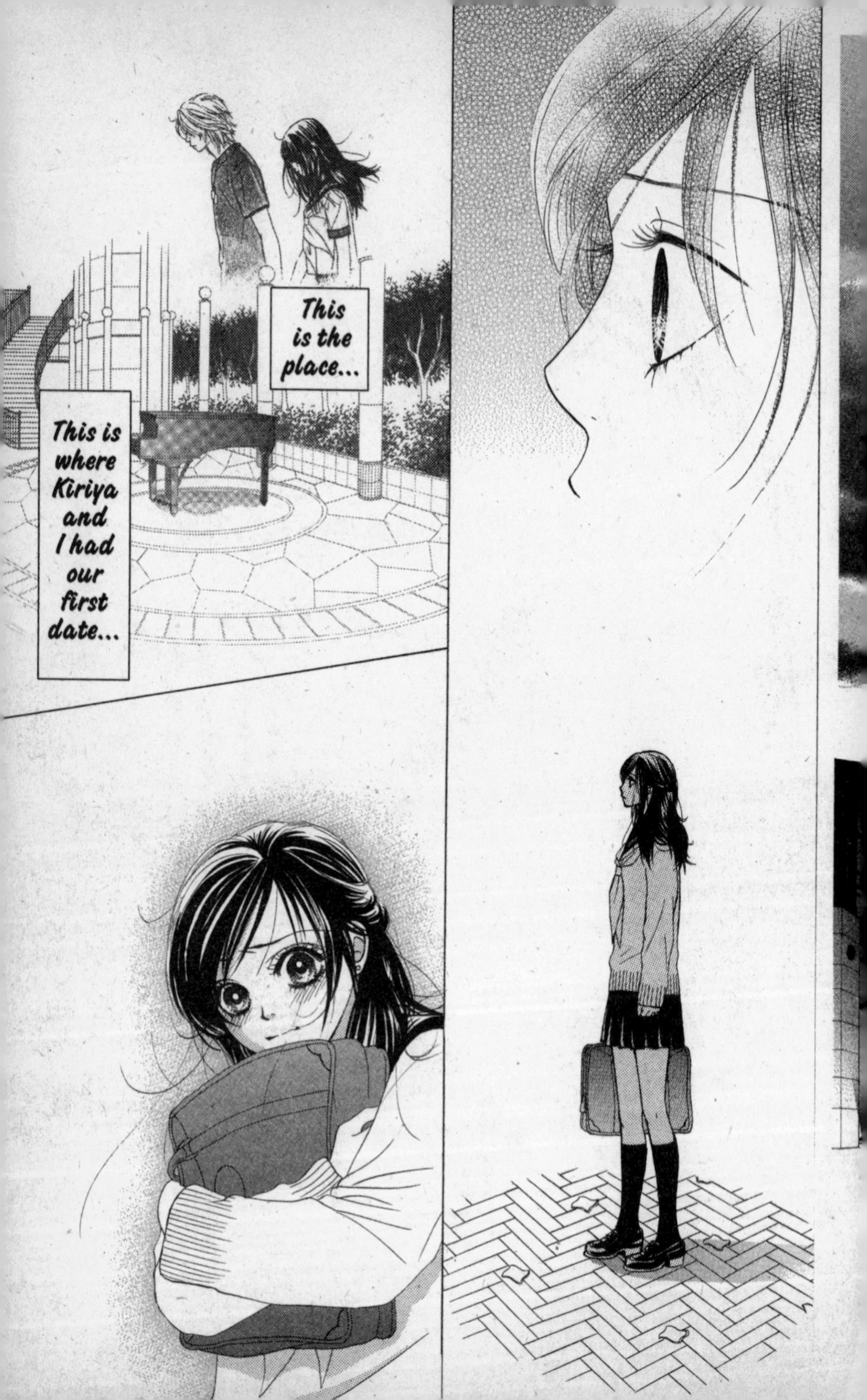
This is the place...
This is where Kiriya and I had our first date...

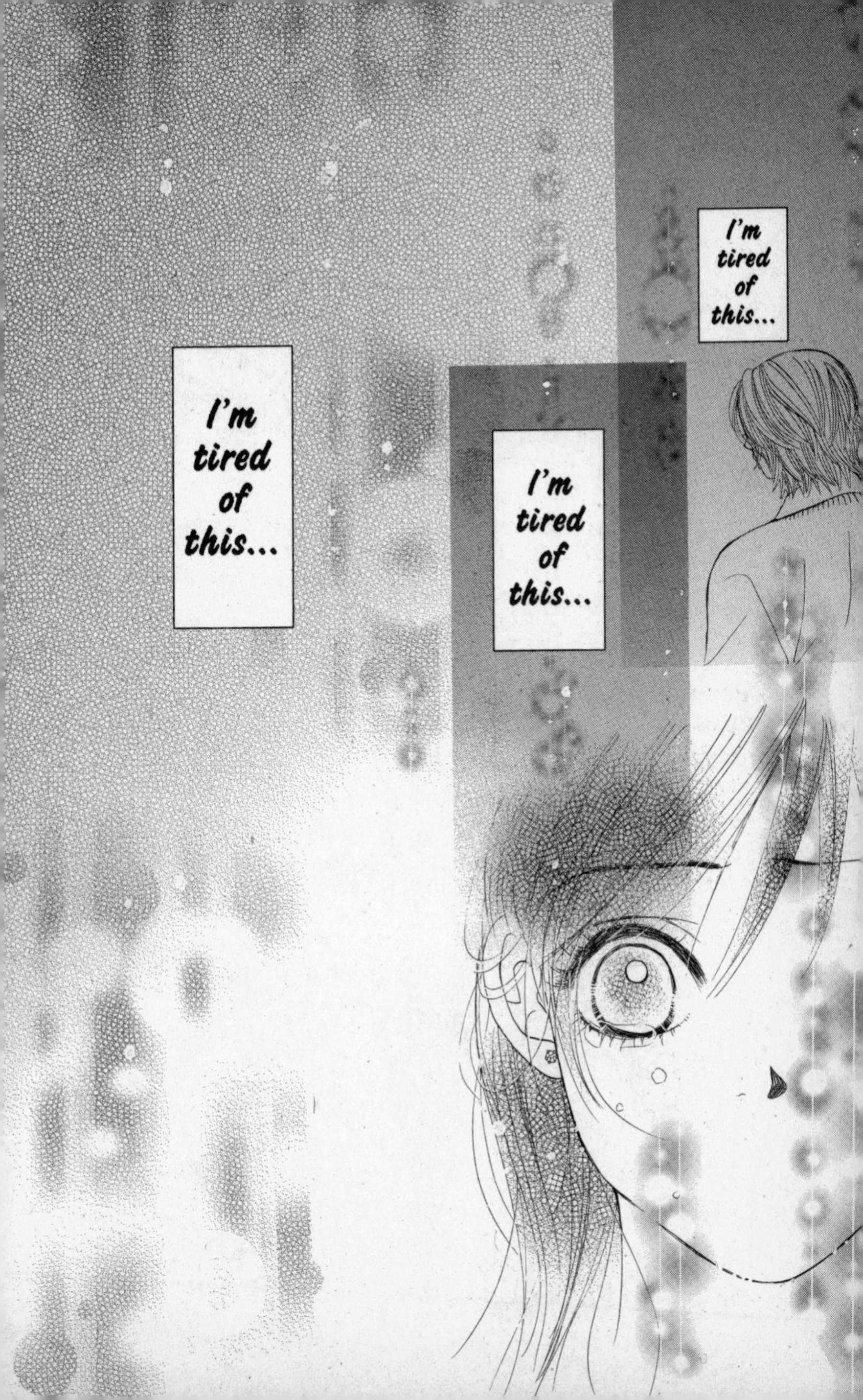
I'm tired of this...
I'm tired of this...
I'm tired of this...

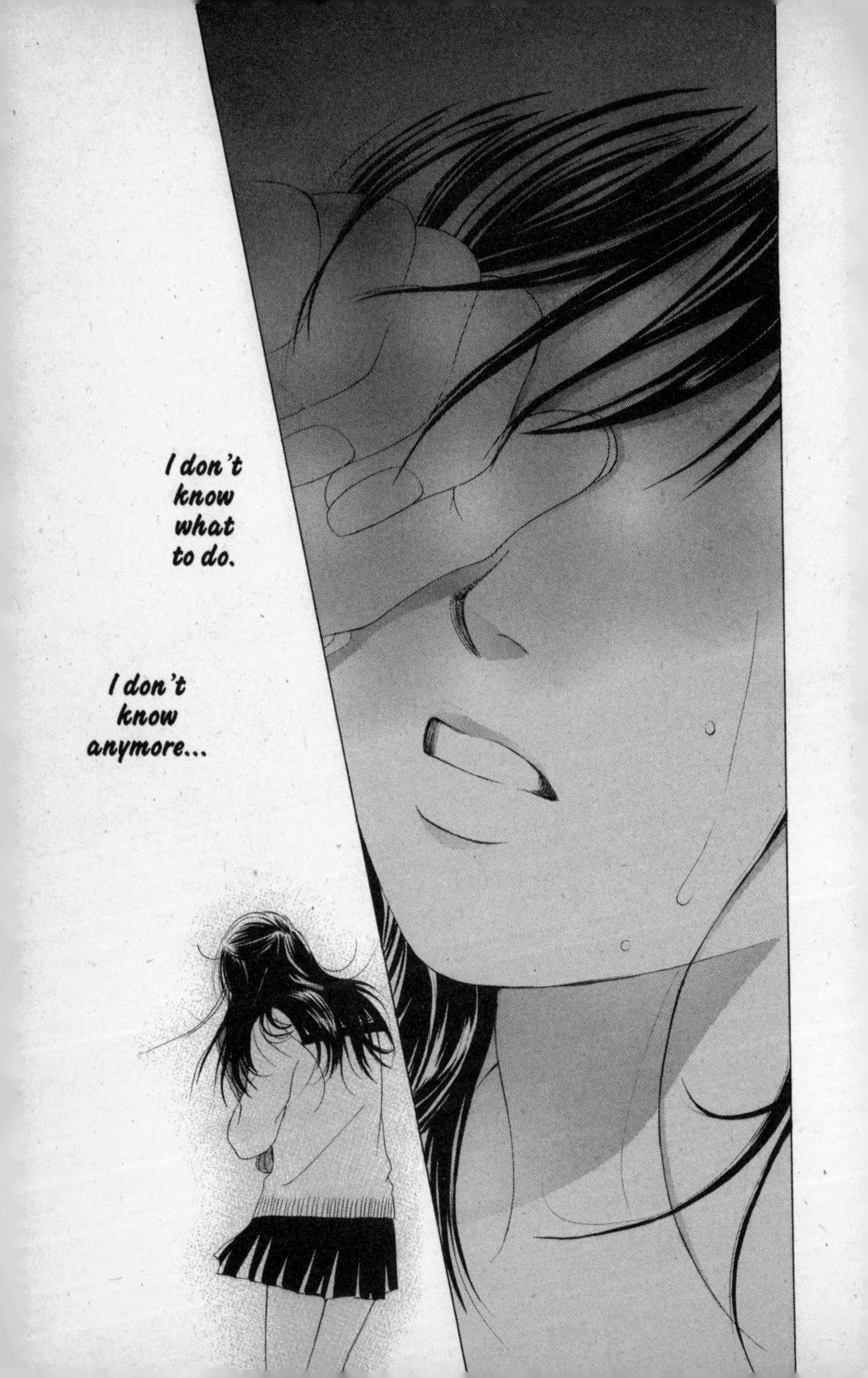
I don't know what to do.
I don't know anymore...

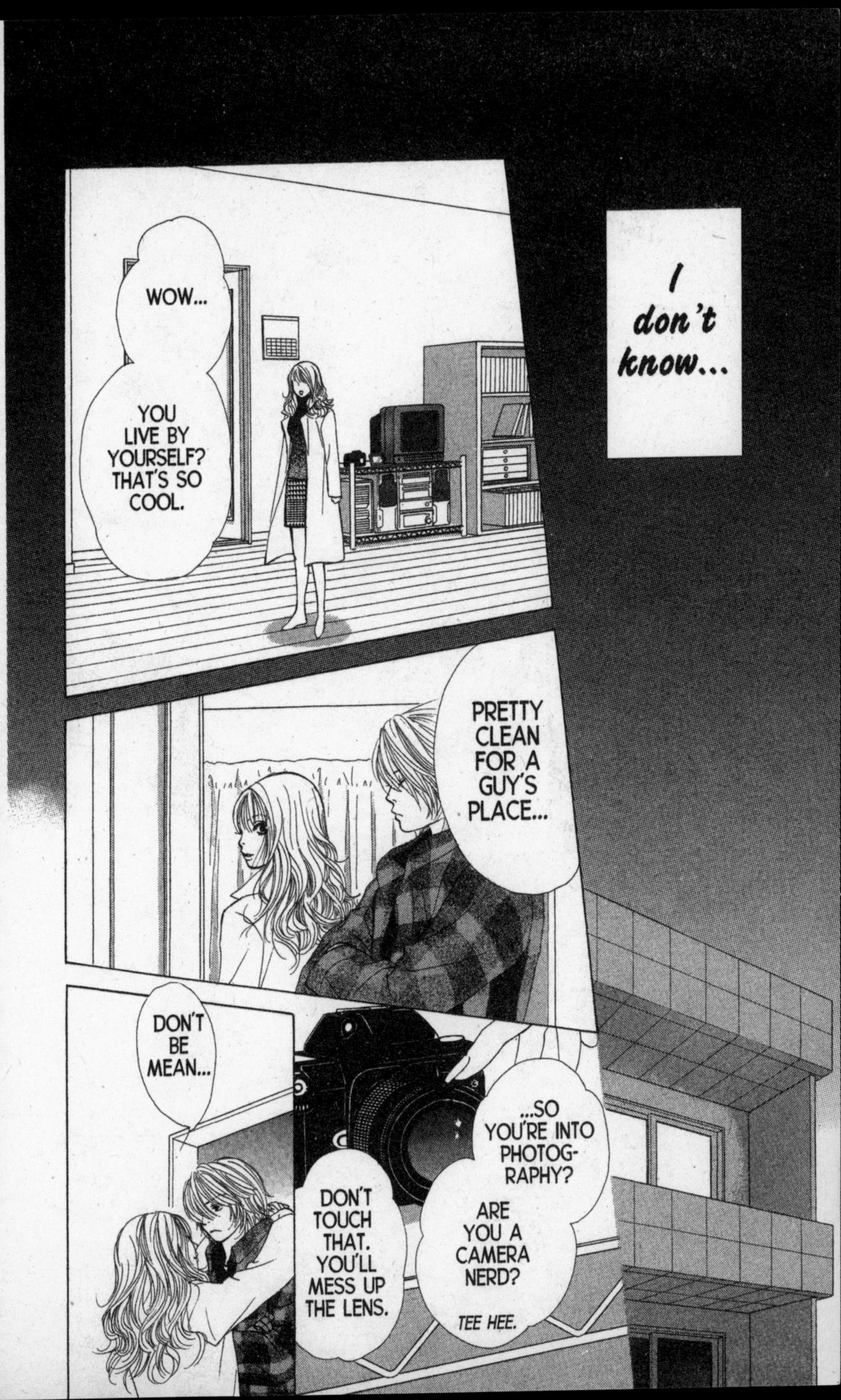
I don't know...
WOW...
YOU LIVE BY YOURSELF? THAT'S SO COOL.
PRETTY CLEAN FOR A GUY'S PLACE...
...SO YOU'RE INTO PHOTOG-RAPHY?
ARE YOU A CAMERA NERD?
TEE HEE.
DON'T TOUCH THAT. YOU'LL MESS UP THE LENS.
DON'T BE MEAN...

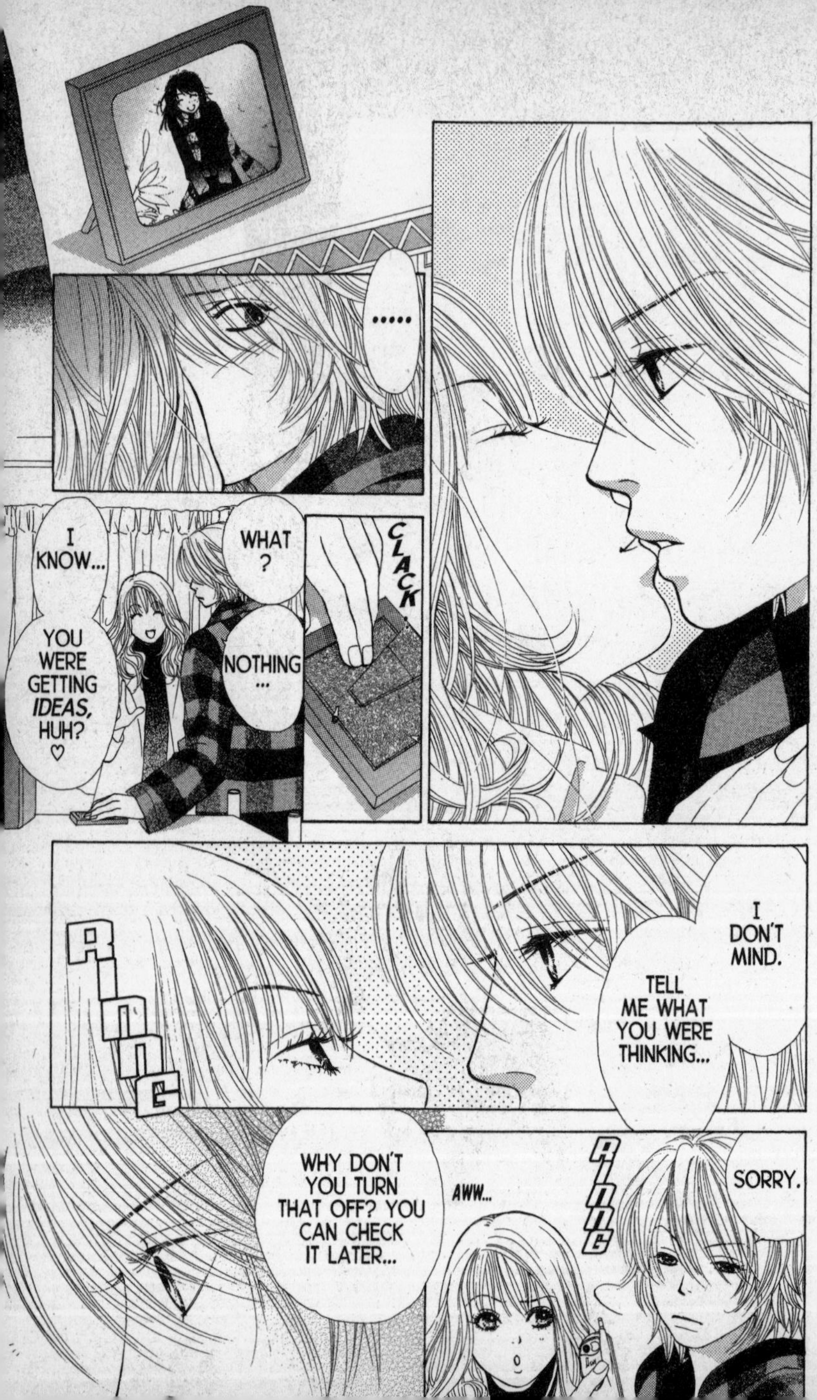

.....
CLACK
WHAT?
I KNOW...
NOTHING...
YOU WERE GETTING *IDEAS,* HUH? ♡
I DON'T MIND.
TELL ME WHAT YOU WERE THINKING...
RING
SORRY.
RING
AWW...
WHY DON'T YOU TURN THAT OFF? YOU CAN CHECK IT LATER...

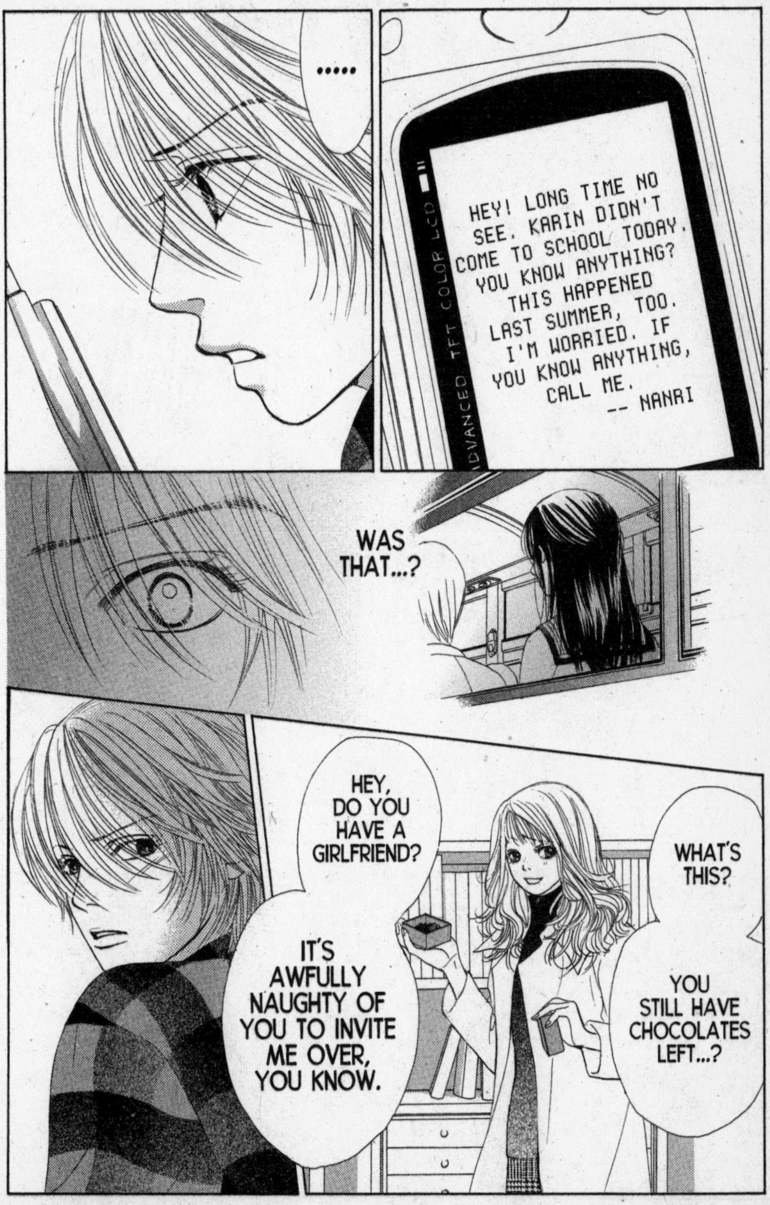
HEY! LONG TIME NO SEE. KARIN DIDN'T COME TO SCHOOL TODAY. YOU KNOW ANYTHING? THIS HAPPENED LAST SUMMER, TOO. I'M WORRIED. IF YOU KNOW ANYTHING, CALL ME. -- NANRI
ADVANCED TFT COLOR LCD
......
WAS THAT...?
WHAT'S THIS?
YOU STILL HAVE CHOCOLATES LEFT...?
HEY, DO YOU HAVE A GIRLFRIEND?
IT'S AWFULLY NAUGHTY OF YOU TO INVITE ME OVER, YOU KNOW.

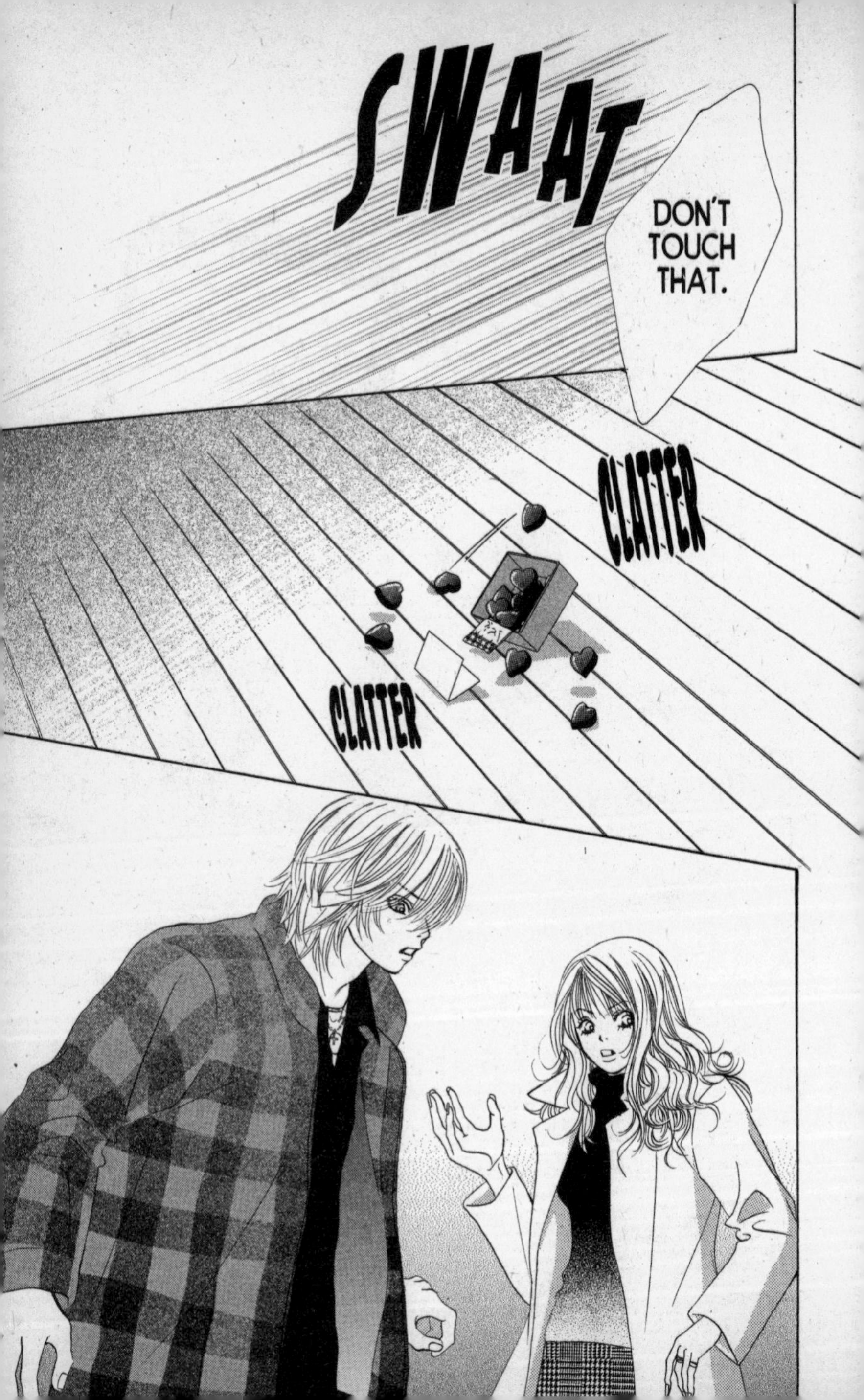
SWAAT
DON'T TOUCH THAT.
CLATTER
CLATTER

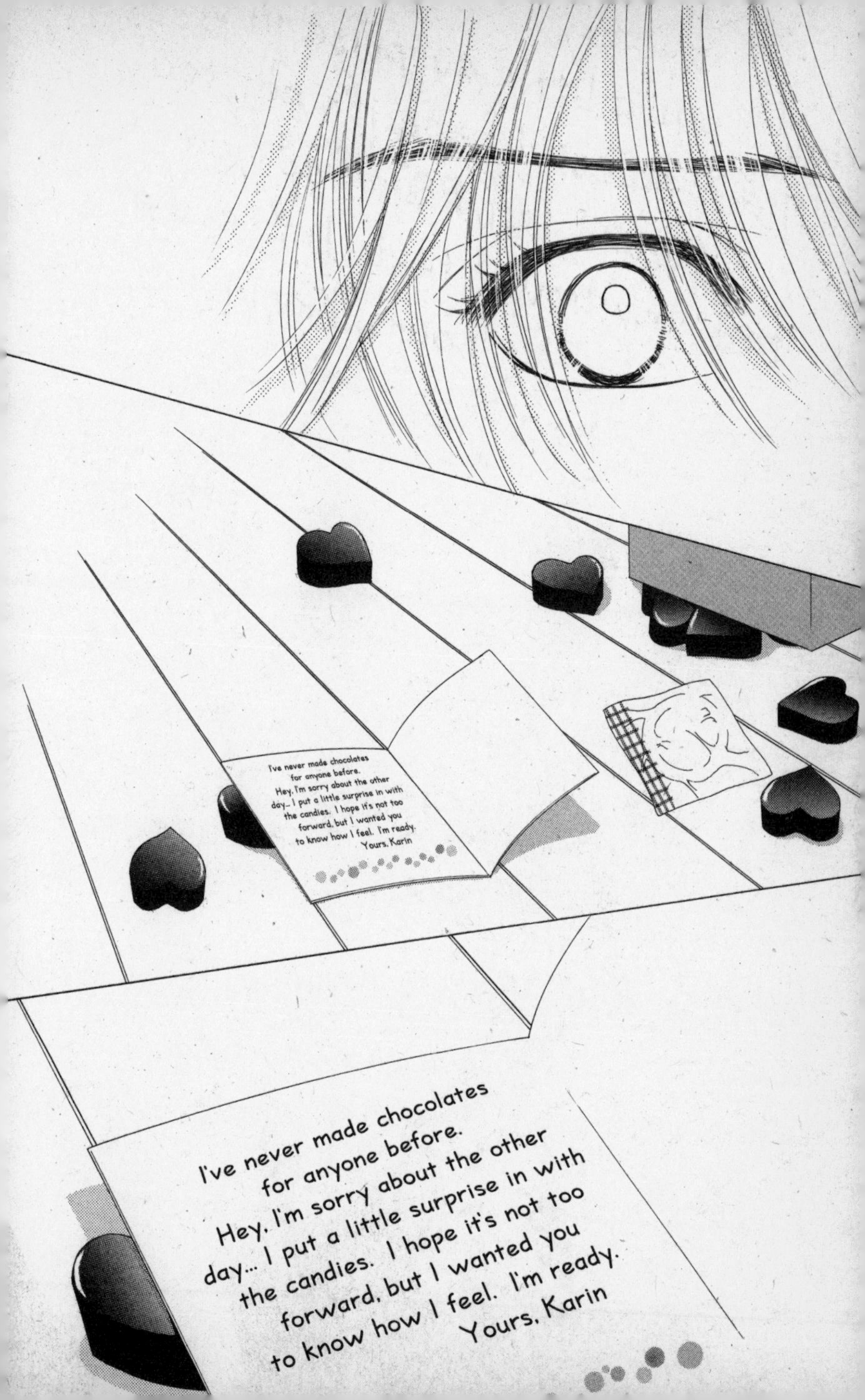
I've never made chocolates
for anyone before.
Hey, I'm sorry about the other
day... I put a little surprise in with
the candies. I hope it's not too
forward, but I wanted you
to know how I feel. I'm ready.
Yours, Karin
I've never made chocolates
for anyone before.
Hey, I'm sorry about the other
day... I put a little surprise in with
the candies. I hope it's not too
forward, but I wanted you
to know how I feel. I'm ready.
Yours, Karin

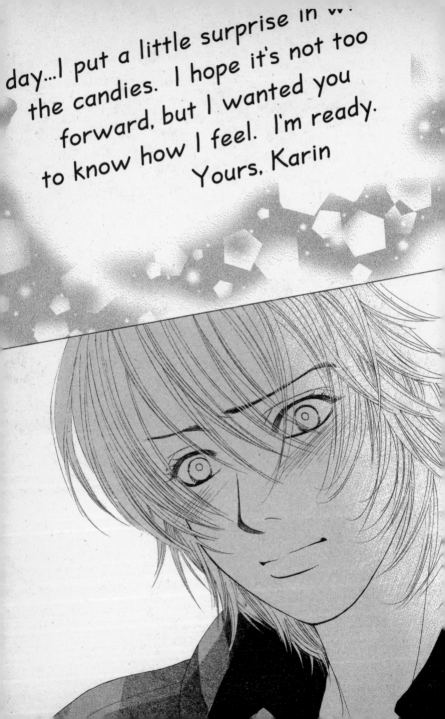

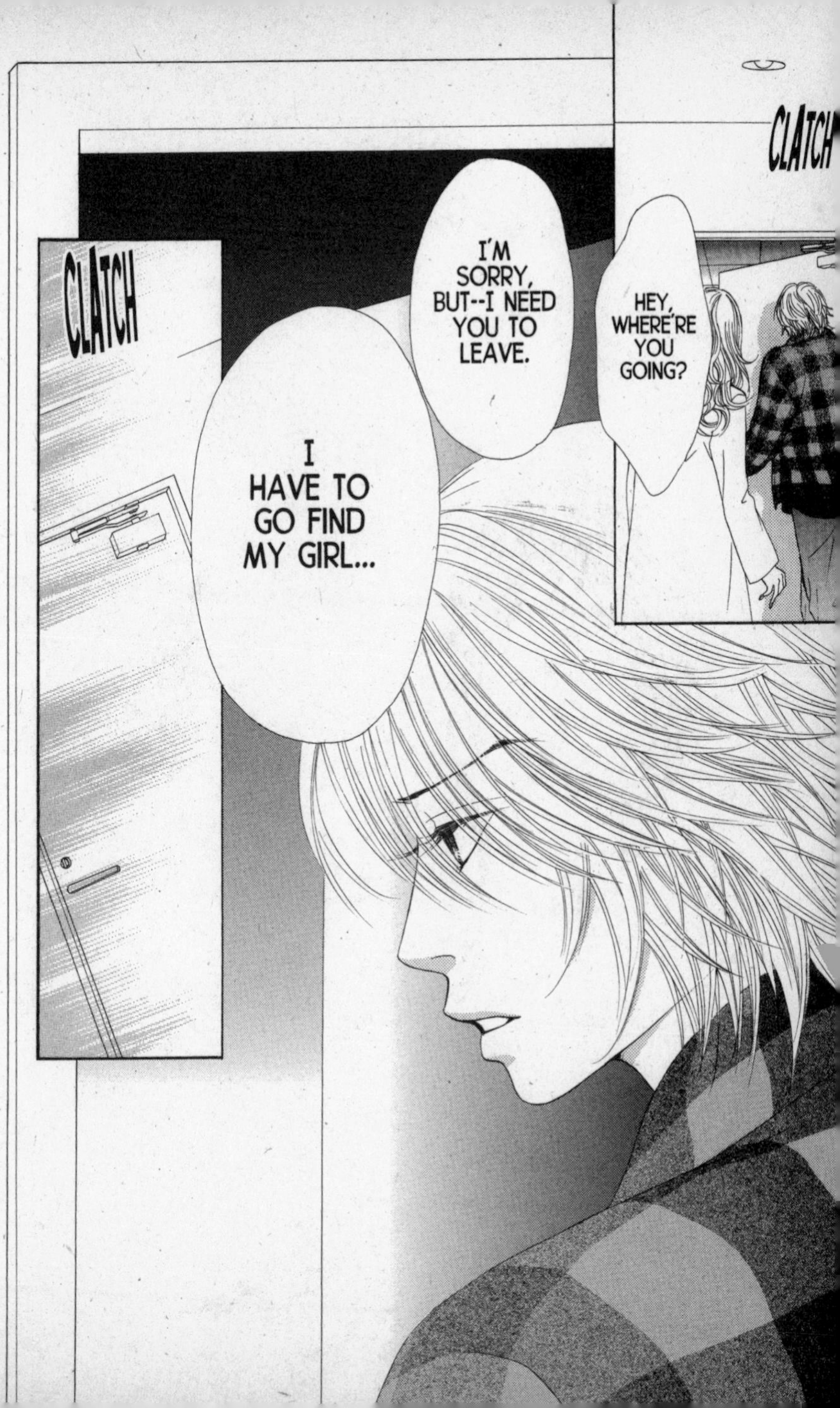
CLATCH
HEY, WHERE'RE YOU GOING?
I'M SORRY, BUT--I NEED YOU TO LEAVE.
I HAVE TO GO FIND MY GIRL...
CLATCH

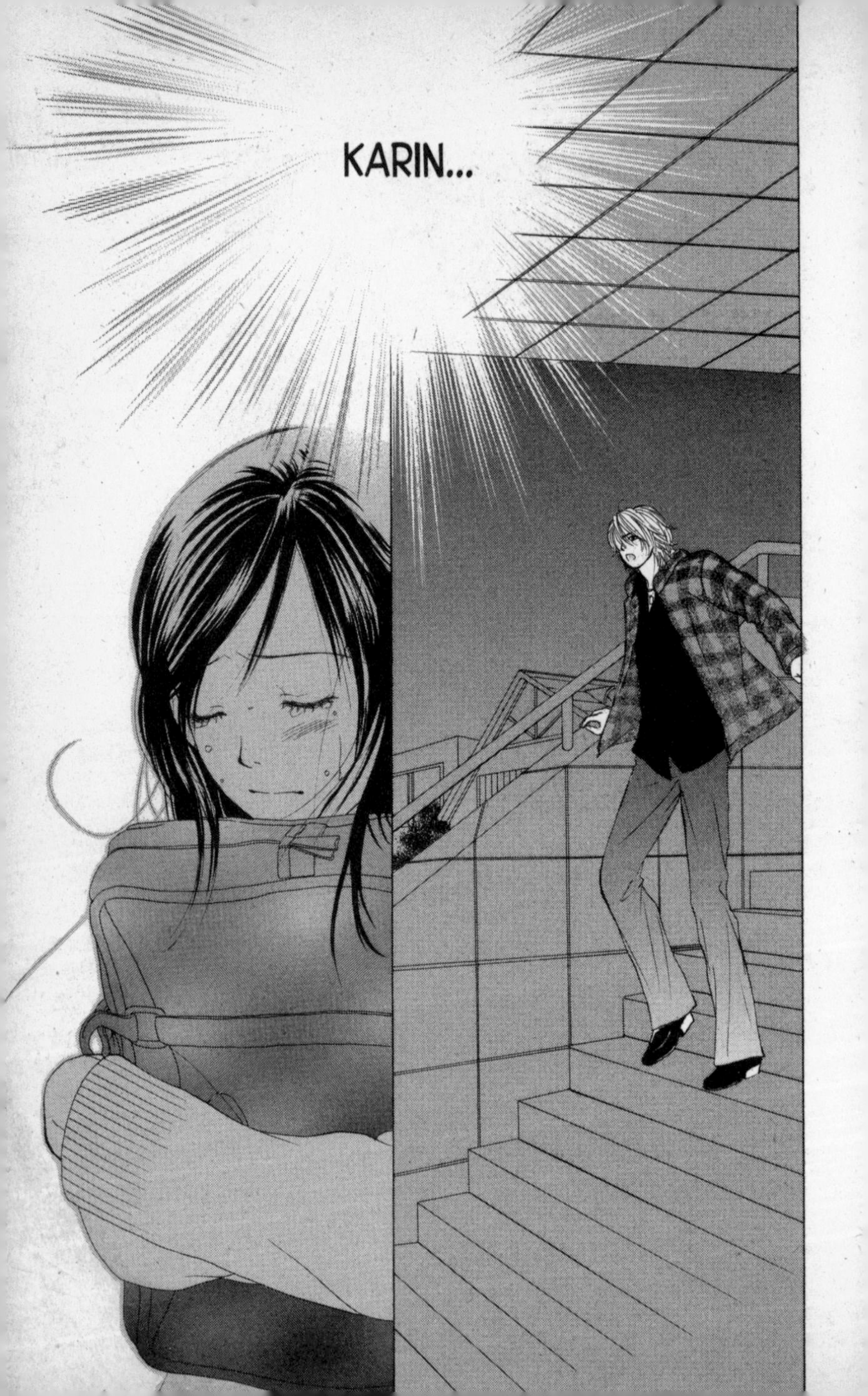
KARIN...

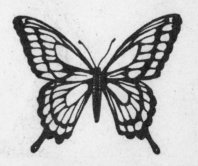

「彼」KARE
First Love

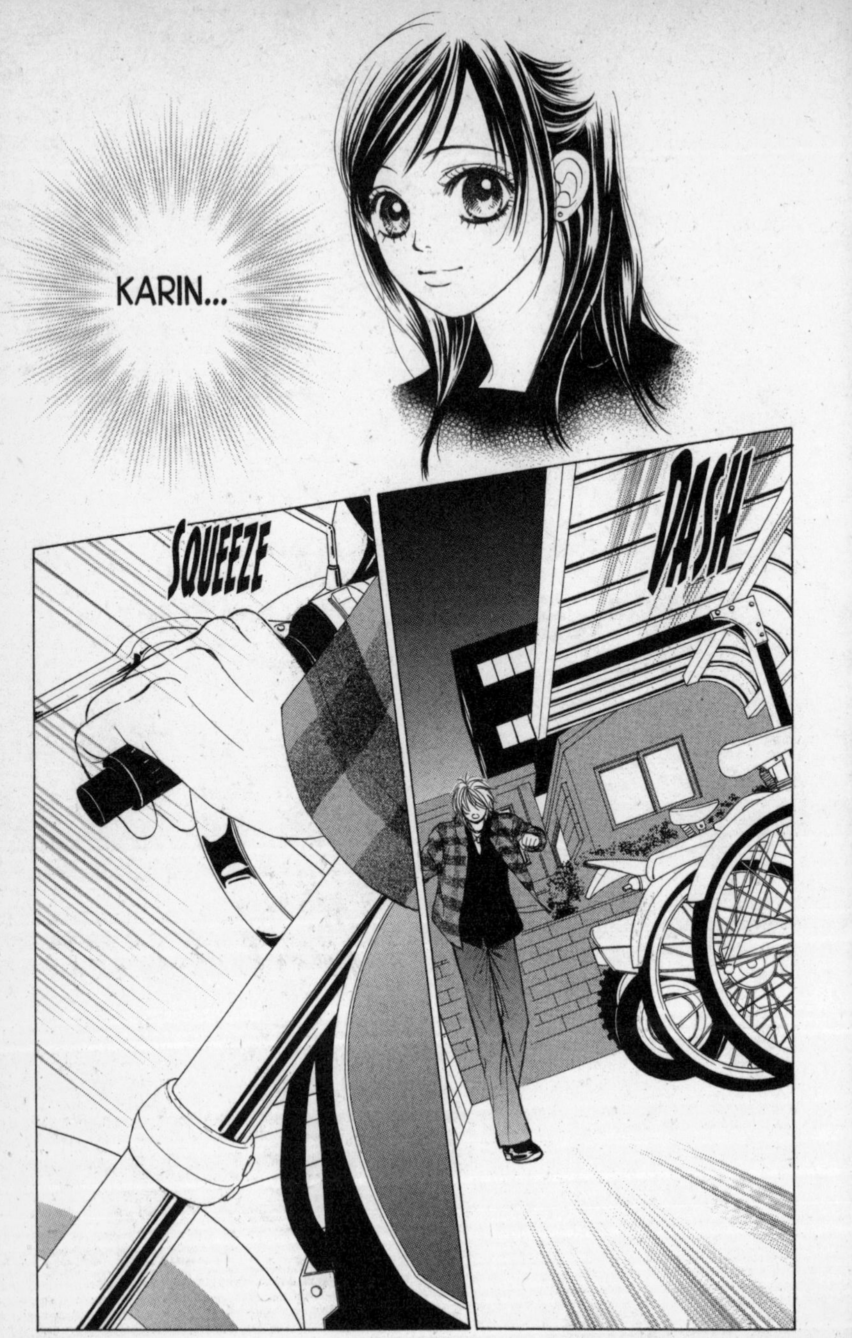
KARIN...
DASH
SQUEEZE

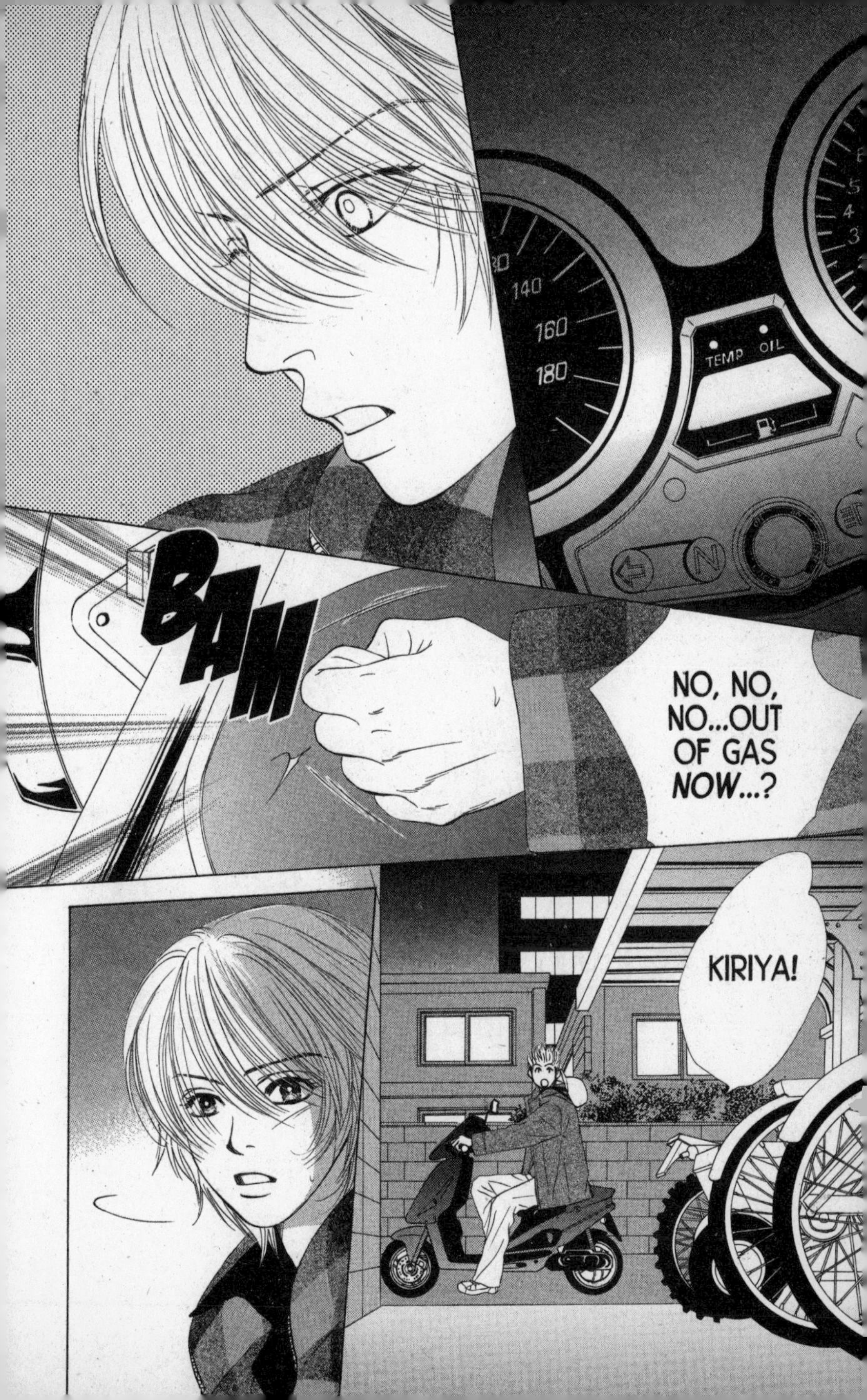
140
160
180
TEMP
OIL
N
BAM
NO, NO, NO...OUT OF GAS *NOW*...?
KIRIYA!

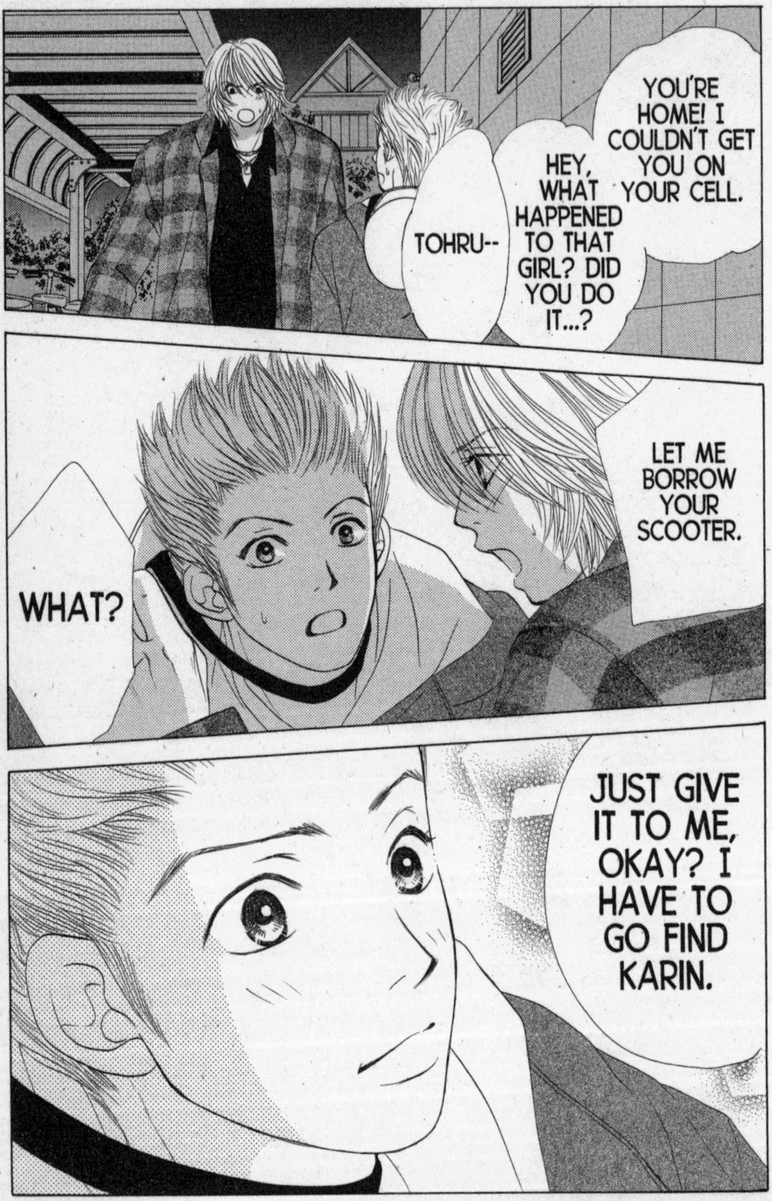
YOU'RE HOME! I COULDN'T GET YOU ON YOUR CELL.
HEY, WHAT HAPPENED TO THAT GIRL? DID YOU DO IT...?
TOHRU--
LET ME BORROW YOUR SCOOTER.
WHAT?
JUST GIVE IT TO ME, OKAY? I HAVE TO GO FIND KARIN.

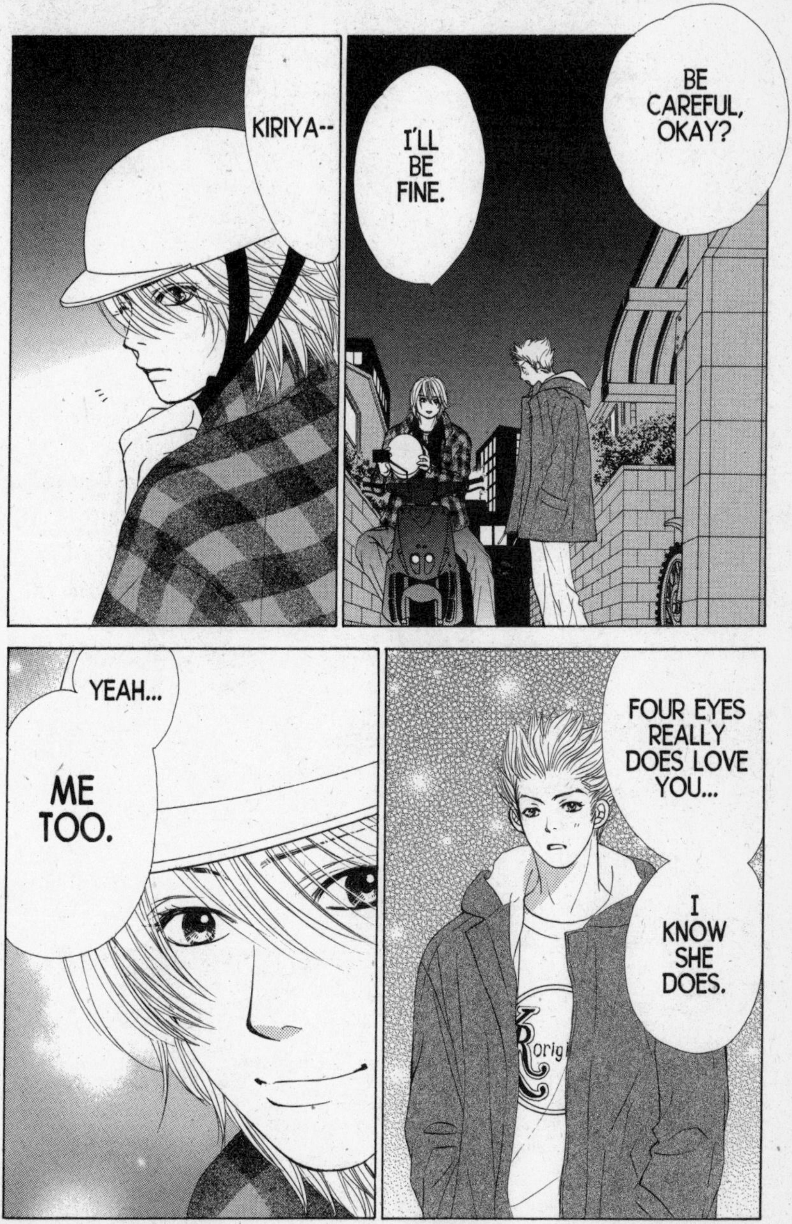
BE CAREFUL, OKAY?
I'LL BE FINE.
KIRIYA--
FOUR EYES REALLY DOES LOVE YOU...
I KNOW SHE DOES.
YEAH...
ME TOO.

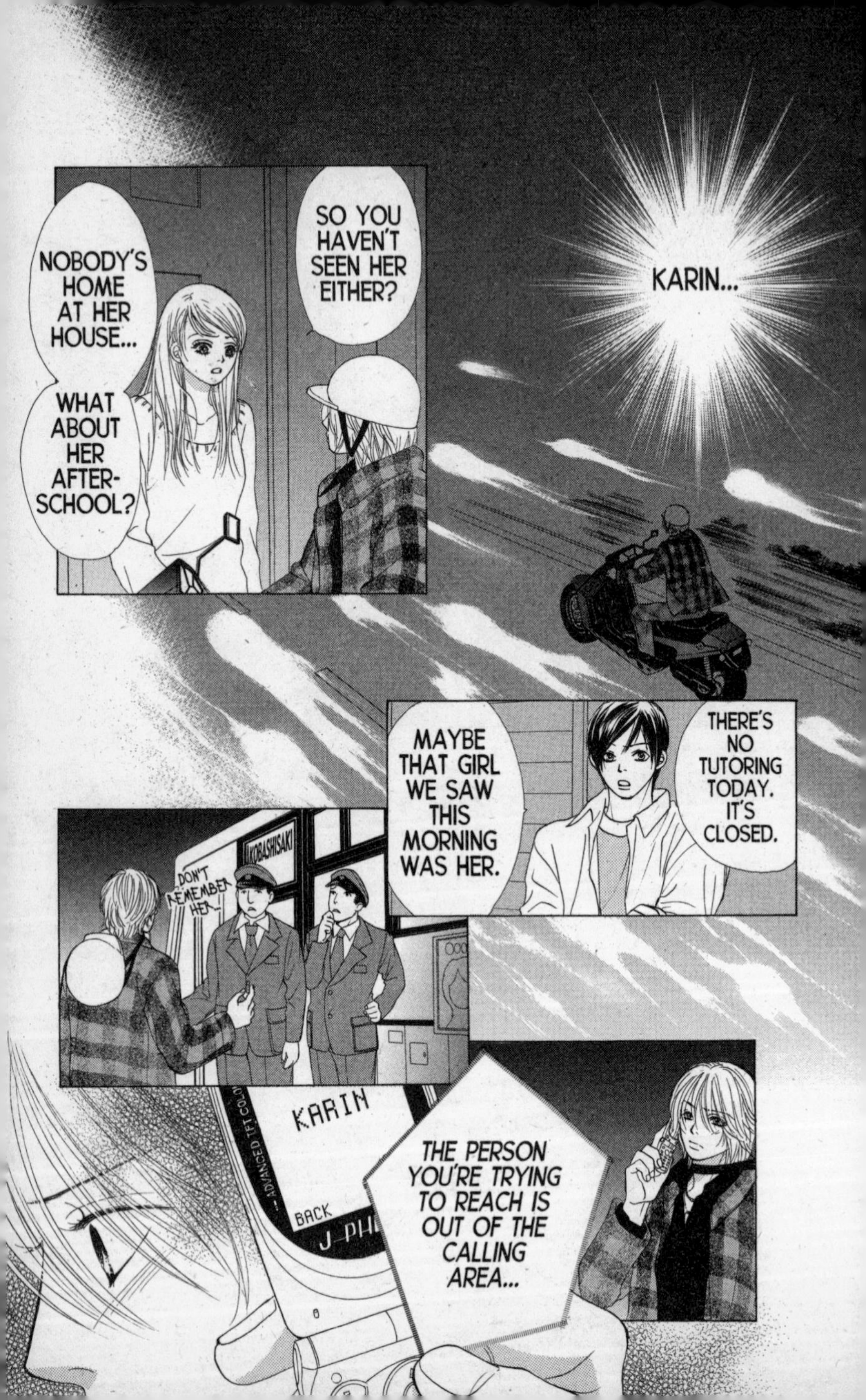
KARIN...
SO YOU HAVEN'T SEEN HER EITHER?
NOBODY'S HOME AT HER HOUSE...
WHAT ABOUT HER AFTER-SCHOOL?
THERE'S NO TUTORING TODAY. IT'S CLOSED.
MAYBE THAT GIRL WE SAW THIS MORNING WAS HER.
KOBASHISAKI
DON'T REMEMBER HER...
KARIN
BACK
THE PERSON YOU'RE TRYING TO REACH IS OUT OF THE CALLING AREA...

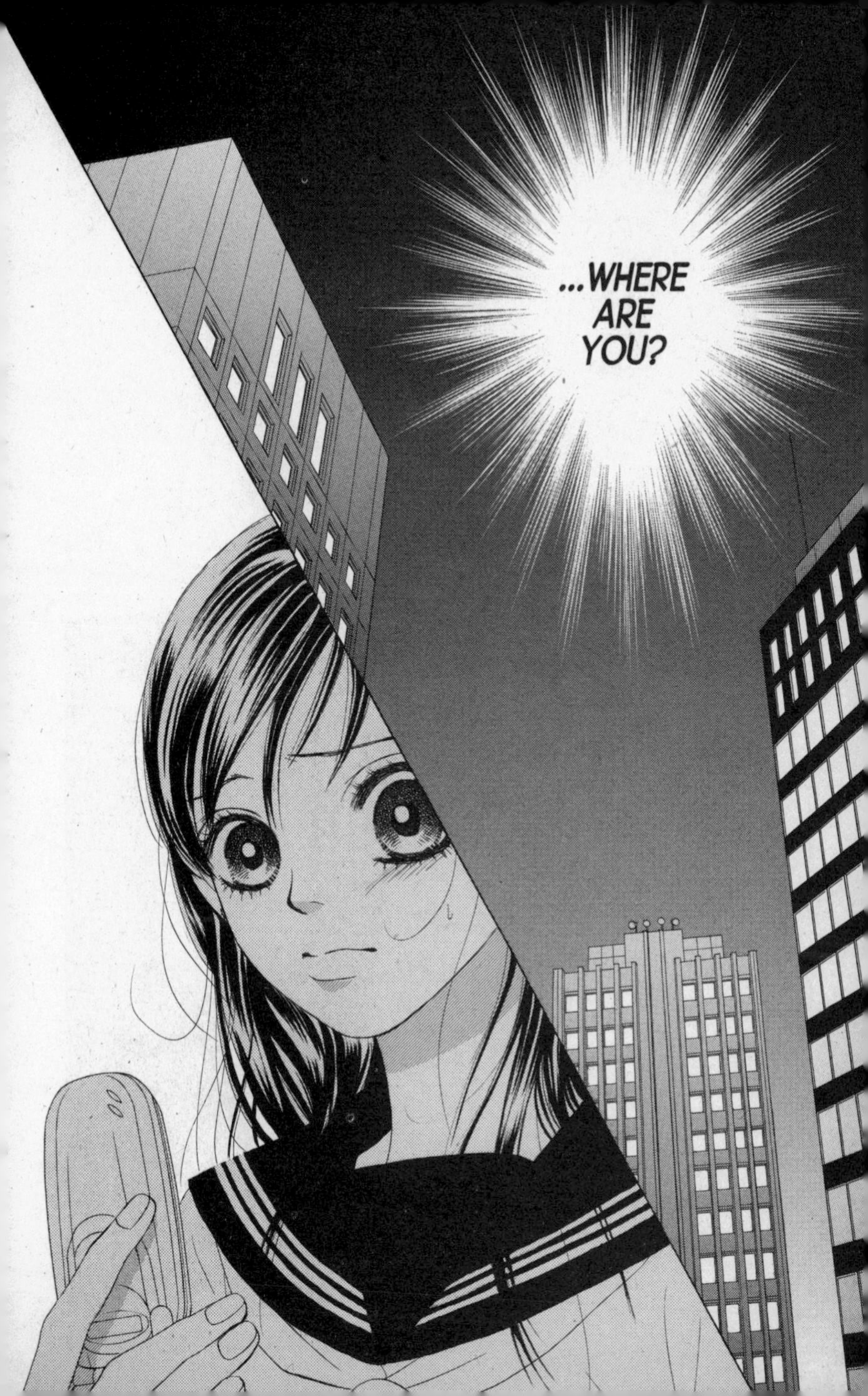
...WHERE ARE YOU?

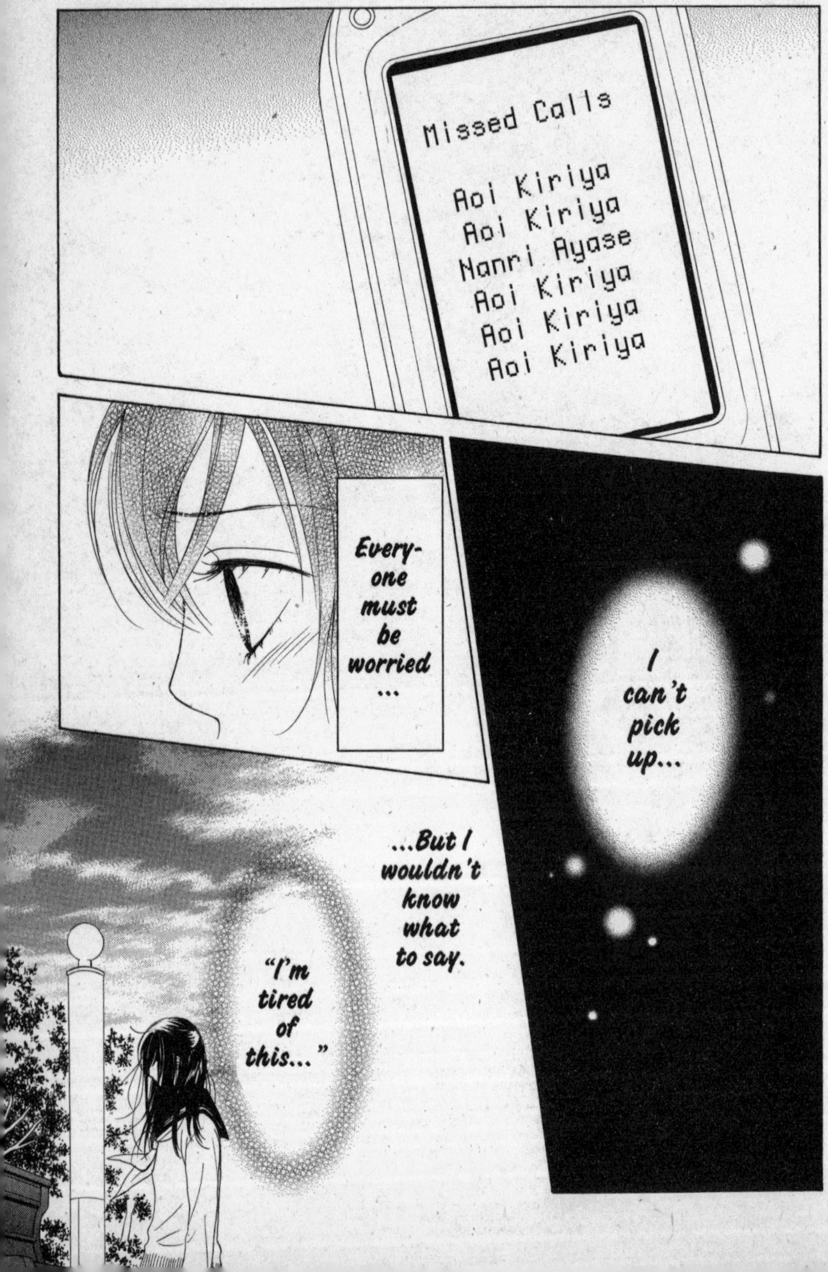
Missed Calls
Aoi Kiriya
Aoi Kiriya
Nanri Ayase
Aoi Kiriya
Aoi Kiriya
Aoi Kiriya
I can't pick up...
Every-one must be worried...
...But I wouldn't know what to say.
"I'm tired of this..."

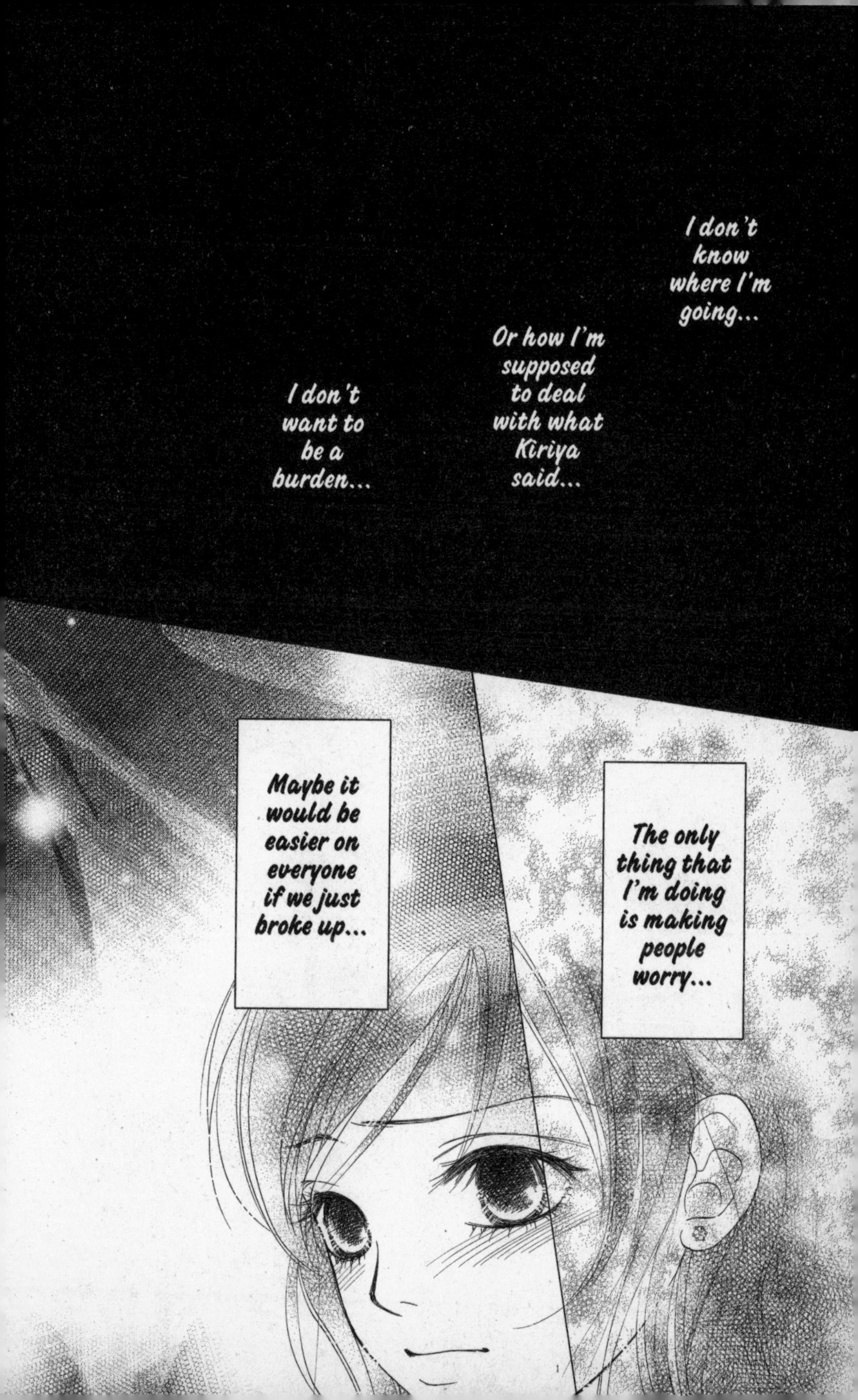
I don't know where I'm going...
Or how I'm supposed to deal with what Kiriya said...
I don't want to be a burden...
The only thing that I'm doing is making people worry...
Maybe it would be easier on everyone if we just broke up...

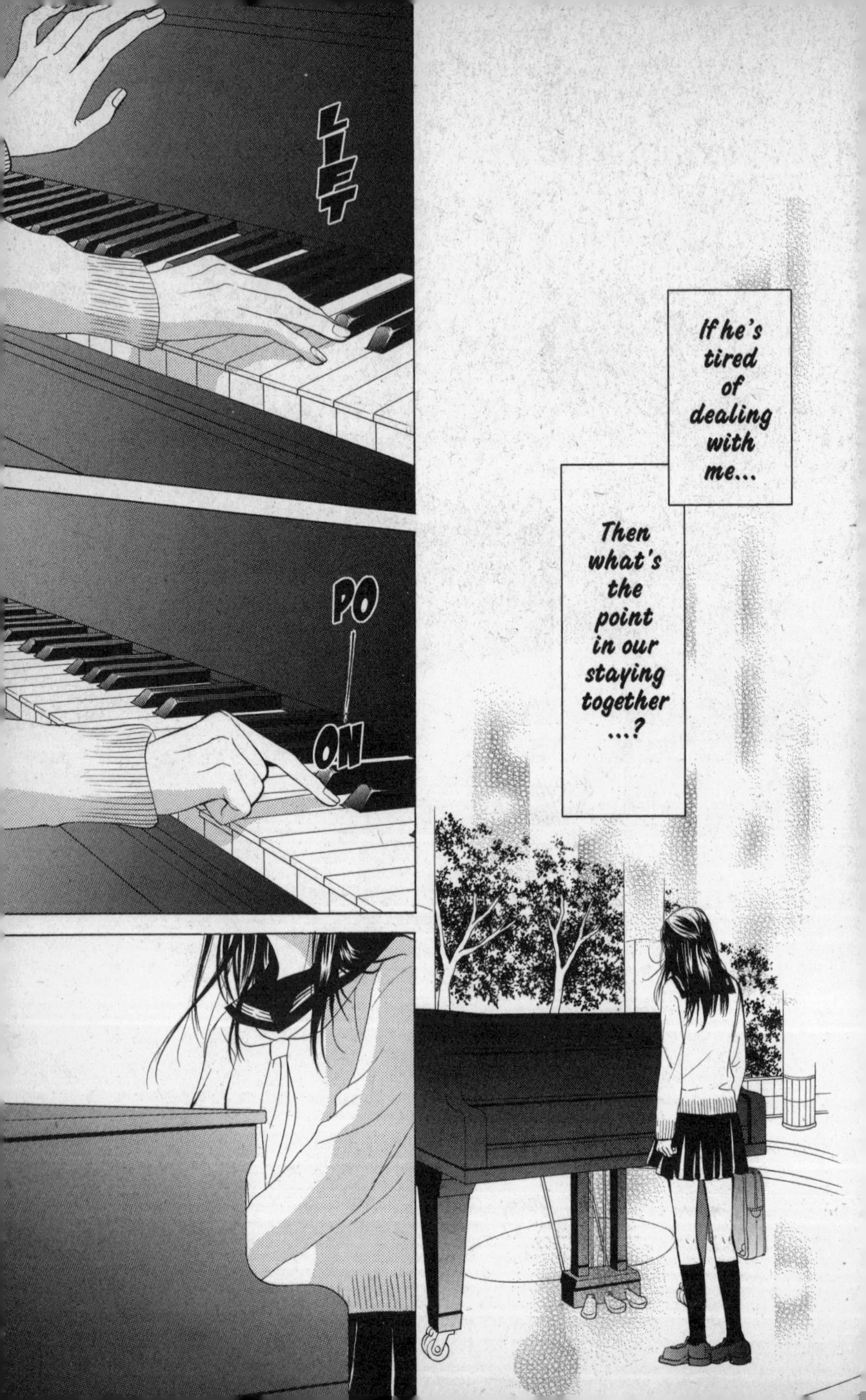
If he's tired of dealing with me...
Then what's the point in our staying together ...?
LIFT
PO-ON

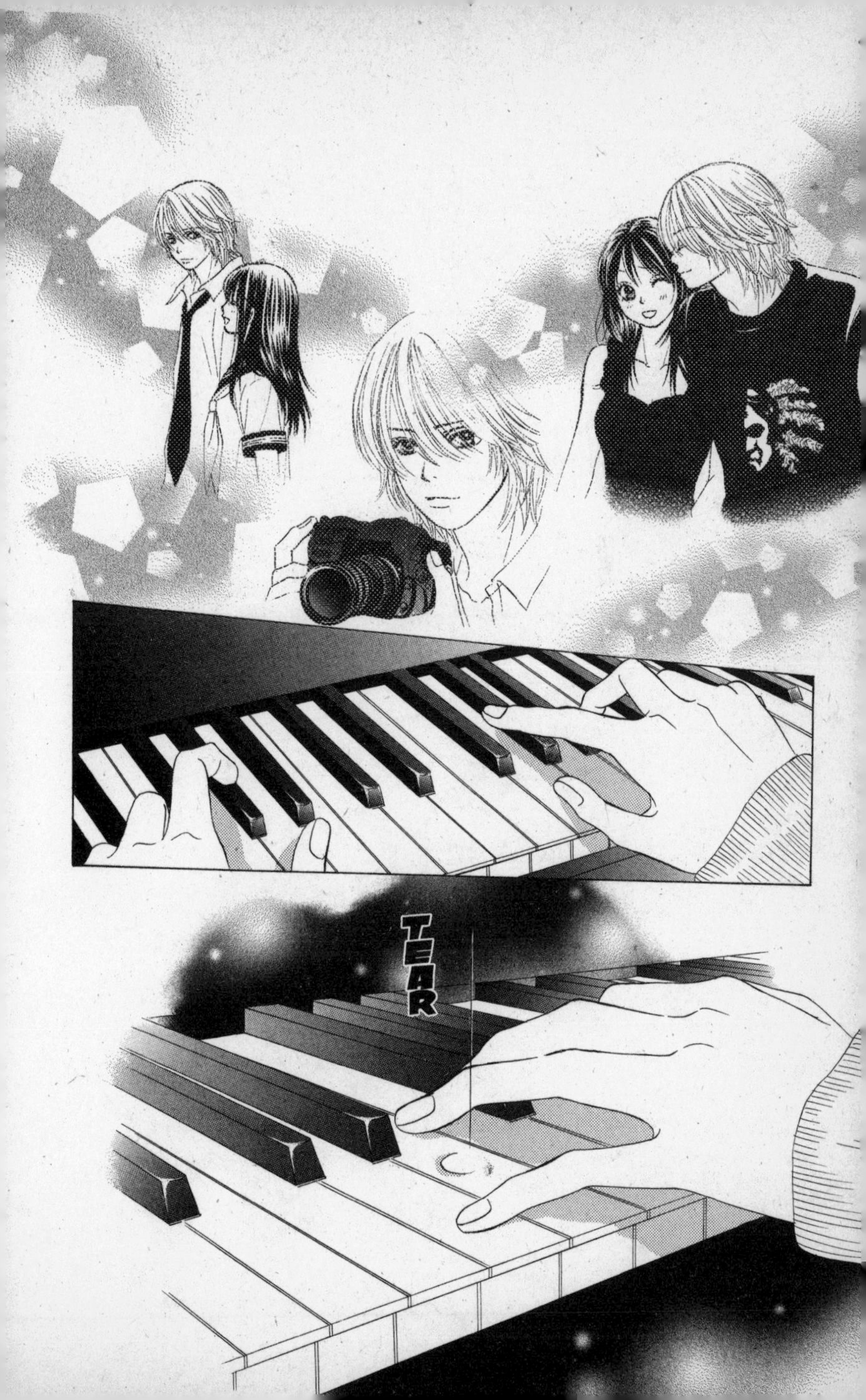
TEAR

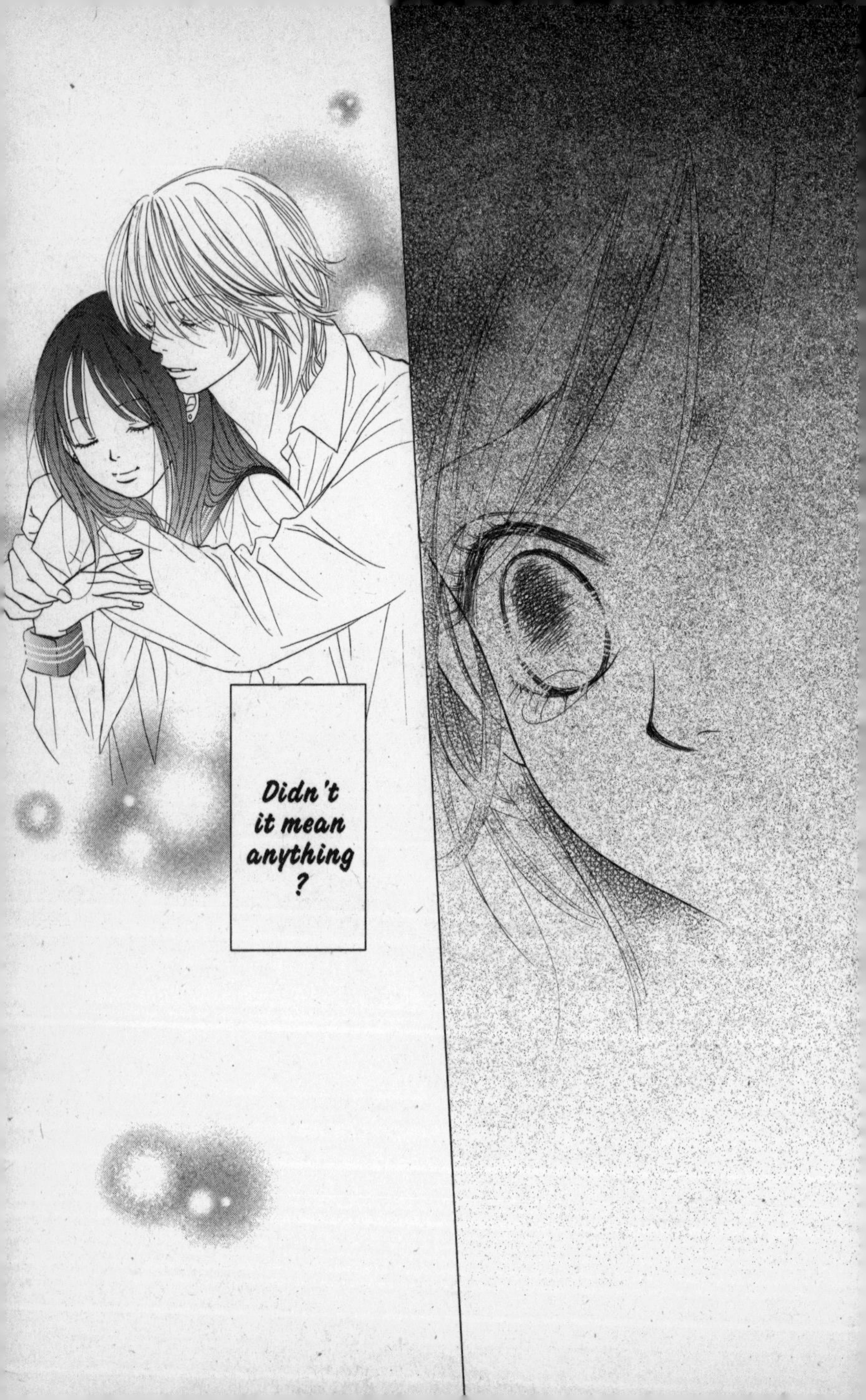
Didn't it mean anything?

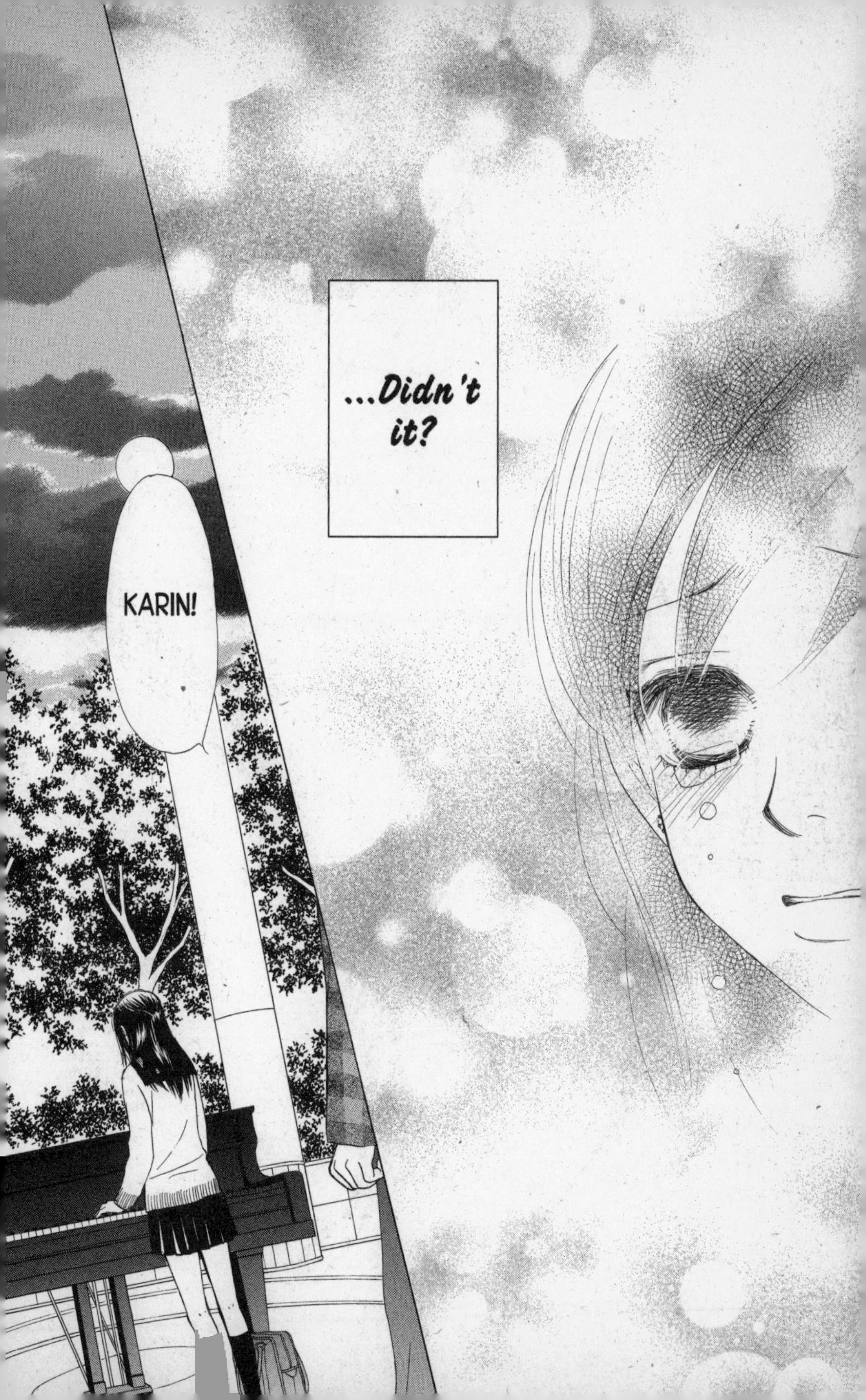
...Didn't it?
KARIN!

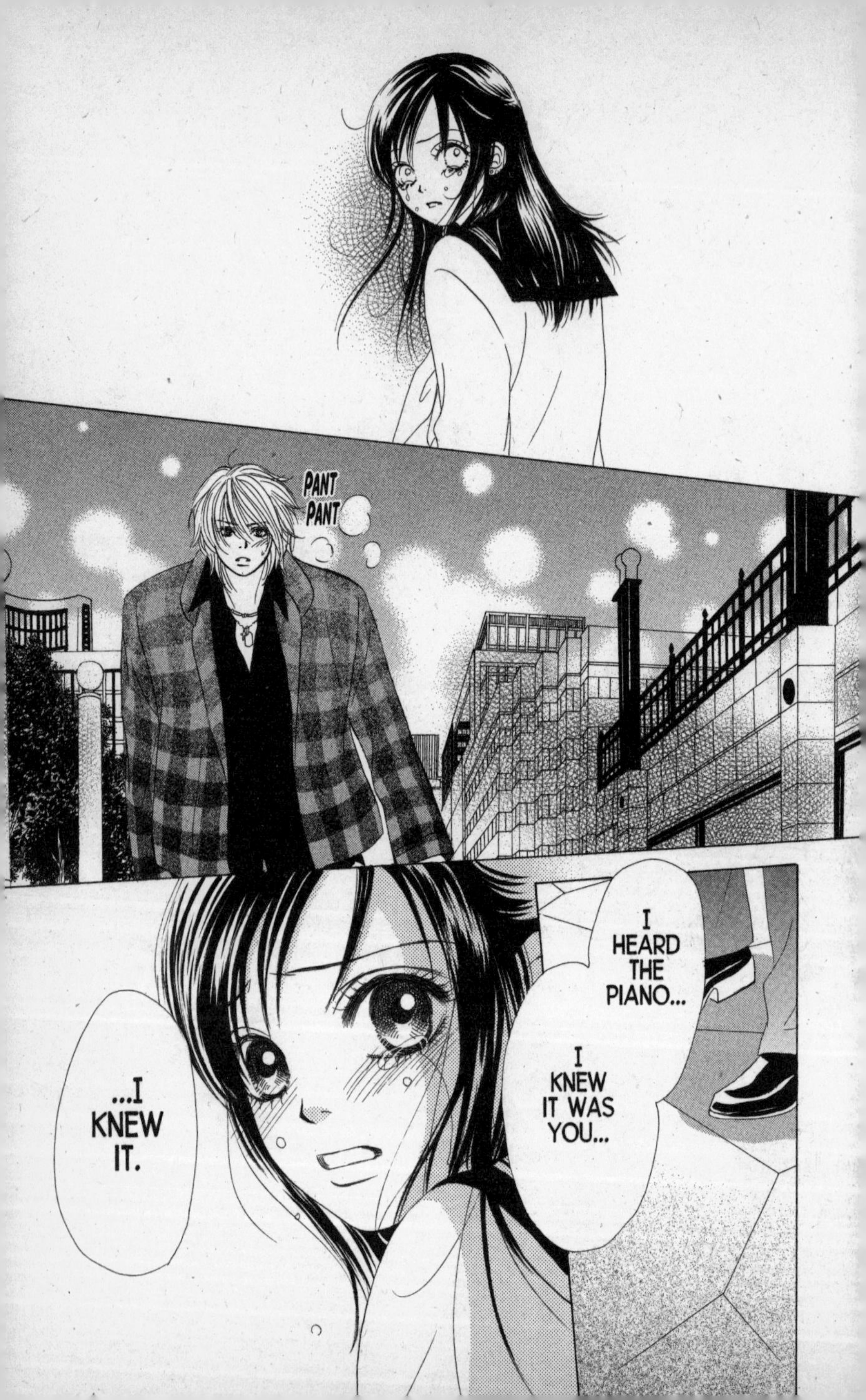
PANT PANT
I HEARD THE PIANO...
I KNEW IT WAS YOU...
...I KNEW IT.

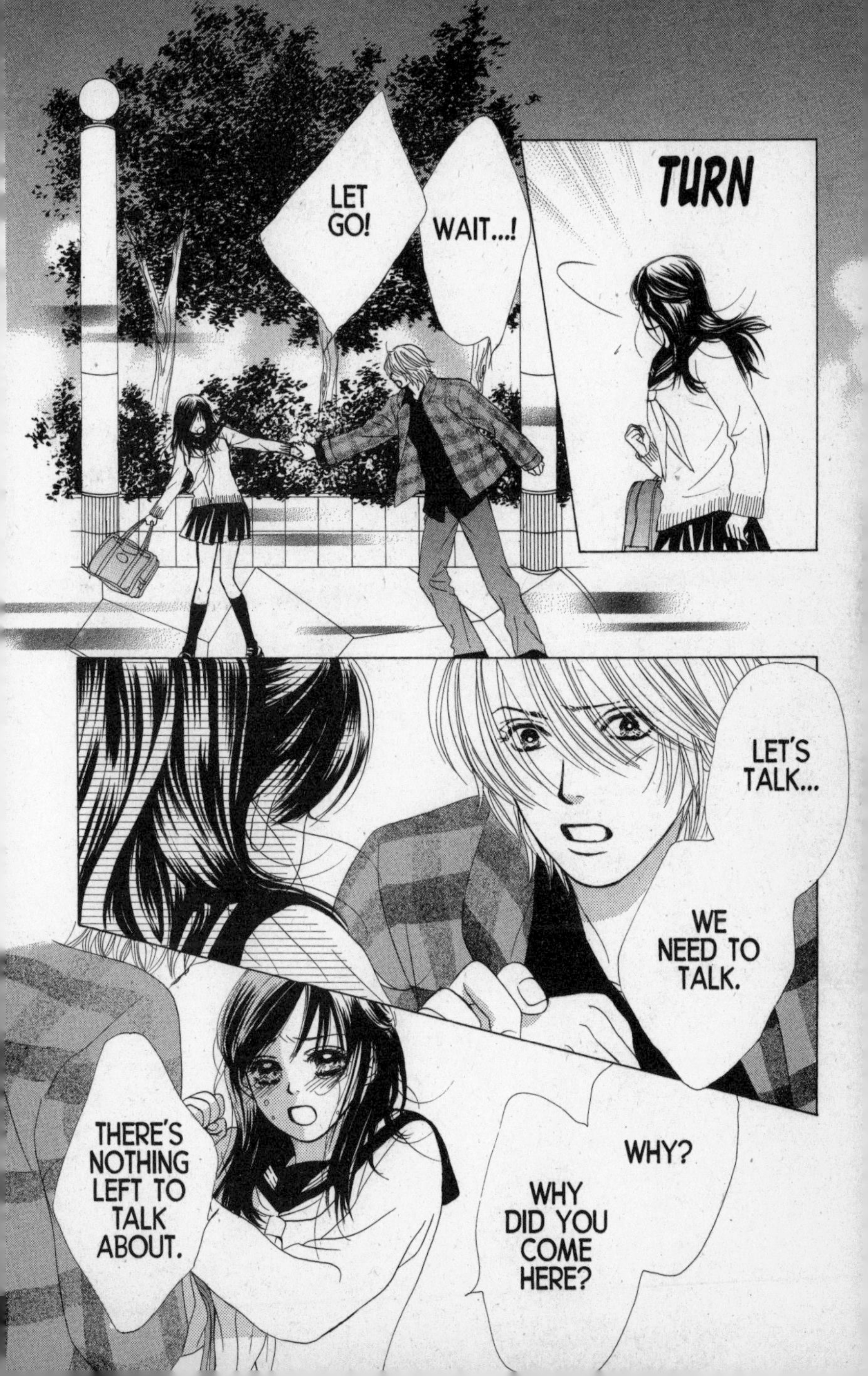
TURN
WAIT...!
LET GO!
LET'S TALK...
WE NEED TO TALK.
WHY?
WHY DID YOU COME HERE?
THERE'S NOTHING LEFT TO TALK ABOUT.

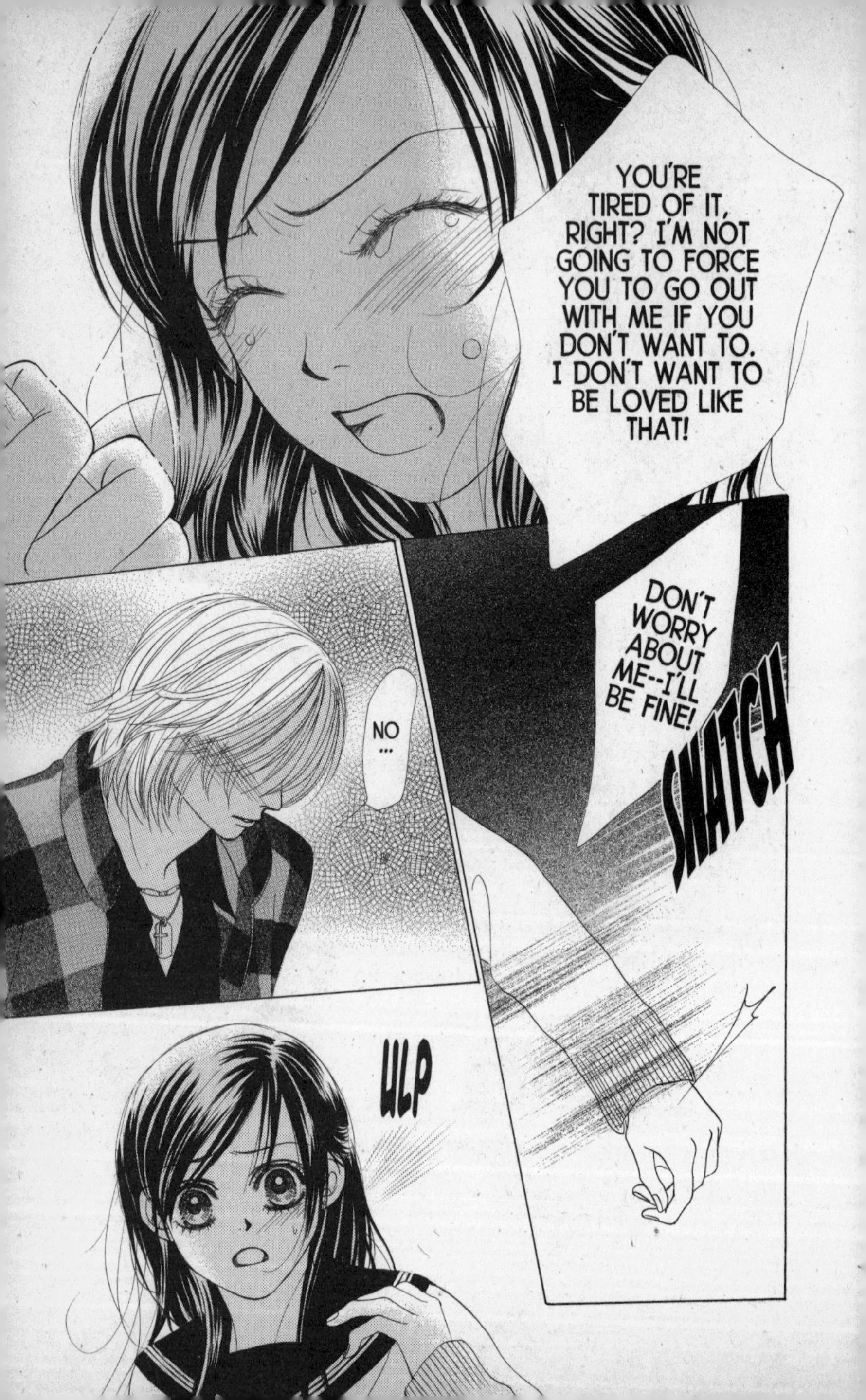
YOU'RE TIRED OF IT, RIGHT? I'M NOT GOING TO FORCE YOU TO GO OUT WITH ME IF YOU DON'T WANT TO. I DON'T WANT TO BE LOVED LIKE THAT!
DON'T WORRY ABOUT ME--I'LL BE FINE!
SNATCH
NO ...
ULP

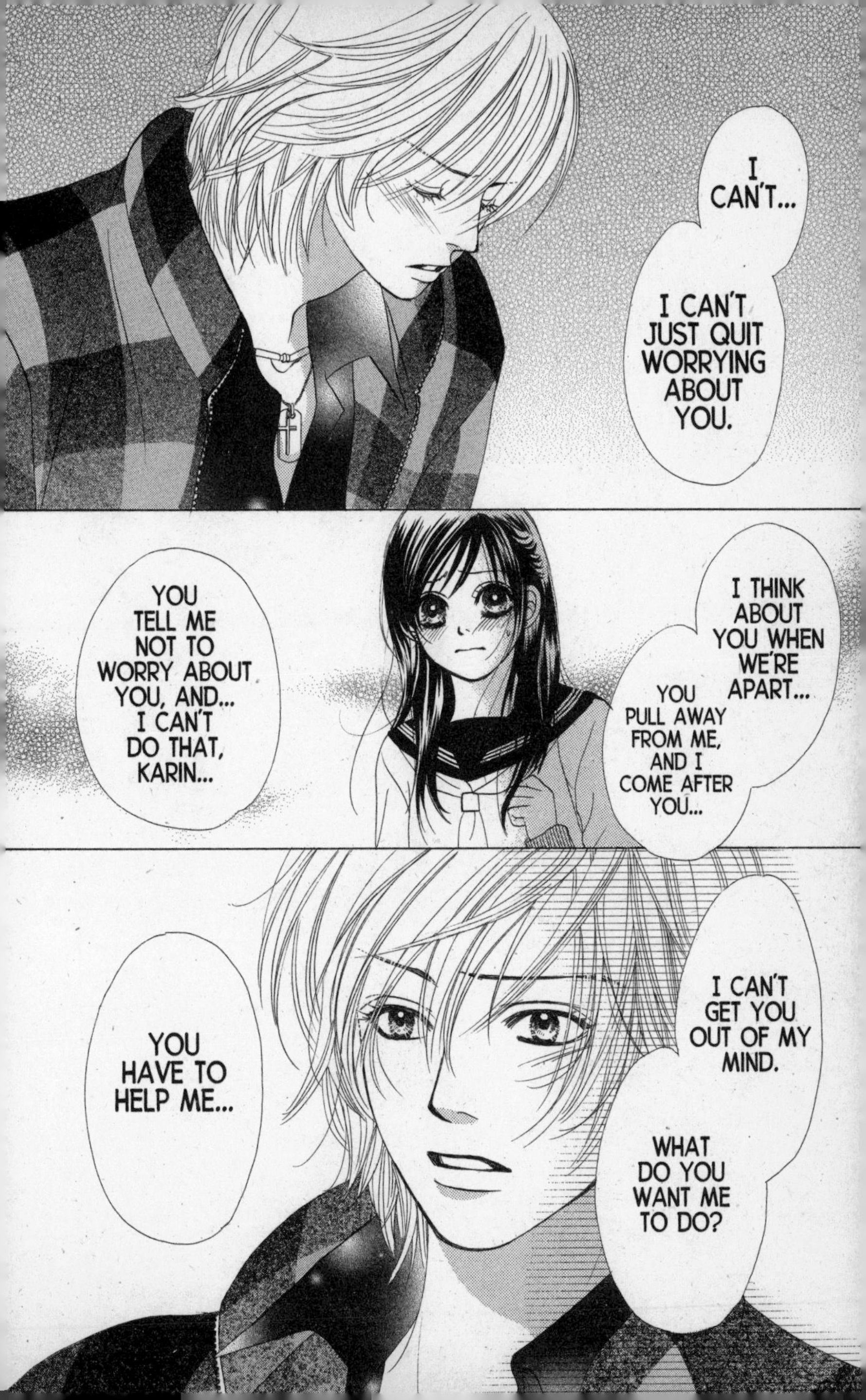
I CAN'T...
I CAN'T JUST QUIT WORRYING ABOUT YOU.
I THINK ABOUT YOU WHEN WE'RE APART...
YOU PULL AWAY FROM ME, AND I COME AFTER YOU...
YOU TELL ME NOT TO WORRY ABOUT YOU, AND... I CAN'T DO THAT, KARIN...
I CAN'T GET YOU OUT OF MY MIND.
WHAT DO YOU WANT ME TO DO?
YOU HAVE TO HELP ME...

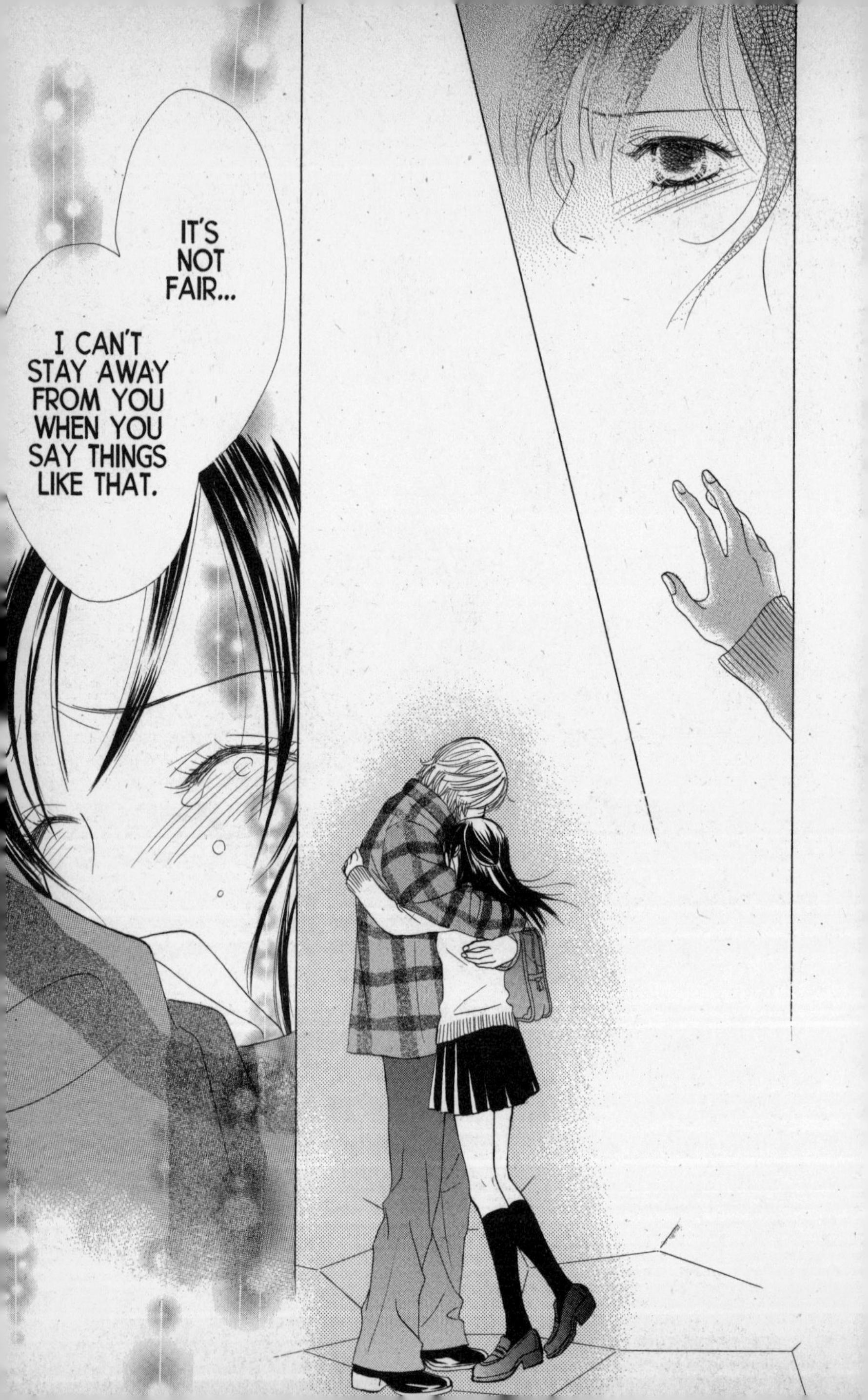
IT'S NOT FAIR...
I CAN'T STAY AWAY FROM YOU WHEN YOU SAY THINGS LIKE THAT.

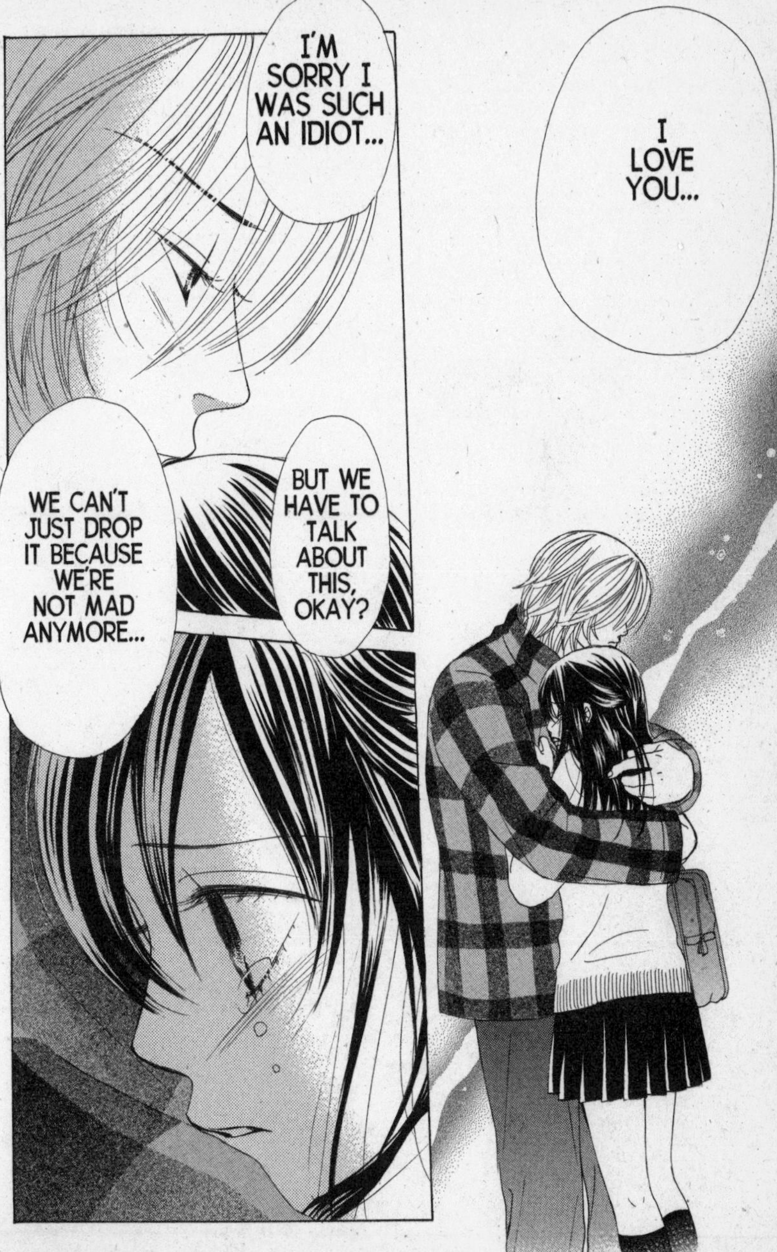
I LOVE YOU...
I'M SORRY I WAS SUCH AN IDIOT...
BUT WE HAVE TO TALK ABOUT THIS, OKAY?
WE CAN'T JUST DROP IT BECAUSE WE'RE NOT MAD ANYMORE...

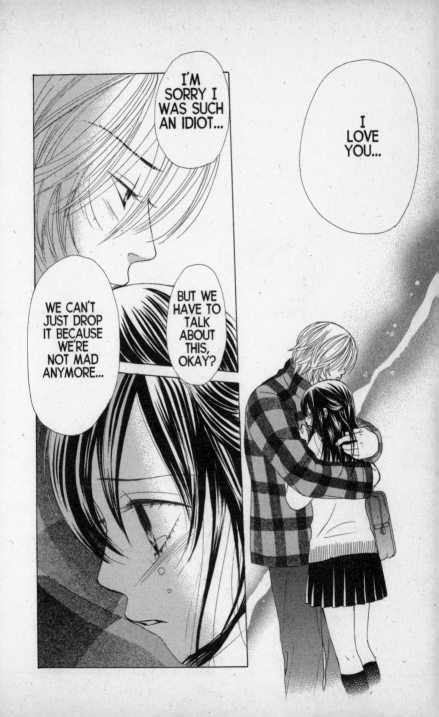

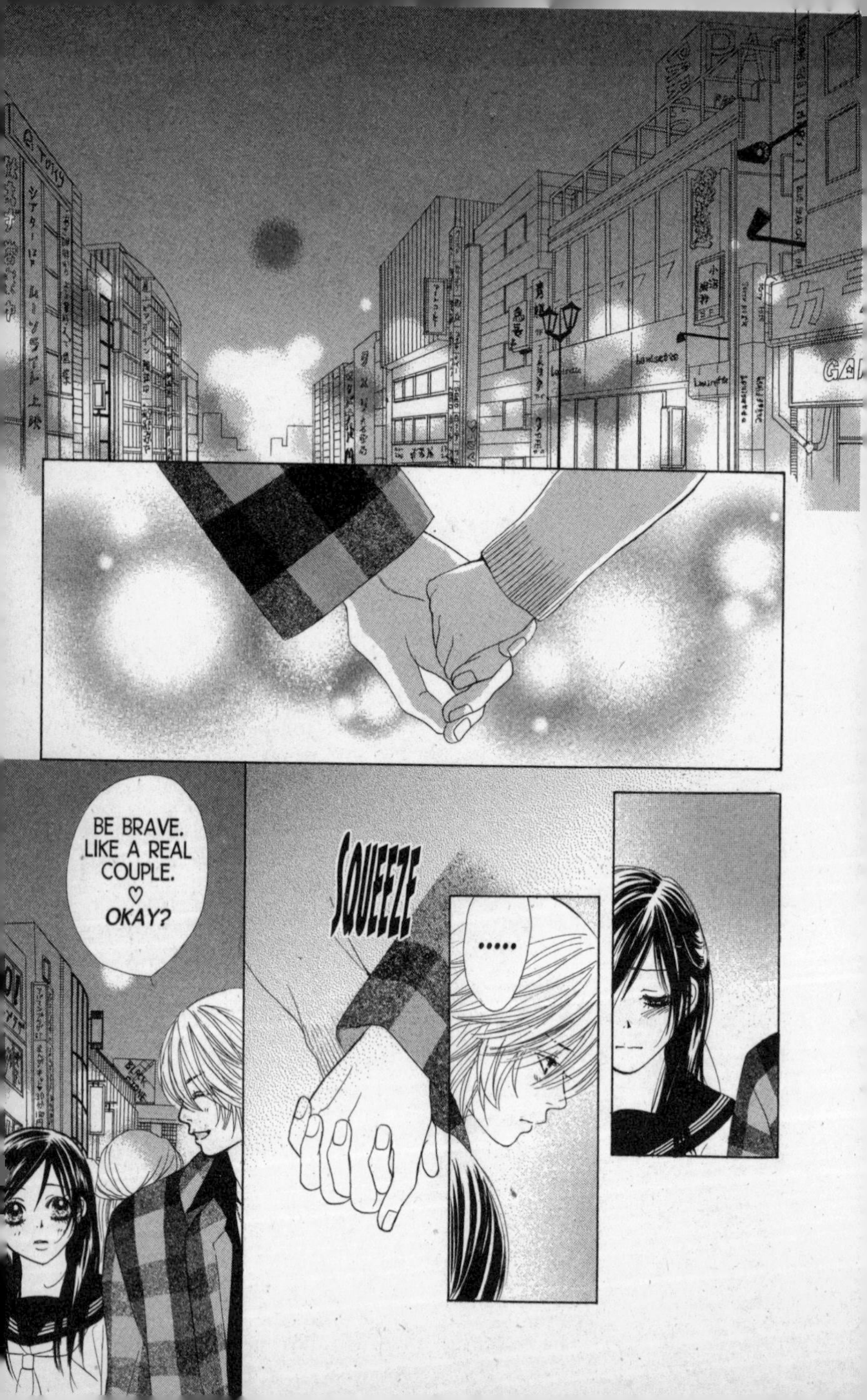
.....
SQUEEZE
BE BRAVE. LIKE A REAL COUPLE. ♡ OKAY?

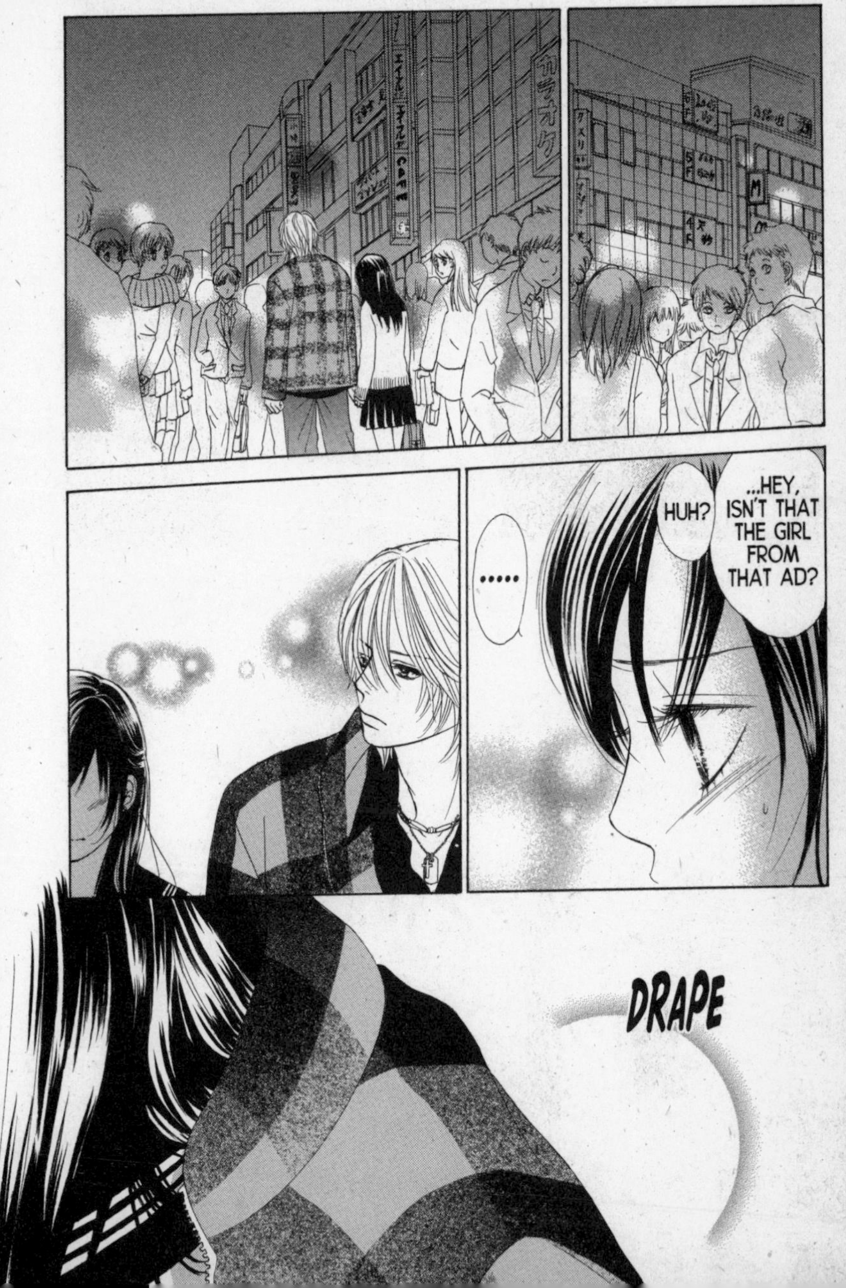
...HEY, ISN'T THAT THE GIRL FROM THAT AD?
HUH?
......
DRAPE

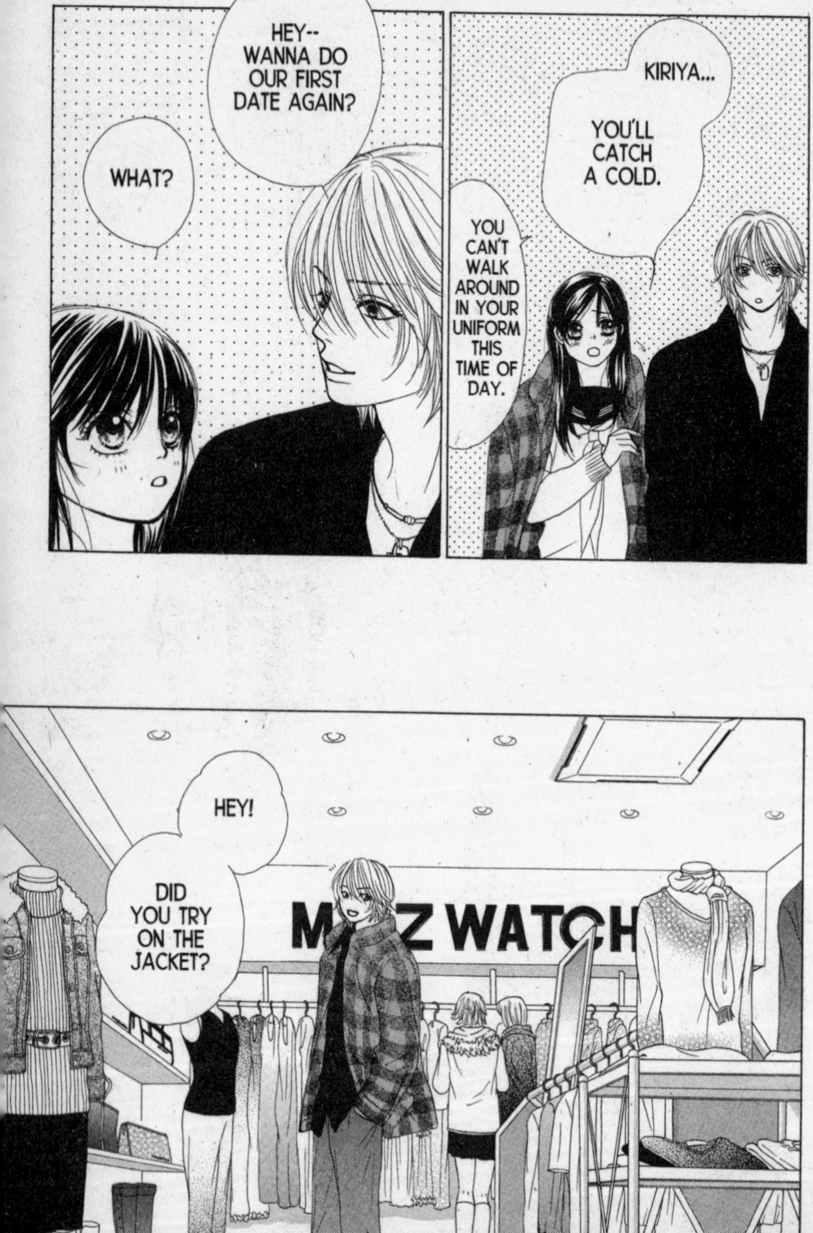
KIRIYA...
YOU'LL CATCH A COLD.
YOU CAN'T WALK AROUND IN YOUR UNIFORM THIS TIME OF DAY.
HEY-- WANNA DO OUR FIRST DATE AGAIN?
WHAT?
HEY!
DID YOU TRY ON THE JACKET?

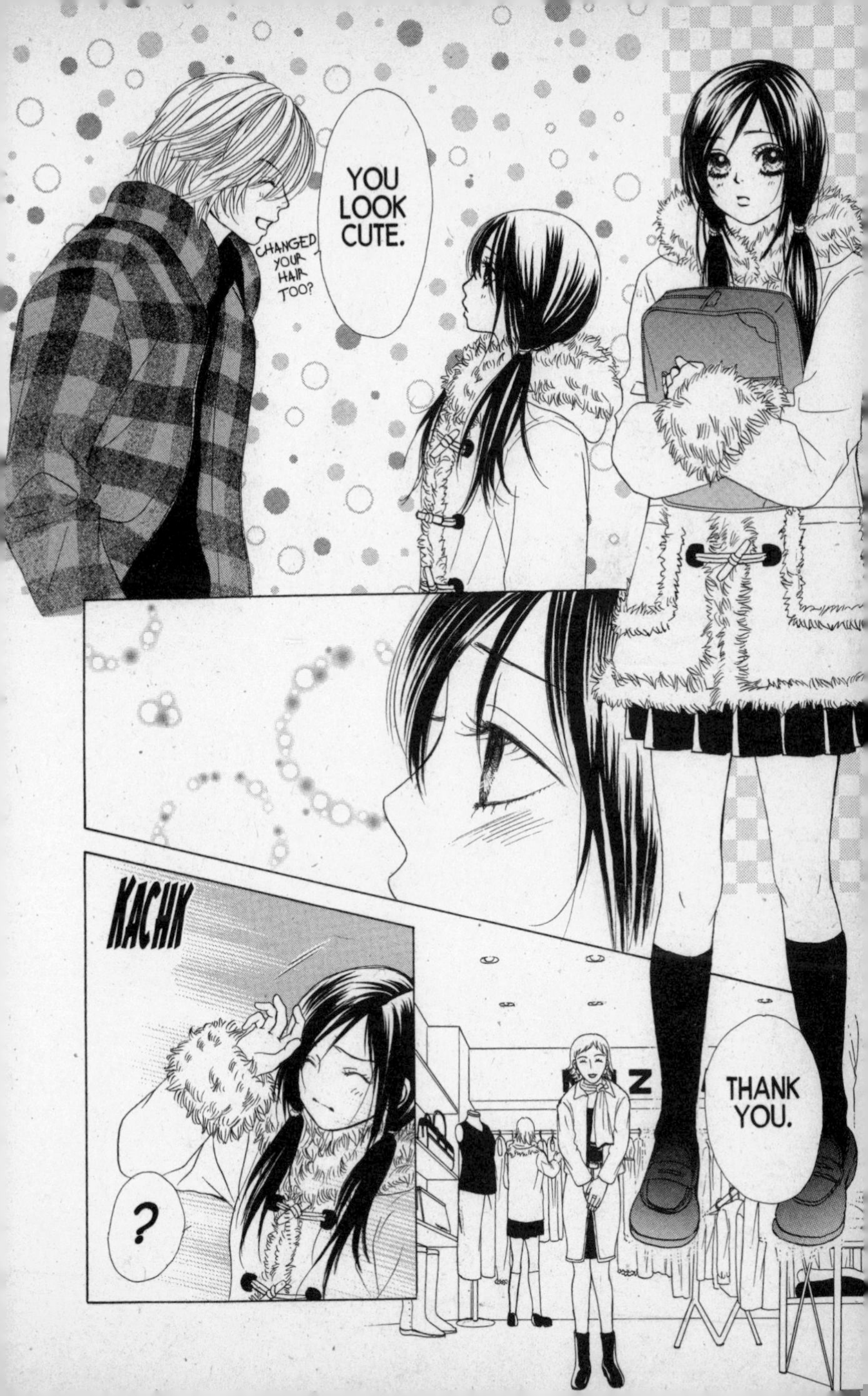
YOU LOOK CUTE.
CHANGED YOUR HAIR TOO?
THANK YOU.
KACHK
?

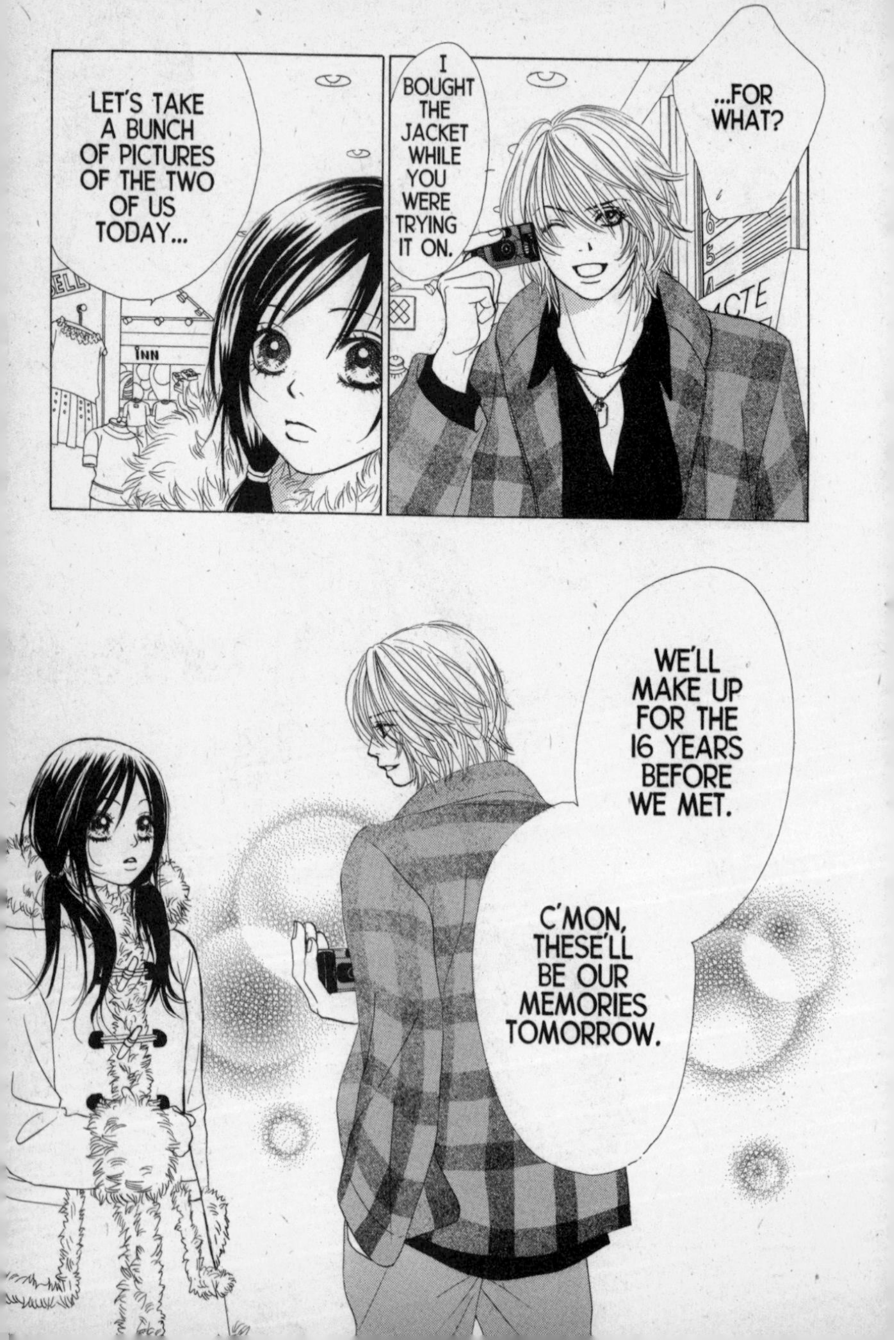
...FOR WHAT?
I BOUGHT THE JACKET WHILE YOU WERE TRYING IT ON.
LET'S TAKE A BUNCH OF PICTURES OF THE TWO OF US TODAY...
WE'LL MAKE UP FOR THE 16 YEARS BEFORE WE MET.
C'MON, THESE'LL BE OUR MEMORIES TOMORROW.

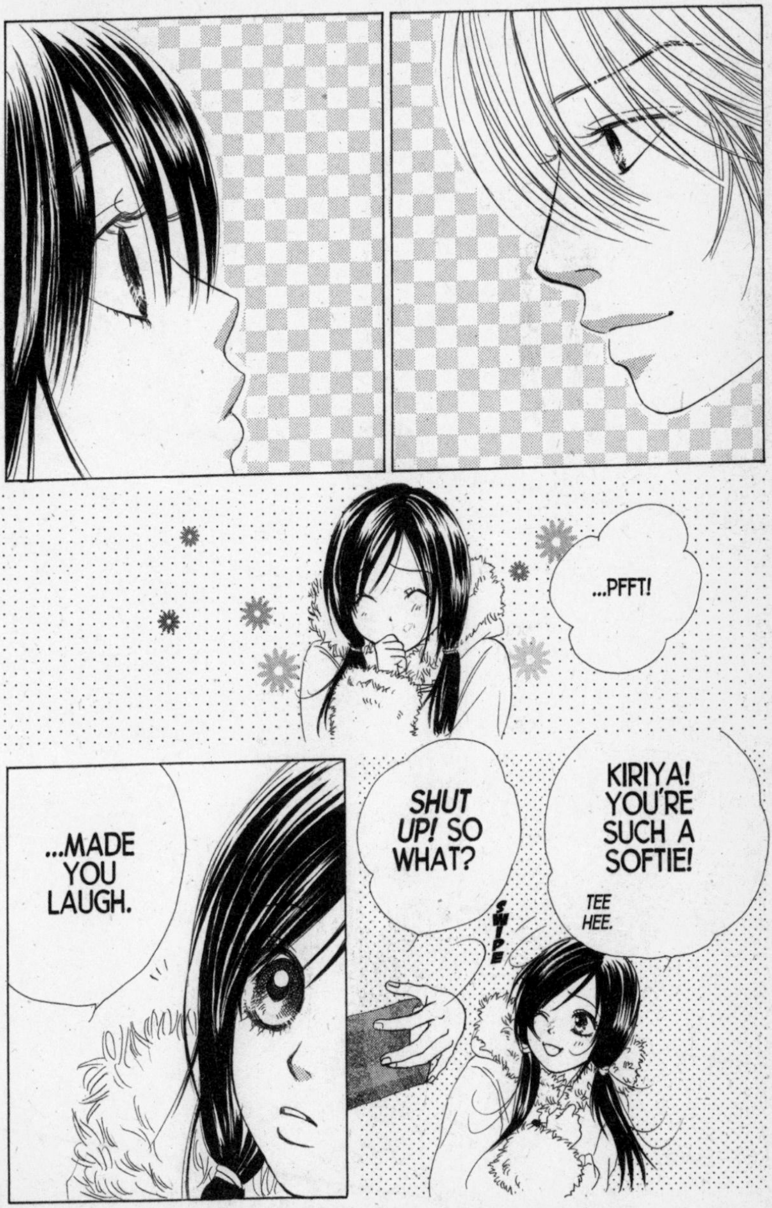
...PFFT!
KIRIYA! YOU'RE SUCH A SOFTIE!
TEE HEE.
SHUT UP! SO WHAT?
SWIPE
...MADE YOU LAUGH.

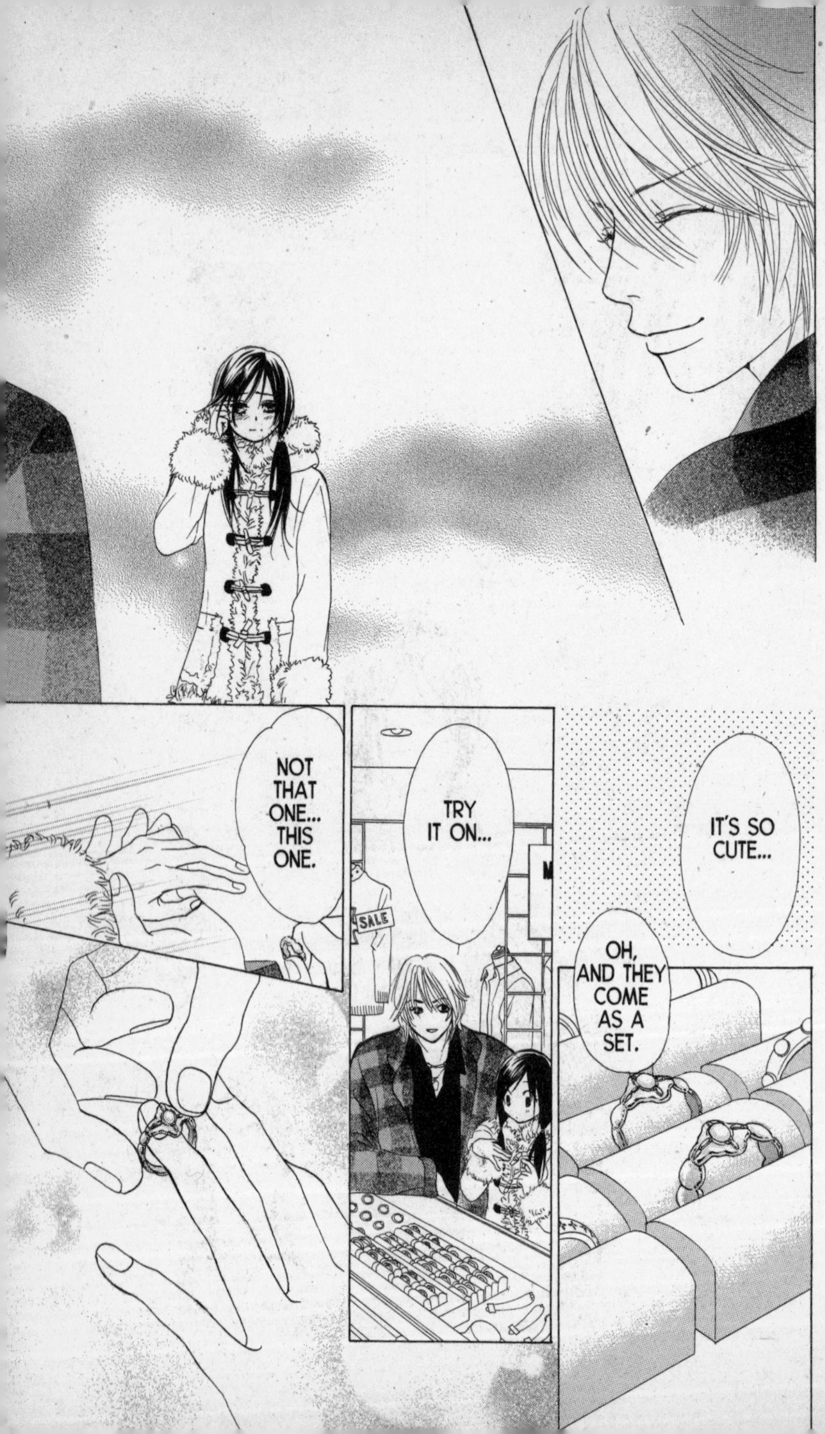
IT'S SO CUTE...
OH, AND THEY COME AS A SET.
TRY IT ON...
SALE
NOT THAT ONE... THIS ONE.

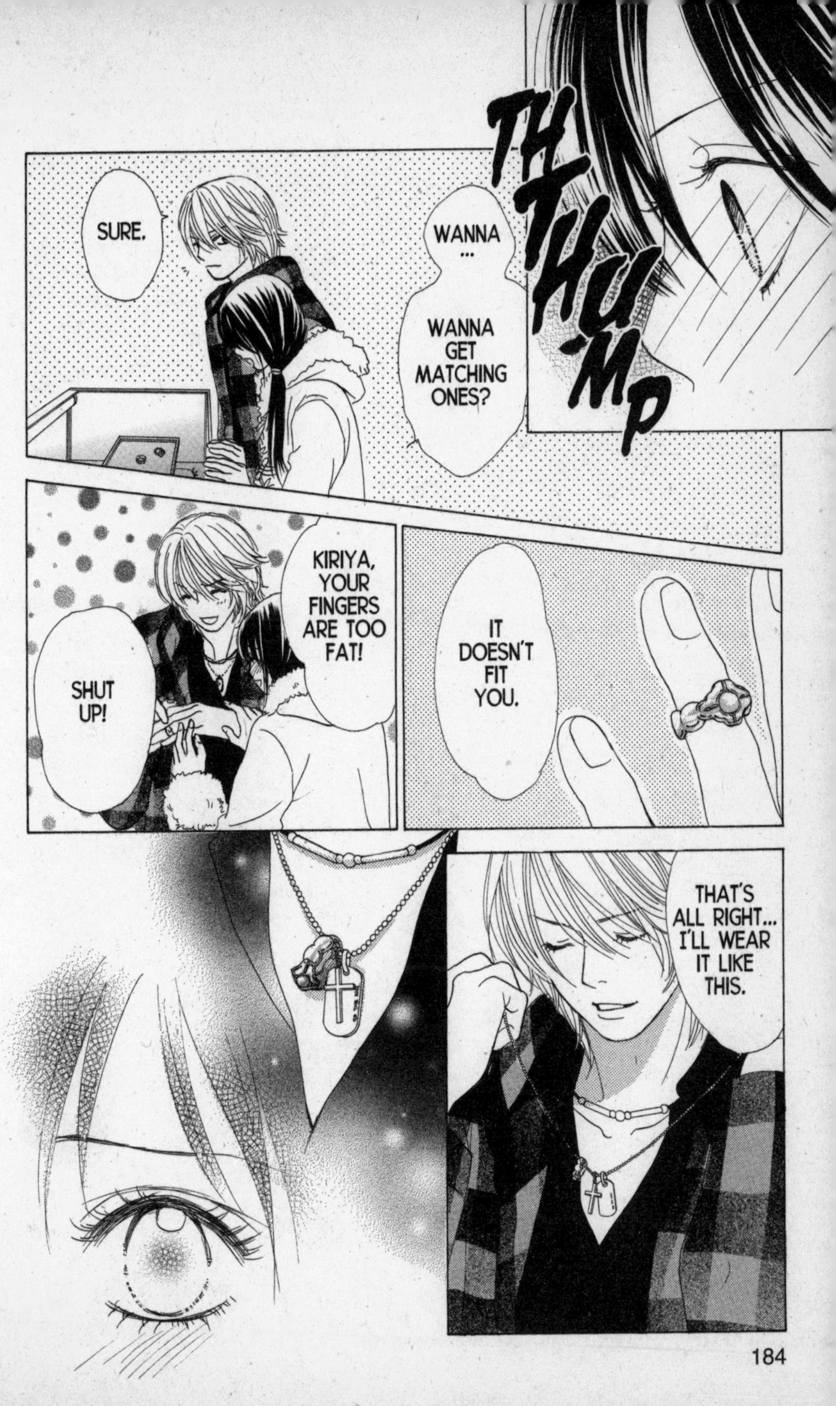
THTHUMP
WANNA ...
WANNA GET MATCHING ONES?
SURE.
IT DOESN'T FIT YOU.
KIRIYA, YOUR FINGERS ARE TOO FAT!
SHUT UP!
THAT'S ALL RIGHT... I'LL WEAR IT LIKE THIS.

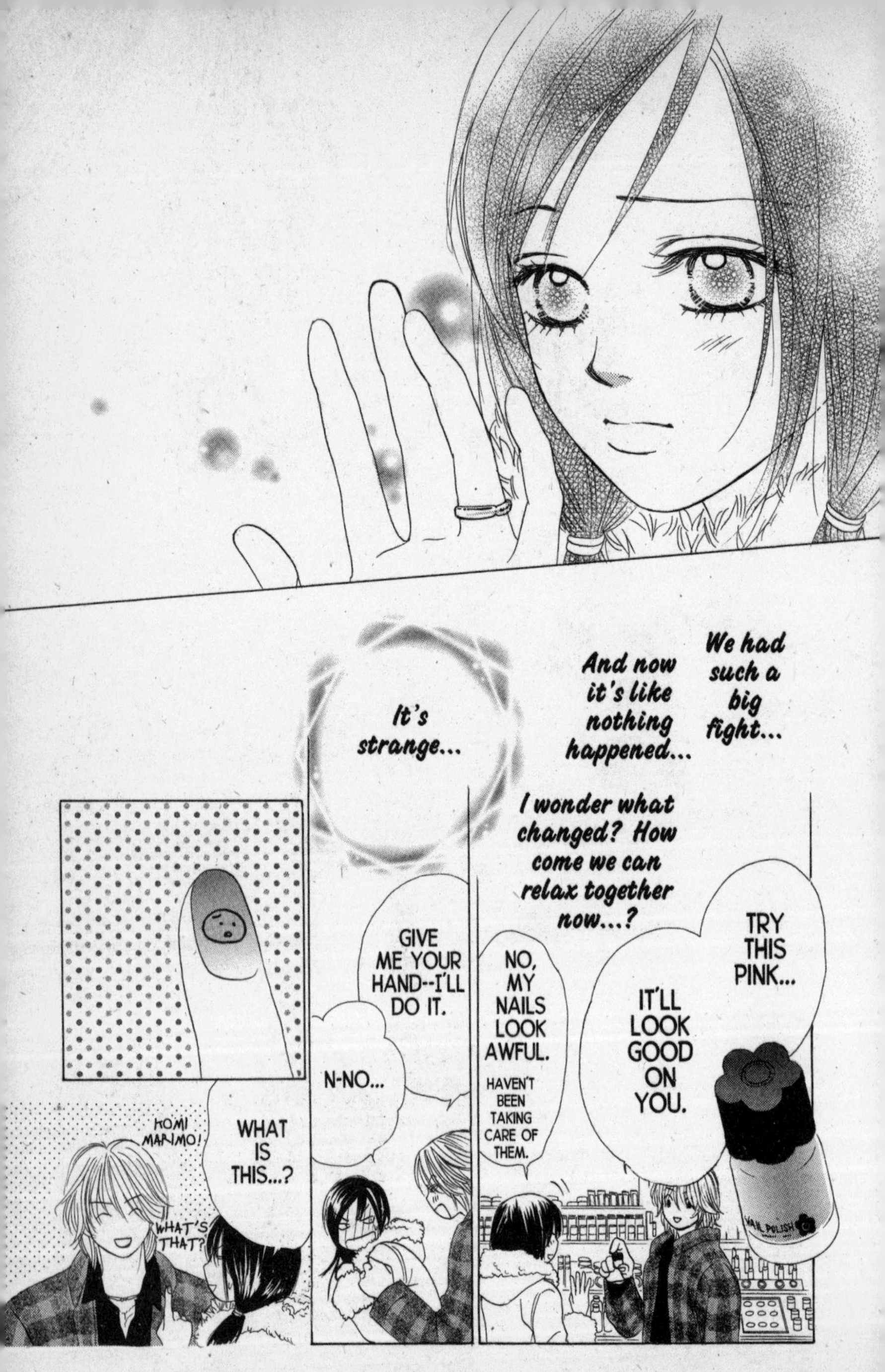
We had such a big fight...
And now it's like nothing happened...
It's strange...
I wonder what changed? How come we can relax together now...?
TRY THIS PINK...
IT'LL LOOK GOOD ON YOU.
NAIL POLISH
NO, MY NAILS LOOK AWFUL.
HAVEN'T BEEN TAKING CARE OF THEM.
GIVE ME YOUR HAND--I'LL DO IT.
N-NO...
WHAT IS THIS...?
KOMI MARIMO!
WHAT'S THAT?

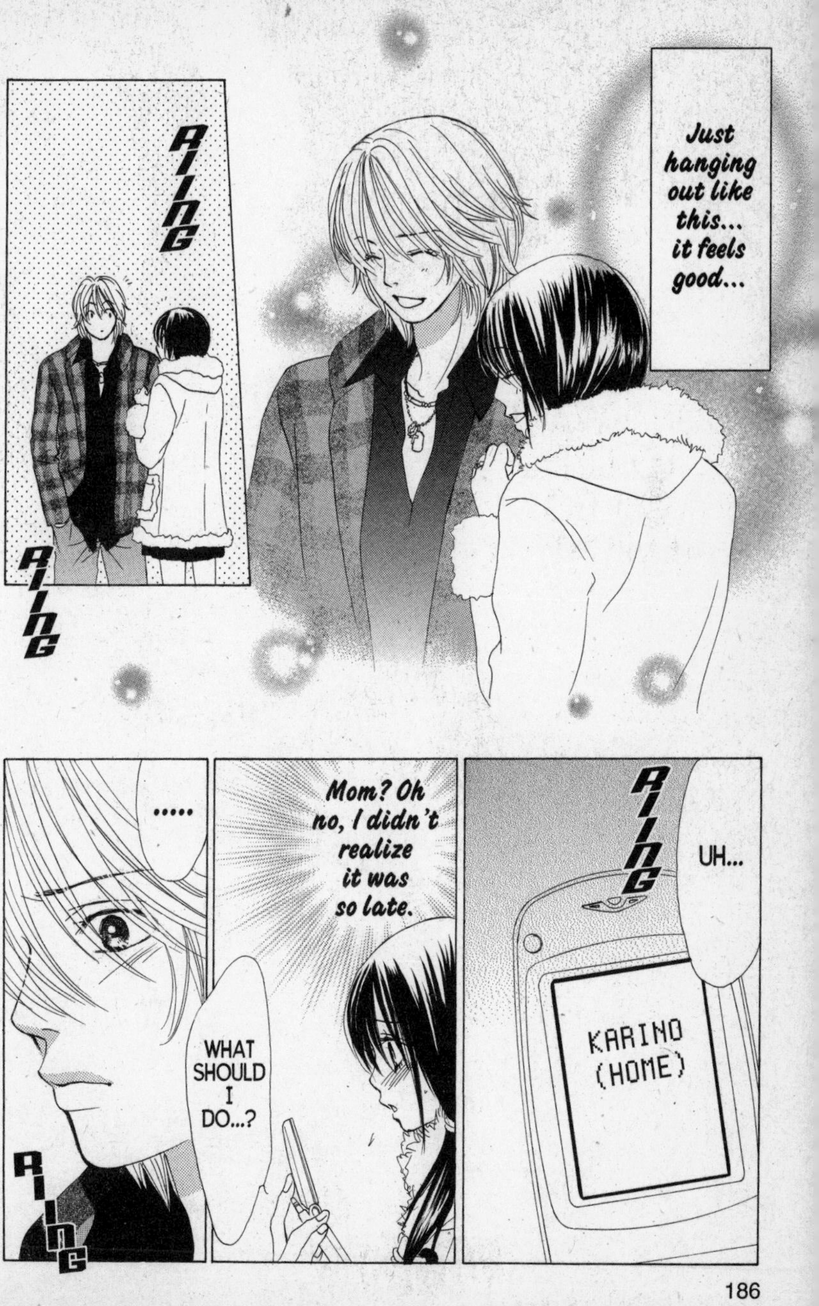
Just hanging out like this... it feels good...
RING
RING
RING
UH...
KARINO (HOME)
Mom? Oh no, I didn't realize it was so late.
WHAT SHOULD I DO...?
.....
RING

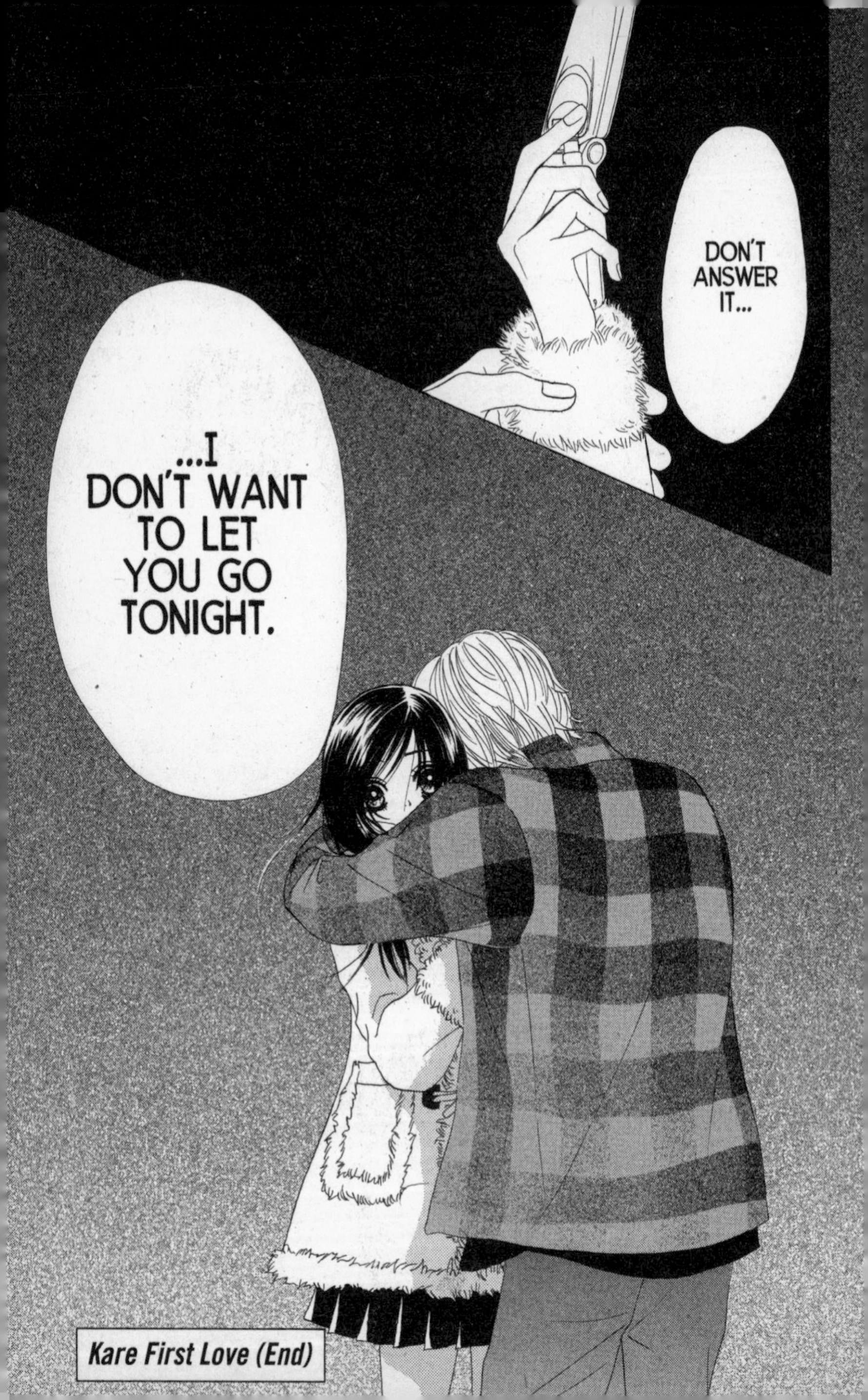
DON'T ANSWER IT...
...I DON'T WANT TO LET YOU GO TONIGHT.
Kare First Love (End)

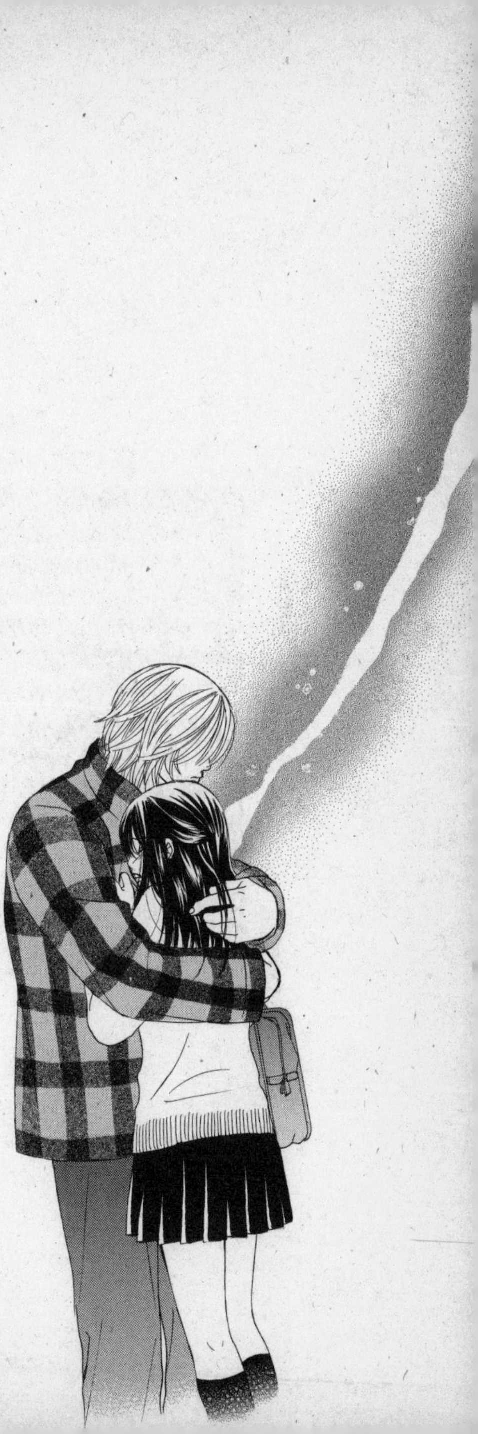

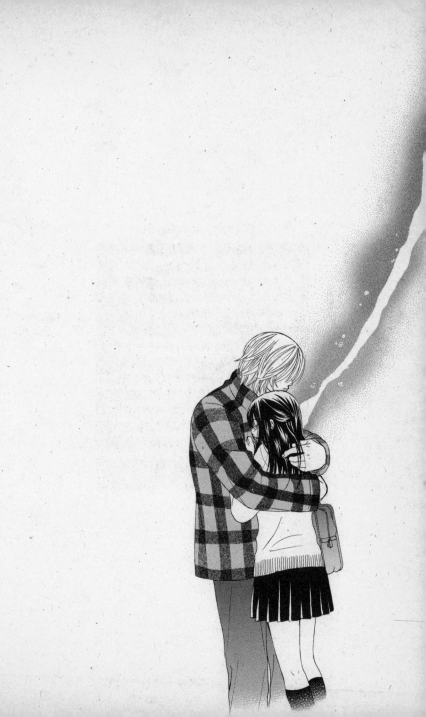

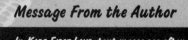

Message From the Author

In KARE FIRST LOVE, text messages often precede an important event. I did that because I'm trying to show how we've come to rely on technology in our daily lives. I know I'VE grown dependent on it! There was a time when I got along without it, so I know intellectually that it isn't a necessity, but it certainly feels like one. The same thing can happen in a relationship. There are no guarantees; feelings change. It's dangerous to take people for granted. Hmm. Does it sound like I'm talking about Kiriya and Karin's relationship...?

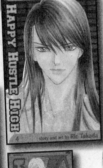

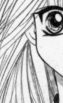
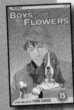
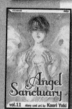
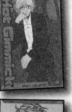
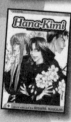
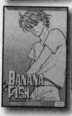
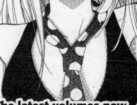
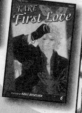
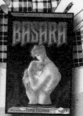

LOVE SHOJO? LET US KNOW!

☐ Please do NOT send me information about VIZ Media products, news and events, special offers, or other information.

☐ Please do NOT send me information from VIZ' trusted business partners.

Name: _____

Address: _____

City: _____ **State:** _____ **Zip:** _____

E-mail: _____

☐ **Male** ☐ **Female**   **Date of Birth** (mm/dd/yyyy): ___/___/_____ (Under 13? Parental consent required)

What race/ethnicity do you consider yourself? (check all that apply)

☐ White/Caucasian   ☐ Black/African American   ☐ Hispanic/Latino

☐ Asian/Pacific Islander   ☐ Native American/Alaskan Native ☐ Other: _____

What VIZ shojo title(s) did you purchase? (indicate title(s) purchased)

_____

What other shojo titles from other publishers do you own? _____

_____

Reason for purchase: (check all that apply)

☐ Special offer   ☐ Favorite title / author / artist / genre

☐ Gift   ☐ Recommendation   ☐ Collection

☐ Read excerpt in VIZ manga sampler   ☐ Other _____

Where did you make your purchase? (please check one)

☐ Comic store   ☐ Bookstore   ☐ Mass/Grocery Store

☐ Newsstand   ☐ Video/Video Game Store

☐ Online (site:_____)   ☐ Other _____

How many shojo titles have you purchased in the last year? How many were VIZ shojo titles?
(please check one from each column)

SHOJO MANGA
- ☐ None
- ☐ 1 – 4
- ☐ 5 – 10
- ☐ 11+

VIZ SHOJO MANGA
- ☐ None
- ☐ 1 – 4
- ☐ 5 – 10
- ☐ 11+

☑ S0-BRX-309

What do you like most about shojo graphic novels? (check all that apply)

- ☐ Romance
- ☐ Comedy
- ☐ Other _____

- ☐ Drama / conflict
- ☐ Real-life storylines

- ☐ Fantasy
- ☐ Relatable characters

Do you purchase every volume of your favorite shojo series?

- ☐ Yes! Gotta have 'em as my own
- ☐ No. Please explain: _____

Who are your favorite shojo authors / artists? _____

_____

What shojo titles would like you translated and sold in English? _____

_____

THANK YOU! Please send the completed form to:

NJW Research
ATTN: VIZ Media Shojo Survey
42 Catharine Street
Poughkeepsie, NY 12601